✦ The Heritage Guides

VENICE

Including the islands of Murano, Burano, and Torcello, the Lido, and the villas on the Brenta

Touring Club of Italy

Touring Club of Italy

President and Chairman: *Giancarlo Lunati*

Chief Executive Officer: *Armando Peres*

Managing Directors: *Adriano Agnati* and *Radames Trotta*

Editorial Director: *Marco Ausenda*

Coordination: *Michele D'Innella*

Managing Editor: *Anna Ferrari - Bravo*

General Consultant: *Gianni Bagioli*

Jacket Layout: *Federica Neeff*

Map Design: *Cartographic Division - Touring Club of Italy*
Authors: *Giorgio Bellavitis* (Venice: A City in the Sea of History); *Rinio Bruttomesso* (S. Marco; S. Polo and S. Croce), *Tiziana Favaro* (Cannaregio; Castello), *Ernesta Serena Mancuso* (The Grand Canal; Dorsoduro; The Islands); *Pierluigi Fantelli* (The Riviera del Brenta); *Francesca Brandes* (Venice: Instructions for Use; Information for Travellers).

Translation and adaptation: *Antony Shugaar*

Copy Editor: *Derek Allen*

Drawings: *Antonello* and *Chiara Vincenti*

Layout: *Studio Tragni*

Production: *Umberto Fattori*

Picture credits: *Action Press: Y.A. Bertrand* 11; *Archivi Alinari/Giraudon:* 67; *Archivio T.C.I./M. Iodice:* 36, 62, 76, 82, 114; *G. Arici:* 12, 15, 22, 86, 118; *Image Bank: A. Becker* 42, *G. Cigolini* 19, *S. Dunwell* 47, *G.A. Rossi* 9, 31; *L. Ronchi: G. Lucci* 3; *L. Ronchi: G. Baviera* 90, 108; *L. Ronchi - T. Stone: J. Garrett* 51, *J. Lamb* 113, *G. Pile* 20; *G.L. Sosio:* 126, 129; *Stradella: Ellebi* 116.

Cover: Venice, bridge and gondola in a canal, by *H. Sund (Image Bank).*

Typesetting and colour separations: *APV Vaccani - Milano*

Printed by: *G. Canale & C. - Borgaro Torinese (Torino)*

Code L2D
ISBN 88 365 1517 7
Printed in October 1998

Foreword

Without Venice, it has been said, "the world would be a little poorer." Indeed, the treasures of art and light, emotion and history with which this lagoon city abounds are, truly, the personal possession of every citizen of this planet.

Venice is utterly unlike any place else on earth. For many centuries it ruled as a world capital, and a mighty sea power; now it is an open-air museum, a mighty treasure chest of stone and water, air and sunlight. It hovers, a delicate miracle of survival and equilibrium, poised between encroaching water and rising silt.

This guide, part of "The Heritage Guide" series, is an indispensable tool for those who wish to visit the city of Venice and its array of islands. An introductory chapter recounts the history of Venice; a second chapter offers a series of suggestions for seeing and understanding the city in the best way possible. Then come eight chapters, broken up into 19 tours. The first tour is devoted to the Grand Canal, while the next 13 chapters follow as many routes through the historic "sestieri", or sixths (instead of quarters: Venice is unique in every detail): these "sestieri" are called San Marco, San Polo, Santa Croce, Dorsoduro, Cannaregio, and Castello, to list them from the historical center, with its monuments, and working outward to the humbler neighborhoods of the "lesser Venice."

The Doge's Palace in the Piazzetta S. Marco

The last five routes are dedicated to the islands of the Venetian lagoon, places of heart-melting loveliness, and the Riviera del Brenta, a rivercourse lined with famous villas, many of them true masterpieces of 16th- and 17th-century architecture.

In the section entitled Information for Travellers there are listings of more than 500 addresses of museums and galleries, shops, hotels, and restaurants. There is an especially rich array of maps and illustrations accompanying the text, with special designs, photographs, city plans, floor plans of buildings and museums, and detailed route maps showing the direction of the tour, as well as a complete city atlas.

Contents

Maps and Plans

How to Use this Guidebook

■ We have attempted to use the original Italian names of all places, monuments, buildings, and other references where possible. This is for a number of reasons: the traveller is thus made more comfortable with the names as he or she is likely to encounter them in Italy, on signs and printed matter. Note also that maps in this book for the most part carry the Italian version of all names. Thus, we refer to Piazza San Marco and Ponte dei Sospiri rather than to St. Mark's Square and the Bridge of Sighs. On first mention, we have tried to indicate both the Italian and the English equivalent; we have renewed this dual citation when it is the first mention in a specific section of text. In Italian names, one of the most common abbreviations found is "S." for "saint" (and "Ss." for "saints"). Note that "S." may actually be an abbreviation for four different forms of the word "saint" – "San", "Sant'", "Santo", and "Santa". Many other terms, while generally explained, should be familiar: "museo" is a museum, "biblioteca" is a library, "torre" is a tower, "giardino" is a garden, "pinacoteca" is an art gallery, "teatro" is a theatre, "battistero" is a baptistery, "via" is a street, "isola" is an island, and so on. Throughout this book, we have used a number of terms that are distinctly Venetian, such as "calle" (for a street), "campo" (for a square), "fondamenta" (for a quay), "rio" (for a small canal), "riva" (for a shore or an embankment), "bàcaro" (for a tavern).

5.3 Cannarégio

Introductory Chapters. This guidebook opens with a chapter on the history of the city, and another chapter, "Venice: Instructions for use," which contains all the information you will need to organize your tour – from the addresses of embassies to tips on how to use public transportation, from shopping suggestions to descriptions of the cuisine, from hints on the best times of year to visit to the most noteworthy cultural and folk events.

The Places to Visit. This section comprises 8 chapters, 7 of which are devoted to Venice and the islands of the Lagoon; the 8th concerns the Riviera del Brenta. Each chapter contains several walking tour.

Information for Travellers. A compendium of useful addresses, hotels and restaurants which suggests a selection of the finest hospitality facilities. Specific criteria are described on page 130. We provide information which is up-to-date as of the writing of this book. The reader should be aware that some subsequent changes may have occurred in hours or schedules.

Maps and plans. Monuments, hotels, restaurants, and other public facilities are marked on the Venice city atlas maps that appears at the end of this guidebook. Througout this volume numeral in parentheses (5) indicate the map in question, while a letter and a number in parentheses (E2) refer to the sector of the map. The notation *off map* indicates that the specific monument or location is not shown on the map.

Notice regarding telephone numbers. As of the 18th December 1998, each location's telephone code must also be dialled for local calls and are listed next to the symbol ☎ in the section "Information for Travellers", page 130. For those calling from abroad, the local code (041 for Venice) must be dialled after international code for Italy, followed by the subscriber's number.

The Church of the Benedictine convent of San Giorgio Maggiore

Conventional Signs Used in the Maps

Highways	quite interesting
Main roads	interesting
Other roads	Other buildings
Railroad lines and stations	Churches
Urban and other lagoon transportation lines	Gardens and parks
Summer lagoon transportation lines	Hotels
Ferry gondolas for pedestrians (Grand Canal)	Restaurants or “bàcari”
Walking tours	Hospitals
Monuments and buildings of exceptional interest	Villas

Venice: A City in the Sea of History

Water is found in many cities, and certainly in every city built on a river, a lake, or on the ocean shore; water usually runs, or flows and ebbs, in areas that are clearly separated from the parts of a city where men and women live, walk, and work. The water of Venice is different. Here – more than in Amsterdam, Bruges, or St. Petersburg, more than in other cities that resemble Venice – the water is found everywhere; it makes its way into every nook and cranny; it runs through broad, sunlit canals or narrow, shadowy "rii"; it extends out in the endless liquid prairies of the lagoon, watery plains upon which, or amidst which, the entire city has been built.

All this constitutes so basic an aspect of Venice's existence that there are countless myths and descriptions of the city based on water: a city that, like Venus, was born of the foam of the sea waves; or flagship of a mighty fleet of islands, riding at anchor in the lagoon; or a city built by beavers, through the gathering of bits of wood into piles to withstand the waves, as Goethe described it during his visit. As early as 1240, Boncompagno da Signa, a lively man with words, described Venice as "a city that has the sea for its floor, the sky for its roof, and the flow of the waters for walls." Much later, in 1912, Thomas Mann, a slightly deeper and more tormented author, wrote that Venice was "an improbable city, which you can reach only by boat and by lengthy travel." Mann, of course, had grasped a basic truth. Certainly, Venice now has two long bridges anchoring it to the land, a railroad bridge built in 1846, and a bridge for automobiles built in 1933, but to understand Venice you should arrive by water; in any case, to get around Venice, you have only two alternatives: on foot, or by boat, either public or private.

The Island of S. Francesco

The three areas of the city of Venice

One fundamental aspect of the city, which you should clearly grasp in order to understand better and tour more thoroughly the city and its surrounding territory – two-thirds of which is watery lagoon – is the differences among the three districts of Venice. Ever since 1927, in fact, Venice has been the administrative, political, and cultural capital of a "Comune," or municipality, that – as of 30 September 1994 – counted a population of 302,187. The inhabitants are distributed as follows: "terraferma," or mainland, 183,650; historical center and Giudecca, 72,271; the estuary, 46,254.

You will have a better understanding of the meaning of these figures if you approach Venice from the air, and from the northeast. Say that you are landing at Marco Polo airport, which is built on the shoals and sandbanks that emerge from the lagoon. With the Po valley stretching out behind it, surrounded by the mighty ring of the Alps, Venice appears as the light tracery of an arabesque; the city is hard to pick out from the reflections in the waters of the lagoon, amidst the long strips of sandy earth that mark the shores of the Adriatic Sea.

The "terraferma"

There is no physical boundary to mark the borders of the municipality, but you can easily guess that it begins with the so-called "terraferma." This area, with its population of 190,000, comprises the vast residential area of Mestre and the industrial and harbor complex of Marghera, built on sandbanks just like the airport. From the area around Mestre, a network of little rivers and canals and roads and railways extend toward the so-called historical center, which is to say, toward Venice proper. The city looms up at the end of the two parallel bridges, each 4 kilometers in length, by which you can drive to Venice, to park your car in Piazzale Roma, or reach Venice by train, arriving in the Station of S. Lucia.

The historical center

If you look at Venice from above, it seems much larger than it does when viewed from a distance. Venice is an array of buildings and thoroughfares that extends 5 kilometers in length, at its widest almost 3 kilometers in breadth; it has the appearance of a vast and compact encrustation of buildings, bristling with bell towers, churches, palazzi, houses, "calli," and "campi" (roads and small squares), that almost entirely cover a surface of about 550 hectares. Through the dense blanket of buildings and pavement, you can see the water glittering through narrow fissures, the internal waterways called "rii" (the singular is "rio"). The only bodies of water you can see clearly are the Grand Canal, the vast basin of the Arsenale, and – above all – the broad harbor-canal of the Giudecca, which runs past St. Mark's (S. Marco) between the island of S. Giorgio and the long island of the Giudecca (which alone almost forms a city quarter of its own).
You can clearly understand that the 76,000 inhabitants of Venice are the result of a slow process that is transforming Venice into a prestigious center for service industries. Every morning, in fact, an average of 50,000 people converge on Venice from their homes or hotels outside of the city: workers, students, and tourists, engaging in various sorts of gainful activities in the many historic buildings, creating a number of problems that are common to every town with an ancient past.

The estuary

As we continue along, we gain a more precise understanding of just what constitutes the estuary, with its population of 47,000.
Here, the vast liquid plains of the lagoon of Venice, extending over nearly 580 square kilometers, are the large picture, so to speak, while the inhabited towns and villages are the painterly details. And this big picture, just like any of the great and luminous frescoes painted by the great Venetian masters, such as Paolo Veronese (1528-1588) or Giovanni Battista Tiepolo (1696-1770), is dominated by a vast but nearly invisible warp and weft, a subtle weave of hidden canals whose flow only becomes evident at low tide. These hidden channels, marked for long stretches by navigational poles ("brìcole"), seem to form a sort of giant tree with its trunk planted in the Adriatic, driving through the mouth of the harbor of S. Nicolò di Lido, and extending its branches into the lagoon in all directions. The deepest of these channels serves the harbor and, as it runs through the city of Venice, takes the name of the Canale di S. Marco (St. Mark's Canal) or the Canale della Giudecca, as it continues on to the industrial area of Marghera.
One of these canals, the Canale dei Marani, runs around the enormous island of S. Erasmo, which once overlooked the sea, and extends to the densely populated island of Murano. Others extend northward, reaching the loveliest little islands in the Venetian territory, Torcello and Burano, located around the ancient mouths of the river Sile, which runs down from Treviso. The largest inhabited island of the estuary, however, is the one that comprises the Lido and Malamocco, the long sandy littoral strip that, along with the two littorals of Pellestrina and Cavallino, separates the Venetian lagoon from the Adriatic Sea. In reality, then, this third zone of the city of Venice – the estuary, with its population of 47,000 – is a vast network of lands, varying greatly in types of inhabitants and wildlife, in size and configuration, accessible only by water. This network represents the filter and the bridge between Venice and the sea, between Venice and the great riverine and agrarian hinterland, to the north of the city. And yet, this great complex really constitutes the first zone of the city, in both historical and geographic terms; it was here that the events that led to the birth of Venice as a port and as a city all had their origins. Torcello – with its Romanesque-Byzantine church, documented as far back as A.D. 639 and now surrounded by vegetable gardens and vineyards – was a more important town than Venice as late as the 9th c. The same, remarkably, is true of Malamocco, known as early as the 8th c. to have been the residence of the Doges. Murano

– with its Romanesque church documented as far back as 1140, now known primarily for its glass industry – had a port of its own, independent from Venice, in the 10th c.

The restless waters of river, lagoon, and sea

Visiting Venice, then, means sharing the memories and history of a community that, over the course of nearly a millennium, has worked – with tireless ingenuity and often with remarkable good fortune – to build a city at the center of converging flows of water, from a scattered network of villages.

One difficulty, which has always loomed large in the history of Venice, has been that of trying to prevent flooding rivers and the tides that rush up the length of the Adriatic from either silting up the lagoon or submerging the city. The various governments that have ruled Venice over the centuries have devoted enormous efforts to this goal. They were by and large successful at limiting the threat posed by the rivers; less so with respect to the dangers of the tidal surges. As of this writing, when the tide rises about 1 m., 4 percent of the surface of the older section of Venice is covered by water; when the tide rises about 1.10 m., 30 percent of the surface is covered. This danger, however, is about to be eliminated, through methods that have previously been used in Amsterdam and London to eliminate similar problems. In Venice the problem is rendered more complex by the coexistence of the three great waters – rivers, lagoon, and sea – that are indivisible, as well as being an intrinsic part of Venice itself. And these waters are inextricably bound up with the history and architecture of the city, as well.

Venice, city of three ecological cultures

We could describe Venice as a unique chemical combination of river culture and maritime culture, created in the laboratory of the lagoon. From the rivers – rivers that, following the collapse of the Roman road system in the wake of the end of the Western Roman Empire, served as the chief communications network in the Po valley – Venice received first its Romanesque, and later its Gothic architecture. Down the rivers came the huge logs that were used to build the houses of Venice and, perhaps more important, Venice's great fleet of ships. From the sea, which served to link Venice with the nearby markets of the Adriatic and the far-flung eastern Mediterranean, Byzantine, and Islamic markets, Venice obtained its taste for precious materials, for golden mosaics and for the more sophisticated variants of the flamboyant Gothic style. And it was from the sea that the merchants of Venice garnered their enormous, proverbial wealth. It was the lagoon, however, with its nearly motionless waters and its peaceful seascapes dotted with little islands, that gave Venice its taste for the minute detail, for the lovely small object, for the prudent and careful use of human resources. It was the lagoon that gave Venice its name of "La Serenissima," meaning "The Serene One."

In the area that now marks the boundary between the Grand Canal and the Canale di S. Marco, the deep water began; this was the area most directly exposed to the force of the sea. The Venetians called these waters the Rivoalto, meaning a "rivo," or river, that is "alto" in

Aerial view of the Grand Canal and the Rialto Bridge

the two-fold sense of "high," as in high banks, and "deep," in the sense of a deep channel. This was also the ancient name of the area where the center of political power, the Doge's Palace (Palazzo del Doge, or Palazzo Ducale), was located. Later, the same name, simplified in form to Rialto, was used to describe the area where trading and business were conducted, along the banks of the Grand Canal; here, in the 12th c., the bridge of Rialto (Ponte di Rialto) was built, at first a drawbridge made of wood.
This bridge, like other famous river bridges, such as the Pont de Nôtre-Dame over the Seine in Paris, or the Ponte Vecchio over the Arno in Florence, is rich in centuries of history. Indeed, it seems indicative that when the Venetians decided, in 1508, to replace the old wooden bridge with the new stone bridge that still spans the Grand Canal (completed in 1592), they did so in part because Francesco Morosini wrote from Paris that King Louis XII was completing a new stone bridge, the Pont de Nôtre-Dame (1499-1507).

The Lion of St. Mark's

The Venetians decided to establish the headquarters of their paramount religious authority, the bishop, on a fortified island, called the Castello (or castle, for the fortifications), located on the Rivoalto, but closer to the sea, where there were other islands occupied by Benedictine monasteries, such as S. Servolo and S. Giorgio. This island, which is now called S. Pietro di Castello, remained separate from the rest of the city. It served as a port for the bishop, until the 12th c.; it was finally joined to the rest of Venice with the construction of the shipyards of the Arsenale.

The early centuries of Venice under the Doges

Around Venice there had existed, ever since Roman times, a number of small harbor towns; they had begun to thrive when, as a result of the barbarian invasions (5th c.), the wars carried on by the Byzantine Greeks (6th c.), and the arrival of the Longobards (7th c.), many of the inhabitants of the surrounding mainland provinces took refuge in the lagoon. The rebirth of the Western Roman Empire through a convergence of interests between the Pope and Charlemagne (A.D. 800) led Constantinople to seek an accord with the Franks (812). One of the consequences was the confirmation, in the area around Venice, of the two authorities whose presence was a prerequisite for the prosperity of a future city: the bishop of Castello (Obeliebato, 775) and the Doge of the Venetians (Agnello Particiaco, 810). Around 827, the Doge obtained from two merchants of Torcello and Malamocco what was believed to be a relic of the evangelist St. Mark; the decision was thus made to build a basilica worthy of containing this relic: St. Mark's, or S. Marco, was rebuilt in 1063 in the Romanesque style, and later decorated in the Byzantine and the Gothic styles.
The Doge and the bishop cooperated in levying customs duties, encouraging the Venetians to organize a thriving harbor for goods arriving from the Byantine and Muslim East, and travelling on to the Italian, German, and French West.
In 992, the Doge Pietro Orseolo II obtained favorable conditions for Venice's river and sea trade from the two empires (East and West); by the year 1000, Venice controlled the coasts of the Adriatic Sea. When the Normans attempted to blockade the Adriatic, the Venetian fleet successfully won through in the eastern Mediterranean (1085), and won recognition in Constantinople through good relations with the Byzantine empire.

The medieval Commune and the Crusades

The First Crusade (1096) represented a great challenge for Venice. If the city wished to maintain its trading networks in the Byzantine Levant, it would now have to compete with the Genoan, Pisan, and Norman fleets, which were doing land-office business, feeding and transporting the Crusaders to the Holy Land. The Venetians' success in the Levant, however, provoked a sharp reaction from Byzantium; the possessions of Venetian merchants in Constantinople were expropriated, and they were briefly imprisoned (1171); in Italy, the

Communal governments were coming to power, while the German emperor, Frederick I Barbarossa, was challenging the authority of the pope. At this point, Venice – finally unshackled from its ancient subjugation to Byzantium – became newly enterprising. The fabulously wealthy doge Sebastiano Ziani convinced the pope, Barbarossa, and the Communes to choose Venice as the site of a major European peace conference (1177), giving the city new and enhanced international prestige. For the conference, St. Mark's Square (Piazza S. Marco) was enlarged, doubling in size; the new wing of the Procuratie Vecchie was built, looking much as it appears in a handsome painting by Gentile Bellini (1496-1500). About twenty years later, the Latin Crusaders, especially the French, selected Venice as the base from which to launch the Fourth Crusade; in this enterprise, the Venetian fleet, led by the doge Enrico Dandolo (1192-1205), sailed to Constantinople, conquered the city, and founded a Latin empire (1205).
This set of events was of considerable importance to Venice, which thus obtained "la quarta parte e mezza" ("A Quarter and a Half-Quarter," i.e., three-eighths) of the territories that were once held by Byzantium, establishing a network of harbors and islands in the Levant that assured Venice of steady and secure maritime connections. Venice also won Corfu (1207) and the island of Crete (1209); despite continual difficulties, Crete remained Venice's most important naval base in the Muslim world until the 17th c. Enormous wealth poured into Venice, which was now not only the capital of the old Lagoon State, or Dogado (Duchy), but also the capital of the Stato di Mare (Maritime State); along with that wealth came priceless relics of Greek and Byzantine art, including the four famed gilded horses, set on the facade of the Basilica di S. Marco. The first great palazzi were built along the Grand Canal, with their long porticoes, used for unloading goods from the ships; these palazzi were also known as Fondachi, or storehouses, as in the Fondaco dei Tedeschi and the Fondaco dei Turchi (storehouses of the Germans and the Turks).

From the Fourth Crusade to the Wars with Genoa in the 14th c.

Constantinople was held by the Latins for sixty years, but in 1261 it fell back into the hands of the Greeks, who were determined to monopolize trade with the Levant, in alliance with Genoa. The Venetians therefore found themselves fighting not only the Turks, but also – and primarily, before long – the Genoans. When the Muslims occupied Acre, the last Christian stronghold in Palestine (1291), the conflict between the two Italian maritime cities became particularly bitter. At this juncture, the Communal government of Venice was consolidated and placed under aristocratic control; only certain families could become members of the Maggior Consiglio, or chief council (1297); the city government also became the sole political power, and all activities were regulated by Statutes and Magistracies, governing the industrial production of wool, hides, and glass (1291), the ownership of property in the lagoon (1282), and the construction and rigging of ships in the Arsenale di Stato (1289). After an attempted palace coup by Bajamonte Tiepolo (1310), a new council, the Council of Ten (Consiglio dei Dieci), was created, and all new problems were resolved through exceptional new powers. Work began on a radical new maintenance of rivers, harbor, and city, a process that continued until the last years of the Republic. The first expansion of the Arsenale (1325) made it possible for the war fleet to provide regular support to the trading fleet, which now ventured out even onto the Atlantic waves, sailing to the English and Flemish markets (1317). Running the Arsenale required specialized craftsmen and laborers, and the city's population swelled rapidly. Large working-class neighborhoods thus grew or sprung up around the Arsenale, and also along the Canale di Cannaregio, to the northwest, still the first point of arrival for those coming from the Terraferma (or mainland). When the bubonic plague (Black Death) struck in 1348, the population of Venice dropped from 100,000 (according to the estimates made by military recruiters) to 70,000, but with the passing of the plague, the population began to grow once again. Venice remained the most populous city in northern Italy in the 14th c., with Florence running a close second. A new attitude seems to have developed in the aristocratic Venice of the time, engendering conflict that was at least in part softened by the charity offered by the State and that practiced by the Mendicant Orders, first established in Venice in the early-13th c. During this period, the great Gothic churches of the Frari (1236-1420), Ss. Giovanni e Paolo (1234-1430), and S. Stefano (1264-1430) were built, along with their enormous convent complexes. In the same period, the enormous grain silos of Terranova (1341) and the new Palazzo Ducale (Doge's Palace; 1334) were built, marking the inauguration of two styles that were to be essential to the fundamental appearance of Venice, the sober practical style of industrial structures, and the lavish, marble-rich, highly adorned style of the "lobate" Gothic, which was to serve

as the model for all of the large private aristocratic palazzi built during the 14th and 15th c. In terms of urban planning, one decisive process that occurred was the elimination of all wooden bridges in favor of arched masonry bridges, putting an end to the presence of horse traffic in Venice
For the rest of the 14th c., while national states were developing elsewhere in Europe, Venice was engaged in land wars with the neighboring Italian seigneuries and in naval wars with Genoa; in 1381 Genoa managed to occupy Chioggia, in the southern lagoon, while Hungary seized the eastern coasts of the Adriatic.

The Golden Century, the Quattrocento

At the end of the 14th c., the Genoan fleet and the Hungarian army had sorely hampered Venice's trade routes in the Adriatic and in the Levant, but by the beginning of the 15th c., the Venetian government managed to emerge from its difficulties, establishing a complex and highly successful network of alliances and counter-offensives by sea and land. By sea, Venice conquered, or reconquered the island of Euboea, or Negroponte (1366), Corfu (1386), Lepanto (1393), Cephalonia (1413), and Cyprus (1490). Moreover, the chief neighboring Italian cities – Treviso (1339), Padua and Vicenza (1404), Verona (1405), and Udine (1420) – which were already linked to Venice by political or commercial ties, fell under Venetian rule, forming the foundation of the Stato di Terra (Land State), the third after those on sea and in the lagoon (Stato Lagunare, Stato di Mare). Credit for this brilliant resurgence should largely be given to the doge Francesco Foscari (1423-1457), who worked in league with Florence; although Foscari was forced to spend heavily on mercenary armies to face off the powerful Lombard dynasties of the Visconti and the Sforza – seizing Bergamo and Brescia in 1433 – he was still able to restore the sound finances of the state, and consolidated all of the financial and legislative mechanisms. The new three-fold state, which took the title of "La Dominante" in 1462, started to become deeply involved in Italian and European affairs; as a result, the city began to acquire the appearance of the early Renaissance. The great Gothic palazzi, their facades decorated with frescoes, gave way to the stern marble facades designed by Mauro Codussi (1440-1509), who blended the strict Florentine style with the courtly magniloquence of the Roman style. This transformation was abetted by a renewal of religious culture, promoted by the Reformed Orders, especially the Camaldolese; for that order Codussi built the church of S. Michele in Isola (1469-1478), which shows clear influence of the work of Leon Battista Alberti.
Venice became the capital of so strong and stable a state – compared with the Italian seigneuries – that it survived the crisis of the century's end, when Charles VIII of France invaded the peninsula (1494) and the Turkish fleet, master of Constantinople from 1453, began to attack Venice's outposts in the Levant (1494).

The terrible and glorious 16th c.

The solidity of the Venetian State – which staved off the thrusting French power, to which Milan succumbed, and the determined Spanish forces, to which Naples fell, after the armistice of Lyons (1504) – decidedly set the lagoon city apart. That solidity was based on the special cultural, political, and financial activism of the city's aristocracy; although this aristocracy ruled a maritime and terrestrial empire, it still considered the Dogado – i.e., the ancient state based in the lagoon (Stato Lagunare) – to be its home territory, a bulwark of security. And yet, it was precisely this territory – the lagoon – that most exposed the city to the natural risks of increasing tidal surges ("acque alte"); on the other hand, due to the accumulation of silt from the rivers and sand from marine currents, the harbor mouth of S. Nicolò di Lido began to fill up, becoming practically unusable. In order to reach the city, ships had to use the Malamocco entrance.
Gaining some control over the lagoon, the rivers, and the sea, in short, was as important to the aristocratic government of Venice as it was to govern the Stato di Mare and the Stato di Terra (the maritime and terrestrial states), where the encroaching dangers took the form of Turkish infidels and Christian armies. With a view to strengthing their land-based state, the Venetians had the ill-advised idea to attack the Papal State in Romagna, prompting a decisive reaction from Julius II (1443-1513), the fiery and brilliant pope of the Roman Renaissance. Julius rapidly organized the League of Cambrai, combining French, Austrian, and Spanish troops to fight Venice (1508), and launched an excommunication against the Venetian Republic. Venice suffered a terrible defeat at their hands at Agnadello, on 14 May 1509. For the moment, Agnadello seemed to spell the end of the Republic, shattering all of Venice's hard-won gains on the mainland.

The powers organized by the pope, however, had troubles of their own, in the form of the Reformation, led by Martin Luther; Venetian diplomats managed to reassemble the entire Dominio Veneto (Venetian Dominions) in just a few years (1517), though the cost was an implicit renunciation of any future plans to expand throughout the Italian peninsula. A few years later, however, when the mighty army of the Hapsburg emperor Charles V struck Rome (Sack of Rome, 1527), putting an end to Rome's preeminence as a center of the Renaissance, Venice became a haven for that culture. Indeed, Venice made Renaissance culture into an instrument with which to rejuvenate and reinforce both itself and its Stato di Terra, or landward empire.

While the great European nations, then, pursued the conquest of new world markets, created by the new ocean routes, 16th-c. Venice became a cautious neutral state that perpetuated its military glory in the creations of art, employing the resources that continued to flow from the sea in the maintenance of its lagoon and agricultural hinterland. This maintenance was overseen by the new magistracies, whose responsibilities included controlling the waters (Magistratura per il Controllo delle Acque; 1505), beautifying the city (Magistratura per il Decoro della Città; 1535), the reclamation of unfarmed lands (Magistratura per i Beni Incolti; 1541), and the maintenance of the rivers (Magistratura per la Regolazione dei Fiumi; 1581). It was chiefly the Venetian aristocrats, however, that helped to develop the taste for the sumptuous Palladian villas built along the very same rivers – Sile and Brenta – that had created Venice in the first place. And those aristocrats returned to the land as amiable and cultivated owners, determined however to make the countryside profitable, as well as to subjugate those troublesome rivers through hydraulic engineering.

The spectacular Regata Storica in the Grand Canal

At the same time, and especially under the guidance of the great doge Andrea Gritti (1523-1538), the city of Venice continued to change its appearance, carrying on with the architectural reforms begun in the 15th c. Major figures in this process were the architects Jacopo Sansovino (1486-1570) and Andrea Palladio (1508-1580); in particular, Sansovino built the Biblioteca Marciana (St. Mark's Library; 1537) and completely transformed Piazza S. Marco (St. Mark's Square); Palladio built the churches of S. Giorgio Maggiore (1565) and the Redentore (1577), giving the Bacino di S. Marco (Basin of St. Mark's) the appearance of a vast ceremonial square, made of water. In brief, a happy state of affairs, though there was a large and painful thorn in Venice's side – specifically, in Venice's maritime side: the unrelenting pressure of the Turks of the Ottoman empire.

The island of Cyprus, the easternmost outpost of the Stato di Mare, obtained through adroit diplomatic and dynastic machinations in 1486, was the first Venetian possession to be threatened by the fleet of Sultan Selim II (1566-1574), an indolent drunkard.

Venice had undertaken in 1473 the third major expansion of its Arsenale di Castello; with the somewhat relaxed pace encouraged by thirty years of peace, it was upgrading its galleys with the latest technology, and building massive new galleasses. The Venetian Senate voted on 20 March 1570 to reject the proposals of peace offered by the Turks – proposals of a peace whereby Venice would simply renounce its claims to Cyprus. The vote to reject the proposals was a close one, though, a clear sign of uncertainty. No one really wanted war, and all of Venice's diplomatic corps was soon deployed to persuade the pope and Spain to join Venice in a united front against the enemies of Christendom. A new League was formed (20 May 1570).

War did come, and Venice was ready for it, emerging victorious from the Battle of Lepanto (7 October 1571), where a Turkish battle-fleet of 230 warships fought a Christian fleet of 208 ships, more than half of them Venetian. Victory did not save Cyprus, but it put the Turkish fleet out of commission for the next thirty years, and it gave Venice renewed rights to free trade in the Muslim Levant.

Heroism at sea and the balance of power on land between the 17th and 18th c.

Despite the loss of Cyprus – with its sugar, salt, and cotton – Venice managed to hold onto the great island of Crete, which produced oil, wine, and raisins, as well as linen and cotton. It was still the capital of a rich maritime and land-based state, a state that looked forward to a long future in the early-17th c. The enormous Baroque monument of the church of the Salute, begun in 1631, as a votive offering for the end of yet another bout of the plague, was certainly a sign of this confidence in the future. The architect of this church, Baldassare Longhena (1598-1682) was, for nearly a century, the unquestioned master of the Baroque style in Venice; let us mention just two of his great buildings, the Palazzo Rezzonico (1657) and Palazzo Pesaro (1665), overlooking the Grand Canal.

This belief in a long future for the city, however, turned into something resembling a religious faith in the wisdom of the Republic; hence the harsh and unbending resistance of the younger members of the Venetian aristocracy in the face of the demands of the pope – resulting in another excommunication (1606-1607) – that the Venetian government adhere to the policies of the Catholic church's Counter Reformation, in such areas as relations with Protestant nations, and that it accept the Inquisition and the new rules on ecclesiastical praebends. This was the dispute by interdict, in which the Republic was defended by Fra' Paolo Sarpi, versus the Cardinal Bellarmin; only the mediation of King Henry IV of England prevented armed conflict.

This was a specialization based on forms of personal "heroism," as became evident at sea in particular, when the Ottomans attacked Crete (1666); after ceding some of their territories (1669), the Venetians saw the Turks take the whole island for good, on 24 October 1671, one century after the Battle of Lepanto.

The Venetians' determined resistance had a hero in the great admiral, and later Doge (1688-1694) Francesco Morosini. Morosini managed to conquer most of the Morea (or Peloponnesus) in 1687, while the Turks were vainly attempting to take Vienna; he thus acquired for Venice a last presence in Greek waters, a presence that endured until the Treaty of Passarowitz (1718), when the Venetian Stato di Mare was whittled down to the Adriatic Sea and nothing more.

Slowly, 18th-c. Venice acquired a contradictory nature. Scientific studies – and especially hydraulic engineering – flourished at the University of Padua; many Venetians continued to travel, learning the new theories and philosophies of the time; view-painting attained unrivalled heights of exquisite beauty with the work of Canaletto (1698-1768), architecture seemed to be ahead of its time, with work that foreshadowed European Rationalism, in particular by Lodoli (1690-1771) and Temanza (1705-1789); the work of protecting the city and the lagoons from the waters of the rivers and the sea proceeded apace. All the same, the genuine participation of the state, as a territorial association of cooperating citizenry in the city's prestige was a dead letter, indeed, seemed to be an impossible dream. Venice acquired the unenviable reputation of being a playground, a European capital of theater and courtesans, crowded with adventurers, but without a real and solid future. Whether this was true, or merely an imagined interpretation seen in hindsight, remains an open and much-debated question.

Certainly, Venice was callow and feeble when the French Revolution, and the Napoleonic Wars that followed it – aimed chiefly at Austria – shook the structures of the Venetian state. Perhaps we should only point out that few aristocracies could have managed to give up their power with such dignified silence.

The French and Austrian 19th c.

When the last doge of Venice left the Palazzo Ducale once and for all, on the evening of 15 May 1797, he entrusted to the provisional democratic government established by Napoleon a city that – beneath the ubiquitous masks and the frenzy of Carnival – possessed a solid and well-run harbor, a prosperous agricultural hinterland, and an enormous cultural and environmental heritage. In this context, the greatest problem that faced the French governors, and the Austrian governors that followed them, in ruling Venice (until it joined a united Italy in 1866), was how to reconcile the efficency of the harbor with the preservation of a city that boasted some of the finest art and architecture in all of Europe. Though it has been denied, historians must admit that both the Austrians and the French – bound to Venice by ancient political and cultural ties – acted for the city's best interests every time they were forced to deal with the knotty problem of the lagoon.

In terms of the preservation of the city structure, even Napoleon – who had stated that he wanted to be an Attila to Venice – may have caused traumas in political terms, but he was still quite careful to preserve the aging jewel of the Adriatic.

Or course, as he had done in other conquered regions, Napoleon expropriated the ecclesiastical institutions, which indeed owned a considerable portion of the city; as a result, a number of churches were demolished. The most notable church to be destroyed was that of the Servites, a great Gothic monument similar to the Frari; only a single portal still stands. The greatest changes that were made concerned the Punta di S. Antonio, which was transformed into a park (now occupied by the Biennale) with the demolition of three convents; the great 14th-c. Granai, or grain siloes, of S. Marco, were replaced by the Giardinetti Reali. One of the facades of St. Mark's Square was also completely rebuilt; the Ala Napoleonica replaced the 16th-c. church of S. Geminiano (1810). The French did some very useful work on the Arsenale, however, building the Porta Nuova, which still allows ships to enter the inner basins directly through the port of S. Nicolò; they also began to dredge the sandbars blocking access to the port of Malamocco. The most decisive intervention, however, was that of the Austrian government (1814-1866), in collaboration with a number of Italian-German joint venture companies: the construction of the Venice-Milan railroad, and the building of a new seaport at the western end of the city. This was followed by a general revamping of the pedestrian walkways throughout the city, with the accompanying construction of many bridges, especially the iron bridges of the Accademia (1854) and the Ferrovia (railroad; 1858).

Venice in 20th-c. Italy

The annexation of Italy to the Kingdom of Italy, marked by the entry of Italian troops into the city on 19 October 1866, was the beginning of a new period of general reforms; among those reforms was, necessarily, a continuation of the French and Austrian projects for Venice's lagoon and harbor. Following the clearance of the entry to the lagoon of Malamocco, the harbor mouth of S. Nicolò was rendered more efficient as well, with the construction of offshore breakwaters that extended out into the Adriatic Sea (1910). A secondary but notable effect of the restored efficiency of the harbor was the development of Lido as a popular beach resort, encouraged by the construction of the Hotel Excelsior (1898-1908); among the effects of this new resort hotel was the return of the popularity of Middle Eastern styles, which had not been seen for many centuries. A more substantial project followed, consisting of the creation of the industrial port of Marghera (1917) and the expansion of the Comune, or municipality (1927); by shifting most of Venice's industrial production onto the Terraferma, or mainland, the ancient city of Mestre was also encouraged to grow; in fact, over half of the population of the municipality now lives there. Lastly, with the construction of the automobile bridge (1933), which intersected roughly with the westernmost end of the Grand Canal, and the resulting excavation of the Rio Nuovo, which links the Piazzale Roma with the Grand Canal, it became necessary to carry out a more thorough rebuilding of the pedestrian walkways.

After WWII, the thrusting industrial expansion of the 1930s was dampened, in the mainland municipality of Venice; part of this discouragement of unbridled development emerged from a growing cultural awareness of the remarkable environmental heritage of the lagoon. Many came to think of the lagoon as a laboratory in which to search for ways of preserving the historic city; scientific studies, however belated, began to be carried out.

The overall zoning regulations established in a single plan in 1963 had completely overlooked the problem of tidal surges ("acque alte"), despite the heavy seas and general flooding that submerged the city in 1951, destroying the breakwaters along the shores of Pellestrina. This regulatory plan has been fiercely attacked by environmentalists, who point in particular to the remarkably high tides of 1966 (1.92 m.); it would soon be replaced by more complete and articulated urban plans. There is a consensus in Venice that steps must be taken to accelerate the process of restoration and conservation, with greater specific attention to the problem of tidal surges ("acque alte").

Venice: Instructions for Use

Those who do not live in Venice tend to form an idea of the city that is substantially flawed and superficial: visitors often think of Venice as if it were all one great archeological museum (without any of the structures and organization of a major urban center), rather than as a living city. With this approach, it is natural that tourists fail to establish a healthy relationship with the city. They cannot fail to see Venice as a powder-puff display, as a sideshow supported by scaffolding like some theatrical production, and ultimately to feel a certain revulsion. J.P. Sartre once referred to Venice as "the pink spider of the Adriatic that has devoured her mate." This sort of theme park can charm you, enchant you, and then toss you back out into the everyday world, sucked dry of everything, (including your umbrella and your change purse).
The only way to establish a solid relationship with Venice is to toss into the sea (or perhaps we should say, into the lagoon) all the misleading cultural baggage associated with Venice, and to start over from the very simple but fundamental concept that Venice is a city. A city with all the unique variations that belong here, but a city nevertheless. And a city with plenty of problems. It is evident that the thriving business and labor force derive chiefly from the inhabitants and infrastructure of the mainland – with a generally younger population and the burgeoning growth of small and mid-sized businesses in the exurban area. It is, all the same, unquestionable that the City on the Sea still has plenty to offer, both potentially, and in actual fact (particularly in the fields of culture and in terms of tools for the advanced service industries). Venice can certainly handle criticism, but the city needs a little respect. And respect should be the byword of visitors and tourists, however brief the stay; a clear show of respect will make it easier for you to win acceptance from the Venetians, who tend to think of themselves as a privileged caste, for better or worse.
There are difficulties involved in living in Venice: there are houses that simply cannot be restored (because of prohibitive cost, or because of bureaucratic red tape), there is the constant humidity, the tidal surges, and the incessant rolling waves that inevitably damage the foundations of buildings. Then, of course, transportation is hardly a simple matter (and certainly slower than in other cities, where you can drive), food and all of the other daily necessities are much more expensive, life is relatively isolated, and there are plenty of other environmental problems, such as the strong smells produced by decomposing algae in the summertime, or the swarms of tiny midges that become tremendously annoying at times. And yet, despite all these negatives, despite the nay-saying of those who call Venice a dying city, it remains an eminently desirable place to live. It has all the charms of a tremendously rich artistic and architectural history; it is also rich in ideas and intellectual stimuli; it is a profoundly multicultural city, far from the growing flames of hatred and racism that are gradually infecting Italian society. Venice is, in short, an international province, with all the pluses and minuses that this profound contradiction in terms can imply.

When to go. If you are making plans to go to Venice, here is an important piece of advice: be sure to go at the right time. If your idea of fun is to mingle with huge crowds, then the high season (from Easter to October) is the right time for you. Even if you avoid the months of July and August (and there are excellent reasons to do so: in August, you may find yourself overcome by the massive heat and humidity, coupled with the considerable difficulties posed by the widespread summer closure of stores and restaurants), going to Venice during the high season is a fine way of seeing a city that looks exactly like its postcards. Unless, of course, you are sufficiently familiar with the city to make your way to some of the lesser-known attractions and areas. It is also true, however, that the spring and summer are the times of year when most of the great events and social and cultural celebrations occur: S. Marco, on 25 April; the day of the Sensa, or Ascension, in late spring, with the evocative ceremony of the Sposalizio del Mare, or Marriage of Venice with the Sea; in May, the Vogalonga, a huge rowing regatta; the Festa del Redentore on the third Sunday in July, with the tradition of night-time boat rides and fireworks over the lagoon. And on the first Sunday in September, there is the spectacular Regata Storica in the Grand Canal (for more information and for tickets, you should contact the offices of the APT and the Assessorato al Turismo del Comune, or city tourist office). Along with all of these events, during the summer, in alternate years, there is the Biennale d'Arte, in the Giardini; there is the annual Venice Film Festival, at the Lido; and then you may wish to see the Supercampiello literary awards, held at the Doge's Palace (Palazzo Ducale).

If, instead, you prefer a less spectacular and a less glitzy Venice, a Venice that is somewhat more down to earth, then the perfect time to visit is in the fall. The major summer art shows are often extended into the fall, the weather is mild (at least until the first "acque alte" are felt), the hotels are still open, and a little less crowded. And, on 21 November, you can watch the Festa della Madonna della Salute, one of the annual religious events most beloved by the inhabitants of Venice. In the winter – despite the many "package" trips to Venice offered by travel agencies – everything is a little more complicated: in some cases, hotels and restaurants close to rest up for the travails of Carnevale, when finding a room in Venice (unless you have reserved well in advance) is a fool's paradise. Carnevale (what Americans think of as Mardi Gras) is a separate issue: it was reborn from its historic ashes as a spontaneous and popular return to tradition, but it was immediately seized upon by the tourist trade, which turned it into a sufficiently massive event that one is inevitably curious and drawn.

In any case, whenever you choose to go, the first step is to get there without problems. It is easy and simple; here is how.

Carnevale, or Mardi gras, in Venice

Getting into Venice. If you should desire to drive to Venice, then you should know that, while this is certainly a possibility, it is most decidedly not a necessity, and it can be – in some cases – an inconvenience. In Piazzale Roma, which is the automotive gateway to Venice, there are plenty of **autorimesse**, or paid parking garages, open 24 hours a day (Garage Comunale, Piazzale Roma 496, tel. 5222308-5237763; Garage San Marco, Piazzale Roma 467/f, tel. 5232213-5235101; fax 5232213). Morever, there is a parking lot, with attendant, run by ACI, the Italian equivalent of the AAA, likewise open 24 hours a day (tel. 5206235). All the same, there is a considerable risk of encountering traffic jams and long lines, especially on your way in and at weekends.

A good solution, especially in view of the newly equipped island, is to leave your car at the parking lot, or Parcheggio del Tronchetto (tel. 5207555), linked with the historical center by public water transportation and private water taxis. The ideal solution, however, is to leave your car on the mainland (Terraferma), in Mestre or Marghera, and to continue from there by bus or train to Venice, over the Ponte della Libertà. For example, at Viale Stazione 10 in Mestre, note the Garage Serenissima, open 24 hours a day (tel. 938021). Or else you can use the parking lot in Via Righi, not far from the overpass ("cavalcavia") of S. Giuliano, or the parking lot of the railroad station of Mestre, toward Marghera. Many buses running to Mestre and Marghera have their terminus in Piazzale Roma: you can count on frequent buses. You should buy bus tickets in "tabaccherie," or tobacconists, news stands, and cafes: if you board without a ticket, you could face heavy fines.

For those who choose to take the **train**, either directly or as a transfer from Mestre to Venice, there are no particular problems; just make sure that the train you take actually does continue to the station of Venezia Santa Lucia. Tickets from Mestre to Venice, which are good for one hour (more than enough time, because there are trains for Venice every few minutes, and the trip itself only requires ten minutes), should be purchased in the train station or at the left luggage, and then stamped just before boarding the train. During the summer, you may also park in the mainland lots of S. Giuliano (ACTV buses for Piazzale Roma numbers 5, 12 with a cross-bar, and 19 weekdays and holidays, 80 and 84, only weekdays) and Fusina (linked with the historic center, at Zattere, by the n. 16 boat line). For those who reach Venice from the littoral of Jesolo, there are the boat lines n. 13 (from Treporti to the Fondamenta Nuove), 14, and 14 with a cross-bar.

The approach is different for those who land at the Marco Polo **airport**, at Tessera, recently upgraded to an international airport, but with a far more modest past, even in recent years (tel. 2606111 switchboard, 2609260 information; fax 2606260). You can reach the historic center by a trans-lagoon water bus, the land buses of the ACTV line n. 5, or in fairly expensive private taxi-powerboats. There is also direct ATVO shuttle bus service to the airport from Piazzale Roma, Venice. For information: tel. 5205530.

Less common, but decidedly available, is access to Venice **by boat**. The landing points are currently at S. Basilio at the end of the Zattere, at the Stazione Marittima (mostly used by commercial sea traffic) and on the Riva dei Sette Martiri in the Sestiere di Castello.

Information. In any case – whether you are in the historical center, at Tessera, Marghera, or the Tronchetto – once you have arrived, it is a good idea to enquire at one of the Servizi Informazioni (information windows) of the APT and the Prenotazione Alberghi (hotel reservations) of the Associazione Veneziana Albergatori (AVA; Venetian Hoteliers Association), scattered at strategic points throughout the city territory.
APT: Castello 4421, tel. 5298711, fax 523099 (weekdays and Saturday 8:30-7); Nuova Rotatoria Autostradale, Marghera, tel. 937764; fax 937764 (weekdays and Saturday 9-4); Stazione Ferroviaria (train station) Santa Lucia, tel. 719078; fax 719078 (weekdays and Saturday 8-7); Ca' Savio, Via Fausta 79/g, tel. 966010; fax 966010 (open during the tourist season); Lido di Venezia, Gran Viale S. Maria Elisabetta 6/a, tel. 5265721; fax 5298720 (winter 8:30-2; summer 8:30-7).
AVA: Cannaregio 3929, tel. 5238032; information office S. Croce 495/9, tel. 5228640; hotel office, Garage San Marco, Piazzale Roma, tel. 5231397; for hotels on Isola Nuova del Tronchetto, tel. 5287833. Information offices: Nuova Rotatoria Autostradale, Mestre, tel. 921638; Rotatoria Autostradale, Marghera, tel. 926981; Strada Romea 1, Marghera, tel. 924213; Aeroporto Marco Polo, Tessera, tel. 5415133; Santa Lucia Railroad Station, tel. 715016. Associazione Veneziana Albergatori Lido, Gran Viale Santa Maria Elisabetta 26, tel. 5261700.

The luxury gondola, one of the symbols of Venice

Arriving without a reservation – aside from the "high season" for Venice (Carnevale, Easter, the heart of the summer, the Film Festival) – is not an insurmountable problem: the city has a well-diversified array of hotels, ranging from 5-star luxury hotels to the modest *pensione*. Here and there, as we point out in the section "Information for travellers" at the end of the book, you may happen on a pleasant surprise: a newly refurbished ancient palazzo, a garden amidst the "calli," views that are as charming as they are unexpected.

Most hotels accept the major credit cards; many – especially those in the top category – offer their guests special services: transportation to the hotel, the use of sports and recreational facilities, garages, and parking areas with attendants. A fair number of hotels have installed special facilities to accommodate the handicapped. The general level of hotels is mid-to-high. An unpleasant situation that could conceivably arise for tourists on the island of Tronchetto, despite the attempts of police and Carabinieri to prevent this sort of fraud, is to fall prey to dishonest boatmen and "fixers," being spectacularly overcharged or cheated (both for the trip to the hotel and the reservations of the room or rooms). If you need a water taxi, you should always rely on authorized companies (and keep in mind that the price, in any case, will be higher than that of a land taxi). A few names: Cooperativa San Marco, tel. 5222303-5235775; Cooperativa Veneziana Taxi, tel. 766124; Cooperativa Serenissima, tel. 5221265-5228538; Società Narduzzi Solemar, tel. 5200838-5231835; Società Marco Polo, tel. 966170.

Transportation. Having reached your destination safe and sound, the time has come to decide how to get around Venice. The simplest thing (aside from walking), is to make use of public transportation, run by the municipal transit service, ACTV; this network can get you close to anyplace in historical Venice (Centro Storico) pretty promptly, as well as to the Terraferma. The main lines are the n. 1 ("vaporetti"), which is a local line that stops at all the landing stations from Lido to S. Marco and then winds along the Grand Canal until it reaches the Tronchetto; the faster n. 2 line, with motorboats, running around the city from Ferrovia (the railroad station) to Lido passing through the Canale della Giudecca; the n. 82, which links the Tronchetto with Lido via the Grand Canal. Lido is also served by the motorboat line n. 6, linking it to the landing station of the Ponte della Paglia. For information, you can contact the Office in Piazzale Roma, tel. 5287886, fax 5222633; the Office in Corte dell'Albero, at S. Marco, tel. 780310, or to its counterpart office in Mestre, in Via Ca' Savorgnan, tel. 972073 (from 7 am to 7 pm). For those not from Venice, ACTV water transportation tickets are fairly expensive (they should be purchased in advance, just as for public transportation on the Italian mainland). The company has therefore established a series of special deals for non-residents: for instance, with a passport sized photograph and proper identification, those who reside in the Venetian Region can buy the Carta Venezia, good for three years, which allows you to enjoy the special resident rates. There is also a 24-hour ticket (except for lines n. 40, 41 and 42, with one piece of carry-on baggage allowed). For slightly longer periods of time, you can buy a three-day and seven-day pass. The ACTV also offers, for the particularly careless, not one but two lost-and-found offices: one in Corte dell'Albero (tel. 780310, 8:30-1 pm) and one in Mestre, in Galleria Teatro Vecchio (tel. 984144, with the same hours, 8:30-1 pm). There is another way – handy and cheap – for crossing the Grand Canal, from bank to bank: the traghetto in gondola, or "gondola ferry." These short-hop ferries operate between S. Maria del Giglio and S. Gregorio (every day, winter 8-6; summer 8-7); between S. Tomà and S. Angelo (weekdays and Saturday 7-9 pm; Sunday and holidays 8-8); between S. Samuele and Ca' Rezzonico (only weekdays and Saturday 7:30-2); between Santa Sofia and Pescaria di Rialto (weekdays and Saturday 7-9 pm; Sunday and holidays 7-7); between Riva del Carbon and S. Silvestro (weekdays and Saturday 8-2); and between Fondamenta S. Simeon Piccolo and the railroad station of Santa Lucia (weekdays and Saturday 7:45-2). The gondolas used for the "traghetti" – a system that is quite popular with the residents of Venice – are the poor cousin of the "gondola di rappresentanza," or the luxury gondola, one of the symbols of this city on the lagoon for nearly a thousand years. Now the gondola deluxe is used only for carrying tourists and honeymooners about, and can be reserved at any of the gondola stops scattered throughout Venice (to mention only a few, at Tronchetto, Piazzale Roma, Rialto, S. Tomà, Calle Vallaresso, Bacino Orseolo, and Riva degli Schiavoni) at official rates, set by the city government. To complete our survey of Venetian water transportation, we should also mention the tours of the estuary organized by the glass manufacturers: they are fairly rapid-fire and mass-audience affairs, and they help to abet the slick postcard image of holidays *Made in Venice*. All the same, if you are in no particular hurry, once you have dropped your luggage at the hotel, the easiest way to get around Venice is on foot, and perhaps exploring routes other than those to the classic tourist attractions; you will need a good map and street directory to find your way. The street numbering, broken up into "sestieri," can be exceedingly confusing. If you begin to lose your way, there are markers indicating the general directions to main landmarks, or even establishing routes of artistic or architectural interest to follow. "Calli" and "campi" (there is only one "piazza"), "fondamenta," "rii terrà" (that is, a "rio" that has been "interrato," or filled in) and "salizzade" (a road that has been paved, or "sel-

ciata"), all have whimsical names, painted on the sides of the buildings that line them; these names are often linked to historical events or specific customs or functions, compiled – as is the Venetian way – in dialect. You may thus find out-of-the-way neighborhoods and quarters that have been spared the onslaught of tourist traffic, where the true soul of Venice can still be found, and where you can still see the structure of the city (the "insule," or block-islands, the layering and incessant renovations that have made Venice what it is over the centuries). You can talk with the real Venetians, and discover that they are much more courteous and friendly than they may seem at first glance.
Another problem can be that of the *acqua alta* (exceptionally high tides or tidal surges), which, particularly in the months of November, December, and February, floods Piazza S. Marco and many other parts of Venice. Often awakening to the sound of high-water sirens, the Venetians resort to little wooden walkways, which allow pedestrians to pass, dry-shod, through the most strategic points of the city, at least along the main routes for pedestrian traffic. Another unwanted presence is that of the Venetian fog (in Italian, *nebbia*; in dialect, *caligo*), which may shroud the city for days at a time, causing considerable problems in lagoon navigation (despite the use of radar equipment), and forcing the populace to take long walks and endure seemingly endless waits at the "pontili," or landing jetties, of the ACTV. Those who are reluctant to wander alone through the maze of Venice can either rely on the organized tours offered by travel agencies, enquire in the tourist office for referral to an authorized tour guide, or directly contact the **Centro Guide Turistiche Autorizzate**,

Lace-tatting, a craft based in Burano

Castello 5448/A, tel. 5239902 or the **Cooperativa Guida Turistica Autorizzata**, Castello 5328, tel. 5209038. For those interested in a novel approach, there is a magnificent way to view Venice from above: an **aerial tour** of the lagoon. For information and reservations, contact the Aeroclub G. Ancillotto at the Aeroporto G. Nicelli di S. Nicolò di Lido (closed Monday, tel. 5260808).

Food in Venice. Another way to explore the city is with your taste buds, instead of your eyes. First of all, we should explode another prejudice that is commonly held concerning Venice: the belief that always and inevitably (unless you go only to restaurants that are famous enough to have become part of the city's mythology), dining is a disappointment here. Here too it depends. If you avoid the black hole of the "menu turistico" (and not all of these are as bad as their reputation), Venice offers some genuine hidden treasures: solid traditions, comfortable and reasonably clean surroundings, fresh food (don't forget the wonderful fish and fruit-and-vegetable markets of Rialto). No, the one thorn that continues to prick is the slight hint of haughtiness, of proud self-aggrandizement on the part of the restaurateurs, and – sadly enough – prices that are decidedly on the high side. But then, come to think of it, everything costs a little more in Venice: leaving aside those absurd cases that have made headlines, the extra cost is primarily due to the problems of transportation. All the same, if you want to eat (relatively) cheaply, you need only dine at a local "bàcaro" or "osteria," which are now quite fashionable (some of them even a little *too* fashionable).

Shopping. Aside from souvenirs for tourists, shopping in Venice and in the various islands of the lagoon can be quite interesting. First of all, there are shops selling handmade faux-marbre paper and notebooks, diaries, envelopes, and boxes made with that paper. Other shops sell cardboard (and also leather) masks for Carnevale; these masks are inspired by characters of the Commedia dell'Arte, and old prints and paintings. And you should not miss the fabrics - silk, cotton, velvet - which are hand-woven and printed. Among the crafts that have made Venice famous, we should mention glass-blowing (vases, glasses, and decorative objects) and lace-tatting; these two crafts are based respectively on the islands of Murano and Burano.
In the section entitled "Information for Travellers" we list the addresses of the most noteworthy shops in Venice and on the islands. We should warn the reader, however, that truly fine handmade lace and glass tend to be quite expensive.

Health-Care and Hygenic Facilities. A less satisfactory matter is the issue of **public toilets**, absolutely indispensable in a city like Venice, with a massive tourist presence. In general, these are substandard, closed at the most remarkable times; in the summer, you sometimes have to stand in line to use them. There is one near the Piazza di San Marco (Albergo Diurno all'Ascension, Ramo Primo de l'Ascension, the cleanest and most acceptable, winter schedule 8-8; summer 7-8:30); other, less inviting toilets are located near the Giardinetti Reali, the Accademia, S. Bartolomeo, in Campo Rialto Novo, S. Leonardo, and in Piazzale Roma (there are other facilities in the two large garages, the Garage Comunale and the Garage S. Marco). Baths and toilets for-a-fee can also be found in the railroad station of Santa Lucia (hours: winter 7-8:30; summer 7-9 pm).
Decidedly more satisfactory is the general situation concerning **health-care facilities** in Venice; they are adequate, efficient, and in some cases, remarkably modern. The Ospedale Civile dei Ss. Giovanni e Paolo has – 24 hours a day – a first-class emergency room (Pronto Soccorso; tel. 5294517), as do the Ospedale al Mare del Lido (Lungomare D'Annunzio 1, tel. 5261750), and the Umberto I in Mestre (Via Circonvallazione 50, tel. 988988). To call a idroambulanza, or water ambulance, the telephone number is 5230000; in Terraferma (the mainland) the number is 988988. The **Croce Rossa Italiana**, or Italian Red Cross, also has a Pronto Soccorso, or first-aid station, in Piazza S. Marco 52 (tel. 5286346). At the Ospedale Civile, in the Department of Nephrology, as well as at the Ospedale al Mare at Lido, there are good **dialysis facilities**, for out-patients as well (you must call ahead).
Venice is still catching up with the times in terms of eliminating barriers for the handicapped: a number of bridges, such as the Ponte delle Guglie, have been equipped with narrow ramps over the steps; in a few cases there are special facilities to help the handicapped across. That is not much, admittedly, in a city that is particularly daunting for the handicapped, where museums and collections have elevators that are too narrow to be used (if they have elevators at all), where the landing jetties are not always easy to use, and where even new buildings do not always take into account the new rules. All the same, steps are being taken.
Among the most recent initiatives launched by the Azienda di Promozione Turistica offering new itineraries (including the installation of 14 information booths in the historical centre and surrounds), a map clearly showing the routes around the city accessible for the disabled stands out. Areas marked in yellow on the map can be visited avoiding bridges or using stair-lift or can be reached directly by the vaporetti, lines 1, 3, 4 and 82. The leaflet also lists all the bridges of the city equipped with stair-lifts (keys for these are offered free of charge to those in need at any of the seven APT offices in the major tourist areas – see the **Information** section – and in the information booths being set up).
In other ways, Venice is still a fairly serene island, where you can get around at night and enjoy its nuanced charm. We may well wonder for how much longer: even in the historical center, crime is growing – mostly petty crime, drug dealing and strongarm protection rackets against shopkeepers. As of this writing, in any case, things are pretty much concentrated on the mainland (Terraferma), between Mestre and the Riviera del Brenta. Here, in any case, are a few numbers for emergency phone calls (they are free from pay phones, and do not require coins or tokens): **Carabinieri** – Emergency Police Aid, or "Pronto Intervento," tel. 112; **Polizia** – Emergency Police Aid, or "Soccorso Pubblico," tel. 113; **Vigili del Fuoco**, or fire department, tel. 115. Among the useful addresses, there is the **Questura**, or police headquarters (Fondamenta S. Lorenzo 5053, tel. 2703511) and the central office of the **Polizia Municipale**, or city police (Ca' Farsetti, tel. 2708203. There are local commands in each "sestiere").

Post Offices and Telephones. The postal service is pretty well distributed throughout the city and quite reliable. The main post office is in the splendid 16th-c. Fontego dei Tedeschi (tel. 5220606), not far from S. Bartolomeo, where – aside from the standard window services, general delivery, and telegram services – you can also send and receive telexes and faxes. Other post offices are located throughout the city and the hinterland.

If you would rather phone than write, the Italian phone company, SIP, has installed phone boothes (wheelchair-friendly) throughout the town. **Public Telephone Offices** are located at S. Bartolomeo (Palazzo delle Poste, weekdays and holidays 8-7:45 pm), at the train station of Santa Lucia (weekdays 8-7:45 pm; Saturday 8-1:45), and at Marco Polo airport at Tessera (weekdays 8-7:45 pm; Saturday 8-1:45).

Venice by night. The daytime Venice, of busy tourist trade and thriving shopping streets, is a world away from the city after sundown. At nightfall, or a few hours thereafter, the city shuts down, and this includes public facilities, bars, restaurants, and most everything else. Even in the summer, it is not easy to find places open after midnight: there are a few "piano-bar," such as the *Martini Scala Club* at S. Fantin or the *Linea d'Ombra* in Punta alla Dogana. Unless you want to try your luck (and test your wallet) at the *Casinò di Ca' Vendramin Calergi*, which moves to Lido in the summer, then you will just have to settle for a solitary and invigorating stroll through a darkened and deserted Venice. Even the most fanatical dancers will have to settle for a minidiscotheque at Accademia, *El Souk Pub* (Calle Contarini Corfù 1056), or else make the trek to the *Acropolis Club 22* (in Lungomare Marconi 22 at Lido). You can listen to good music at the *Paradiso Perduto* in Fondamenta della Misericordia, at *Le Bistrot de Venise*, in Calle dei Fabbri, or *Da Codroma* at the Ponte del Soccorso. For those with more refined tastes, there is the "piano-bar" of the *Do Leoni*, in Riva degli Schiavoni. In the section "Information for travellers" there is more information.
In conclusion, let us say then that the somewhat sleepy nightlife is matched by the less than excellent entertainment: not so much the theater (there is some fine theater at the Teatro Goldoni); rather, it is the disheartening situation of movie houses, which are closing one after another. In the city that, every year, plays host to the prestigious Venice Film Festival (Festival del Cinema della Biennale), there are almost no movie houses, and almost all of them are concentrated in the Sestiere di S. Marco, and shut down for much of the summer. In the rest of Venice, there is a virtual absence of theaters, except for the *Accademia* in the Sestiere di Dorsoduro and the *Astra* at the Lido. The Circuito Cinema del Comune (the city film program) does what it can. There are some fine film series, the movies from the film festival are shown in the center of Venice and in the "terraferma", and there is the very nice custom of open-air movies in Campo S. Polo, for some years now a must for tourists and residents.
After the fire of 29 January 1996 completely destroyed the Teatro La Fenice, one of the architectural and acoustic jewels of Europe, its services and functions (maintaining an international standard) have been tenaciously guaranteed. The operatic and concert seasons are being hosted by the PalaFenice mobile structure, on the Isola del Tronchetto, tel. 5204010, with efficient ACTV link-ups. The Theater's direction, awaiting reconstruction (objective: year 2000), is temporarily housed at Palazzo Franchetti, San Marco 2847, tel. 786500, while the box office is in the headquarters of the Cassa di Risparmio di Venezia, Campo San Luca, tel. 5210161. For information contact the Internet site: **http://www.tin.it/fenice**. Reservations can be made by telephone to Box Office Italia, tel. 940200. For online reservations, the Internet address is: **http://www.cosi.it/fenice**.

Italy: Useful Addresses

Citizens of Australia, Canada, New Zealand, and the United States can enter Italy with a valid passport, and stay for a period of not more than 90 days; citizens of Great Britain and Ireland, as members of the European Union, can travel either with valid passport or with valid identification card.

Foreign Embassies in Italy

Australia:
Corso Trieste 25, Rome, tel. (06) 852721

Canada:
Via G.B. de Rossi 27, Rome, tel. (06) 445981

New Zealand:
Via Zara 28, Rome, tel. (06) 4402928

United States of America:
Via Vittorio Veneto 119/A, Palazzo Margherita, Rome, tel. (06) 46741

Great Britain:
Via XX Settembre 80/A, Rome, tel. (06) 4825441

Ireland:
Piazza Campitelli 3, Rome, tel. (06) 6979121

Foreign Consulates in Italy

Australia:
Via Borgogna 2, Milan, tel. (02) 777041

Canada:
Via Vittor Pisani 19, Milan, tel. (02) 67581

New Zealand:
Via G. D'Arezzo 6, Milan, tel. (02) 48012544

United States of America:
- Lungarno A.Vespucci 38, Florence, tel. (055) 2398276
- Via Principe Amedeo 2/10, Milan, tel. (02) 290351
- Piazza Repubblica 2, Naples, tel. (081) 5838111
- Via Re Federico 18/bis, Palermo (consular agency), tel. (091) 6110020

Great Britain:
- Via S. Paolo 7, Milan, tel. (02) 723001
- Via Crispi 132, Naples, tel. (081) 663511

Ireland:
Piazza San Pietro in Gessate 2, Milan, tel. (02) 55187569

Italian Embassies and Consulates Around the World

Australia:
12 Grey Street - Deakin, Canberra, tel. (06) 273-3333
Consulates at: Adelaide, Brisbane, Melbourne, Perth, Sydney.

Canada:
275 Slater Street, 21st floor, Ottawa (Ontario), tel. (613) 2322401/2/3
Consulates at: Montreal, Toronto, Vancouver.

New Zealand:
34 Grant Road, Wellington, tel. (4) 4735339 - 4729302

United States of America:
1601 Fuller Street, N.W., Washington D.C., tel. (202) 328-5500/1/2/3/4/5/6/7/8
Consulates at: Boston, Chicago, Philadelphia, Houston, Los Angeles, Miami, New York, New Orleans, San Francisco.

Great Britain:
14, Three Kings Yard, London W.1, tel. (0171) 3122200
Consulates at: London, Manchester, Edinburgh.

Ireland:
63/65, Northumberland Road, Dublin 4, tel. (01) 6601744

ENIT

In order to have general information and documentation concerning the best known places in Italy, you can contact the offices of the Ente Nazionale Italiano per il Turismo (ENIT), run by the Italian government; they are open Mon-Fri, from 9 to 5.

Canada:
Office National Italien du Tourisme/Italian Government, Travel Office, Montreal, Quebec H3B 3M9, 1 Place Ville Marie, Suite 1914, tel. (514) 866-7667/866-7669, fax 392-1429

United States of America:
- Italian Government Travel Office, New York, N.Y. 10111, 630 Fifth Avenue, Suite 1565, tel. (212) 2454822-2455095, fax 5869249
- Italian Government Travel Office, Chicago 1, Illinois 60611-401, North Michigan Avenue, Suite 3030, tel. (312) 644-0996, fax 644-3019
- Italian Government Travel Office, Los Angeles, CA 90025, 12400, Wilshire Blvd., Suite 550, tel. (310) 820-0098/820-1898, fax 820-6357

Great Britain:
Italian State Tourist Board, London W1R 6AY, 1 Princes Street, tel. (0171) 408-1254, fax 493-6695

The Places to Visit: Sestieri and Routes

Venice, though not everyone who visits the city realizes it, is a mosaic of over 120 islands, separated by canals, and linked by more than 400 bridges. An unobtrusive but crucial presence is that of the "pozzi," or "wells," capacious cisterns built to capture and filter the rain water, so as to provide the city with an adequate supply of drinking water. Each "insula," or "block" is built around squares called "campi" or "campielli."
The "insule," literally "islands," are the tiles of the mosaic, or the pieces of the puzzle, if you will. Ever since the 12th c., Venice has been divided into six sections, known as "sestieri," or sixths (compare with "quarter"). Three of them are called "sestieri de citra," and three are called "sestieri de ultra," literally, "on this side" and "on that side," with reference to the Grand Canal. The "sestieri de citra" are S. Marco, Castello, and Cannaregio; they have always been the political, economic, and religious center of Venice; the "sestieri de ultra" are S. Polo, S. Croce, and Dorsoduro. The island of Giudecca is part of Dorsoduro, just as the island of S. Giorgio Maggiore is part of the Sestiere di S. Marco. The other islands are separate administrative entities: S. Elena (though this island is commonly treated as part of the nearby Sestiere di Castello), Sacca Fìsola, and Lido, as well as Murano, Burano, and Torcello.
The Venetians have their own ways of doing things; one might go so far as to call them eccentric. One historical example is the number of churches dedicated to figures from the Old Testament (consider the churches of S. Moisè, S. Geremia, and S. Zaccaria, dedicated respectively to Moses, Jeremiah, and Zacharia; the only other place in Europe where this practice is found is Ireland); equally unusual, and of more immediate concern, is the way in which the Venetians number their street addresses.
All of the buildings in each "sestiere" are simply numbered in succession – though just how you are supposed to know in what "sestiere" you happen to be at any given moment is not clear. Thus, the highest street address in Cannaregio is 6419; in Castello, 6828. The little Sestiere di S. Polo must settle for 3144. In other words, nobody in Venice lives at Calle Large n. 22 or Piscina del Fornèr n. 7; the address is given by the name of the "sestiere" followed by the house number. The exceptions to this rule are Lido, S. Elena, and Sacca Fìsola; here the streets are numbered as in any modern city or town.

In the descriptions that follow, an asterisk is set next to those monuments or sites (*) that are considered to be noteworthy or of particular interest.

Sestieri

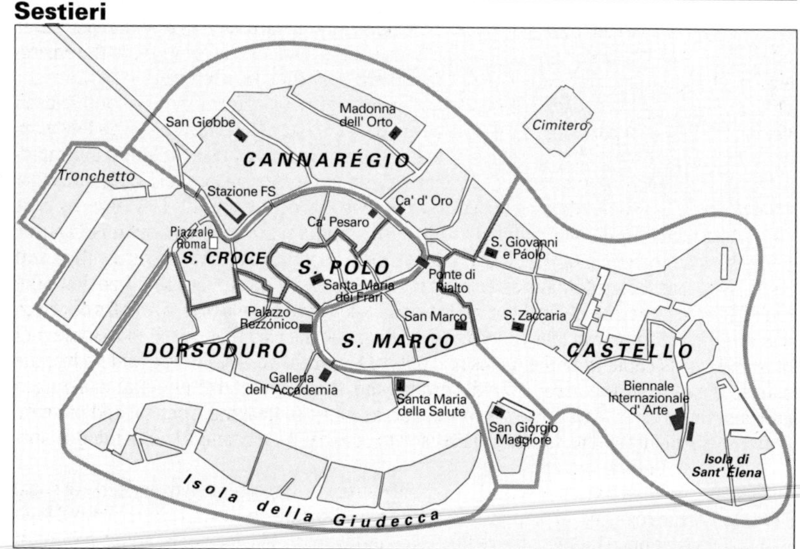

1 The Grand Canal

There is nothing like a visitor's first experience of the Grand Canal: this remarkable thoroughfare, formed by the ever-changing surface of the water and the unbroken succession of buildings, many of them exquisite pieces of timeless architecture, forming an endless series of new vistas along the broad curves of the canal: it is here that Venice and the water of the Venetian lagoon most completely blend together.

This is an exquisitely urban space – "the loveliest thoroughfare, I believe, in the whole world," as a 15th-c. French visitor described it – a long water-filled street, lined with palazzi, their entrances and portals and landing jetties opening directly out onto the water. Each palazzo is marked by painted "brìcole," the barber's pole-like mooring masts, and fronted by loggias and mullioned windows. The Grand Canal links all the various "insule" – the word for "island" and "city block" is the same – and joins the different functional sections of Venice: the area of communication with the mainland (the twin bridge-head; the parking garage of Piazzale Roma and the train station of S. Lucia), the center of trade (Rialto), the religious and political center (S. Marco). The Grand Canal is also necessary to the physical survival of Venice: its long winding channel distributes the oscillating waters of the tides, as they rise and fall, ebb and flow; the Grand Canal is a giant feeder and drainage channel for the 45 smaller "rii" (plural of "rio," or small canal), ensuring that the tides are accommodated and that the water is filtered and replaced. With its broad S curve, it allows in wind, light, and direct sunshine. It is the principal avenue of Venice, allowing traffic to move easily, providing a reference point for all directions.

Long ago the Grand Canal was broader than it is now; we are not sure where its banks originally lay. It may have been the bed of an ancient river, the Rivus Businacus. Its modern course (3,800 m. long, from 30 to 70 m. in width, an average of 4 m. in depth, at most, 5 m.) is the result of centuries of alignment and consolidation of its banks, a process that began in the 14th c. Originally, the Grand Canal served as a port-canal, perhaps a major harbor for shipping on the lagoon, and was certainly the only way to bring cargo boats to the new and growing marketplace of Rialto (where the only bridge in Venice existed as early as the 12th c., a drawbridge to allow vessels to pass). It also provided access to the "case-fondaco" (homes-qua-storehouses) of the first merchants (some of those that survive are now Ca' Farsetti, Palazzo Loredan, and Ca' da Mosto); to the great "fondachi" of the communities of outsiders in Venice (note the modern Fondaco dei Turchi and Fondaco dei Tedeschi, storehouses and residences, respectively, of the Turks and the Germans); to the Granai della Repubblica (grain siloes of the Republic; the Megio still stands). The Grand Canal in time lost its role as a harbor or port, and was gradually replaced by the Basin of St. Mark's (Bacino di S. Marco). The rebuilding of the Ponte di Rialto in stone in 1588, eliminating the drawbridge function, marked the official end of that function; shipyards and maritime repair yards were already forbidden by the 14th c. The Grand Canal became the area where the emerging Venetian nobility chose to display its wealth by building lavish homes.

The reader should keep in mind that the intensity of the transformations of buildings in Venice is at least in part due to the limited amount of land available; it is exceedingly difficult to expand physically; since the nature of the city tends to make buildings age rapidly, the tendency has been to rebuild or renovate frequently. Another consideration was that all of the building materials used to create Venice were brought in from elsewhere, by boat (the white stone used abundantly in the structure and decoration of many buildings, for bridges and embankments, etc., was brought from Istria; the lumber for beams, attics, and roofs, as well as for scaffolding, came from the forests of Cadore, and were rafted down the river Piave; the trachyte – a fine-grained igneous rock – used to build the sidewalks of Venice was quarried in a range of hills called the Colli Euganei; the clay that was fired to make roof tiles and bricks came from the plains and hills of the area around Treviso and Padua; the marble came from the area around Verona, and from Friuli; all the metal came from mines in the area around Belluno). Moreover, as you can imagine, specific and often ingenious expedients and techniques were used to construct a city amidst something as hostile to solid structures as water.

Many buildings therefore were raised, or rebuilt entirely to a greater height; indeed, we could say that Venice rose like so much yeast, in time swallowing up the tall churches and high bell towers that once loomed above the surrounding city. The lack of building materials,

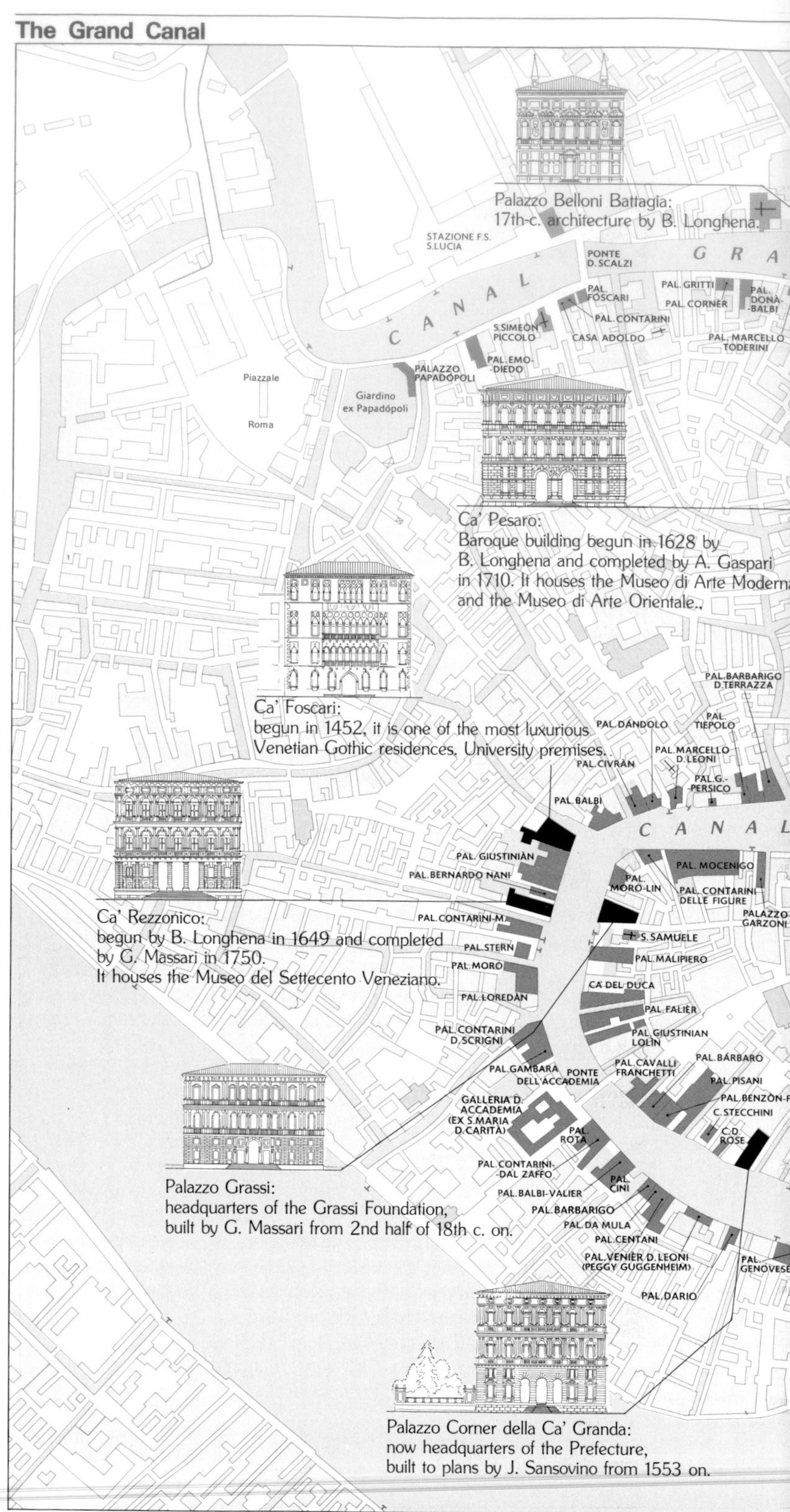

Palazzo Belloni Battagia:
17th-c. architecture by B. Longhena.

Ca' Pesaro:
Baroque building begun in 1628 by B. Longhena and completed by A. Gaspari in 1710. It houses the Museo di Arte Moderna and the Museo di Arte Orientale.

Ca' Foscari:
begun in 1452, it is one of the most luxurious Venetian Gothic residences. University premises.

Ca' Rezzonico:
begun by B. Longhena in 1649 and completed by G. Massari in 1750.
It houses the Museo del Settecento Veneziano.

Palazzo Grassi:
headquarters of the Grassi Foundation, built by G. Massari from 2nd half of 18th c. on.

Palazzo Corner della Ca' Granda:
now headquarters of the Prefecture, built to plans by J. Sansovino from 1553 on.

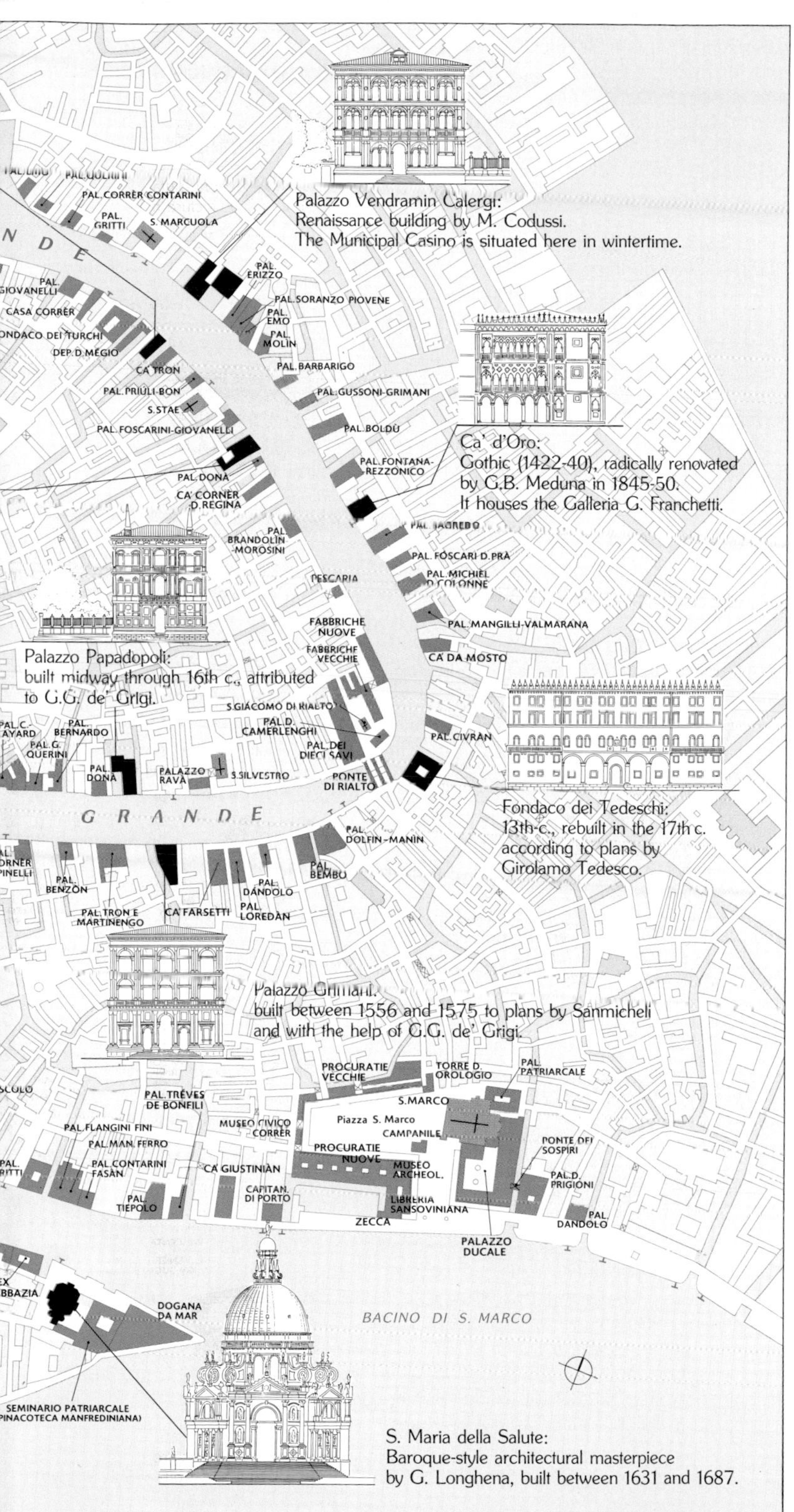

Palazzo Vendramin Calergi:
Renaissance building by M. Codussi.
The Municipal Casino is situated here in wintertime.
PAL. CORRER CONTARINI
PAL. GRITTI
S. MARCUOLA
PAL. GIOVANELLI
CASA CORRER
FONDACO DEI TURCHI
DEP. D. MEGIO
PAL. ERIZZO
PAL. SORANZO PIOVENE
PAL. EMO
PAL. MOLIN
CA' TRON
PAL. BARBARIGO
PAL. PRIULI-BON
S. STAE
PAL. GUSSONI-GRIMANI
PAL. FOSCARINI-GIOVANELLI
PAL. BOLDÙ
Ca' d'Oro:
Gothic (1422-40), radically renovated
by G.B. Meduna in 1845-50.
It houses the Galleria G. Franchetti.
PAL. FONTANA-REZZONICO
PAL. DONÀ
CA' CORNER D. REGINA
PAL. BRANDOLIN-MOROSINI
PAL. FOSCARI D. PRÀ
PAL. MICHIEL D. COLONNE
PESCARIA
PAL. MANGILLI-VALMARANA
FABBRICHE NUOVE
FABBRICHE VECCHIE
CA' DA MOSTO
Palazzo Papadopoli:
built midway through 16th c., attributed
to G.G. de' Grigi.
S. GIACOMO DI RIALTO
PAL. D. CAMERLENGHI
PAL. BERNARDO
PAL. G. QUERINI
PAL. CIVRAN
PAL. DEI DIECI SAVI
PAL. DONÀ
PALAZZO RAVÀ
S. SILVESTRO
PONTE DI RIALTO
G R A N D E
Fondaco dei Tedeschi:
13th-c., rebuilt in the 17th c.
according to plans by
Girolamo Tedesco.
PAL. DOLFIN-MANIN
PAL. BEMBO
PAL. BENZON
PAL. DANDOLO
PAL. TRON E MARTINENGO
CA' FARSETTI
PAL. LOREDAN
and with the help of G.G. de' Grigi.
built between 1556 and 1575 to plans by Sanmicheli
PROCURATIE VECCHIE
TORRE D. OROLOGIO
PAL. PATRIARCALE
PAL. TREVES DE BONFILI
S. MARCO
Piazza S. Marco
MUSEO CIVICO CORRER
CAMPANILE
PAL. FLANGINI FINI
PAL. MAN. FERRO
PROCURATIE NUOVE
PONTE DEI SOSPIRI
PAL. CONTARINI FASAN
CA' GIUSTINIAN
MUSEO ARCHEOL.
PAL. D. PRIGIONI
CAPITAN. DI PORTO
PAL. TIEPOLO
LIBRERIA SANSOVINIANA
PAL. DANDOLO
ZECCA
PALAZZO DUCALE
DOGANA DA MAR
BACINO DI S. MARCO
SEMINARIO PATRIARCALE
PINACOTECA MANFREDINIANA
S. Maria della Salute:
Baroque-style architectural masterpiece
by G. Longhena, built between 1631 and 1687.

or the high cost of transporting those materials from considerable distances, led to the frequent re-use of the same elements whenever a building was rebuilt or renovated.
In this context, we should mention one of the reasons that Venetian builders preferred to build or rebuild on existing foundations: of all the aspects of construction in Venice, the most challenging and expensive was the foundation, due to the presence of water. The lagoon has a soft muddy bed; in order to construct anything as heavy as a palazzo, it became necessary to develop a composite system, with several layers. The lowest layer consisted of wooden poles, sunken vertically in great numbers, so as to create a platform or an outline corresponding to the load-bearing walls, and then pounded down into the muck. Atop this series of poles, planking was laid. And atop that, white Istrian stone was laid, and the walls were built on top of that.
Over time, the wooden poles underwater were calcified, or fossilized, if you will, increasing their solidity; the stone base easily withstood the ebb and flow of the tides.
Sinking a foundation, then, was a time-consuming procedure, requiring considerable amounts of materials – wood and stone – that was at a premium in Venice; once the material was put into a foundation, it could not be reused, unless it remained where it stood. Thus, every time that it became necessary to rebuild a palazzo or other structure, the building material was re-used elsewhere, but the foundation remained just where it was. That is why the general layout of Venice has not changed much over the centuries. This is true of small buildings and larger, more important ones. Many churches, for example, were entirely rebuilt during the Renaissance, but still maintain their Byzantine floor plan. The re-use of building fragments – architraves, cornices, capitals, columns, and window casements that were often mass produced, and were therefore used in different constructions at different times – and the reappropriation of the foundations of older buildings, have together given Venice its remarkable mixture and cross-pollination of architectural languages and styles, succeeding each other over time, resulting in extraordinary juxtapositions. This is one of Venice's most intriguing qualities.
Along the Grand Canal, the construction of the 13th- and 14th-c. Byzantine "case-fondaco" (homes-qua-storehouses) was replaced by the building of palazzi (beginning in the 15th c.; among the first were Ca' Foscari and the two Palazzi Giustinian; and ending practically in the 18th c.). The palazzi of the Grand Canal express nearly every style, ranging from Gothic and Renaissance to Baroque, all translated into a distinctive Venetian architectural idiom. From Ca' Foscari to the two Palazzi Giustinian, and on to the famous Ca' d'Oro (15th c.), from the Renaissance architecture of Palazzo Vendramin Calergi, Palazzo Grimani, Palazzo Corner della Ca' Granda, and Palazzo Dario (end 15th c./16th c.) and on to the increasingly impressive Baroque structures of the Ca' Corner della Regina, Ca' Pesaro, Palazzo Grassi, and Ca' Rezzonico (17th/18th c.)
The stately personality of this area is echoed, and concluded, by the few public buildings erected in the 17th and 18th c.: the enormous church of the Salute and the Punta della Dogana at the southern entrance of the Grand Canal, and the churches of the Scalzi and S. Simeon Piccolo rebuilt at the northern entrance.
This theatrical waterway remains as a record of deeds and a true "Golden Book" of the Venetian aristocracy: every building is haunted by memories, quotes, stories, and links with great names of history. And thus, a gambler betting on black or on red in the Municipal Casino may recall that Richard Wagner lived, composed, and died in those rooms; and the magnificent palazzo, at one point called Palazzo Vendramin Calergi, was built at the behest of Leonardo Loredan, the doge who ruled Venice and the Serenissima during the terrible years (1501-1521) of the League of Cambrai and the wars of Italy.
From the end of the 18th c., with the fall of the Republic, the definitive decline in wealth and power of the leading families and the center of trade and finance of Rialto, the Grand Canal also lost its role as a showcase: the construction in the mid-19th c. of the two new bridges, the Ponte dell'Accademia and the Ponte degli Scalzi, clearly marked the triumph of foot traffic over water traffic. Nowadays, even though presitigious institutions (museums and art collections, universities, public and private institutions of all sorts) occupy the palazzi that were gradually abandoned as homes, the watergates are almost never used now, the lights on the interior are always dark, the ferries (there were 78 of them until around 1850) are now only 7 in number, while the damage done to the buildings by the wakes of motorboats is becoming increasingly serious.

2 San Marco

The Sestiere di San Marco comprises the heart of Venice, and encloses the city's symbol: Piazza San Marco (St. Mark's Square). The fairly small size of this "sestiere" (just 46 hectares) is, however, crowded with ancient buildings, articulated around the most important "campi" (Campo S. Stefano and Campo S. Angelo), and stretches out into the great plaza that marks the city's enduring relationship with the sea and water.
The "sestiere" is bounded in good part by one of the majestic oxbow curves of the Grand Canal, which opens out into the Bacino di S. Marco directly in front of the great square; the Basin of St. Mark's was, for centuries, the site of the harbor of the Serenissima. The other boundary of this "sestiere," on the landward side, is represented by the commercial thoroughfare of the Mercerie, Venice's shopping street by definition (the meaning of the word "merceria" in Italian is, roughly, "shopping") ever since the Middle Ages; this street links St. Mark's Square with Rialto.

Piazza S. Marco seen from above

Actually, the area between St. Mark's Square and Rialto was the original core of the entire urban structure of Venice. Beginning in Byzantine times, and continuing on through the centuries of the Gothic and Renaissance periods, the city of Venice developed largely along the shores of the Grand Canal, with special focus around the churches and the activities revolving around those churches. Leaving aside the great convents, such as S. Stefano and S. Salvador, it was the major churches – such as S. Samuele, S. Fantin, S. Zulian, S. Maria del Giglio, and S. Moisè – that stimulated, promoted, and organized the local interests of much of the populace of Venice.
Certainly, this "sestiere" is physically in the heart of Venice, but it is at Venice's heart in many other senses: culturally, financially, commercially. It is of course the most crowded, especially in summer, when throngs of tourists press through it, experiencing little more of Venice than a stroll through the city's "drawing room" – St. Mark's Square.

2.1 Piazza San Marco

Piazza San Marco (St. Mark's Square) is often described in Venice simply as the "piazza"; it is a universally recognized symbol of the city on the lagoon, a splendid epitome of a thousand years of Venetian history, as well as a remarkable expression of an urban culture that has steadily been enriched and deepened over the centuries.
St. Mark's Square first began to take its present shape sometime in the 12th c., under the Dogado (or reign as doge) of Sebastiano Ziani, when the Canale Batario was filled in (the canal still runs under the pavement of the square) and the church of S. Geminiano was rebuilt in a new location, further west. As a result of these two changes, it became possible to double the size of the existing square, which had lain before St. Mark's

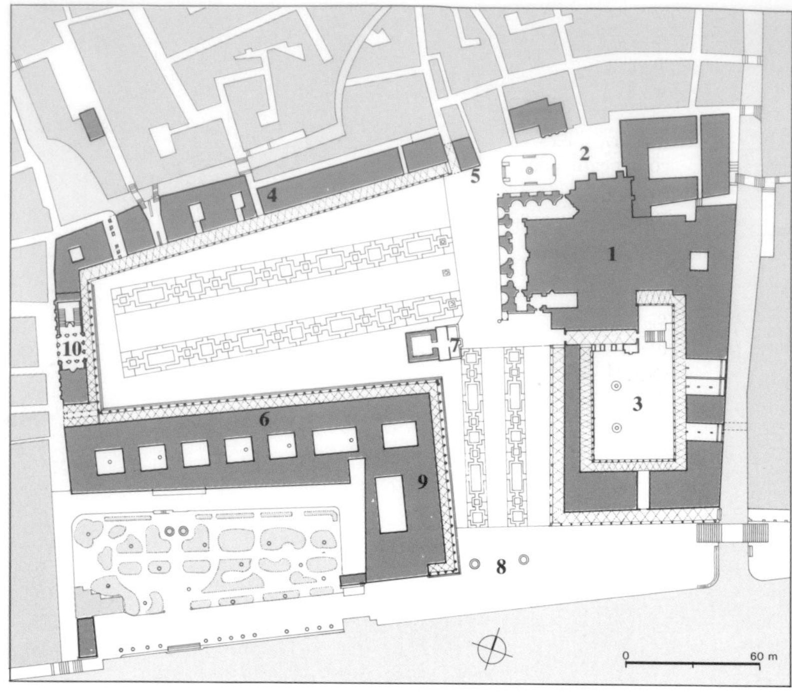

The Marciana Area Today

1 St. Mark's Cathedral
2 Piazzetta dei Leoni
3 The Doge's Palace
4 Procuratie Vecchie
5 Clock Tower
6 Procuratie Nuove
7 St. Mark's Bell Tower
8 Piazzetta S. Marco
9 St. Mark's Library
10 Napoleonic Wing

since the 9th c. The square thus attained a length of about 175 m. The area in front of the Basilica and the Doge's Palace (Palazzo Ducale) was further defined by the construction of the Procuratie – a building that was to house the residences and offices of high magistrates – along with the bell tower, the Torre dell'Orologio (clock tower), the Libreria Sansoviniana (a library), and the Zecca (or mint). Over the centuries this square evolved until it attained its modern-day majesty and sweep, overlooking the great Basin of St. Mark's (Bacino di S. Marco). Now, if the 16th c. was the time of great and radical transformations, the 18th c. witnessed major shifts in the overall appearance of the square; new paving was laid down in 1722 (by Tirali). In the 19th c., the church of S. Geminiano (by Sansovino) was demolished to make way for the new Ala Napoleonica. Moreover, the Granai di Terranova (large grain silos) were torn down; where they once stood, overlooking the Basin of St. Mark's, you will now find the Giardinetti (public gardens).
The Piazza San Marco that we see today, therefore, is not the product of a single, well thought-out plan; rather, it is the culmination of numerous separate projects, from the first settlement in the 9th c. right up to the last major changes in the 19th c. The setting that was thus created is a vast and intricate array of spaces – exterior and interior; it is not limited, as many erroneously seem to believe, just to the broad square that lies before the Basilica. We should consider this as the central core of the square, but we should realize that it also extends toward the Piazzetta San Marco, before the Palazzo Ducale, as well as along the waterfront quay, or "molo," once the harbor of ancient Venice. Other sections of this vast space extend along the facade of the Procuratie and toward the Piazzetta dei Leoni, even reaching into the Basilica and the Palazzo Ducale.
Even the apparent uniformity of the facades that enclose the square – when examined more carefully – proves to be a subtle composition, rich in differences of size, proportion, and style. For instance, consider the facades of the Procuratie Nuove and the Procuratie Vecchie, and note how the facade of the Procuratie Nuove is actually

more impressive and ornate than the facade of the Procuratie Vecchie, while maintaining the same organizational motif. Note also the way in which the vertical courses of the windows on the second and third floors of the Procuratie Nuove punctuate the arches of the portico beneath, coinciding on a one-to-one basis, while each arch of the portico of the Procuratie Vecchie is matched by two windows in the upper stories.

This melding together of diversity has been done with such cunning ability that the radically different architectural styles facing off in the square (the Byzantine-Gothic of the Basilica against the Neoclassical Ala Napoleonica) blend perfectly into a harmonious whole, without discordant notes. The view you can enjoy from above (from the Campanile di San Marco, or from the terrace of the Basilica), lastly, will help you to form an overall idea of the array of spaces involved, their configuration, and how they interlink.

St. Mark's Square, as you see it today, has probably lost the standing it once had as the heart of public life in Venice, a central polarizing spot, because the city is now organized around a series of "centers"; there is no question, all the same, that this is the loveliest and most deeply moving space in Venice (and not only for tourists).

Basilica di San Marco*, or St. Mark's Cathedral (5 D6). This church served as the official chapel of the Doge until 1807, when it replaced S. Pietro di Castello as the cathedral of Venice. It has always really been the chief church of Venice, however; it is the place where the doges were consecrated, the center of Venice's religious and public life, and a recognized and cherished symbol of its history (see plan on page 34). Its complex and intricately arrayed structure reflects the various phases of construction and later modifications. It was founded in the 9th c. and renovated for many centuries thereafter, so that the original Byzantine structures were overlaid with features in the Gothic and 16th-c. styles.

Construction began in A.D. 829; it was meant as a church to house the relics of St. Mark (the evangelist was buried in Alexandria, following his martyrdom), relics which had been stolen by the Venetians the year previous. The church dedicated to the patron saint of Venice (St. Mark) replaced the church of S. Teodoro (St. Theodore), Venice's first patron saint.

Although the Basilica was heavily renovated on more than one occasion, it retained its original foundation, taking on the distinctive silhouette of Byzantine churches, built to Greek-cross plan, with a central dome, and with four other smaller domes on each bay; the interior was gradually adorned with a facing of exquisite mosaics. In the 13th c., as the square spread out before the church expanded in size, it was decided to heighten the effect of the building's size by constructing, atop each dome, a further lantern structure, terminating in a small onion dome. Later, in the 16th c., Sansovino carried out a number of modifications designed to reinforce the stability of the structure; in the 17th c., radical changes were made in the altars of the Virgin Nikopoeia (Greek for "Victory-Worker") and of the Sacrament, marking the completion of the cathedral. Decoration continued unabated, however, and as late as the 19th c. a number of mosaics were redone. It is precisely these mosaics, with their gold backgrounds, extending over a total area of 4,240 sq. m., that represent one of the principal treasures of the cathedral. The building, including the vestibule, measures 76.5 m. in length, 43 m. in height (at the exterior top of the central dome; 28.15 m. on the interior); its facade is 51.8 m. in width, while the transept measures 62.6 m. in length.

The **facade** is largely horizontal in extension, extending over two stories and five arcades. The lower story presents an intricate array of small jutting arches, stacked orders of columns, reliefs, and decorations, creating a lavish interplay of light and shadow that shifts incessantly throughout the day, with the movement of the sun.

In the vault of the first arcade (1) note the only original mosaic still found on the facade, the *Transfer of the Body of St. Mark into the Church* (1260-70); in the lunette of the second arcade (2), note the 18th-c. mosaic, based on a cartoon by Sebastiano Ricci, *The Body of St. Mark Being Venerated by the Doge*; in the center, around the lunette of the third arcade (3), note three arches decorated with splendid 13th-c. *bas-reliefs*, which constitute one of the most important series of Romanesque sculptures in Italy (*Months, Virtues, Prophets*), while in the intrados of the main arch are bas-reliefs of the *Vocations*, representing the main trades pursued in Venice. The last figure, with crutches, to the left of the intrados, is said to depict the architect of St. Mark's; he is shown biting his finger, supposedly out of regret at having lost his job, once the cathedral was finished, for having boasted that he could build an even finer one. In the fourth arcade (4), *The Body of St. Mark Being Welcomed by the Venetians*, an 18th-c. mosaic;

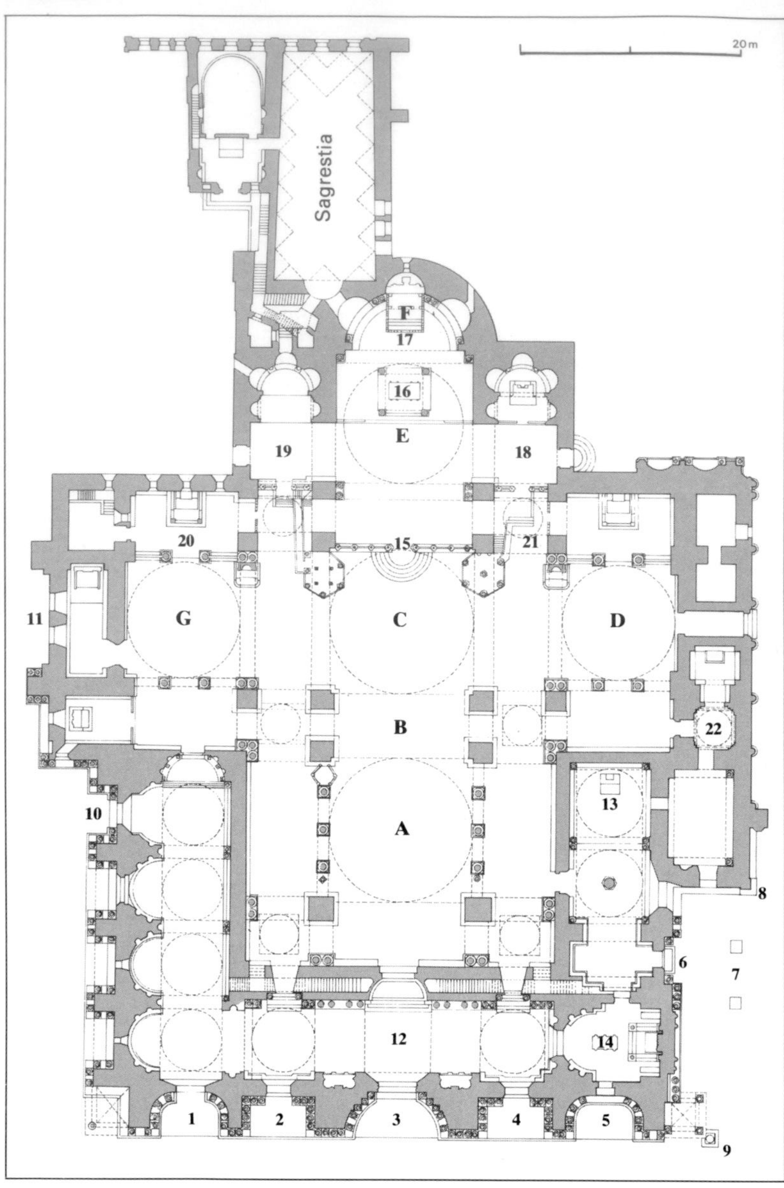

St. Mark's: interior layout

lastly, in the fifth arcade (5), another 18th-c. mosaic, *Theft of the Body of St. Mark*.

On the upper terrace (which you can reach from the galleries) you will find copies of the four statues of horses taken from Constantinople by Doge Enrico Dandolo. The originals can be seen in the Museo di S. Marco (Museum of St. Mark's). In the large lunettes are early-17th-c. mosaics, while cusps, aedicules, and statues date from the work done in the Gothic period.

On the **southern side** of the church (overlooking Palazzo Ducale), of the two original side entrances, only the portal giving access (6) to the Battistero, or Baptistery, still survives; before it stand two *pillars* (7), brought here from Acre after 1256.

At the corner nearest the Porta della Carta of Palazzo Ducale is the statuary group of the *Tetrarchs* (8), in porphyry, probably 4th-c. Syrian work; some say this is a depiction of the emperor Diocletian and the three other emperors who reigned with him at the end of the 3rd c. According to popular legend, these are four Moors, turned into stone for having attempted to steal the Treasure of St. Mark's. Near the corner extending out into the Piazza is the *Pietra del Bando* (9), or stone of decrees, which was knocked over and shattered when the bell tower collapsed in 1902. This is the shaft of a Syrian column, where the decrees of the Republic were read aloud.

The **northern side** (toward the Piazzetta dei Leoni) has the same decorative motif as the facade, but a misguided 19th-c. restoration dimmed the ancient splendor of the original decorations; under the fourth arcade is the side entrance known as the Porta dei Fiori (10); further along (11) is the *tomb of Daniele Manin*, a 19th-c. Venetian patriot.

The **atrium** (or narthex) is the area lying before the entrance to the church, a transition space, leading from the bright light of the outdoors to the shadows and diffuse golden color of the interior. The floor dates from the 11th/12th c.; it is said that, on the slab of red marble (12) in front of the central entrance, Pope Alexander III and Frederick I Barbarossa, the Holy Roman Emperor, once met. The ceiling is covered with splendid mosaics done between the 12th and 13th c., on subjects taken from the Old Testament. To the right of the main entrance portal is the stairway leading up to the galleries.

The **interior** is majestic, stern, and impressive; particularly striking is the remarkable interplay of volume between domes and arches, covered with golden mosaics; beneath your feet are the vivid geometric patterns of the floors.
The floor plan is a Greek cross, with pillars and columns surmounted by splendid Byzantine capitals; they divide the interior into three aisles; above, note the galleries. The upper surfaces of the walls are decorated with **mosaics** with gold backgrounds, partly original (12th/14th c.), and partly dating from a later period; they follow a precise compositional scheme, based on the glorification of the Church of Christ, the Church of Venice, and – in particular – the Cathedral of St. Mark's.

The mosaics in the domes are perhaps the loveliest, as well as some of the oldest mosaics in the cathedral (for the best view of them, keep in mind that they are lighted every day from 11:30 to 12:30, on Saturday after 5 pm, and all day on Sunday). In the Cupola delle Pentecoste (A), note the *Preaching of the Apostles* (2nd half of the 13th c.); the vault (B) has *Scenes of the Passion*, which date from the beginning of the 13th c., showing the clear influence of Romanesque art. In the central dome, or Cupola dell'Ascensione (C), and in the dome to the right, or Cupola di S. Leonardo e del SS. Sacramento (D), note the 13th-c. frescoes with *Christ Offering Benediction* (C) and depictions of saints (D).
In the dome of the presbytery (E), note 12th-c. depictions of Christ and the Prophets; while the mosaics in the apse, be-

St. Mark's Cathedral

tween the windows (*Saints Nicholas, Peter, Mark*, and *Hermagore*) may be the oldest frescoes in the cathedral, as they were completed prior to the fire of 1105.

The **Battistero**, or Baptistery (13), built during a reconstruction project in the 14th c. (the project involved enclosing the atrium that overlooked the Piazzetta San Marco), contains tombs of doges; before the altar is the Tombstone of Jacopo Sansovino, one of the greatest architects of the Renaissance and the most illustrious "Proto," or chief architect of St. Mark's; he created the *baptismal font* set in the center of the Baptistery. The altar stands on a block of granite (orig-

St. Mark's Cathedral: interior

inally from Tyre); it is said that Christ preached while standing on this stone.
On the wall facing the altar is the entrance to the *Cappella Zen* (14), built in the16th c. as a funerary chapel for Giovanni Battista Zen, who bequeathed his estate to the Venetian Republic, with the proviso that he be buried in the cathedral; the 16th-c. tomb is in the center of the chapel (both the Baptistery and the Cappella Zen are currently undergoing restoration).

The **presbytery** is raised over the crypt, and is separated from the rest of the church by a majestic *iconostasis*, or screen (15) made of polychrome marble; at the center of the architrave, note a large bronze and silver Cross (2.5 m.); on either side, note the paintings of the *Virgin, St. John*, and the *Twelve Apostles*, masterpieces by Jacobello and Pier Paolo Dalle Masegne (1396).
The main altar (16), made of marble, contains an urn with the relics of St. Mark, found in a casket, supposedly inside a stone in the crypt, during the restoration carried out in 1811.
A ciborium with baldachin is held up by four splendid alabaster columns, carved with scenes from the Gospels and the Apocrypha. Estimates of their age range from the 5th to the 13th c.
Behind the main altar is the renowned *Pala d'Oro**, or golden altar piece (1.4 x 3.48 m.), a remarkable masterpiece of Byzantine and Venetian goldsmithery, executed in stages, over a period beginning in the 10th c. and ending in 1342. According to an inventory made in 1796, this altar piece is encrusted with 1,300 pearls, 400 garnets, 300 sapphires, 300 emeralds, 90 amethysts, 75 balas rubies, 15 rubies, 4 topazes, 2 cameos, and more than 80 enamels.
In the apse, in the central niche, note the Altare del Sacramento, or Altar of the Sacrament (17); before it stand remarkable marble and translucent alabaster columns.
On either side of the presbytery are, to the right, the Cappella di S. Clemente (18), and, to the left, the Cappella di S. Pietro (19); standing before each of them is a handsome iconostasis.
In the left transept, in the Cappella della Madonna Nicopeia, is the icon of the *Virgin Nikopoeia*, or Victory-Worker, a Byzantine icon from the early-13th c., set in a precious frame. It was brought from Constantinople as booty from the Fourth Crusade, and is believed to be the protectress of Venice. It is displayed on the main altar on solemn occasions.

You reach the **crypt** by descending the stairway to the right of the presbytery; here, behind the altar, is the boulder inside of which, in 1811, a casket was supposedly found, containing the bones of St. Mark.
At the end of the right aisle of the right transept is the **Tesoro di S. Marco** (Treasury of St. Mark's), an exquisite collection of liturgical objects and reliquaries taken from Constantinople (1204); despite subsequent theft and plundering, this is considered to be one of the world's richest troves of religious art. The treasure is contained in three rooms (one of them, the *Santuario*, or *Sanctuary*, is closed to the public to preserve its holiness), and comprises vases, chalices, goblets, evangeliaries, and other objects of 11th- and 12th-c. Byzantine goldsmithery; among them, note the temple-shaped silver *incense burner* (12th/13th c.), two *icons of*

the Archangel Michael (1st half of the 11th c.), and on the left wall, two gilt silver *frontals*.

The **Museo di San Marco (Museum of St. Mark's)** is arranged on the same floor as the galleries, and is accessible from the atrium. It comprises notable collections of art and historical items from the Basilica, including fragments of mosaics, a handsome polyptych by Paolo Veneziano (1345), tapestries, and Persian carpets.
Here you will also find the four *horses* from the chariot of St. Mark, in gilt bronze, which were removed from their centuries-old location atop the terrace of the Basilica in 1974, and subjected to restoration in order to halt the dangerous process of deterioration. There is no certain verdict concerning their origin (they are either Greek statues from the 4th or 3rd c. B.C., or masterpieces of Roman sculpture of the 4th c.); it is known that they were taken from the hippodrome of Constantinople and that they arrived in Venice in 1204 as booty of the Doge Dandolo, following the Fourth Crusade. They remained above the entrance to St. Mark's until 1798, when Napoleon took them to Paris, whence they were returned in 1815.

Piazzetta dei Leoni (5 D6). Opening out on the left of the Basilica, this little square takes its name from the two lions carved of red marble (1722); it is raised to allow water to be collected in the well; note the well head designed by Andrea Tirali. Closing off the square at one end is the Neoclassical facade of the *Palazzo Patriarcale*, built to plans by Lorenzo Santi (1837-1870), while on the north side of the square is the former church of *S. Basso*, with side elevation by Baldassare Longhena (1676): no longer used for worship.

Palazzo Ducale*, or the Doge's Palace (5 D-E6). This building symbolizes the government of the Republic of Venice; it was the home of the doges and the headquarters of the highest magistracies of the Serenissima; it remains one of the most admirable pieces of Venetian Gothic architecture.
Founded as a castle in the 9th c., after a number of fires it underwent its first radical transformation under Doge Sebastiano Ziani (1172-78), who converted it into a palazzo designed to house the ducal apartments, as well as the most important institutions of the Republic – the Maggior Consiglio and the Minor Consiglio – and other offices of various magistracies. At the beginning of the 14th c., a decision was made to enlarge the building, and work went on practically without interruption until 1463; the original Byzantine-style building now had an appearance that was almost entirely in the new Gothic style; still it maintained the original architectural concept of the palazzo: it was, so to speak, empty below and full above (later, Andrea Palladio harshly criticized this approach, which he considered to be contrary to the laws of nature). Indeed, the ground floor opens out onto the "piazzetta," or little square, with a continuous portico; on the second story this is surmounted by a loggia; above this is a high wall with few windows, decorated with pink and white stone arranged in geometric patterns.
Fires played a major role in the history of this building, leading in 1484 and again in 1577 (when the Sala del Maggior Consiglio was reduced to ashes) to the rebuilding of sections of the palazzo; the building by this point was truly an immense structure, and the two projects of reconstruction were undertaken by Antonio Rizzo first (he was forced to flee Venice in 1498 when he was accused of embezzlement) and, after a few others, by Antonio Da Ponte (the architect of the Ponte di Rialto) who persuaded the Senato to respect the existing architectural style while preserving the damaged parts of the building, and not to adopt the approach advised by Andrea Palladio, of rebuilding completely. The last major construction dates from the beginning of the 17th c., and was done by Bartolomeo Manopola; it involved reorganizing the arrangement of rooms on the inside of the building. The palazzo is now used for exhibitions and holds the offices of the Soprintendenza per i Beni Ambientali e Architettonici di Venezia (Commission for the Protection of the Environmental and Architectural Heritage of Venice).
The two facades, overlooking the quay and the Piazzetta San Marco, are identical, a little more than 70 m. in length, punctuated by pointed-arch windows with handsome balconies on the central window (the balcony on the southern facade dates from the early-15th c., by members of the Dalle Masegne family; the other balcony dates from 1536, and was built by Scarpagnino and Sansovino).
Sentences of death were read from the ninth arch of the loggia in the facade overlooking the Piazzetta San Marco; note the two red marble columns.
Also note the capitals of the stout columns, without plinth, in the portico, which is ar-

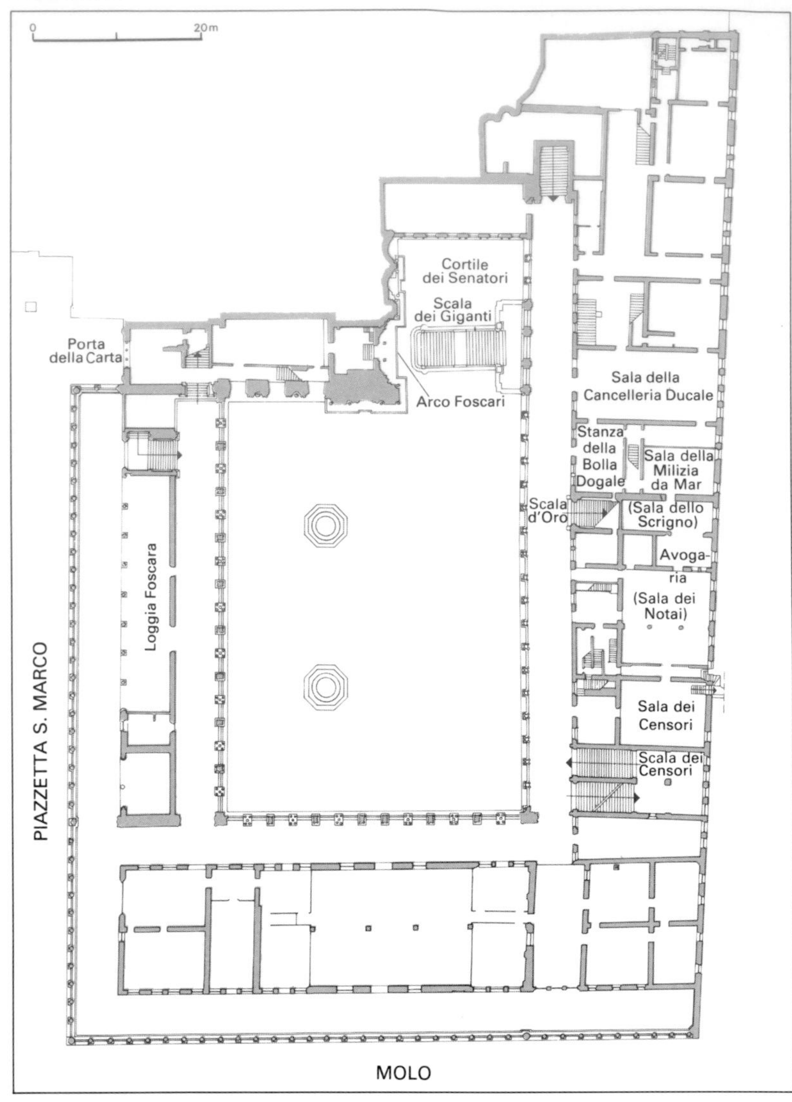

The Doge's Palace: layout of the courtyards and Floor of the Logge

ticulated in a right-angle corner: they are by masters of the 14th and 15th c.

You enter the Doge's Palace (note plan, above) through the *Porta della Carta* (literally, Door of Paper; possibly a name taken from the presence of offices of scribes in the building), a lavish creation by Giovanni and Bartolomeo Bon (1438); note the doge, Francesco Foscari, kneeling before a winged lion, symbol of Venice (19th-c. copy of original, destroyed at the fall of the Republic). The door opens into the *Porticato Foscari* (built by members of the Bon family), which in turn gives onto the courtyard, and ends at the *Arco Foscari*, an arch in the Gothic style, set at the foot of the monumental *Scala dei Giganti*, a staircase by Antonio Rizzo (1484-1501). The top of the staircase is decorated with impressive statues of *Neptune* and *Mars*, carved by Sansovino (1554). The ceremony of the coronation of the new doge was held on the landing, behind the two statues. In this ceremony, the doge swore allegiance to the laws of Venice, and received from the oldest of the councillors (*consiglieri*), the *zoia* – the ducal biretta, or hat.

The **courtyard** is really a full-fledged "piazza" stretching out beneath the high walls of Palazzo Ducale, almost an extension of the public square of Piazza San Marco; the interior facades feature the same design as the

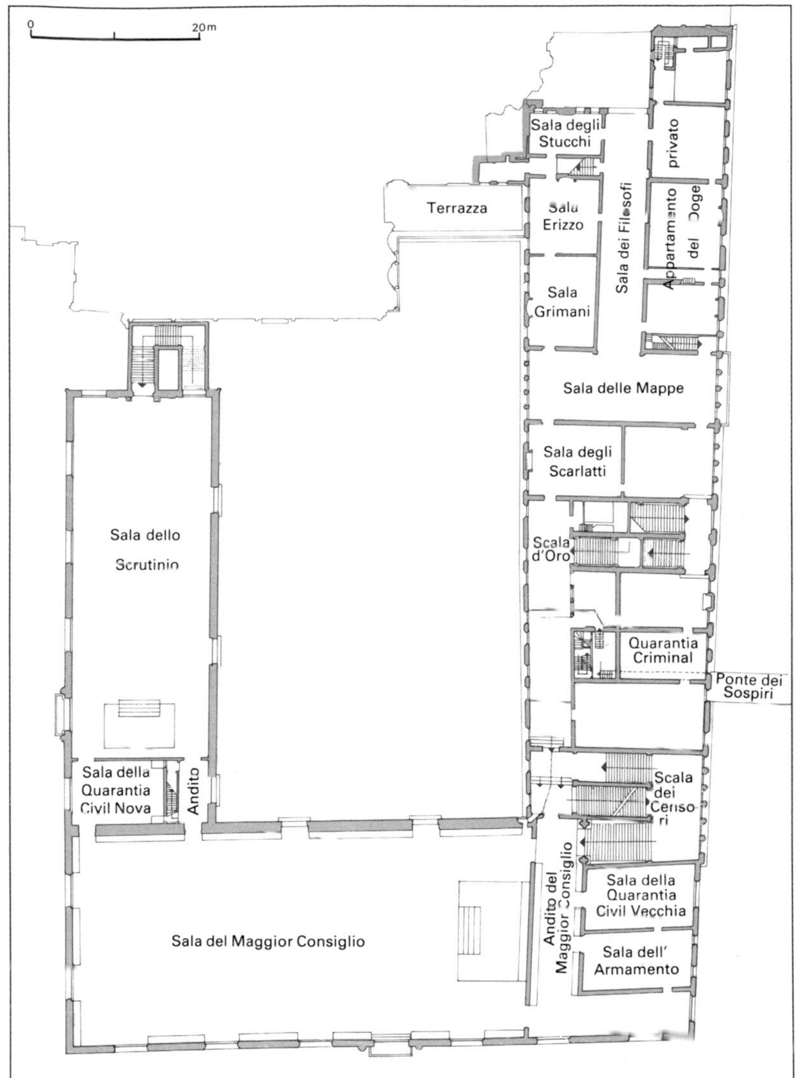

The Doge's Palace: layout of the Primo Piano Nobile (second floor)

outer facades; the space of porticoes and loggias is surmounted by solid walls, on the southern and western sides, while on the eastern side, Antonio Rizzo installed tall windows that bring light to the upper stories.

The original terracotta pavement was replaced in 1773 with the paving that you see now; the two well heads date from the mid-16th c.

At the southeast corner of the courtyard, the *Scala dei Censori* (stairway) leads up to the *Piano delle Logge* (or Floor of the Loggia), and, on the right, you reach the *Scala d'Oro**, begun prior to 1549 by Sansovino and Scarpagnino, and completed in 1559: this stairway was used exclusively by Magistrates and illustrious personages; note the lavish decoration by T. Aspetti, A. Vittoria, G.B. Franco, and F. Segala.

The **Appartamento Ducale** (private apartments of the doge) is set on the second story (the Venetians called this the "first noble story," "primo piano nobile"; the third story was the "secondo piano nobile"), in rooms that were rebuilt after a fire in 1483.

The first ten halls are used for temporary exhibits, and can be toured only when a show is being held. From the *Sala degli Scarlatti* ("sala" means "hall"; the name of this hall comes from the fact that the councillors of the doge, who

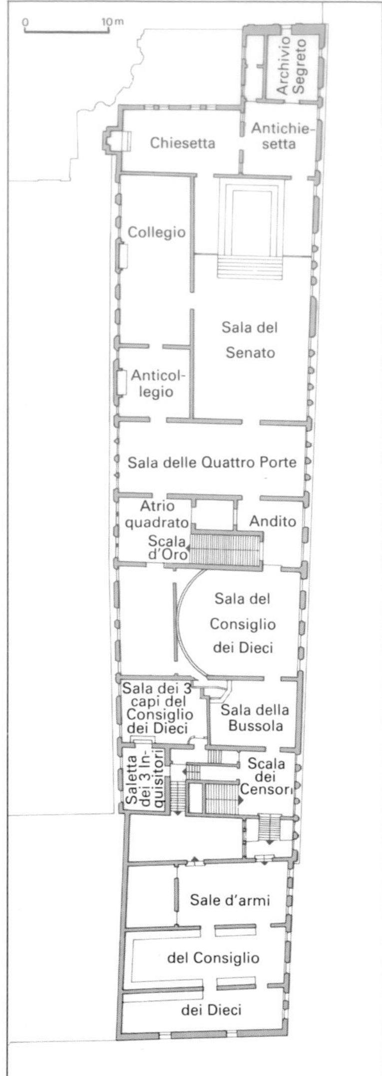

The Doge's Palace: layout of the Secondo Piano Nobile (third floor)

wore scarlet robes, would meet here), you will then continue on to the *Sala della Mappe* (Hall of Maps), with interesting geographic charts on the walls. Then you will enter the *Sala Grimani* (used for private audiences), with a painting by Giovanni Bellini, *Christ Mourned**, and an elegant fireplace by the Lombardos. Then you will enter the *Sala Erizzo*, and then the *Sala degli Stucchi* (named for the stucco decorations in the vault).

In the *Sala dei Filosofi* (Hall of Philosophers), named for the 12 paintings of philosophers hanging on the walls; note the fresco of *St. Christopher*, by Titian (1523-24) on the right, over the door leading to the stairway.

You will then encounter three rooms which were once the private apartment of the doge (Sala delle Volte with a *Lion of St. Mark's*, by Carpaccio; *Sala Corner*, and *Sala dei Ritratti*, or hall of portraits). Completing the apartment is the *Sala degli Scudieri*, used by aides and guards of the doge; note two paintings by Domenico Tintoretto.

On the third floor (plan on the left), in the east wing, you will find the halls in which the highest magistracies of the Venetian Republic would convene: the Signoria, the Senato, the Consiglio dei Dieci (Council of Ten) and the Tre Inquisitori (Three Inquisitors).

You will pass back by the Scala d'Oro, and then into the *Atrio Quadrato* (Square Atrium): on the ceiling, note paintings by Jacopo Tintoretto; on the walls are paintings by Veronese and Bassano.

The *Sala delle Quattro Porte*, or Hall of Four Doors (this room served as an antechamber), was built by Da Ponte to plans by Palladio and G.A. Rusconi; note the four monumental doors, decorated with statues and columns. The ceiling, designed by Palladio, is decorated with frescoes by Jacopo Tintoretto. On the wall by the entrance, note the famous painting by Titian, *The Doge Antonio Grimani Kneeling Before Faith, While St. Mark Looks On**, completed after the artist's death (1576).

The *Anticollegio* served as a waiting room for illustrious guests about to be received by the doge. This room was rebuilt to plans by Palladio and Scamozzi; it is certainly one of the most renowned rooms in the Doge's Palace, largely because of the splendid paintings on walls and ceiling. In the vault, center, fresco by Veronese (1577); between the windows, monumental fireplace by Vincenzo Scamozzi. On the walls, on either side of the entrance, note four paintings* with mythological subjects, by Jacopo Tintoretto (1577); on the wall facing the fireplace, on the left, *Rape of Europa**, by Paolo Veronese (1580).

You then continue on to the *Sala del Collegio* (where the Signoria met); note carved ceiling, with paintings by Paolo Veronese (1575-78); on the walls, paintings by Tintoretto and Veronese. In the large adjoining *Sala del Senato*, the senators would meet in the presence of the doge and the Signoria, seated in tiers. The ceiling dates from the late-16th c.; at the center, note the painting *Venice Seated Among the Gods Receives the Gifts of the Sea*, by Jacopo and Domenico Tintoretto (1581-1584); on the walls are a number of paintings by Palma the Younger.

You then enter the *Sala del Consiglio dei Dieci*, a magistracy presided over by the doge, comprising 10 members and six councillors; the gilt carved ceiling features works by Paolo Veronese. In the *Sala della Bussola*, near the facing door, is the mail slot through which secret letters of denunciation could be slipped.

A number of the rooms that follow (and the Prigioni, or prisons) form part of a route called "itinerari segreti," or "secret passages," and can only be toured with a guide, by advance reservation.
In the *Sala dei Tre Capi del Consiglio dei Dieci* (Hall of the Three Chiefs of the Council of Ten), the secret letters of denunciation were opened; note paintings by Paolo Veronese, on the ceiling, and by Hieronymous Bosch, on the walls (1500-1504). Next door is the *Saletta dei Tre Inquisitori di Stato*, or Little Hall of the Three State Inquisitors; this was a magistracy assigned to the most delicate matters of the Republic. They were greatly feared for their unbridled powers (from here you could go straight upstairs to the Camera del Tormento and the Prigioni – the torture chamber and the prison cells).

Sala d'Armi del Consiglio dei Dieci: this was the armory of the Doge's Palace; sadly, it was plundered at the end of the Republic. With its collection of 2,031 items, it remains of enormous historical interest. Note the armor of King Henry IV of France and of the condottiere Gattamelata, as well as weapons, busts of doges, and trophies of war.
Then you head back downstairs, to the *Andito del Maggior Consiglio*, a vestibule (note paintings by Domenico Tintoretto, with references to the Battle of Lepanto, and by Palma the Younger) that leads into the *Sala della Quarantia Civil Vecchia* (this magistracy was composed of forty members, and it had jurisdiction over the civil affairs of the state) and on into the *Sala dell'Armamento*, where you can see all that remains of the great fresco done by Guariento (1365-67) – *Paradise* – for the *Sala del Maggior Consiglio*; it was badly damaged by a fire in 1577. In the succeeding loggia (or *liagò*), toward the *Molo*, or quay, are statues of *Adam* and *Eve*, masterpieces by Antonio Rizzo (1464); together with a statue of an *Alfiere*, or standard-bearer, these statues once formed part of the Arco Foscari. Then you will enter the *Sala del Maggior Consiglio*, where a council met that, after 1297, was composed only of those Venetian aristocrats who were listed in the Libro d'Oro, or golden book. This is the largest room in the palace (52.7 m. long, 24.65 m. wide, and 11.5 m. high); it was rebuilt after the fire of 1577 by Antonio Da Ponte. This is where the assembly of all officials and magistrates of the Republic would meet in plenary session. This very large hall, meant to accommodate the roughly 1,500 members of the assembly, was also used on more than one occasion for banquets and celebrations. The east wall, behind the dais where the doge (center) and his six chief councillors sat, was entirely covered by *Paradise**, an enormous painting (7.45 x 24.65 m.) by Jacopo Tintoretto and his son Domenico, with the assistance of Palma the Younger and others, between 1586 and 1594. It was painted on a number of canvases that were subsequently joined and hung here; the painting is meant to honor the proper and benevolent government of the Republic, showing that it would enjoy its just rewards, much like the Virgin Mary, shown here being crowned by Christ at the center of the painting. In the middle of the ornate ceiling, note the *Apotheosis of Venice**, by Paolo Veronese; in the large ovals on either side, canvases by Palma the Younger and Jacopo Tintoretto. The hall contains works by other artists as well, among them Leandro Bassano, Carlo Saraceni, Aleinze, and Paolo Veronese. In the upper section of the walls, the Tintorettos (father and son) painted portraits of the doges, right up to Francesco Venier (1554-56). In place of the portrait of Marin Faliero, who was beheaded in 1355 for having conspired against the State, there is a black space with a legend denouncing his turpitude.
Next door is the *Sala della Quarantia Civil Nuova* (a sort of appeals court, comprising forty magistrates); following that is the *Sala dello Scrutinio* (here elections were held for membership in the Maggior Consiglio; the doge was also elected here). Built in the 15th c., it was rebuilt after 1577 by Antonio Da Ponte*. At the end of this large hall is a *Triumphal Arch* by Antonio Gaspari, in honor of Franceso Morosini, "the Peloponnesian"; on the opposite wall is a large canvas of *The Last Judgement*, by Palma the Younger (1587-92). Many of the canvases in this room commemorate great sea battles fought by Venice; on the east wall in particular, note the *Victory of Lepanto*, by Andrea Vicentino (1571). At the top of the walls, the series of portraits of the doges is completed, down to the very last one, Lodovico Manin (1789-1797).
Then you cross the **Ponte dei Sospiri**, or Bridge of Sighs (built in the late-16th c.; 5 D6) to reach the Prigioni Nuove, or new prison. This famous bridge comprises two corridors, one above the other, connecting both the Palazzo di Giustizia, or Hall of Justice and the Prigioni Vecchie, or old prison, with the cells on the other side of the Rio di Palazzo. The *Prigioni Vecchie*, ancient prison

The Bridge of Sighs

cells in the Palazzo Ducale, were divided into the "Piombi" (cells located under the lead roof of the Palazzo Ducale, hence the name, literally, "lead"; Giacomo Casanova was imprisoned here, and claims to have escaped) and the "Pozzi," or wells (cells located on the ground floor; they were dank, damp, and narrow; only those imprisoned for the worst crimes and political prisoners were held in the "Pozzi").
On the ground floor of the Palazzo Ducale is the *Museo dell'Opera del Palazzo*, with an array of interesting artifacts from the building, pertaining to its construction over the years (original capitals, ornamental fragments; currently closed for restoration).

Procuratie Vecchie (5 D5). This long structure (152 m.) is the north side of St. Mark's Square; it was built one story tall in the 12th c. and was rebuilt after 1514; Jacopo Sansovino took over the project in 1532, and raised the building to two stories. It was used as the residence and offices of the Procuratori di San Marco (the most important magistrates in Venice after the doge); it now belongs to Assicurazioni Generali, a major Italian insurance company. The building will house the offices of Venice's city government; behind it is the *Bacino Orseolo*, created in 1863 as a picturesque mooring spot for gondolas.

Torre dell'Orologio, or Clock Tower (5 D5). Terminating the eastern side of the facade of the Procuratie Vecchie, at the mouth of the Mercerie; it was built between 1496 and 1499, and probably designed by Mauro Codussi, with a later renovation (1755) by Giorgio Massari, who reinforced its structure. The hour is rung by the Moors, two bronze statues (1497) that strike a large bell with long hammers; the clock face shows the time, the phases of the moon, and movement of the Sun through the Zodiac.

Procuratie Nuove (5 E5). This building marks the south side of the square, and was built to replace the Procuratie Vecchie as the residence of the Procuratori di S. Marco. Construction was begun by Vincenzo Scamozzi in 1582; a floor was added, continuing the compositional theme of the Libreria Sansoviniana; the building was completed by Baldassare Longhena around the middle of the 17th c. In Napoleonic times, the building was used as Palazzo Reale, or Royal Palace; it now houses a number of rooms of the Museo Correr, the Museo del Risorgimento, and the Museo Archeologico, as well as administrative offices, and the library of the Museo Correr. Under the porticoes, note the 18th-c. *Caffè Florian*, rebuilt in the 19th c., one of the best known meeting spots in Venice.

Campanile di San Marco, or St. Mark's Bell Tower (5 D6).
Standing nearly 100 m. tall, this bell tower is the chief landmark for those who see Venice from a distance. It was rebuilt in the 12th c., on the structure of what was probably a watchtower; it was heavily renovated at the turn of the 16th c. under the supervision of Bartolomeo Bon, to plans by Giorgio Spavento, who added a higher belfry, terminating in a cusp covered with copper, surmounted by a statue of the *Archangel Gabriel*, set on a revolving platform, as a weathervane.
The bell tower collapsed suddenly on 14 July 1902; the town council of Venice ordered that it be rebuilt "as it was and where it was"; reconstruction was completed in 1912. You can still hear the one bell (the "marangona") that, amazingly, survived the collapse.
The **Loggetta***, or little loggia, at the base of the bell tower is by Jacopo Sansovino (1537-49); it became the building of the Corpo di Guardia degli Arsenalotti, a police unit. Destroyed when the bell tower collapsed in 1902, it was reassembled from the fragments of the original structure. The bronze statues – *Minerva, Apollo, Mercury*, and *Peace* – are also by Sansovino, while the terrace with balustrade was added in the 17th c.

Piazzetta San Marco (5 D-E6). This remarkable space has the Basin of St. Mark's on one side, the facade of the Palazzo Ducale on the left and that of the Libreria Sansoviniana on the right. The horizon, across the water, is enclosed by the island of S. Giorgio, set between the two *monolithic columns*, made of Eastern granite, surmounted by Veneto-Byzantine capitals, with statues of the *Lion of St. Mark's* and *Todaro* (St. Theodore), the first patron saint of Venice. Executions were carried out between the two columns.

Libreria Sansoviniana, or St. Mark's Library (5 E6). This masterpiece by Jacopo Sansovino was originally built to house the Library established by John Cardinal Bessarion, a Byzantine theologian who fled Constantinople after it fell to the Turks in 1453, bringing Greek culture to the West for the first time. Since 1907 part of the library is also housed in the Zecca. The building was begun in 1537, and was completed after Sansovino's death (1570) by Vincenzo Scamozzi (between 1583 and 1588)

Through the central portal, under the portico (n. 13), recognizable by the two giant *caryatids*, you can climb upstairs, to the old Library, now only open for temporary exhibits.

Take the monumental *stairway* up to the *vestibule* – in the center of the ceiling, note the painting of *Wisdom**, a late work by Titian (1564) – and to the great hall (*salone*), an enormous space designed by Sansovino. On the walls, note paintings of *philosophers* in false niches, by Veronese, Jacopo Tintoretto, and Andrea Schiavone; on the ceiling note framed paintings of allegorical subjects, executed by seven artists selected in 1556-57 by Titian and Sansovino, including Veronese; so fine was the latter's contribution, that he was given the gold necklace awarded by the two great artistic "judges."

Museo Archeologico, or Archeological Museum (5 E6). With an entrance at n. 17 of the Portico della Libreria, arranged in a number of halls in the Procuratie Nuove, this museum has notable collections of Greek statuary, Roman architectural fragments and sculpture, busts, inscriptions, marble, and a collection of Roman coins (from the 3rd c. B.C. to the 1st c.)

The museum originated with a bequest from Domenico Cardinal Grimani (1523), who donated to the Venetian Republic marble and bronze statues unearthed in Rome. The collection has been housed in this building since 1924. Among the most notable items, *Greek statues of goddesses**, from the 5th and 4th c. B.C. (Demetra, Hera, Athena), the *Grimani Ara**, a late-Hellenistic work of extreme technical virtuosity; three statues of *Gauls*, from the late-3rd c. B.C.; busts of *Trajan* and *Vitellius*; casket for relics, early-Christian art, 5th c., ivory.

Zecca, or Mint (5 E5-6). In this building, Venice once minted its coins (entrance at n. 7 from the portico of the Libreria Sansoviniana); designed and built by Jacopo Sansovino (1537-1566), it now houses the **Biblioteca Nazionale Marciana**, a major library. The inner courtyard, with the later addition of a skylight, is now used as a reading room.

The Library, based on a bequest by John Cardinal Bessarion (1468) of about a thousand Greek and Latin codices, gradually grew with the incorporation of the libraries of suppressed convents, and now includes more than 900,000 volumes and more than 13,000 manuscripts. Among the most important works is the *Grimani Breviary* (end of the 15th c.), one of the most exquisite codices in Europe, with excellent illuminated miniatures.

Ala Napoleonica, or Napoleonic Wing (5 D-E6). This building faces St. Mark's Square across from the Cathedral, joining the Procuratie Vecchie to the Procuratie Nuove. On this site, until the early-19th c., stood the church of S. Geminiano, rebuilt by Jacopo Sansovino in the 16th c.; demolished in 1808 (a plaque on the site has a depiction of it), the Fabbrica Nuova, or Ala Napoleonica, was built in its place, to commemorate the glory of Napoleon's victories (designed by Giuseppe Maria Soli).

The facade overlooking the square is topped by an attic with statues of *Roman emperors*. Inside, at the end of the monumental double staircase, you enter the sumptuous *Salone Napoleonico* (1822) designed by Lorenzo Santi, with Neoclassical decorations by Giuseppe Borsato.

Museo Correr* (5 E5). In 1922 the Civico Museo Correr was installed in the Ala Napoleonica (and in a few rooms in the Procuratie Nuove). This museum contains a major art gallery and interesting collections of objets-d'art, historic memorabilia, and documents concerning the glorious history of the Venetian Republic.

From the *Loggia Napoleonica*, or gallery, where noteworthy maps and views of Venice are on display, dating from the end of the 15th c., you enter the first hall (*Sala Canoviana*). In a Neoclassical setting, note works by Antonio Canova, including *Daedalus* and *Icarus*. The subsequent halls are dedicated to the office of the doge, and all the pomp and circumstance that surrounded it, with portraits of doges, paintings and prints that document various phases of their lives (audiences, feasts, regatas). Other halls have original costumes, banners, arms and armor; a considerable portion of the collection is devoted to memorabilia that once belonged to the doge Francesco Morosini, known as "The Peloponnesian" for his military triumphs, and came originally from his palazzo in Campo S. Stefano.

Reopened in 1960 after a renovation by Carlo Scarpa, the **Quadreria** or **Pinacoteca** (gallery of paintings) contains works from the 14-/16th-c. Venetian School, as well as work by Ferrarese, Flemish, and German artists.

Particularly noteworthy is the hall devoted to the work of Cosmè Tura (*Pietà**, 1468), Antonello da Messina (note the only work still in Venice from that artist's sojourn here, another *Pietà*, 1475-76), the Bellini family – the father Jacopo and the two sons, Gentile and Giovanni (*Crucifixion**, by Jacopo, 1450; *Virgin with Child*, *Pietà*, *Transfiguration*, and *Crucifixion*, works* painted between 1455 and 1464 by Giovanni; *Portrait of the Doge Giovanni Mocenigo*, unfinished work by Gentile, 1479), Alvise Vivarini (*Antonio da Padova*, or St. Antony of Padua, with the original frame), Vittore Carpaccio (*Two Venetian Ladies**, also known by the original title of *The Courtesans*, 1510-15, and *St. Peter Martyr*, part of a polyptych that is scattered in various museums, 1514, and *Visitation*, painted around 1514 for the Scuola degli Albanesi) and Lorenzo Lotto (*Virgin with Child*).

Also housed in this building is the **Museo del Risorgimento e dell'Ottocento Veneziano**, a museum devoted to the Italian unification movement and to 19th-c. Venice, with collections of prints, documents, and memorabilia covering the period from the late-18th c. to the annexation of Venice to the Kingdom of Italy in 1866.

2.2 From St. Mark's to the Ponte dell'Accademia

This route winds basically along the thoroughfare that links the complex space of St. Mark's Square with the vast Campo S. Stefano, a favorite meeting spot in Venice; the route ends at the Ponte dell'Accademia, a bridge that leads over to the Sestiere di Dorsoduro.

The area through which you will be walking has a splendid sequence of "campi" and "campielli," in an assortment of shapes and sizes (Campo S. Moisè, Campo S. Fantin, Campo S. Maria del Giglio, Campo S. Maurizio, Campo S. Stefano, Campo S. Vidal, and Campo S. Samuele), linked by elegant streets lined with shops. This is the financial and business district of Venice (stock exchange, banks, insurance companies); there are numerous prestigious cultural institutions (the Biennale, Palazzo Grassi, the Musical Conservatory) and famous hotels, in a welter of structures that is so densely packed that this is one of the most popular areas with both tourists and Venetians.

Frezzeria (5 D4-E5). After you leave Piazza S. Marco via the Ala Napoleonica, and after crossing the *Calle Larga dell'Ascensione* (note in particular, at n. 1241, the low 19th-c. building of the *Corpo di Guardia*, by L. Santi and A. Pigazzi; once a guardhouse, it is now a post office; at n. 1239-42, note the former Albergo del Selvadego, Venetian-Byzan-

tine architecture, now an office building of Assicurazioni Generali) you will reach the intersection (on the right) with the Frezzeria, which takes its name from the vendors of arrows ("frecce") who lived and traded here during the Middle Ages, when every man between the ages of 16 and 35 was obliged to practice archery once a week on the beach of Lido, with bows and crossbows.

Calle Vallaresso (5 E5) runs toward the Grand Canal, and at n. 1332 is the entrance to the *Teatro del Ridotto*, a theater located in Palazzo Dandolo, which in the 18th c. contained the renowned "Ridotto," a public house and gaming house for the nobility (though the bourgeoisie could enter wearing masks); the Venetian Republic shut it down in 1774, because too many family estates had been squandered on gaming; in 1768 a restoration by Bernardino Maccaruzzi (with fresocs by Jacopo Guarana) gave the palazzo a new face.
At the end of the "calle," on the left, is *Harry's bar*, opened in 1931 and a favorite haunt of Ernest Hemingway.

Campo S. Moisè (5 E4). The regular shape of the "campo" is bounded by the Rio di S. Moisè and is dominated by the 17th-c. facade of the church of S. Moisè; note the modern elevation of the more recent wing (1949) of the 19th-c. *Hotel Bauer-Grünwald* (which overlooks the Grand Canal).

S. Moisè (5 E4). Founded in early times (8th c., according to tradition), rebuilt repeatedly until the 17th c., its facade was built (1668) by Alessandro Tremignon, who created one of the most radical expressions of Venetian Baroque, with the theatrical arrangement of statues celebrating not the Holy Faith, but rather the family of the clients, the Fini, with overabundant decorations (by Heinrich Meyring). On the right is the old 14th c. campanile.
The interior has a single rectangular aisle and a vault ceiling; it focuses on the main altar, a Baroque creation designed by Alessandro Tremignon and carved by Heinrich Meyring, depicting *Mount Sinai with Moses Receiving the Ten Commandments*. On the second altar on the right, note the *Discovery of the Cross* by Pietro Liberi. In the chapel to the left of the main chapel, on the left, is the *Washing of the Feet*, a late painting by Jacopo Tintoretto.

Calle Larga (Via) XXII Marzo (5 E4). The name commemorates the date (22 March) on which the Austrian occupying troops were driven out of the city, in 1848; the "calle" was widened in 1880. In a certain way this is the "City" of the lagoon city, since the main economic and financial activities of Venice are concentrated here: at n. 2032-34, note the broad facade of the *Palazzo della Borsa e della Camera di Commercio* (Stock Exchange and Chamber of Commerce; 1924-26), while on the other side of the street are numerous banks.

As soon as you cross the bridge over the Rio di S. Moisè, on the left, take Campiello Barozzi and Sottoportego Barozzi to get to Corte Barozzi: at n. 2155-58, is the *Palazzo Treves de' Bonfili* (5 E4), rebuilt at the beginning of the 17th c., probably with help from Bartolomeo Monopola. On the inside (open upon request) you should note two large statues by Antonio Canova, *Hector* (1808-16) and *Ajax* (1811-12), set in a specially designed and decorated hall (by Giuseppe Borsato).

Campo S. Fantin (5 D-E4). This enchanting old square, enclosed by the once splendid white facade of the Teatro La Fenice, and by the church of S. Fantin and the former Scuola di S. Fantin. The well heads, made of Istrian stone, date from the 15th c.

Teatro La Fenice (5 E3-4). The city's principal theater, one of the most famous opera theaters worldwide (praised in particular for its acoustic and decorations); some "absolute debuts" include *Rigoletto*, 1851, and *La Traviata*, 1853, by Giuseppe Verdi; *Tancredi*, 1813, and *Semiramide*, 1823, by Gioacchino Rossini; as well as *La carriera di un libertino*, 1951, by Igor Stravinsky. It was completely destroyed by a fire on 29 January 1996.
The original construction had suffered the same tragedy in 1836, built in 1790-92 by Giannantonio Selva – only the perimetral walls survived. La Fenice rose up from the ashes (*nomen omen*) thanks to the works of Tommaso and G.B. Meduna, while in 1936 Eugenio Miozzi supervised the stage renovations.
The facade and the canal prospect, before the last fire, were the original Neoclassical constructions with sculptures by G.B. Meduna in the niches. The project to reconstruct the theater aims to finish for the year 2000 " where and how it was before," while taking advantage of avantgard technology and new services.

S. Fantin (5 D4). Rebuilt in 1507 by Scarpagnino and, after the death of that architect, by Jacopo Sansovino, this church faces the entrance of the theater. A number of studies have determined that Pietro Lombardo was the actual designer. In the three-aisle interior, with barrel- and cross-vaults, note, on the

counterfacade, the *marble choir chancel* (1563), possibly by Jacopo Sansovino.
Linked to Venetian history are, in the right aisle, above the side door, *Saints John the Evangelist, Rocco, and Theodore Intercede with the Virgin Mary for the Cessation of the Pestilence of 1630, in the Presence of the Parish Priest Giovanni Pomelli*, a large canvas by Joseph Heintz the Younger and, on the left wall of the presbytery by Sansovino, with two pulpits, *The Doge Alvise Mocenigo Thanks the Virgin After the Victory of Lepanto*, large canvas by Palma the Younger; on the main altar: two marble carvings, *St. Fantin* e *St. Martha*, by Giuseppe Torretti (1756).

Scuola di S. Fantin (5 D4). Formerly the headquarters of the Confraternita di S. Girolamo e di S. Maria della Giustizia, a religious confraternity whose chief act of justice was that of assisting and accompanying those under sentence of death to their executions (this building was thus also known as the Scuola dei "Picai," i.e., of the gallows-birds, or the Scuola della "Buona Morte," i.e., of the Good Death), since 1812 this has been the headquarters of the *Ateneo Veneto*, an academy of sciences and letters, ordered built by Napoleon.
The building as it stands today was built at the end of the 16th c., after a fire destroyed the original building; the architect was Antonio Contin (1592-1600), who worked with Alessandro Vittoria (he did the statues in the pediment) as did Tommaso Contin after the death of his brother Antonio.
The interior (access from the left side) is divided into two halls. On the ground floor is the Aula Magna (or great hall), formerly Oratorio della Scuola, with a wooden ceiling; in the thirteen panels are depictions of *Suffrage for the Souls in Purgatory* and *Doctors and Fathers of the Church* by Palma the Younger (1600). On the second floor, in the *Sala Tommaseo*, formerly Albergo Piccolo della Scuola, are two works by A. Zanchi: on the ceiling, an enormous *Last Judgement* (1674) and on the wall to the right of the door, *Jesus Driving the Moneylenders from the Temple* (1667).
As you walk along the right side of the Teatro La Fenice, you will reach the *Campiello della Fenice (or Campiello Marinoni)* overlooked by a building dating from 1869 (now a hotel) studded with projectiles and small cannon used by the Austrians in 1849 to bombard Venice, and a bronze portrait of Daniele Manin.

Campo S. Maria del Giglio (5 E3). This "campo" is irregular in shape, and is actually made up of two spaces, one lying before the church, the other preserving the base of the bell tower (demolished in 1775 because it was hazardous) and now used as a shop; the space extends into the nearby Campo del Traghetto, with the distinctive wooden piers for gondoliers, and, on the left, the Gothic *Palazzo Gritti*, now one of the most renowned hotels in Venice or Italy. From this spot, on 21 November, the Feast of the Madonna della Salute, a bridge of boats is extended across the Grand Canal, stretching to the church of the Salute.

S. Maria del Giglio (Zobenigo; 5 E3). Founded in the 10th c. by the Jubanico family (hence Zobenigo), it was renovated several times, and rebuilt entirely in the second half of the 17th c. The facade was built by Giuseppe Sardi (1678-83), at the expense and for the glory of the Barbaro family, depicted in the statues set in the various niches, while, lower down, there are six plans of as many cities *(Zara, Candia, Padua, Rome, Corfu* and *Spalato, or Split*).
The interior, which has a single rectangular aisle, has a flat ceiling with canvases by Antonio Zanchi, painted between 1690 and 1696 (*Birth of the Virgin Mary, Coronation, Assumption*). Note the interesting Stations of the Cross, or *Via Crucis* (1755-56), by various artists. On the right side, you can enter the Cappella Molin, with a bust of *Girolamo Molin*, by A. Vittoria and, on the ceiling, the *Virgin Mary* attributed to Domenico Tintoretto; on the walls, note various canvases, including a *Virgin Mary with Christ Child and Young St. John* by Peter Paul Rubens. On the 3rd altar on the right, *Visitation* by Palma the Younger. Note in particular the 17th-c. sacristy, with a handsome canvas by Antonio Zanchi, *Abraham Teaching Astrology to the Egyptians*. Behind the main altar, on either side of the organ, note the original doors, with the *Four Evangelists* by Jacopo Tintoretto (1552) and the *Mater Dolorosa* by Sebastiano Ricci. On the 3rd altar on the left, note the *Christ and Saint Francis of Paula Justine* by Tintoretto.

Behind S. Maria del Giglio, and beyond the Rio del Giglio, extends the charming Campiello della Feltrina, overlooked by the 15th-c. *Palazzo Malipiero* (n. 2514). After you cross the Ponte Zaguri on the left, the "fondamenta" terminates at the landward entrance of *Palazzo Corner della Ca' Granda* (headquarters of the Prefecture and the Provincial Administration; 5 E-F3). This is one of the largest Venetian palazzi, and was designed and built by Jacopo Sansovino (construction began in 1533 and dragged on for more than 30 years), on behalf of Jacopo, the nephew of Caterina Cornaro, queen of Cyprus. Famous for its splendor, only a few of its rooms still reflect the antique glory.

Campo S. Maurizio (5 E3). The regular shape of the quiet square is bounded by the church of S. Maurizio and by 15th- and 16th-c. palazzi. The well head dates from 1521. On the right of the church, you can see the leaning bell tower of the church of S. Stefano. This "campo" is used during certain festive occasions as an antiques marketplace.

S. Maurizio (5 E3). Rebuilt to plans by P. Zaguri, between the end of the 18th and the beginning of the 19th c., with work by G.A. Selva and A. Diedo, who designed and built the facade.
The Greek-cross interior and the central dome are by Selva, as is the main altar and the design of the organ and pulpit, decorated by Giuseppe Borsato.

In the narrow Calle del Piovan is the former *Scuola degli Albanesi* (now private) from the late 15th c., with elegant reliefs of the Lombard school. As you cross the Rio del Santissimo you may note, on the right, the choir of the church of S. Stefano stretching over the water, and on the left, the elevation of Palazzo Morosini overlooking the "rio" (the landward entrance is in Campo S. Stefano), marked by the distinctive winged horse that juts from the arch of the central door.

Campo S. Stefano or Campo F. Morosini (5 E2). One of the favorite meeting places for Venetians, who like to meet at the cafes in this "campo," located at the intersection of major walking routes (toward S. Marco, Rialto, the Ponte dell'Accademia).
Extending over, and articulated in a number of open spaces and "campielli," with the bronze statue of the *Monument to Niccolò Tommaseo* (1882) at its center, and embellished by two well heads built in 1724, this "campo" is closed off to the north by the side of the church of S. Stefano, and is bounded by an unbroken curtain of elegant palazzi.
At n. 2803 is the monumental entrance of *Palazzo Morosini*, which was the home of Doge Francesco Morosini, known as the Peloponnesian; he commanded the cannons that bombarded the Acropolis in Athens in 1687. Comprising two buildings with a common courtyard, it was unified at the end of the 17th c. by Antonio Gaspari. When the Morosini dynasty died out in 1884, the furnishings were auctioned off and scattered (the ceiling, painted by G.B. Tiepolo, now adorns Palazzo Isimbardi in Milan), and the building itself is now the headquarters of the Consorzio Venezia Nuova, which represents the Italian state in the safeguarding of Venice and its lagoon.
At n. 2945 stands the *Palazzo Loredan*, a long building, originally Gothic, rebuilt in the 16th c. to plans by Scarpagnino, and now the headquarters of the *Istituto Veneto di Scienze, Lettere ed Arti*, an institute for the sciences, letters, and arts, founded in 1810; with a long tradition of studies and research of Venetian history and affairs, it has a library of more than 185,000 volumes.

The Campo S. Stefano with the Monument to Niccolò Tommaseo

The Campiello Pisani, practically a private courtyard, is dominated by the impressive facade of **Palazzo Pisani** (5 E2), which now houses the Conservatorio di Musica Benedetto Marcello. The building, begun in the early-17th c., was completed by Girolamo Frigimelica in 1728 on behalf of the wealthy Pisani family. The interior is now bare of its luxurious furnishings, although there are still a few rooms with 18th-c. decorations and frescoes. Of particular interest are the chapel and the grand ballroom, now used for concerts.
Note also the handsome 16th-c. *Palazzo Barbaro* (n. 2947); its facade was once frescoed.

S. Stefano* (5 D-E3). One of the most important Gothic religious complexes in Venice, in terms of history, architecture, and art. Founded by the Eremitani Agostiniani toward the end of the 13th c., the church was completed in the elegant style of the 15th-c. Gothic, which also shaped the splendid portal, possibly a creation of Bartolomeo Bon (1442).
The interior is enormous (63 m. long, 25 m. wide, 23 m. tall) and has three aisles, spanned by a rare and exquisite wooden ship's-hull ceiling, while the walls are decorated in a diamond-shaped pattern, with clear reference to the exterior of the Doge's Palace (Palazzo Ducale). On the floor of the nave, note the *seal of the tomb of Doge Francesco Morosini*, the Peloponnesian (F. Parodi, 1694); the church contains a number of funerary monuments, in accordance with the custom in large Gothic churches; note, on the right counterfacade, the Renaissance *Monument to Giacomo Surian** or else, in the chapel to the left of the main chapel, on the right, *Monument to the Jurist G.B. Ferretti*, attributed to Michele Sanmicheli (1557). In the sacristy, on the right wall: *Last Supper**, *Washing of the Feet**, *Jesus Praying in the Garden**, three large canvases by Jacopo Tintoretto, and a *Crucifixion,* panel by Paolo Veneziano (1348). On the walls to either side of the altar, *St. Peter* and *St. Lawrence*, parts of a polyptych by Bartolomeo Vivarini, and two chest/armoires to contain relics: the one on the right holds the Byzantine icon of the Madonna Ortocosta (Our Lady of Grace), booty from the war in Morea, taken by Francesco Barbaro. On the left wall: *Sacred Family with St. Catherine of Alexandria* by Palma the Elder.
The presbytery is raised above the ancient crypt, and terminates in a large polygonal apse from the turn of the 15th c. On the walls are remains of the ancient marble choir chancel, which until the turn of the 17th c. was set, as was customary, in the center of the nave: the wooden stalls (1488) are now in the apse. The majestic main altar with a large ciborium is made up of three soaring arches; the two side arches contain wooden sculptures attributed to Girolamo Campagna (*St. Mark* and *St. Clare*). At the foot of the left aisle is the entrance to the Cappella del Battista, or Chapel of St. John the Baptist; at this altar, note the *Baptism of Christ* by Pomponio Amalteo, and on the wall *funerary stele of Giovanni Falier* by Antonio Canova. On the 3rd altar on the left, note the *statue of St. Nicholas of Tolentino*, a creation of the Lombardesque school in the late-15th c.; between the columns, *St. Paul* and *St. Jerome* by Pietro Lombardo. The 2nd altar is a lovely Baroque creation by Antonio Gaspari.
From the side door of the left aisle – beneath the funerary monument erected by the Senato for Bartolomeo d'Alviano, and planned and executed by Baldassarre Longhena (1633) – you emerge into the *cloister* (1529), attributed to Scarpagnino; note the portico with Ionic columns and a handsome well head: there was a time when the facades were decorated with frescoes by Pordenone. From the right arm, you can enter the 2nd cloister, from the 14th c., with wooden architraves and a fine well head.
After the Convent was suppressed (1810), the Financial Adminstration (Intendenza di Finanza) set up offices here. From the 16th-c. cloister, you exit onto the Campo S. Angelo (see page 44); from here you can see the *leaning campanile* of the church of S. Stefano, one of the tallest in Venice, 15th-c. in the lower half, completed in the mid-16th c.

S. Vidal (S. Vitale; 5 E2). Founded in early times, and rebuilt in the 18th c. to plans by Antonio Gaspari, with facade (originally planned to commemorate Morosini) by Andrea Tirali. Now this church is deconsecrated and is the headquarters of the Centro d'Arte S. Vidal, an art center; it still has its original furnishings and decorations, such as *St. Vitale on Horseback, with Eight Saints** by Vittore Carpaccio (signed and dated, 1514) and *The Archangel Raphael with St. Antony of Padua and St. Louis** by G.B. Piazzetta (ca. 1730).

As you proceed toward the Grand Canal, in Campo S. Vidal, you will be faced with the impressive and peculiar structure of *Palaz-*

zo *Cavalli Franchetti*, built in the 15th c. but heavily renovated in the 19th c.

Ponte dell'Accademia (5 F2). This bridge spans the Grand Canal, and was built in 1934 to replace a prior, iron bridge, built in 1854. The existing wooden structure was designed by Eugenio Miozzi as a temporary structure; nonetheless, it was recently reinforced with steel fittings. From here, with a fine view of the Punta della Dogana, you enter the Sestiere di Dorsoduro.

2.3 From St. Mark's to Palazzo Grassi

This route is made up of three sections. The first, stretching from San Marco to Rialto, runs through one of the oldest areas in Venice, and allows you to observe all that survives of the original urban structure, which is a patchwork of shops and homes; this leg leads to the Ponte di Rialto, one of the symbols of Venice. The second leg runs along the Grand Canal, whose shores are occupied by the many gondola piers. Lastly, the third part of the route wends its way, first inland, between Campo S. Luca, Campo Manin, and Campo S. Angelo, along one of the busiest streets in Venice, the Calle della Mandola; it then returns to the Grand Canal.

Mercerie* (5 C-D5). This route leads straight from the religious and political center of the Piazza S. Marco (Torre dell'Orologio, or clock tower) to the shops and crowds of Rialto, which has always been a varied marketplace of Venice ("merci," Italian for "merchandise," is the source of the name "Mercerie"); this was the site of 10th-c. Byzantine Venice. Note the dense urban structure, interrupted by numerous "calli," or lanes; paved in the 13th c. to allow horses to pass (horses were prohibited however as early as 1340), the Mercerie are broken up into numerous sections, with different names.
At the beginning of the first stretch, the *Merceria dell'Orologio*, note on the left (at n. 149) the commemorative relief, "old woman with a mortar," referring to the historical episode from 1310, when the standard-bearer who was leading the conspirators under Bajamonte Tiepolo in revolt against the Doge Gradenigo was struck by a mortar, dropped by an elderly woman from a high window (on the pavement, a white cobblestone indicates where the mortar struck the ground).

S. Zulian* (S. Giuliano; 5 C-D5). This church dominates the "campo" with its facade, sheathed in Istria stone. According to tradition, this church was founded in A.D. 829; rebuilt in 1105, it was again rebuilt in its modern form by Jacopo Sansovino (1553-55), who also modeled, according to some, the bronze *statue of Tommaso Rangone* (who commissioned the construction of

2.3 San Marco

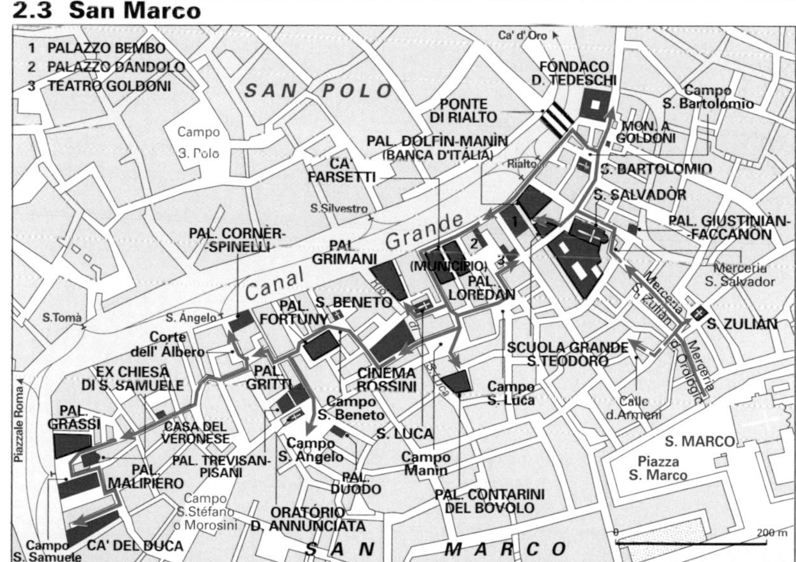

the church, marking the beginning of a Venetian custom of self-glorification), set above the portal. The interior, with a single aisle, has a square plan.
By Palma the Younger: the *Glory of St. Julian*, on the wooden ceiling; *Our Lady of the Assumption*, panel on the second altar on the right; *St. John the Evangelist, St. Joseph, and St. Antony*, in the chapel to the right of the main altar; the *Resurrection* in the extrados of the arch of the chapel to the left of the main altar; in the altar of this chapel, note the *Pietà**, a marble high-relief by Gerolamo Campagna. Also note Paolo Veronese's *Pietà*, a panel on the first altar on the right.

From this "campo," you can reach the Calle Fiubera (5 D5), and from there, running off to the right, the Calle degli Armeni, at the end of which (n. 965 B) stands the entrance to the church of *S. Croce degli Armeni* (open only Sunday mornings), operated by the Padri Mechitaristi of the Isola di S. Lazzaro degli Armeni. The 15th-c. building was enlarged at the end of the 17th c., and is enclosed by the buildings of a quarter once inhabited by the Armenian community of Venice. Further along is the intersection with the *Rio Terrà delle Colonne*, filled in in 1840; note the portico that once ran along the water-filled "rio."

Campo S. Salvador (5 C5). Opening out to the left at the end of the Mercerie, with the white facades of S. Salvador and the Ex-Scuola di S. Teodoro framing the passageway of the Calle dell'Ovo, with odd paving in red granite. At the center is a commemorative column (1898) honoring the revolt of Venice against the Austrians in 1848.

S. Salvador* (5 C5). Built in earliest times, this church was restored repeatedly. The modern structure, which dates from the 16th c., was designed also by Tullio Lombardo and Jacopo Sansovino, while in 1574 Scamozzi built the lanterns on the three domes, and in 1663 Giuseppe Sardi designed the impressive facade.
The interior, with three broad aisles, is rich in artworks. In the right aisle, after the 1st altar, *Monument to the Procurator Andrea Dolfin and Benedetta Pisani Dolfin* by Giulio del Moro; after the 2nd altar (*Virgin Mary with Christ Child and Angels*, a marble group by Campagna), *Monument to the Doge Francesco Venier** by Jacopo Sansovino (1556-61). At the 3rd altar, *Annunciation** by Titian (1566).
In the chapel to the right of the main altar, on the right wall, *Martyrdom of St. Theodore*, attributed to Paris Bordon. In the presbytery, on the main altar, a *Transfiguration** by Titian (1560) covers a 14th-c. silver altarpiece. In the left aisle, the 3rd altar is by Alessandro Vittoria, who also carved the statues of *St. Rocco* and *St. Sebastian*.
Surrounding the side door, by Jacopo Sansovino (1530), note the organ, with ports decorated by paintings by Francesco Vecellio (1530): outside, note *St. Augustine* and *St. Theodore*, inside, *Resurrection* and *Transfiguration*.
To the right of the church, n. 4826, entrance portal of the former convent of *S. Salvador*, 16th c., with two cloisters. The entire convent complex was restored (1987-92) by SIP, the Italian phone company, which owns the property; the goal was to install one of the most advanced telephone switchboards in Europe.

Scuola Grande di S. Teodoro (5 C4). The building of the Confraternity dedicated to Venice's first patron saint was begun in 1578 and completed at the end of the 17th c., by several different architects, among them, Baldassarre Longhena, who designed the left side, and Giuseppe Sardi (he did the facade, 1655).
Headquarters of the Associazione Culturale di S. Teodoro, this building is now used for temporary art exhibitions; the interior, like all of Venice's "Scuole," is split into two floors, linked by a monumental staircase: on the upper floor, in the chapter hall, note the two organ doors by Palma the Younger depicting the *Annunciation*.

Campo S. Bartolomio (5 B5). This was once a busy marketplace, and is now one of the favorite meeting spots for residents of Venice; it is especially lively in the evening, when young people gather here and in the nearby Campo S. Luca for preprandial socializing. At the center is the *Monument to Carlo Goldoni* (1883), while on the left you can glimpse the silhouette of the Ponte di Rialto (see below) and the Fondaco dei Tedeschi; on the right, note the 14th-c. *Palazzo Moro* (n. 5308).

S. Bartolomio (5 C5). Long the house of worship for the German community that inhabited the nearby Fondaco dei Tedeschi, the church, built in 1170, was radically restored during the 18th c. The Baroque campanile was built by Giovanni Scalfarotto (1754). The interior, built to a Latin-cross plan, has three aisles; all of the artwork has been removed, to allow its use for temporary exhibitions.

Ponte di Rialto* (5 B4-5). This is certainly one of the most famous bridges on earth,

Rialto Bridge from the Grand Canal

with a major archway (spanning the narrowest part of the Grand Canal); until the nineteenth century it was the only permanent link between the two halves of the city.
The bridge as it now stands has a span, with an opening of 28 m. and a height of 7.5 m.; three pedestrian walkways cross the bridge, between the two lines of shops, joined in the center by two larger arches. On the sides, note the 16th-c. bas-reliefs. The bridge is a symbol of Venice, and has long assured links between the commercial area of Rialto and the political and religious center of S. Marco.
A first permanent structure in wood was built in 1264 to replace a previous raft bridge; the 13th-c. bridge collapsed in 1444, and was rebuilt, again in wood, with a passageway between two lines of shops, and a central swing-bridge, to allow boats through (as it is depicted by Carpaccio in his large painting, now in the Gallerie dell'Accademia). At the turn of the 16th c., the Venetian Republic examined a number of plans for a new bridge – plans by Sansovino, Palladio, and perhaps Michelangelo, among others – but, after much dispute, they decided to entrust the project to Antonio Da Ponte, who rebuilt it in stone between 1588 and 1591.

Fondaco (Fontego) dei Tedeschi (5 B5). Now occupied by a post office, for centuries it housed the German merchants who spent time in Venice for business.
It existed as early as the turn of the 13th c., and was ruined by fire and rebuilt in the 16th c., to plans by Girolamo Tedesco, under the supervision of Giorgio Spavento and the Scarpagnino.
The facade overlooking the Grand Canal (visible from the Ponte di Rialto) was decorated with frescoes by Giorgione and Titian (fragments at the Ca' d'Oro and in the Gallerie dell'Accademia). The interior overlooks a vast courtyard (topped by a skylight in 1937), which was once lined by warehouses and shops.

Riva del Ferro and Riva del Carbon (5 B-C4). These are the two "fondamenta" that, along the southern bank, run from the Ponte di Rialto for some distance along the Grand Canal, overlooked by such notable palazzi as *Palazzo Dolfin-Manin* (offices of the Banca d'Italia), with a distinctive "sottoportego" along the Grand Canal, built to plans by Jacopo Sansovino between 1536 and 1573; on the side, along Calle Larga Mazzini, stands a *Monument to Giuseppe Mazzini* (1951).
Beyond the Rio S. Salvador stands, n. 4792, the 15th-c. *Palazzo Bembo*, with splendid five-light mullioned windows; here lived the cardinal Pietro Bembo, poet and author (1470-1547).
On the 14th-c. Gothic *Palazzo Dandolo*, n. 4172, a plaque commemorates Doge Enrico Dandolo, who, though blind, led the Fourth Crusade to the conquest of Constantinople.
Next to it are two Venetian Byzantine palazzi (12th/13th c.), now the site of Venice's city hall: Palazzo Loredan and Ca' Farsetti.
Palazzo Loredan (n. 4137), formerly the residence of the Corner del Ramo Piscopia, so-named after the fief they obtained from the Lusignano of Cyprus, later the home of the Loredan, and after 1868, city property. In the "sotoportego," note the boulder of Is-

tria stone and the Roman column, taken in 1947 from the tomb of Nazario Sauro in Pola, and brought in 1954 to Venice. A plaque on the left side commemorates Elena Lucrezia Cornaro Piscopia, the first women to earn a degree, in 1678.
Ca' Farsetti, which belonged first to the Dandolo family, and later to the Farsetti family, has housed the Accademia Farsetti since the 18th c.; this academy, frequented by many artists, including Canova, once had a collection of plaster casts of ancient sculptures, which was transfered to the Gallerie dell'Accademia. In 1826 the building became municipal property, and the city government moved its offices here from the Doge's Palace (Palazzo Ducale). Inside, note the staircase by Andrea Tirali (18th c.) and rooms frescoed and decorated in stucco, with works by 18th-c. masters.

S. Luca (5 C-D4). Separate from the Campo di S. Luca, this church turns its right side to the Campiello della Chiesa and its facade overlooks the Rio di S. Luca. Built in ancient times, it was rebuilt more than once, and finally in 1832; it still has the 15th-c. campanile, however.
The interior has a single aisle; note, on the main altar, the *Virgin Mary in Glory and St. Luke* by Paolo Veronese (1581) and, on the 2nd altar on the left, the 17th-c. *Miracle of St. Lorenzo Giustiniani* by Carl Loth, a Bavarian painter whose funerary monument is located in the corridor of the sacristy.
On the "fondamenta" (n. 4041) note the landward entrance of **Palazzo Grimani*** (now houses judiciary offices) with facade overlooking the Grand Canal. Built to plans by Michele Sanmicheli (after 1556), it was completed in 1575.
Facing the church is the modern building of the theater and movie house Cinema-Teatro Rossini.

From the Campiello della Chiesa (at n. 4038, note the 13th-c. terracotta portal of *Palazzo Magno*) take Salizzada S. Luca to the *Campo S. Luca* (5 C4), a lively meeting point, with late-19th-c. buildings; then take Calle del Forno, passing by the *Teatro Carlo Goldoni*, built in the 16th c. and more than once rebuilt, given its current form in 1979.

Campo Manin (5 D4). This "campo" acquired its present appearance and shape following extensive demolition in the 19th c. (among other things, the church of S. Paternian was destroyed; this was once Campo Paternian) and the new space was named for Daniele Manin, leader of Venice's anti-Austrian resistance movement in 1848-49; Manin's house stood across the "rio": a monument in the center of the "campo" is dedicated to Manin (1875). Where the church once stood is now the Cassa di Risparmio di Venezia, a bank designed and built (1968) by Pierluigi Nervi and Angelo Scattolin.

Midway along the southern facade, Calle della Vida leads to the *Palazzo Contarini del Bòvolo*

Palazzo Contarini del Bovolo

(15th/16th c.; 5 D4), with its splendid Renaissance exterior spiral staircase* (*bòvolo*, in Venetian dialect).

Campo S. Beneto (5 D3). This "campo" preserves in its center the high platform that indicates the presence of wells for the collection of rainwater; it is dominated by the majestic facade of *Palazzo Fortuny* formerly Palazzo Pesaro degli Orfei, dating from the 15th c., and adorned by two large seven-light mullioned windows. The palazzo, which once housed the Accademia degli Apollinei (hence the name "degli Orfei"; Orphic and Apollonian being linked concepts), was purchased at the turn of the 20th c. by Mariano Fortuny y Madrazo, a Spanish painter, set designer, and collector; it now houses the *Museo Fortuny*, which displays the artist's work in the halls that he himself furnished.
On the upper floors are the *Centro di Documentazione Fotografica*, a center of photography, and the *Donazione Virgilio Guidi*,

with 80 works by this Roman artist who lived much of his life in Venice.
Nearby is the church of *S. Beneto* (Ss. Benedetto e Scolastica), rebuilt after 1619, which preserves, in its single-aisle interior, on the 2nd altar on the right, a panel by Bernardo Strozzi, *Martyrdom of St. Sebastian* and on the 1st altar on the left, *S. Francis of Paula* by Gian Domenico Tiepolo.

Campo S. Angelo (5 D3). This broad space is the product of the demolition, in 1837, of the ancient church of Angelo Michele, which stood near the "rio"; two broad elevations mark the pavement over the wells, marked by late-15th-c. well heads; in the background is the silhouette of the leaning bell tower of S. Stefano. Overlooking the "campo" are the 15th-c. *Palazzo Duodo* (n. 3584), where the composer Domenico Cimarosa died, *Palazzo Gritti* (opposite, n. 3832), and the 17th-c. *Palazzo Trevisan-Pisani* (n. 3831).
At the center (n. 3817) stands the *Oratorio dell'Annunciata*, founded by the Morosini in the 10th c. and repeatedly rebuilt; this building housed the Scuola dei Sotti (Zoppi): inside, note the fine wooden *Crucifix*, of the 15th-c. Venetian school.

Corte dell'Albero (5 D3). This irregularly shaped courtyard opens out among tall palazzi; among them are *Casa Nardi*, an interesting example of a housing complex in the Venetian-Byzantine style (by G. Alessandri and V. Fantucci, 1913) and, toward the Grand Canal, n. 3870, *Palazzo Sandi*, by Domenico Rossi (1720), with a splendid fresco, in the hall of the main floor, or "piano nobile", by the young G.B. Tiepolo, *Story of Orpheus*.
Further along, on the Riva del Canal Grande, n. 3877, is the landward entrance of **Palazzo Corner Spinelli*** (5 D3), built by Mauro Codussi at the end of the 15th c., with later work by Sanmicheli.
Along the Rio di S. Angelo you will reach the Piscina S. Samuele and the *Salizzada S. Samuele* (5 D2) where (n. 3338) the painter Paolo Veronese lived and, on 19 April 1588, died. A short way further along is the building (n. 3216) that once housed the *Scuola dei Mureri* (masons), with a relief depicting the emblems of the mason's craft: miter-square and hammer.

Campo S. Samuele (5 D-E1-2). This is one of the most distinctive "campi" on the Grand Canal, with trees that shade the area between the majestic Palazzo Grassi (to the right) and, on the left, the 17th-c. *Palazzo Malipiero*, as well as the church of S. Samuele with its 12th-c. Venetian-Romanesque campanile.

On the rear of Palazzo Malipiero, you can take Calle Malipiero (a plaque, high and on the right, notes that, on 2 April 1725, Giacomo Casanova was born here); on the right you will reach the *Corte del Duca Sforza*, distinguished by the presence of a large tree not far from the "sottoportego" that overlooks the Grand Canal, and known for the so-called *Ca' del Duca* (5 E2). The building that now stands here was erected in the 19th c., and encloses the remains of the previous 15th-c. residence of the Cornaro family, which sold this entire area in 1461 to Francesco Sforza, duke of Milan. Inside is the private art collection (Collezione Ca' del Duca), normally open to the public but now closed for restoration, with remarkable artwork from the 18th c.

S. Samuele (5 D2). Dating from the 11th c., heavily rebuilt toward the end of the 17th c., this church has not yet been deconsecrated, yet it is used largely for art exhibits. The interior, with three aisles, still preserves the Gothic 15th-c. apse; note the triumphal arch adorned by thirteen lunettes by various artists.

Palazzo Grassi (5 D1-2). This impressive construction was built by Giorgio Massari around 1750, and it represents the last great aristocratic home built in Venice before the fall of the Serenissima. Headquarters of the Grassi Foundation, funded by Fiat, it is used for major art shows

3 San Polo and Santa Croce

The Sestiere di San Polo and the Sestiere di Santa Croce are treated together here because of the close ties that link the two areas; indeed it is quite difficult in some areas to make out the boundaries separating these two "sestieri," because they are not separated by a "rio" or canal, as most "sestieri" are. Both "sestieri" are contained within the "peninsula" surrounded by the northern oxbow curve of the Grand Canal and, roughly, by the course of the Rio Nuovo, although the Sestiere di Santa Croce also has the considerable addition of the area around Piazzale Roma, the Isola Nuova del Tronchetto, and the piers of the Stazione Marittima. The ages of the urban structures contained between the eastern boundary of the "sestieri" – Rialto – and their westernmost extremity – the Tronchetto – correspond perfectly to the history of the construction of Venice itself: that is to say, from Venice of the high Middle Ages to modern Venice.
Indeed, if the commercial area of Rialto, with its typical "case-fondaco," or "homes-qua-storehouses," along the banks of the Grand Canal, and, behind them, the compact medieval quarters, represents one of the earliest sections of Venice to have developed, the Terminal del Tronchetto is the most recent and the most hotly debated project to have been built in the historical center, while both the area around Piazzale Roma and the Stazione Marittima are recently built projects that have radically redefined the image of Venice's historical center (and in part its functions).
As we follow the routes described here, in the direction that corresponds to a voyage forward through time, we may notice the variations in the composition, quality, and characteristics of both public and private spaces, from the earliest area around Rialto to the areas of 20th-c. construction and even some buildings from the late-1980s. Let us cite just one example: the absolute lack of public spaces or green parks in the area around Rialto, and, on the other hand, the great number of gardens – with the accompanying network of "campi" and "campielli" – on the other side of the Rio di S. Polo.
While the predominant quality that can be detected in these two "sestieri" is that found throughout much of the city – the close ties between "casa e bottega," i.e., "home and workshop," or between residential houses and commercial operations – we should also point out the presence of numerous university buildings, as well as the incomparable monuments of the Frari, S. Rocco, and S. Giovanni Evangelista.

3.1 From Rialto to Piazzale Roma

From Rialto, one of the areas that is truly emblematic of Venice, the route winds around the upper curve of the Grand Canal. Along this route, you will be able to visit the major palazzi that overlook the waters of the Grand Canal (especially, Palazzo Corner della Regina, Ca' Pesaro, and the Fondaco dei Turchi) as well as the churches that front on that waterway (S. Stae and S. Simeon Piccolo); you can also work your way into the intricate fabric of this "sestiere" to see a number of "campi" of particular note (Campo S. Maria Mater Domini, the tree-lined Campo S. Giacomo dell'Orio, Campo S. Zan Degolà, and Campo S. Nicolò da Tolentino), while keeping in mind that the churches that form the heart of these "campi" contain genuine art treasures.
The route terminates in the area around Piazzale Roma, an area that is now being transformed in a way that will radically reorganize this automobile terminal.

Rialto* (5 B4; map on page 55). Traditionally thought to have been one of the first settlements in the city's history, Rialto can be considered, with S. Marco (the religious and political center) and the Arsenale (center of maritime power), to be the third stonghold of the ancient urban structure of Venice. This was the site of the marketplaces as early as the 11th c., and over time it absorbed the city's financial activity and the leading magistracies connected with business. It is still a busy and thriving area, even though it is limited to retail trade (open mornings).
The original arrangement of the marketplace, by trades, can still be seen in the names of the streets and squares: Ruga degli Orefici (goldsmiths), Pescaria (fish market), Erbaria (vegetable and herb market), Beccarie (meat market). This organization of Rialto presents aspects that are typical of medieval marketplaces, with the

juxtaposition of shops selling remarkably different products: alongside the goldsmiths, for example, were the insurers (Calle Sicurtà); the Cordaria (cords and ropes) stands next to the Erbaria (vegetable and herb market) and not far from the Casaria (cheeses), near the spice vendors.
Note the dense urban layout, with a crowded network of shops, storehouses, and homes, without waterways, and with long "calli" alternating with short "calli"; the absence of bridges made it easier to transport goods.
After the structures of the medieval market were destroyed by a great fire in 1514, the reconstruction done by Scarpagnino basically followed the original organization, with the addition of the 16th-c. Fabbriche Vecchie and Fabbriche Nuove and the Palazzo dei Camerlenghi.
The Rialto area lies between the Ponte di Rialto, described above (page 50), the Pescaria, the Campo delle Beccarie, and the churches of S. Aponal and S. Silvestro.

At the foot of the bridge, on the left, note the *Palazzo dei Dieci Savi* (magistrates who supervised taxation) built by Scarpagnino following the great fire, and now the headquarters of the Magistrato alle Acque (supervising Venice's water); opposite is the *Palazzo dei Camerlenghi* (magistrates responsible for the finances of the State); on the ground floor of this building are the cells of the old prisons for debtors as well as jails for criminals awaiting transfer elsewhere (it is now the headquarters of the Corte dei Conti, or administrative courts).

Campo S. Giacomo di Rialto (5 B4). Once the center of financial activity in Venice, this "campo" is bounded by the church of S. Giacometto and by the porticoes of the *Fabbriche Vecchie*, offices built by Scarpagnino (1520-22); here the bankers set their tables ("banks," or literally benches), awaiting business from merchants, who applied for the transfer of credit through bank books (this service was later provided by the government with the first state banks: the Banco della Piazza in 1587 and the Banco del Giro, in 1619).
Facing the church is the statue of the *Gobbo di Rialto* (Hunchback of Rialto; 16th c.), which supports the staircase up to the Colonna del Bando, a column from atop which sentences of punishment and decrees were read aloud to the populace. In popular tradition, this statue became the Venetian version of Rome's Pasquino, a sort of bulletin board for the posting of public satires and lampoons.

S. Giacomo di Rialto (S. Giacometto; 5 B4). Said to be the oldest church in Venice (5th/6th c.), but rebuilt later (12th c.), it survived the great fire of 1514. It has been restored, and conserves its original portico; in the little bell tower, note the 15th-c. clock, rebuilt in 1749.
The interior, heavily renovated in the 17th c. and raised because of constant flooding, still preserves the original structure with a

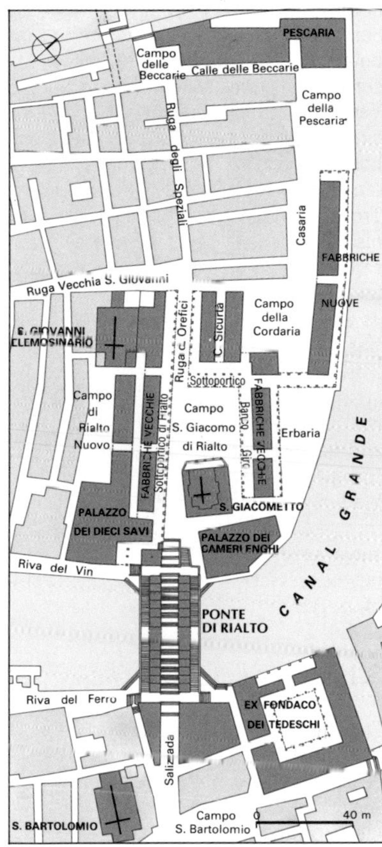

The area around Rialto

Greek-cross floor plan; note the handsome medieval columns and the capitals. Vincenzo Scamozzi created the altar on the left, or Altare degli Orefici (goldsmiths), with noteworthy bronzes by Girolamo Campagna (1604). On the right wall, note the *Annunciation* by Marco Vecellio, near the Altare Devozionale dei Garbeladori (altar of the guild of grain inspectors).

To the left of the Ruga degli Orefici, beyond the Fabbriche Vecchie, lies the *Campo di Rialto Nuovo* (5 B4), established in the 13th c. as a functional appendage to the increasing bulk of activity revolving around the Ponte di Rialto; on the

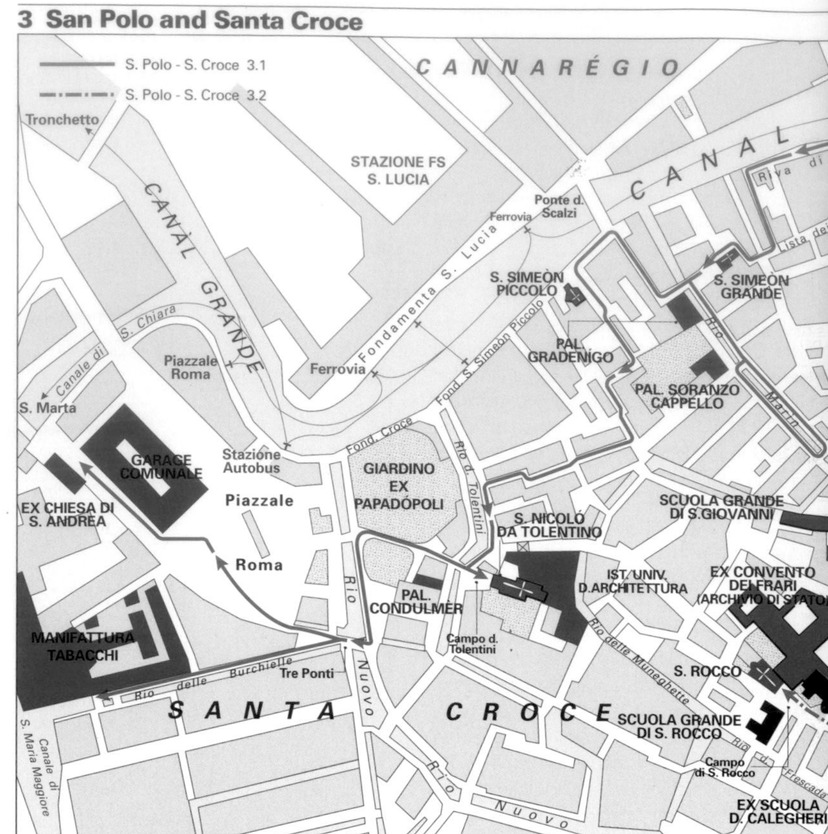

left (n. 554) note the building of the former *Scuola degli Oresi* (goldsmiths). Continuing along the nearby Calle dei Preti, and taking a right into the Calle Toscana, you will reach the *Ruga Vecchia S. Giovanni*, the chief thoroughfare linking Rialto and S. Polo, set back from the Grand Canal by the narrow and deep structure of the Byzantine Case-Fondaco (warehouses-cum-homes) that overlook the waterway.

Campo della Pescaria (5 A4; 2 F4). Opening out onto the Grand Canal, this large "campo" is occupied, in the mornings, by the canopy-covered stands of the food vendors. Overlooking this "campo" is the end of the long structure of the *Fabbriche Nuove*, a building originally occupied by the offices of the Magistrates who oversaw trade; built by Jacopo Sansovino (1554-56), it is now occcupied by the Tribunale, or trial courts; on the opposite side of the "campo" stands the porticoed structure of the *Pescaria*, or fish market, built in 1907 in the Neo-Gothic style, by Domenico Rupolo and Cesare Laurenti; the thriving and noisy fish market is quite a show, and worth seeing for the skill and good humor of the vendors.

Campo delle Beccarie (5 B4; 2 F4). This "campo" is the NW boundary of the Rialto area. Once the site of the Macello Pubblico, or Municipal Slaughterhouse, it is now a lively meeting ground for early-morning market browsers and shoppers. Overlooking the "campo" is one wing of the *Casa dei Querini*, with 13th-c. arcades and a three-light mullioned window; the building was demolished by the government of the Venetian Republic after 1310, because the Querini family took part in the unsuccessful conspiracy of Bajamonte Tiepolo.

From the "campo," *Calle dell'Angelo* runs into an area with a strong Gothic flavor, where the workers in the market of Rialto once lived.

S. Cassiano (5 A3; 2 F3). The featureless right side of the church of S. Cassiano overlooks the Campo S. Cassiano, more a thoroughfare than a meeting place. Founded in the 10th c., the church was repeatedly renovated and little survives of the original buildings; the handsome 13th-c. terracotta bell tower, however, still stands.
The three-aisle interior features, in the pres-

bytery, on the main altar, a *Resurrection, with Saints Cassian and Cecilia*, attributed to Jacopo Tintoretto (1575), and, on the walls, also by Tintoretto, *Descent into Limbo* and *Crucifixion** (1568).

If you take the Calle del Campanile and then turn right into the Calle di Ca' Michiel, you will reach the *Corte del Teatro Vecchio* (or Corte Michiel: 5 A3; 2 E-F 3), site of one of the earliest theaters built in Venice, founded around 1580 with tiers and stages; according to the late-16th-c. denunciations of the Jesuits, great "infamy" attached to the performances in said theater, and shortly thereafter, it was shut down.
At the mouth of the Calle del Campanile onto the Grand Canal you enjoy a fine frontal view of the Ca' d'Oro and the other palazzi on the opposite bank.

From Campo S. Cassian, after you cross the bridge, take a right into the Calle della Regina: at n. 2214 is the landward entrance to the *Ca' Corner della Regina* (2 E3; 5 A3) built by Domenico Rossi after 1724, on the site of an existing Casa Corner; the architecture has numerous similarities with that of the nearby Ca' Pesaro. This building belonged to the branch of the Corner family that produced Caterina, the famous queen of Cyprus, who was born here in 1454.

Campo S. Maria Mater Domini (5 A2-3; 2 F2-3). One of the most distinctive and charming "campi" in Venice, with a regular and well-proportioned shape bounded by handsome and intact late-Byzantine and Gothic buildings. Among them, you should note: at n. 2174, *Casa Zane*, dating from the 13th c., which has one of the very few overhanging roofs left in Venice; at n. 2120-22, *Casa Viaro-Zane*, with splendid five-light mullioned windows and different architectural styles on different floors; at n. 2177, *Casa Barbaro*, dating from the 14th c.

S. Maria Mater Domini (5 A2-3; 2 F2-3). This Renaissance reconstruction was probably designed by Giovanni Buora; note the facade in Istrian stone, attributed to Jacopo Sansovino.
The exceedingly simple and elegant interior is built to a Greek-cross floor plan, and clearly shows its Renaissance roots. In particular, note *St. Christine Surrounded by Angels Kneels in Adoration Before Christ Risen** (1520), by Vincenzo Catena, on the 2nd altar on the right, and, in the left transept, *Dis-*

*covery of the Cross**, a youthful work by Jacopo Tintoretto.

On the Fondamenta di Ca' Pesaro, at n. 2060, the late-14th-c. *Palazzo Agnusdio* (2 E3; note the inset "patera" with an Evangelical lamb, or "Agnus Dei," set over the canal door), with a handsome five-light mullioned window adorned with an *Annunciation* and *Symbols of the Evangelists* (bas-reliefs from the 14th/15th c.). At the end of this little quay is the landward entrance (n. 2076) of Ca' Pesaro.

Ca' Pesaro* (2 E3). This is one of the largest Venetian palazzi overlooking the Grand Canal, and was once the home of the very wealthy Pesaro family; in the 16th c. this family held a monopoly on the transport by cart of vessels over the embankment of the river Brenta, at Fusina. It houses the Museo d'Arte Moderna (a museum of modern art, closed since 1983, and until it can be restored) and the Museo d'Arte Orientale, a museum of Asian art.
Begun in 1628, designed by Baldassarre Longhena, the building was completed – after Longhena's death – by Antonio Gaspari, in 1710. The complex and articulated facades overlooking the Grand Canal and the Rio delle Due Torri were restored recently; note the lovely light hue of the Istrian stone, the statues and fanciful decorations.

The **Museo d'Arte Moderna** (the modern art section of the Musei Civici) was founded in 1897; its collection was greatly enlarged by an early body of works from the first few editions of the Venice Biennale d'Arte; it is one of the leading collections of painting, sculpture, and drawing, Italian and worldwide, covering the period from the late-19th c. to modern times.
Among the 20th-c. artists featured here, note: Morandi, Boccioni, Savinio, De Chirico, Carrà, Sironi, Rosai, Miró, De Pisis, Chagall, Kandinskij, Klee, Ernst, and Klimt; the sculptors include: Moore, Messina, Martini, Arp, Cascella, Pomodoro, and Calder. There is also a major collection of 19th-c. art.

The **Museo d'Arte Orientale** possesses one of the largest collections of Japanese art from the Edo period (1614-1868) and other sections devoted to China (porcelain and jade) and Indonesia (weapons, fabrics, shadow-theater puppets). The collection was created by Enrico di Borbone (a member of the Bourbon family), Count of Bardi who, in the late-19th c., traveled frequently to the Far East and assembled some 30,000 items; part of the collection was sold at auction, following his death, while the central core of the collection has been on display in this museum since 1929.

Campo S. Stae (2 E3). Practically a large terrace overlooking the Grand Canal, this "campo" is dominated by the facade of the church of S. Stae, while on either side, you may note: to the left, the side of *Palazzo Foscarini-Giovanelli* (2nd half of the 16th c.) and, on the right, the side of *Palazzo Priuli-Bon* (15th-c. Gothic); note, on the facade overlooking the Grand Canal, traces of the ancient "casa-fondaco," or storehouse-cum-home, from the 13th c.
Adjacent to the church is the lovely facade of the former *Scuola dei Tiraoro e Battioro* (1711), once the headquarters of the confraternity of goldsmiths, now privately owned.

S. Stae (S. Eustachio; 2 E3). Rebuilt in the 17th c., atop an existing church, to plans by Giovanni Grassi; the facade was rebuilt in 1709 by Domenico Rossi. This church is often used for temporary exhibitions and for concerts.

Not far from the Campo S. Stae, along Calle di Ca' Tron, you can reach the *Ca' Tron* (16th c.; 2 E2), the lavish home of the Tron family, once a leading power in Venice; it is now part of the university (Institute of Architecture). Standing on the Salizzada di S. Stae, to the left, is the impressive *Palazzo Mocenigo* (2 E3), a 17th-c. construction; the Mocenigo family gave Venice no fewer than seven doges. Palazzo Mocenigo now belongs to the city, and it houses a *museum*, with 5th-/7th-c. Coptic fabrics, 14th-/19th-c. Italian and French cloth, and 18th-/19th-c. costumes.

Campo S. Giacomo dell'Orio (2 F2). One of the few tree-lined spaces in the center of Venice; this "campo" is an intricate structure surrounding the church, and a very pleasant one at that. In the summer, performances and popular festivals are held here, especially for the feast of the patron saint, St. James the Great, on 25 July. The name refers to the rich Orio family, which once lived nearby.

S. Giacomo dell'Orio (2 E-F1-2). Certainly one of the oldest churches in Venice (possibly 10th c.), it was rebuilt in 1225, undergoing various modifications and additions in later centuries. The facade, overlooking the "rio," features inset works of Byzantine art; on the left side stands the handsome 13th-c. terracotta campanile.
The interior, with a Latin-cross floor plan,

The Campo S. Giacomo dell'Orio

not only maintains intact the medieval structure; it is also itself a treasure chest of art. Among the remarkable treasures in this church, let us mention the handsome wooden keel roof (14th c.), the *holy water font* (13th c.) in the nave, and the Lombardesque *pulpit*, standing against a 6th-c. column from Ravenna.
Among the many paintings, in the presbytery, note the *Virgin Mary with Christ Child and Saints* (1546) by Lorenzo Lotto; in the ceiling of the Sagrestia Nuova, canvases painted in 1577 by Paolo Veronese; on the altar of the left transept, *Saint Lawrence, Saint Jerome, and Saint Prosper of Aquitaine* by Paolo Veronese (1572).

Fondaco dei Turchi (2 E2). At the end of the Salizzada dei Turchi is the landward entrance (n. 1730) of this noteworthy 13th-c. Venetian-Byzantine "casa-fondaco," or storehouse-cum-home; it originally belonged to the Pesaro family, but from 1621 until 1838 it belonged to the Venetian government, and was used as a storehouse and hotel for Turkish merchants.
A deplorable 19th-c. restoration damaged the original appearance of the palazzo, which now houses the *Museo Civico di Storia Naturale*, a municipal museum of natural history.

S. Zan Degolà (S. Giovanni Decollato; 2 E2). Standing on the NE corner of the Campo S. Zan Degolà, this church is surely quite ancient (10th/11th c.); it has been rebuilt repeatedly, and still has the 18th-c. facade. The interior is divided into three aisles, with columns made of Greek marble, and 11th-c. Byzantine capitals; note the keel roof.

Riva di Biasio (2 E1; 1 E6). This is the "fondamenta," or quay that runs along the Grand Canal, within sight of the mouth of the Canale di Cannaregio, embellished and made particularly majestic by the set of facades of the church of S. Geremia, the facade of Palazzo Labia, overlooking the water, and the handsome Ponte delle Guglie. The Riva di Biasio may take its name from the *luganegher* (or sausage maker) Biagio Cargnio, who had a shop in this area in the early 16th c. He was executed after he admitted using the flesh of children that he had killed in the preparation of *sguazeto*, a Venetian-style gravy.

S. Simeon Grande (S. Simeone Profeta; 1 E5). Founded in early times, it once had a cemetery in front of the present facade (hence the name Campo Santo, literally, cemetery); it was heavily restored in the 18th c.
The three-aisle interior with a basilican plan still has ancient columns with Byzantine capitals. Among the artworks, note, in the right aisle, *Presentation in the Temple and Clients*, by Palma the Younger; on the wall of the left aisle, *Last Supper*, by Jacopo Tintoretto.

Rio Marin (1 E5-F6: 4 A5-6). From the Ponte della Bergama, immediately following the Campo Santo, you can enjoy an overall view of this distinctive area of the Sestiere di S. Croce, comprising the Rio Marin, which takes its name from Marin Dandolo, who ordered it dug in the 11th c., and from the two "fondamenta," also called the Fondamenta dei Garzoti (wool carders), that line it. Overlooking these "fondamenta" are, on the left, adjacent to the bridge, *Palazzo Gradenigo*, an imposing 17th-c. construction built by Domenico Margutti, possibly to plans by Longhena and, a little further along, the late-16th-c. *Palazzo Soranzo-Cappello*, with a lovely garden that is mentioned by Gabriele D'Annunzio in his novel *Il Fuoco*.

Ponte degli Scalzi (1 E5). This was the last of the bridges over the Grand Canal to be built. It was rebuilt in 1934, to plans by Eugenio Miozzi, replacing the original iron structure built by the Austrian occupying forces in 1858. The arch has a span of 40 m., and a height of 6.75 m.

S. Simeon Piccolo (1 E5; 4 A5). Built in 1718-38 by Giovanni Scalfarotto and dedicated to the Holy Apostles Simon and Judas, it has a tall distinctive copper dome and an elegant pronaos, atop a broad stairway.
The interior has a circular floor plan and features an interesting main altar, in marble, with a tabernacle surrounded by statues of *Saints Simeon and Matthias* (18th c.); in the sacristy note the marble *Crucifix* attributed to Giovanni Marchiori.

Campo dei Tolentini and Campazzo dei Tolentini (4 B5). This interesting open space lies near the church of the Tolentini, split into two sections ("campo" and "campazzo") by tall residential buildings. The "campo" lies before the pronaos of the church, overlooking the "rio," with an unusual stone balustrade; the Campazzo, running along the side of the church, is distinguished by the entrance – built by Carlo Scarpa in 1984 – to the main building *Istituto Universitario di Architettura*, which has occupied the halls of the former Convento dei Padri Teatini since 1964.

S. Nicolò da Tolentino (4 B5). Designed and begun by Vincenzo Scamozzi (1591-95) and completed by the clients themselves, the Padri Teatini (1602), this church features, on its unfinished facade, a tall pronaos with pediment by Andrea Tirali (1706-14).
The interior, with a Latin-cross floor plan, designed by Scamozzi, has a rich 18th-c. decoration, and contains various paintings by Jacopo Palma the Younger and Sante Peranda; a splendid *Annunciation* by Luca Giordano (right wall of the presbytery), a *St. Jerome Visited by an Angel* by the Flemish painter Liss (left wall, on the exterior of the presbytery); and the *Charity of St. Lawrence*, by Bernardo Strozzi.

Giardino Papadopoli (4 B4). Beyond the Ponte dei Tolentini extends an immense park, all that survives of a far larger estate that once belonged to the 16th-c. Palazzo Foresti-Papadopoli (n. 250; now an elementary school), still famous at the turn of the 20th c. for the number and variety of plants that grew here. The excavation and dredging of the Rio Nuovo (1932-33) cut this splendid garden in two, depriving Venice of an inestimable heritage of green space.

Tre Ponti (4 C4). This is a distinctive intersection of canals and bridges, not far from Piazzale Roma. Note the unusual triangular plaza of the *Campazzo dei Tre Ponti* and, on the left, the *Fondamenta delle Burchielle*, with a handsome series of 17th-c. row houses with notable chimneys.

Piazzale Roma (4 B3-4). This immense, oddly shaped space is the landward "gate" of Venice. Built at the same time as the long car bridge across the lagoon (1931-33), it serves as the terminus of all automotive traffic to town: therefore an enormous, city-owned garage was built on the west side of the "piazzale."
A recent international architectural competition, assigned by the Municipal Government, in cooperation with the Biennale (1991), resulted in a project (by the British architects Dixon and Jones) for the complete reorganization of this area.

To the left of the Garage is the church of *S. Andrea della Zirada* (4 B3), founded in the 14th c. and rebuilt toward the end of the 15th c.; it still preserves its 15th-c. terracotta facade and a campanile with an 18th-c. onion dome, set atop the original shaft. No longer used as a church, it has been stripped of its original furnishings.

3.2 From Rialto to the Frari

This route (map on page 56) runs through the interior of the Sestiere di S. Polo, which, ever since the earliest centuries of Venetian history, revolved around the centers of S. Polo, the Frari, and S. Rocco. The complex based around the church and the convent of the Frari, which developed in what was once a marsh, soon became one of the centers of religious and social life in Venice.
Next to the church of the Frari, the church and the Scuola Grande di S. Rocco on one side, and the church and the Scuola Grande di S. Giovanni Evangelista on the other, formed a complex system of private and public spaces, around which major charitable institutions had developed.
Not far away, the immense Campo S. Polo constitutes the only evident "tear" in the

dense architectural "fabric" of the two "sestieri."
The route, in its final section, winds through little-known areas, largely forsaken, which offer interesting glimpses of what is wrongly considered a "less important" part of Venice.

Riva del Vin (5 B-C4). This "riva," or embankment (the name comes from the fact that boats transporting wine would dock here) and the opposite embankment (Riva del Carbòn and Riva del Ferro; here coal and iron were unloaded, as the name clearly indicates) are the only section of the Grand Canal – aside from the embankments around the railroad station and the Riva di Biasio – to be lined by pedestrian sidewalks; the sidewalks here worm their way under the blocks of buildings, through "sottoporteghi." Unassuming facades now overlook the "rive," though in bygone days this area was occupied by the handsome "case-fondaco" of aristocratic families.
Marking the end of the Riva is the *Palazzo Ravà*, a Neo-Gothic building by Giovanni Sardi (1906), built on the site of the ancient Palazzo dei Patriarchi di Grado.

Campo S. Silvestro (5 C3). This "campo" lies at the intersection of a number of walking routes, since it is located quite close to the vaporetto stop. The "campo" has a regular shape, though that shape was radically altered by the filling in (1845) of the "rio" that once flowed in front of and along the left side of the church.

S. Silvestro (5 C4). Founded in ancient times (9th c.), this church was entirely rebuilt to plans by Lorenzo Santi (1837-1843), but the facade dates from the turn of the 20th c.
The Neo-Classical interior has a single central aisle. Note the paintings by Jacopo Tintoretto, *Baptism of Jesus** (1580), on the 1st altar to the right, and, on the 2nd altar to the right, *Holy Family* by Carl Loth (1681); between the altars stands the entrance to the *former Scuola dei Mercanti di Vino* (16th c.; wine merchants); note the ceiling of the upstairs hall, decorated with canvases by Gaspare Diziani.

Campo S. Aponal (5 B3). This small but busy thoroughfare along the route from Rialto to S. Polo is dominated by the bell tower and the facade of the former church of *S. Aponal* (S. Apollinare), with a simple brick Gothic elevation, embellished by 5 aedicules with statues.
Along the "calle" that leads to S. Polo, just after the Campiello dei Meloni, is the *Calle del Forno* (5 C3), which leads to the Corte Petriana, originally a private courtyard, a lovely setting that still preserves its Gothic structure as well as a handsome Renaissance well head.
At the end of the Calle del Traghetto you can enjoy a fine view of the Grand Canal and the facades of the palazzi on the opposite shore.

Campo S. Polo (5 B-C2). This is one of the largest and most attractive "campi" in Venice; over the centuries it was used for feasts and games, as many 19th-c. paintings show: there were bull fights, dances, fires, parades. It is still used, especially in the summer, as a great open-air theater and cinema.
The "campo," bounded by the apse of the church of S. Polo, is lined on its eastern side by a long curving row of palazzi, which represents the line of the "rio" (filled in, 1761) that once ran along the edge of the buildings. Among the palazzi, you should note: at n. 1957, *Palazzo Maffetti-Tiepolo*, a 17th-c. building by Domenico Rossi; at n. 2169 and n. 2170 note the *Palazzi Soranzo*, splendid examples of Gothic architecture; at n. 2177, the early-16th-c. *Palazzo Donà*.
On the opposite side of the "campo" juts the corner of the imposing *Palazzo Corner Mocenigo*, built by Michele Sanmicheli (mid-16th c.) and now headquarters of the Guardia di Finanza (Italy's financial police); a former printing shop, Tipografia Tasso (n. 2156; 1840); and a former brewery – note the mosaic sign (n. 2168).

S. Polo (S. Paolo Apostolo; 5 C2). Byzantine in origin, this church was modified in the 15th c. and further radically renovated in 1804, with the addition of a Neo-Classical decorative scheme over the simple Byzantine-Gothic style decorations. The terracotta campanile dates from the mid-14th c. The facade is entirely hidden by a block of buildings between church and canal, completely modifying the original spatial arrangement. On the interior, a further 19th-c. restoration has eliminated some of the modifications done in the early-18th c. The three-aisle basilican plan has a wooden keel roof (15th c.).
On the interior elevation of the facade, note the *organ* built by Gaetano Callido (1763); on the left, *Last Supper* by Jacopo Tintoretto; also by Tintoretto, on the 1st altar to the right, *Our Lady of the Assumption and Saints*. Of particular interest are the canvases by Palma the Younger, on the walls, and, on the 2nd altar on the left, *The Virgin Mary Appears to St. John Nepomuk* by G.B. Tiepolo (1754).

In the 18th-c. Oratorio del Crocifisso, note a number of works by G.D. Tiepolo.

In the nearby Calle dei Nomboli, which runs off to the left from Calle dei Saoneri, at n. 2793, is the entrance to the 15th-c. *Palazzo Centani* (5 C2), with the original exterior staircase; here, on 26 February 1707, the dramatist Carlo Goldoni was born.
Since 1953 it has housed the Istituto di Studi Teatrali Casa Goldoni, an institute which documents and carries out research into the field of theater.

Campo S. Tomà (5 C1). Handsome in array, rectangular in shape, this "campo" is bounded by the facades of the former *Scuola dei Calegheri* (cobblers; 15th c.), with handsome 15th-c. frescoes inside, and the church of *San Tomà* (San Tommaso; or St. Thomas), founded in the 9th c. Rebuilt more than once (most recently in the 18th c.), its facade is by Francesco Bognolo (1742).
The church is closed to the public, and has been stripped of all its original furnishings.

Campo S. Rocco (5 C1). This "campo" is not served by any canals; it has an uncommon, triangular shape, and is a remarkably charming little plaza, given the presence of magnificent architectural masterpieces, in close array: the church of S. Rocco, the monumental facade of the Scuola Grande di S. Rocco, the apse of the church of the Frari. A cunning interplay of solids and space, enhanced every year on 16th August, the day of the Festa del Santo, by the procession that winds through the "campo" along a "corridor" defined by the strips of marble on the pavement; there are still holes in the marble in which poles were once placed, to support the white cloth canopies that were erected to keep off the sunshine.

S. Rocco (5 C1). The earliest structure of this church, built by Bartolomeo Bon, was in the Renaissance style, and was completely renovated in 1725 by Giovanni Scalfarotto. The facade too was reconstructed in 1771 by Bernardino Maccaruzzi, who took his inspiration from the facade of the Scuola. Among the more notable artworks, we should mention: on the 1st altar on the right, *St. Francesco di Paola Revives a Child* by Sebastiano Ricci; on the next wall, *La piscina probatica* (1559) and *St. Rocco Being Led into Prison* (1577-84) both by Jacopo Tintoretto, who also did the large canvases* on the walls of the presbytery. On either side of the altar is all that survives of the frescoes by Pordenone that once adorned the presbytery and the dome. Also, on the left wall, after the 2nd altar, *Saints Martin and Christopher* (1528) by Pordenone, and, on the 1st altar, *Discovery of the Cross*, a late painting by Sebastiano Ricci. To the right of the church is the late-15th-c. *Scuoletta di S. Rocco*.

Scuola Grande di San Rocco* (5 C1). This headquarters of the Scuola di Devozione (School of Devotion) dedicated to St. Rocco (patron saint of plague victims), was built initially to plans by Bartolomeo Bon, after 1516, and continued under the supervision

The Scuola Grande di San Rocco

of Sante Lombardo and the Scarpagnino, with some assistance from Gian Giacomo de' Grigi; it was completed in 1560. The long period of construction is immediately evident in the appearance of the facade; note the style on the ground floor, reminiscent of the early Renaissance, while the upper floor shows signs of the Baroque style. The opposite facade, with a porch overlooking the "rio," is more uniform in style.
The interior, on two stories, features the entire cycle of **teleri***, or large canvases, painted by Jacopo Tintoretto between 1564 and 1587, after he won the competition for the project (among those competing was Paolo Veronese); instead of presenting the judges with the sketches required, Tintoretto secured the commission by donating a finished canvas of St. Rocco in glory to the Scuola Grande free of charge.
The tour begins, for chronological reasons, from the upper floor, which you can reach by climbing the splendid *stairway** designed by Scarpagnino (1544-46), with a barrel vault; on the right wall, note *The Plague of 1630**, a masterpiece by Antonio Zanchi (1666).

In the *Sala dell'Albergo*, decorated by Tintoretto (1564-66): in the wooden ceiling, the painting *St. Rocco in Glory*, mentioned above, and on the wall facing the entrance, note the *Crucifixion** (1565). In the imposing Sala Maggiore, decorated by Tintoretto between 1576 and 1581, you can see, in the ceiling panels, 21 canvases by the Maestro (1576-1578); on the walls, also by Tintoretto, are the *Stories from the New Testament* (1578-1581). On the altar, by Francesco Fossati (1588), is another painting by Tintoretto, the *Glory of St. Rocco*. Between the stairway and the altar is the entrance to the *chancery*, an 18th-c. hall. In the *Salone Terreno*, the great three-aisle hall on the ground floor, note the eight canvases that Tintoretto painted between 1583 and 1587: from the left, *Annunciation, Epiphany, Flight into Egypt, Slaughter of the Innocents, St. Mary Magdalene, St. Mary Egiziaca, Circumcision, Assumption*; on the altar, *St. Rocco*, statue by Girolamo Campagna (1587).

Behind the Scuola is the *Campo di Castelforte*; note the steps that lead down into the water where the two "rii" intersect.

Campo dei Frari (5 C1). Extending along the "rio," this square extends around the immense brick bulk of the church of the Frari, specifically the left side and the facade. Toward the "rio," note the succession of elevations of palazzi; in particular, n. 2998-99, the former *Scuola della Passione* (1593), and n. 3005, a 15th-c. building, once the site of the *Scuola dei Milanesi* and the *Scuola di S. Francesco*.

S. Maria Gloriosa dei Frari* (5 C1). From afar, you can see the massive structure of the bell tower (70 m. tall), one of the highest in Venice. Nothing remains of the ancient church, built in the 13th c. by the Franciscan Minorite friars (Frari). The church that now stands here is stern and magnificent; it was begun in 1340 and completed more than a century later. It contains memories and splendor from five centuries of history and culture of La Serenissima, the Most Serene Republic of Venice. With the church of Ss. Giovanni e Paolo, this is the pantheon of the glories of Venice.

In the late-Gothic facade, the Florentine lily appears alongside the lion that symbolizes St. Mark, and thus Venice, a clear reference to the Cappella dei Fiorentini; a pointed-arch portal in flamboyant Gothic style (sculptures by B. Bon, P. Lamberti, and A. Vittoria) leads inside. On the interior, note the three solemn aisles, divided by twelve mighty piers, linked by wooden chains. Also note the altars, hanging urns, and funerary monuments; the transept features seven chapels, the main chapel and six side chapels, once pertaining to confraternities or important families. In its original location, closing off the nave, is the *Coro* dei Frati*, or choir of the monks: on the interior of the marble enclosure, completed in 1475, are 124 wooden stalls dating from the 15th c. and two 18th-c. organs. Though the **Assumption*** by Titian, commissioned in 1516 and completed two years later (main altar), is certainly the best-known artwork in the entire complex, you should also note such masterpieces as the **Virgin Mary Enthroned, with Christ Child and Saints***, a triptych by Giovanni Bellini, signed and dated 1488 (altar in the sacristy); a *St. John the Baptist** by Donatello, a wooden sculpture (ca. 1450 , Cappella dei Fiorentini, to the right of the main chapel) badly repainted in the 19th c.; also by Titian, note the altar piece known as the **Madonna di Ca' Pesaro*** (1526, second altar on the left), hailing the deeds of the bishop Jacopo Pesaro, who was a captain in the wars against the Turks. Among the funerary monuments, note the one dedicated to Titian (second bay on the right), built in the 19th c. on the site where the artist is traditionally said to lie buried; in the Cappella dei Milanesi, decorated with sepulchral seals and scenes from the life of St. Ambrose, is the *tomb of Claudio Monteverdi* (d. 1643); a masterpiece of the Venetian Renaissance, on the left wall of the presbytery, is a *marble facade** with the funerary urn of the doge Niccolò Tron (d. 1473), by Antonio Rizzo and assistants; note the colossal "macabre machine" designed by Baldassarre Longhena for the doge Giovanni Pesaro (d. 1659), which frames the side door of the left aisle; lastly, in the second bay on the left, note the funerary pyramid built for Antonio Canova (d. 1822) by his pupils, to plans by Canova himself, originally drawn up for the tomb of Titian.

Convento dei Frari (Archivio di Stato; 5 B-C1). This convent, founded long ago and repeatedly rebuilt, extends along the right side of the church (entrance at n. 3003), and is organized around two cloisters: the *Chiostro della Santissima Trinità* and the *Chiostro di S. Antonio*. The former, built in the 17th c., features a portico with large arcades, and at the center, a monumental well head by Antonio Pittoni (1714), decorated with statues by Cabianca. The latter is attributed to Sansovino and is surrounded

The Campo dei Frari and the Church of the Frari

with a portico set on pillars surmounted by round arches; at the center of the cloister is a well head with a statue of S. Antony (17th c.). Adjoining this cloister is a third, smaller cloister, belonging to the convent of S. Nicolò dei Frari.
The convent, suppressed in 1810 with a Napoleonic decree, has housed since 1815 the *Archivio di Stato*, one of the most important state archives in the world, with a trove of some 15 million documents relating to the history of Venice from the 9th c. until its fall (1797).

Campiello di S. Giovanni Evangelista (5 B1). This harmonious and elegant setting, built during the Renaissance, was given its present appearance toward the end of the 15th c. by Pietro Lombardo; it is divided into two areas by a marble partition, composed of a portal and windows topped with pediments. On the inner Campiello della Scuola, an area that was once closed off and used privately, the entrances of the church (on left) and the Scuola Grande (on right) face each other.
In the lunette that decorates the screen, note the *eagle*, symbol of the Evangelist St. John (S. Giovanni Evangelista).

S. Giovanni Evangelista (5 B1). Founded in ancient times, rebuilt in the Gothic era, this church has been through numerous renovations, the last of which in the 18th c. by Bernardino Maccaruzzi, resulting in its present appearance.
The interior has a single aisle; only the presbytery and the apse survive from the Gothic structure. Among the various decorations note, on the right wall, *Christ on the Cross, and the Faithful* by Domenico Tintoretto (1626); also note the doors of the venerable organ, built by G.B. Piaggia and painted by Pietro Liberi.

Scuola Grande di S. Giovanni Evangelista (5 B1). The long history of its construction (from the 14th to the 18th c.) explains why this Scuola is so different from its counterparts. You can see the process of stylistic sedimentation on the facade, with the 14th-c. reliefs, the Gothic windows, the Renaissance portal and the mullioned window, by Mauro Codussi (end-15th/early-16th c.). The interior is separated into two grand, vast stories, linked by a monumental *staircase* by Codussi (1498), with two converging flights of stairs, surmounted by a barrel vault. The *Salone Terreno*, or downstairs hall, originally Gothic, is divided into two aisles by handsome columns. The *Salone Superiore*, or upstairs hall, still shows the luxurious splendor of the renovation by Giorgio Massari (1727). On the ceiling, note the *Scenes of the Apocalypse* by G. Angeli, G. Diziani, J. Marieschi, J. Guarana, and G.D. Tiepolo. On the walls, note works by Domenico Tintoretto, Sante Peranda, and Pietro Longhi. The marble altar is by Massari, while G.M. Morlaiter carved the statue of *St. John the Evangelist*.
Facing the altar is a door that leads to the *Oratorio della Croce*, once adorned with renowned "teleri," or large canvases, by Gentile Bellini, Vittore Carpaccio, and others; these are now in the Gallerie dell'Accademia. On the altar, inside a magnificent Gothic gilt-silver reliquary, is the priceless *Reliquia della Croce, or Relic of the Cross*, which the confraternity received as a gift in 1369. Next comes the Sala dell'Albergo, decorated with episodes depicting the *Apocalypse*, by Palma the Younger.
This building, when the confraternity was suppressed in 1806, was stripped of much of its artwork, and was almost demolished. Now it has been restored as the site of the Scuola Grande and the headquarters of the Arciconfraternita.

Campo S. Stin (5 B1). Once bounded, on the "rio" side, by the church of S. Stin (or S. Stefano Confessore, named for St. Stephen), which was demolished in 1810, this "campo" is now surrounded by Gothic buildings, some of them heavily renovated; in the center, note the well head (1508) decorated

with reliefs of St. Stephen and others.
On Calle di Ca' Donà (5 B1-2), on the right, n. 2515, note the 16th-c. *Palazzo Donà delle Rose* and, facing it, n. 2514, *Palazzo Molin*, a 13th-c. Byzantine structure, rebuilt at the turn of the 19th c., and now housing offices of the Venetian Regional government.

Rio Terrà Secondo (5 B2). After you cross Rio S. Agostin, follow Calle della Chiesa, which will take you to *Campo Sant'Agostin* (5 B2), an area of ancient tradition, dating from the Byzantine period, with strong accents of the Gothic era. Then you will enter Rio Terrà Secondo, where, in the "palazzetto" at n. 2311, the print shop of Aldo Manuzio (Aldus Manutius), a renowned Venetian publisher and printer, once stood. At n. 2278 is the Gothic *Palazzo Soranzo Pisani*, with a 14th-c. relief: *Faith and Justice Enthroned.*

With a short detour on the left, from Rio Terrà Secondo, you reach a small "campo," particularly entrancing because of its apparent perfection, diminutive size, and tranquillity, off the beaten track as it is. The ancient church of S. Boldo (St. Uboldo) once stood here, until it was demolished in 1826 (all that remains is the terracotta campanile, lost among the surrounding houses); note at n. 2271, the imposing 17th-c. facade of the *Palazzo Grioni* (5 A2).

Ponte delle Tette (5 B3). From Rio Terrà Secondo, take a right into Calle dello Scaleter, and you will reach the Ponte di Ca' Bernardo; from here you can see, straight ahead, and slightly to the right, the splendid facade of *Ca' Bernardo* (5 B2), a 15th-c. Gothic palazzo with a porticoed courtyard and a spiral staircase; retrace your steps, and then take Calle del Cristo (5 B2) and Calle Longa, and again, on the right, Calle di Ca' Bonvicini and Calle dell'Agnello (5 B3), you will reach Ponte delle Tette, (literally, Bridge of Breasts), so called because prostitutes used to lean out of the windows of the houses here, displaying their breasts to attract customers. This entire area, known as the *Carampane*, was once dotted with bordellos; it is said that this phenomenon was encouraged expressly by laws passed by the government of the Serenissima, which wished in this way to stem the increasingly common phenomenon of homosexuality, punished in that period by burning at the stake in the Piazzetta S. Marco.

Palazzo Albrizzi (5 B3). The Campiello Albrizzi, a quiet square off the beaten tourist track, is dominated by the great bulk of the facade of the Palazzo Albrizzi (n. 1940), built at the end of the 16th c. and enlarged into the "campiello" two centuries later. On the side facing the Rio di S. Cassiano, a graceful bridge links the palazzo to the garden that stands across the "rio," on the site once occupied by the Teatro di S. Cassiano, demolished in 1812.
Here Isabella Teotochi Albrizzi held her renowned literary salon, frequented by Ugo Foscolo, Ippolito Pindemonte, and the sculptor Antonio Canova. The interior is renowned for its spectacular rooms, richly decorated with stuccoes, which frame paintings by Pietro Liberi and Antonio Zanchi and perhaps by Luca Giordano. In the notable halls there are canvases by Pietro Longhi and a bust of *Helen* by Antonio Canova. The palazzo is very well preserved, and can be toured by request.

Palazzo Molin-Cappello (5 B3). Not far from the Campiello Albrizzi, along Calle del Tamossi, you reach the Ponte Storto, spanning the Rio delle Beccarie; from here, on the left, you can see the 16th-c. palazzo, where Bianca Cappello was born (1548) and grew up; in 1563 she fled to Florence with an employee of the nearby Banco Salviati, and later became the wife of the Grand Duke of Tuscany, Francesco I de' Medici.

Rio Terrà S. Aponal (5 B3). The winding course of this thoroughfare clearly mirrors the original waterway, which was filled in in 1844-45 during Austrian occupation, in the context of the revamping of the city grid; the idea was to make it easier for pedestrians, rather than boats, to get around.

Take Ruga del Ravano (5 B3), and then Ruga Vecchia S. Giovanni (5 B4) to get back to the Market of Rialto; here the face of the city is quite different: on the left, the blocks are more compact and truly dovetailed together; on the right, the blocks are long and lie in parallel formations.

4 Dorsoduro

The Sestiere di Dorsoduro (the name, according to the most reliable scholars, comes from the fact that the ground is higher here than in surrounding areas; it means, literally, "hard-back") is very large (covering 92.25 hectares), and is bounded to the north by the Sestiere di San Polo and by the Sestiere di Santa Croce and by the tail end of the Grand Canal; to the south it is bounded by the Canale della Giudecca, and to the west by the Canale della Scomenzera.
The eastern section of Dorsoduro, running from the Accademia to the Punta della Dogana, along the Grand Canal, is not far, but is clearly separate from the Sestiere di San Marco (to which it has been linked since 1854 by the Ponte dell'Accademia); rich in cultural activities of the finest sort (Gallerie dell'Accademia, and many other art collections), this is a quiet, largely residential area, now considered one of the finest parts of Venice, and much sought after, especially by non-Venetians.
The central and the western sections of Dorsoduro, on the other hand, are more greatly affected by the major public works undertaken on the western side of Venice (in chronological order, the railroad bridge, the Stazione Marittima, and the automobile bridge and parking garage in Piazzale Roma), and are therefore busier and less tranquil. Among the institutions found here is the University, with many of the buildings it occupies scattered in this area, from the original headquarters in Ca' Foscari to the buildings on the outskirts of S. Marta. Students and professors bring life and excitement to the neighborhood. All the same, this remains a lively working-class quarter; the heart of the area is the Campo S. Margherita, with its marketplace, a meeting place for the local inhabitants and students, and a playground for children.
The nature of the parts of Venice that are found in the Sestiere di Dorsoduro vary greatly. Stately and uniform is the row of palazzi lining the Grand Canal, broken up only by the large former convent of the Carità, now housing the Gallerie dell'Accademia, a new attraction and magnet for the quarter. The spectacular church of the Salute, which dominates the Punta della Dogana, was the culmination of an enormous construction project of the 17th c., which affected the whole eastern section of the "sestiere," and completed the view over the Bacino di S. Marco.
Equally homogeneous, though perhaps less spectacular, is the long front of the Zattere, along the Canale della Giudecca. This was originally a working area, as you can see from the warehouses ("saloni") and "squeri" still standing, while the renovation done after the embankment and paving can be seen in little "palazzetti" and in the 16th-c. convent complexes of S. Spirito and S. Maria della Visitazione and in the 18th-c. church of the Gesuati. Inland, you can see the various "insule," city blocks that correspond to islands, each with their own little church and network of roads, at times regular and orderly, as in S. Barnaba, in other cases more complex and chaotic, as in Borgo di S. Trovaso.
If the Zattere are homogeneous, the far western section of the "sestiere" is decidedly heterogeneous, where age-old working-class residential neighborhoods (7th c.), Angelo Raffaele and S. Nicolò dei Mendicoli, have largely been replaced by nondescript public housing and by great buildings from the early industrial age of Venice, in the 19th and 20th c. – the run-down and abandoned facilities of the giant natural gas tanks, built on the reclaimed land of the Sacca dell'Angelo; the facilities of the water mains, to the enormous buildings of the Ex-Cotonificio Veneziano, once a huge cotton mill; the Magazzini Generali, old storehouses that are intriguing pieces of industrial archeology, in some sense striking features of the Venetian skyline.

4.1 From the Ponte dell'Accademia to the Gesuati

This route runs through the section of Dorsoduro that extends between the Grand Canal and the Canale della Giudecca, with an easternmost extremity that ends in the Punta della Dogana. At first you will walk along behind palazzi that overlook the Grand Canal, in shaded and quiet "calli," with sudden views along "rii" that, by linking the Grand Canal with the Canale della Giudecca, slice this section of the "sestiere" into regular "insule," or blocks.
This is a particularly lovely section of

Venice, small but packed with fine art and architecture, large museums and private collections. One odd thoroughfare here is the broad Rio Terrà Antonio Foscarini, a road that is larger than the immediate needs of the city would seem to require.
The second section of this route, beyond the extraordinary panoramic point of the Punta della Dogana, is a pleasant stroll on the "lungomare," or seafront (approximately 1 km. in length), of the Fondamenta delle Zattere as far as the Ponte Lungo; you have a fine view of the island of Giudecca, opposite, and you can stop at open-air cafes and restaurants along the way.

Campo della Carità (9 B2). This small "campo" looks out over the Grand Canal and is bounded by the buildings of S. Maria della Carità (see Gallerie dell'Accademia); ever since the construction of the Ponte dell'Accademia in 1854, it has been a major thoroughfare, with busy foot traffic from and to S. Marco. The *Rio Terrà Antonio Foscarini*, which was covered over in 1863, following the construction of the bridge, runs into the "campo."

Gallerie dell'Accademia* (9 B1-2). This is the most notable collection of painting from Venice and the Venetian region, and was established in 1807 in conjunction with Napoleon's suppression of various civic and religious institutions. It is located in the complex of S. Maria della Carità, formerly a church, monastery, and "Scuola Grande," the product of years and centuries of rebuilding, additions, renovation, and transformation, a typical case of the slow accretion of Venetian architecture.
Nothing survives from the earliest settlement (12th c.) by Lateran canons; the pointed-arch structure of the church that now overlooks the "campo" dates from the reconstruction of 1441-45, though other further changes date from the 19th c. While the 14th-c. portal (in the right corner; you now enter through the Accademia di Belle Arti) with three aedicules (*Virgin with Child*, 1345, and *St. Christopher* and *St. Leonard*, 1378) belongs to the Scuola Grande di S. Maria della Carità, further inside, in the second courtyard, there is still a wing with portico and loggias, part of a project by Palladio (1555-62; it can be viewed while the Accademia is open, and from the balcony of the Gallerie, between halls 20 and 21). The entrance of the Gallerie opens into the more recent, Neoclassical facade of the former Scuola Grande di S. Maria della Carità, which was rebuilt, along with the interior stairway, between 1756 and 1765 by Giorgio Massari and Bernardino Maccaruzzi, and further renovated in 1830 with the construction of the entrance. The wings behind it and the clearly visible reconstruction on the exterior were the result of work begun in 1807 by Giovanni Antonio Selva and continued until 1845 by Francesco Lazzari, in order to accommodate the Accademia di Belle Arti and the Gallerie.
The current installation of the Gallerie, not strictly in chronological order, due to the size and nature of the structure itself, was done in 1945-48 (with further modifications up to 1955) by Carlo Scarpa.

Giorgione, The Tempest

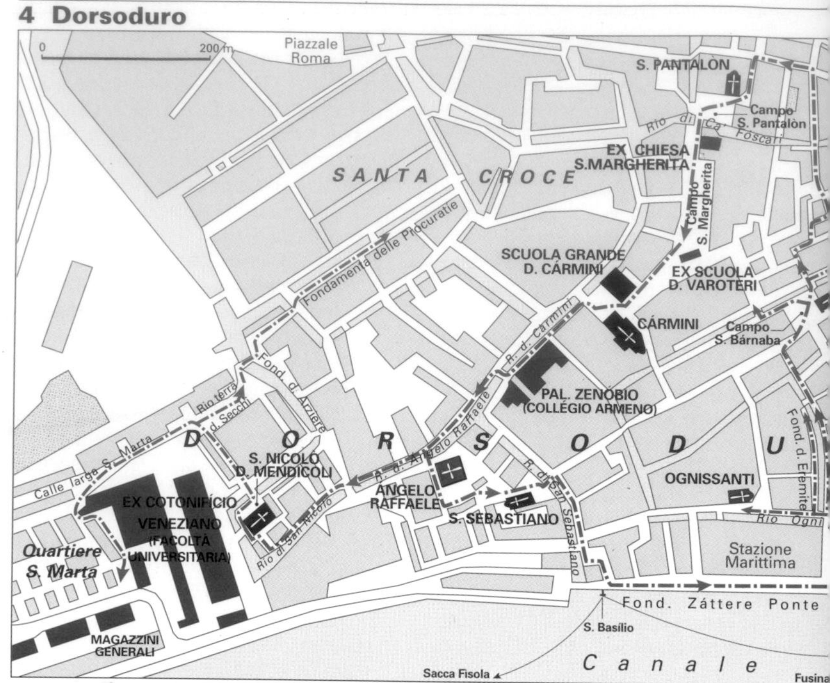

From the earliest artists, working between the end of the 14th c. and the mid-15th c. (hall 1), you will immediately pass on to the works of one of the greatest of Venetian painters, Giovanni Bellini; particularly notable are his **Virgin Mary Enthroned, with Christ Child and Saints*** (ca. 1480; hall 2), the *Virgin with Child, between St. Catherine and Mary Magdalene* (ca. 1490; hall 4), and **Pietà***, a later work, dating from 1505 (hall 5). It is easy to compare this latter work with paintings by Giorgione, in the same room, hall 5, **The Old Woman*** (ca. 1505-1506) and **The Tempest***; in so doing, you will note the unprecedented aspects of Venetian painting of the early-16th c., particularly in the treatment of landscape and light, as opposed to the work of Andrea Mantegna (*St. George*) or Piero della Francesca (*St. Jerome and a Worshipper*), clearly influenced by Tuscan art, both in hall 4.
Among the paintings by artists working in the first half of the 16th c., displayed in halls 6, 7, 8, and 9, and all worthy of note, special mention should be made of the exquisite **Portrait of a Gentleman*** by Lorenzo Lotto (hall 7). Continue on to hall 10, where you will find the work of the leading painters in Venice, the city, and Venetia, the region, during the second half of the 16th c.: note the renowned **Dinner in the House of Levi***, painted by Paolo Veronese in1573 for the Dominican monks of the church of Ss. Giovanni e Paolo (it was given its present title, rather than being called The Last Supper, to skirt the restriction imposed by the Court of the Inquisition), and the impressive *Mystical Wedding of St. Catherine* (ca. 1575). Jacopo Tintoretto painted the "teleri," or large canvases intended for the Scuola Grande di S. Marco, the *Theft of the Body of St. Mark* (1562), the *Miracle of St. Mark* (1548), and *St. Mark Rescues a Saracen* (1562). Here you can see Titian's last painting, **Pietà***, finished after his death (1576) by Palma the Younger (restored in 1983); Titian intended this painting for the Altare del Crocifisso in the church of the Frari, where he wished to be buried.
In hall 11 you will find more paintings by Tintoretto (*Adam and Eve* and *Cain and Abel*, painted around 1550-53). Beyond hall 12, which features 18th-c. landscapes, and hall 13, with several works by Jacopo Bassano, halls 14, 15, 16, 17, and 18 display genre paintings by artists working between the 16th and 18th c.
We return to the great Venetian painting of the 15th c. in halls 20, 21, and 23 (with a few early works in hall 19). In hall 20 (hall of the Miracles of the Cross), note the eight "teleri" (painted at the end of the 15th c. by the leading "cerimonial painters" of the era: Gentile Bellini, V. Carpaccio, G. Mansueti, and L. Bastiani) prepared for the hall that contained the relics of the Cross in the Scuola

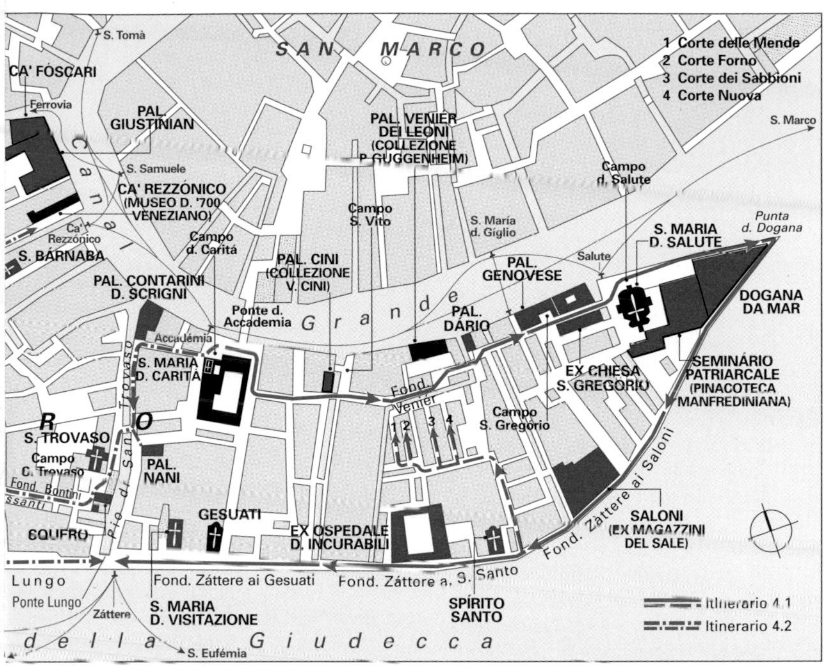

Grande di S. Giovanni Evangelista; they should be considered both in terms of their artistic excellence and as historical documents illustrating life in Venice of their time. The celebrated **Procession in Piazza S. Marco*** (1496) by Gentile Bellini, is as remarkable as his *Miracle of the Cross Fallen into the Canale di S. Lorenzo**. Note the extraordinary narrative, set in airy Venetian landscapes, of the life of St. Ursula (S. Orsola), painted by Vittore Carpaccio between 1490 and 1495 (hall 21); note in particular the **Dream of St. Ursula***. Beneath the rafters of the former church of S. Maria della Carità (hall 23), lastly, you will find another group of works with a coherent theme, the large **triptychs*** by Giovanni Bellini and workshop. Hall 24, once a hall of the Albergo della Scuola della Carità, has a gold and light-blue ceiling, and contains paintings done expressly for this hall; note the glittering *Virgin Mary in Throne, with Christ Child and Saints**, a triptych by Antonio Vivarini and Giovanni d'Alemagna (1446), and the **Presentation of the Virgin Mary in the Temple***, painted by Titian between 1534 and 1539.

Campo San Vio (9 B2). Enlarged in 1813, in the wake of the demolition of the church of Ss. Vito e Modesto, this "campo" is bounded to the east by the side of the 16th-c. *Palazzo Barbarigo* (n. 730), which was the headquarters in the 19th c. of the Compagnia Venezia Murano, which commissioned Giulio Carlini to do the spectacular mosaic facing with gold background. Facing it, with a facade overlooking the "rio," is Palazzo Cini.

Palazzo Cini (9 B2). The Renaissance facade overlooks the little Rio San Vio, rather than the Grand Canal, which would have been the norm. This palazzo houses the great art collection known as the *Raccolta d'Arte della Collezione Vittorio Cini*, part of the Fondazione Giorgio Cini. In the various halls of the two main floors ("piani nobili"), furnished with remarkable furnishings and objets-d'art, note the thirty or so paintings by artists of the Tuscan school, working from the 13th to 15th c. (B. Daddi, F. Lippi, Piero della Francesca, and Pontormo).

Peggy Guggenheim Collection (9 B3). This prestigious collection of European and American avant-garde artwork is housed in the *Palazzo Venier dei Leoni*, for thirty years the Venice home of the American art collector and patron Peggy Guggenheim. The palazzo was purchased by Guggenheim in 1949, and it was immediately filled with the art that she had been acquiring since 1939; it consists of only the ground floor, all that was built in 1749 of an immense project by Lorenzo Boschetti. The museum overlooks the Grand Canal and a garden, which is now enclosed by a lovely fence, embellished with colored glass. Peggy Guggenheim continued to build her collection, and after her death (1979), both the art and the palazzo were left to the Solomon R. Guggenheim Foundation in New York. The palazzo was renovated to accommodate the museum, between 1980 and 1983, eliminating the living quarters (only the bedroom was preserved; note the oils and pastels by Peggy's daughter, Pegeen Vail); the exhibits follow a strict arrangement by school: in the garden, there is a mixture of sculpture of various schools. Here Peggy Guggenheim is buried, with her dogs.

In the section devoted to Constructivism and De Stijl (hall 2 and corridor), note works by Piet Mondrian, *The Sea* (1915-16) and *Oval Composition* (1913-14), and by Paul Klee, *Magic Garden* (1924) and *Portrait of Madame P. in the South* (1924). In hall 3, which features Abstract Expressionism, Bauhaus, and Futurism, note works by Giacomo Balla (*Automobile: noise+speed* ca. 1913) and Gino Severini (*Sea=dancer* 1913-14). There is an exceedingly rich collection devoted to Surrealism and related schools (hall 5, corridor and hall 6), with major works by Max Ernst, such as (hall 5) the *Antipope* (1941-42) and the *Vesitition of the Bride* (1940); equally important are three paintings by Joán Miró, *Dutch Interior* (1928), *Seated Woman II* (1939) and *Painting* (1925); *The Red Tower* (1913) by Giorgio De Chirico and *La Baiguada* (1937) by Pablo Picasso. Among the works of the post-war period, note ten paintings by Jackson Pollock, a great protégé of Peggy Guggenheim's, done between 1942 and 1947; in particular *Moon-Woman* (1942), *Circumcision* (1946) and *Enchanted Forest* (1947) (hall 7).

A little way past the building of the Collezione Guggenheim, in the little Campiello Barbaro, is the rear of **Palazzo Dario** (9 B3), with its large chimney, "altana," or covered roof terrace, and Gothic windows. Palazzo Dario was built around 1487, with a lavish facade with polychrome marble facing, and overlooks the Grand Canal. Gabriele D'Annunzio described it as leaning slightly, "like a decrepit courtesan, weighed down with her glittering jewels."

Campo San Gregorio (9 B3). This "Gothic" space is bounded by the 15th-c. *church of San Gregorio*, which was deconsecrated in the 19th c., when it was used as the Gold Refinery of the Zecca, or Mint; and by the garden of the Neo-Gothic *Palazzo Genovese*, built in 1892 following the demolition of part of the medieval *abbey of S. Gregorio* (9 B4).

From the "campo," the narrow passageway of the Calle dell'Abbazia and the Sottoportego dell'Abbazia makes for a particularly startling first view of the immense white Baroque structure of S. Maria della Salute.

Campo della Salute (9 B4). This is one of relatively few "campi" overlooking the Grand Canal; it offers a spectacular view of the Grand Canal and of the Bacino di S. Marco. Dominated by the great marble mass of S. Maria della Salute, rearing high above its stepped base, this "campo" is linked to the water by the long "riva," or embankment; on its other sides, it is bounded by austere buildings that contrast sharply with the immense church.

S. Maria della Salute* (9 B4). This major landmark in the Venetian skyline, visible from all over the city, from land as well as from sea, is considered to be the masterpiece of the Baroque architect Baldassarre Longhena. Built to fulfill a vow taken by the Senato, following a major outbreak of the plague in 1630, the church was erected between 1631 and 1687; in time, it became a site of civic importance as well as of religious worship; beginning in 1681, on the day of the Presentation of the Virgin Mary, 21 November, a solemn religious celebration has been held here, with a procession from Piazza S. Marco to the Salute passing over the Grand Canal upon a bridge of boats, extending on a line with the church of S. Maria del Giglio.

Built, as Longhena himself once wrote, "in the form of a crown, and dedicated to the Virgin," the church is a composition comprising a main octagonal structure with a central plan topped by a large hemispherical dome buttressed by immense and enchanting volutes; adjoining this structure is a presbytery expanding into the side apses, in turn surmounted by a dome and steeples: you can enjoy a splendid view of the church from the Rio Terrà dei Catecumeni, which was, until the turn of the 20th c., the only land route to the church.

A dense array of statues and figures (attributed to F. Cavrioli, J. Le Court, M. Ungaro, and T. Ruer) swarms around the statue of the Virgin Mary, dressed as a "capitana da mar," or maritime commander; the statue stands with a "bastone di comando," or "captain's baton," atop the lantern of the cupola, in a noteworthy overlapping of the cult of the Virgin and the celebration of Venice.

On the interior, you will pass from the central octagonal hall, surrounded by chapels,

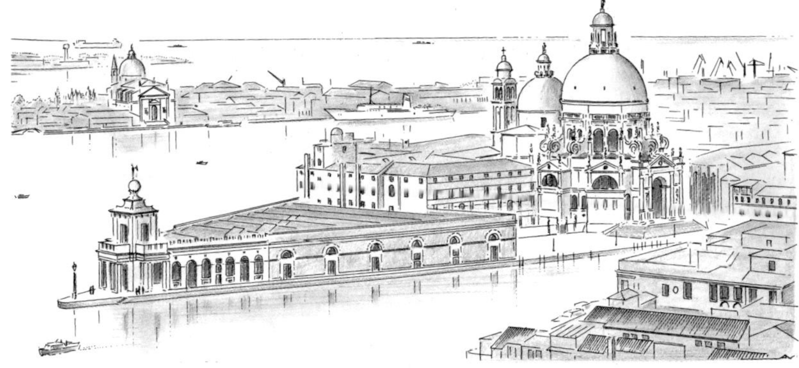

The Punta della Dogana and the Church of the Salute

to the presbytery; note the gradual shift in the light that pours down from the cupolas as you approach the spectacular *main altar.* Designed by Longhena and built by Josse Le Court, this altar frames a venerated Greco-Byzantine icon that was brought to Venice from Candia in 1672; in the upper section, note the statue depicting *The Virgin Mary with Christ Child Looking at Venice, Kneeling at Her Feet*; the city is thanking the Virgin for the cessation of the plague, shown fleeing. While the paintings and sculpture in this church, chiefly devoted to the theme of the Virgin Mary, are not particularly noteworthy, there are plenty of fascinating artworks in the sacristy: by a youthful Titian (1512), *St. Mark Enthroned with Saints Sebastian, Rocco, Cosma, and Damian**, on the altar, and, on the ceiling, three later canvases* (ca. 1543) depicting the *Sacrifice of Abraham, David and Goliath, Cain and Abel.* By Jacopo Tintoretto note the large canvas *The Wedding at Cana** (wall to the right of the altar).

Seminario Patriarcale (9 B4). This immense and solemn palazzo, built by Baldassarre Longhena in 1671, is arrayed around a cloister and a monumental staircase decorated with statues and reliefs. Originally built for the religious order of the Padri Somaschi, it has been the site of the Seminario Patriarcale (Patriarchal Seminary) of Venice since 1817. Since then, it has also housed a notable collection of paintings and statuary taken from the religious institutions suppressed by the new Napoleonic government; alongside this collection, note the **Pinacoteca Manfrediniana** a collection of paintings from the 15th/18th c., left as a bequest by the Marchese Federico Manfredini (1743-1829). Thus, among the sculpture, you will find such exquisite works as the two Renaissance reliefs by Tullio Lombardo, *Virgin Mary and Mary Magdalene* and *Eternal Father and the Holy Ghost* in the Cappella della SS. Trinità on the ground floor, the five terracotta *busts* by Alessandro Vittoria, and a terracotta bust, fashioned by a young Antonio Canova, depicting Gian Matteo Amadei.

Punta della Dogana* (9 B4-5). This dividing point separates the Grand Canal and the Canale della Giudecca, extending into the Bacino di S. Marco, concluding in a certain sense the great wreath of monuments. Note the somewhat theatrical construction, built by Giuseppe Benoni in 1677, conceived as the prow of a ship, with a loggia ending in a little tower, that is surmounted by a great sculpture by Bernardo Falcone: the two bronze Atlases, bowing under the weight of the great gold ball (the World), are topped by a slight and airy weathervane, fashioned in the person of Fortuna, or chance.
The loggia ends in the low structure of the *Dogana da Mar*: estabished as early as the 15th c. as a port for goods from the sea, it now has a 17th-c. section, by Benoni, toward the point, and a 19th-c. section (1835-38), by Alvise Pigazzi, toward the Campo della Salute, overlooking the Fondamenta delle Zattere.

Zattere* (9 C1-2-3-4). This is the long Fondamenta, or quay, that extends from the Punta della Dogana all the way to S. Basegio (Basilio), running for about 1.5 km. along the broad Canale della Giudecca (with an average width of 300 m. and a length of 1,680 m.). This was the landing quay for the rafts, or lighters (in Italian, "zattere"), used to transport lumber from the mainland along waterways and rivers; the quay was paved and shored up by decree in 1519. This was Venice's great loading dock and work area, lined with storehouses – especially for the storage of salt; "Magazzini del Sale" – furnaces, and "squeri," as well as with monasteries, hospitals and hospices. Today it is one of the pleasantest promenades in the city, sunny and sheltered from the cold north wind, or "bora," lined with cafes and trattorias, where you can dine on wooden terraces set on piles over the water; from here you can see, in a single sweeping panoramic view, the entire front of the Island of Giudecca, from the Zitelle all the way to the enormous mass of the Nordic Mulino Stucky and, further on, the smokestacks of the industrial area of Marghera and Fusina. This long quay is broken into four sections by name; these names come from the building or other landmark that most distinguishes them; from east to west: Fondamenta delle Zattere ai Saloni, Fondamenta delle Zattere allo Spirito Santo, Fondamenta delle Zattere ai Gesuati, and Fondamenta delle Zattere al Ponte Lungo.

The first stretch of the Zattere, then, takes its name from the salt storehouses, the *Saloni* (9 C3-4; n. 258-266), nine huge halls set in a row, built in the 14th c., and rebuilt for the same function in 1830 by Alvise Pigazzi with the current Neoclassical facade and large arches.

The church of the *Spirito Santo* (9 C3) gives its name to the next stretch of the Zattere, and, with the adjoining Scuola dello Spirito Santo (today, oddly enough, a private home), it presents a simple Renaissance facade (1506): from here, on the occasion of the Festa del Redentore, in accordance and a vow, a bridge of boats links the Zattere with the Isola della Giudecca. Adjoining (n. 423), note the long 16th-c. facade of the former *Ospedale degli Incurabili* (9 C2), part of an enormous building erected between 1527 and 1591, originally meant to house those infected with syphilis; the project was soon abandoned, however: one of the numerous institutions established by the Venetian government and then taken over by private citizens, for the care of the sick and the helpless.

I Gesuati* (S. Maria del Rosario; 9 C1). Still called the church of the Gesuati, from the name of the order, later suppressed, which founded the adjoining monastery, this church was built at the behest of the Dominican order, which replaced them; the church was built between 1724 and 1736, with contributions from the various Guilds (Arti) and confraternities. The product of a financial effort by the entire city, it is also the result of exemplary cooperation between several of the leading artists of the 17th c. The architect was Giorgio Massari who, in the exterior volumes – dome flanked by two bell towers, semicircular apses – successfully provided a new interpretation of Palladian compositional motifs, taking the model of the church of the Redentore on the opposite shore; on the interior, he invented – at the end of the rectangular nave, behind the main altar – a truly luminous apsidal chamber with an ellipsoidal plan, where the choir has been placed.

Statues and bas-reliefs by Giovanni Maria Morlaiter, a veritable gallery of this sculptor's work, punctuate the walls, while the chapels are decorated with paintings, notable among them "Le Tre Sante," by G.B. Tiepolo (*The Virgin Mary with Saint Rose, with the Christ Child, St. Catherine of Siena, and St. Agnes of Montepulciano*, 1748, on the 1st altar on the right) and the luminous *St. Vincent Ferrer, St. Hyacinth, and St. Lodovico Bertrando*, considered a masterpiece, by G.B. Piazzetta (1738, 3rd altar on the right); also, note a 16th-c. painting restored by Piazzetta, the *Crucifixion* by J. Tintoretto (ca. 1526, 3rd altar on the left). The atmosphere, rich in light and color, is completed by the ceiling, frescoed by G.B. Tiepolo, 1737-39, on the theme of the Festa del Rosario.

Alongside the church is the former *Monastero dei Gesuati*, comprising a Renaissance section and an 18th-c. section (n. 919); at the entrance, note the "bocca delle denunce pubbliche," a slot for letters of denunciation, rare in that it is still in its original location.

4.2 From the Ponte dell'Accademia to the Zattere of Ponte Lungo

The route (map on page 68) runs from the Accademia all the way to S. Nicolò dei Mendicoli, at the heart of the working-class neighborhood at the westernmost tip of the "sestiere," allowing you to savor an unusual array of settings and atmospheres. Part of the way you will be walking along quiet, sun-kissed quays ("fondamenta") and part of the way through a lively shopping area and strolling ground, the fulcrum of which is the Campo S. Margherita, passing such centers of great cultural interest as the Ca' Rezzonico, the Scuola dei Carmini, and many university buildings.

The second section of this route runs through working-class neighborhoods of ancient origin, reaching the campo and church of S. Nicolò dei Mendicoli, with the rarefied and modest atmosphere of an early lagoon settlement.

Rio di S. Trovaso (9 A-B1). From the Campo della Carità (9 B2) you take Calle Corfù to the edge of the "rio," along a lively waterway linking the Grand Canal with the Canale della Giudecca, almost entirely lined by a Fondamenta, or quay; since the 14th c. this has been a prime site for aristocratic homes; the names of the Fondamenta, or

Rio of S. Trovaso

quay, reflect the noble families who lived here. The most notable one, at the intersection with the Grand Canal, is the *Palazzo Contarini degli Scrigni* (9 A-B1), also known as Palazzo Corfù, made up of two buildings that have been joined. Also worthy of note are buildings that have been turned into schools and university facilities; note the17th-c. *Palazzo Giustinian-Recanati* (Fondamenta Priuli, n. 1012; 9 B1), with a small garden; *Palazzo Nani* (Fondamenta Nani, n. 960-61; 9 B1), in the 14th-c. pointed-arch style, with stuccoes added during the 16th-c. restoration by Alessandro Vittoria; lastly, the 16th-c. *Palazzo Sangiantoffetti* (on the opposite bank, n. 1075), also known as Ca' Bembo, from the atrium of which it is possible to glimpse one of the largest and most astonishing private gardens in all of Venice.
Clearly visible from the Fondamenta Nani is the 17th-c. *squero di S. Trovaso* (9 B1), the oldest of all those still operating in Venice. The small brick-and-wood structure stands amidst the greenery, with a wet-dock sloping toward the "rio," bounding the eastern side of the *Campo S. Trovaso* (9 B1; 4 F6), which extends around the church, partially tree-lined and dotted with three fine well heads.

S. Trovaso (Ss. Gervasio e Protasio; 9 B1; 4 F6). This church features the Palladian style of the reconstruction begun in 1585. Two nearly identical facades, overlooking the two intersecting waterways of Rio di S. Trovaso and Rio di Ognissanti, enclose an interior with a single aisle and a broad presbytery, where, aside from the *organ* by Gaetano Callido (1765), there is a noteworthy Renaissance relief depicting *Angels with Symbols of the Passion* (right transept, chapel on the right wall), attributed to the Maestro di S. Trovaso, and *St. Crisogono on Horseback* by Michele Giambono (right chapel, left wall). You can hardly fail to note the many paintings by Jacopo and Domenico Tintoretto.

Fondamenta di Borgo (4 E-F6). This distinctive and quiet "fondamenta" bounds the "insula" of S. Trovaso, which was called "borgo" in bygone times. On the facing Fondamenta delle Eremite you may note a small palazzo (n. 1333-35) built in Lombard style around 1850, and variously attributed to G. Fuin or L. Cadorin, as well as a convent with a little 17th-c. church, formerly the church of the Eremite, now closed.

Campo S. Barnaba (4 E6). This "campo" is not very big, but it is quite lively, with grocery stores and open-air cafes; it is dominated by the massive facade of the church of *S. Barnaba*, built between 1749 and 1776 by Lorenzo Boschetti, on the foundation of a much earlier church (9th c.), rebuilt several times over the centuries: from this church, the *campanile* survives, with a conical cusp which was added in the 14th c. The "campo" lies in the heart of the Insula di S. Barnaba, a long, narrow block between the Rio del Malpaga and the Rio di S. Barnaba; it is distinguished by the dense urban fabric, as it were, clustering around the central thoroughfare, the Calle Lunga S. Barnaba, from which "calli" run out, serving rows of buildings.

Ca' Rezzonico* (4 D-E6). This palazzo, one of the largest on the Grand Canal, was restored in 1936 to its appearance as an 18th-c. aristocratic residence, furnished with paintings, statues, and other items of that era, from the Civico Museo Correr. Since then it has housed the **Museo del Settecento Veneziano***, or museum of 18th-c. Venice. It was built in two stages, a century apart: begun in 1649 by Baldassarre Longhena for the Bon family, work halted on the second floor; when the building was sold to the Rezzonico family in 1750, the third floor and a ballroom were added by Giorgio Massari. Note the slight differences in style, especially evident in the facade overlooking the Grand Canal. The ground floor features a long sequence of rooms from the atrium (where, set in a fountain-niche, is the Rezzonico family crest) all the way to the bank of the Grand Canal. On the two "piani nobili," or main floors, note the typical floor plan, with a large central salon ("portego") overlooking both courtyard and canal, and rooms along either side: more unusual is the part added in the rear by Massari, comprising the staircase and the ballroom, the largest single hall (24 x 14 x 12 m. tall) ever built in Venice for a private palazzo; the Rezzonico family crest, an enormous *Allegory of the Four Parts of the World* on the ceiling (by G.B. Crosato, 1753), and the famous furniture, carved by Andrea Brustolon (early 18th c.) are the most notable features of this room.

The various halls, on the two main floors ("piani nobili"), should be considered each for its specific qualities and for the overall harmony of the setting. Note the remarkable frescoes by Giambattista Tiepolo, on the second floor (first "piano nobile"), on the ceilings of the Sala della Allegoria Nuziale, or Hall of the Nuptial Allegory (*The Wedding of Ludovico Rezzonico with Faustina Savorgnan*), the Sala del Trono, or throne room, formerly the wedding chamber of the Rezzonico family (note the luminous *Allegory of the Merits of Nobility and Virtue**, 1758), and the Sala del Tiepolo (note the canvas *Strength and Wisdom**). Equally interesting documents of this era can be found in the *furniture* by Andrea Brustolon, in the hall that bears his name, and the *portraits* (many of them by Rosalba Carriera) in the Sala dei Pastelli, or hall of pastels. On the third floor (second "piano nobile"), with smaller and more intimate rooms, you will find 18th-c. paintings in the Portego dei Dipinti, including a number of *landscapes* by F. Zuccarelli and G. Zais and *The Death of Darius** by G.B. Piazzetta; the *telette*,* or small canvases, by Pietro Longhi and *frescoes** by G.A. Guardi in the halls devoted to those two painters; the Camera dell'Alcova, a reconstruction of an 18th-c. bedroom, with furnishings for the wedding dowry and, adjoining it, the Camerino degli Stucchi, a small room with exquisite stuccoes. Giandomenico Tiepolo, son of Giambattista, is the artist featured in a series of rooms (Portego del Mondo Novo, Camera dei Pulcinelli, Chiesetta, Camerino dei Centauri, Camera dei Satiri), with a series of detached *frescoes**, arranged as they originally were in the Villa di Zianigo, purchased by the Tiepolo family around 1753. Lastly, note two masterpieces by Francesco Guardi, *The Visiting Room of the Nuns at S. Zaccaria** and *The Foyer**, concluding the gallery of paintings, in the Sala del Ridotto.

Palazzi Giustinian and Ca' Foscari* (4 D6). The Palazzi Giustinian, twin buildings, were built during the maturity of Venetian Gothic, for the Giustinian family (who produced Lorenzo Giustinian, the first patriarch of Venice, canonized in 1690); the Ca' Foscari was built in 1452 for Francesco Foscari, doge from 1423 until 1457. These buildings are prime examples of the unification in the 15th c. of the architectural style of the large aristocratic palazzi along the banks of the Grand Canal. The Grand Canal was thus being transformed from a river port to a spectacular drawing room of an increasingly wealthy and powerful city.

The Palazzi Giustinian have an "L"-shaped floor plan, opening on the courtyard and exterior staircase; the Ca' Foscari is more imposing, with a large central hall, an exterior stairway, and a large crenelated courtyard; together, they all have long facades that practically form a single elevation overlooking the Grand Canal. Palazzo Giustinian was home to Richard Wagner for a certain period (in 1858-59 he composed the second act of *Tristan and Isolde* here); Ca' Foscari was made into a school building (1867), beginning with the Scuola Superiore di Commercio, a business school; together, they are now the main building of the Università di Venezia.

After crossing Rio di Ca' Foscari (from the bridge, fine view of the Grand Canal) take Calle Larga Foscari and you will reach (left) Campo S. Pantalon.

Campo S. Pantalon (4 C-D6). Looking out over the Rio di Ca' Foscari, this "campo" is bounded by the long 16th-c. *Palazzo Signolo* now Palazzo Loredan (n. 3708-3707), rebuilt, and, on the north side, by the brick church of S. Pantalon.

S. Pantalon (S. Pantaleone; 4 C-D6). As early as the 11th c., this was a major parish church; it was rebuilt in the 17th c. (1684-1704) by Francesco Comino.

The interior is given a further sumptuous note by the enormous painting (40 canvases) that stretches across the ceiling of the nave; it depicts, in remarkable perspective, the *Martyrdom and Glory of St. Pantaleone* (1680-1704) by Giovanni Antonio Fumiani.

Works by Paolo Veronese (*St. Pantaleone Heals a Child*, 2nd chapel on the right, and *St. Bernardino*, 3rd chapel on the right), and by Palma the Younger (*Decapitation* and *Miracle of St. Pantaleone*, 2nd chapel on the right) decorate the church, but the artistic high point is attained all the same in the *Cappella del Sacro Chiodo* (literally, Chapel of the Holy Nail, to the left of the main chapel): in this small room there is a profusion of masterpieces, among them the *Coronation of the Virgin Mary** by Antonio Vivarini and Giovanni d'Alemagna, *gold backgrounds* by Paolo Veneziano and a reliquary *altar* (school of the Bon family) with a remarkable *altar frontal* by Marino Cedrini.

Campo S. Margherita (4 D5-6). Tree-lined, this is one of the largest, liveliest, and most authentic of all Venice's "campi," and has long served as a marketplace and as the center of the social life in the "sestiere." Note the truncated campanile of the former church of *S. Margherita*, set on the north corner, and on the western side of the "campo," a series of remarkable little "palazzetti," in the Byzantine style (n. 2962, n. 2961, and n. 2496) or the Gothic style (from n. 2935 to n. 2927), and in particular, the 14th-c. *Palazzetto Foscolo-Corner* (n. 2931-33); some of the buildings still have the original and distinctive ground-floor workshops with a little display window and door framed in Istrian stone. This "campo" has long been a center for merchants, and is served directly from the waterway of Rio di S. Margherita, behind it, through "calli" and "sottoportici." Set in the middle of the "campo" are two large public well heads, dating from 1529; standing alone is the former *Scuola dei Varoteri* (furriers), dating from 1725, with a bas-relief dating from 1501.

Scuola Grande dei Carmini* (4 D5). This was the headquarters of the prestigious confraternity founded in 1594 in devotion to the Virgin of Carmelo, becoming exceedingly powerful after about a hundred years (in 1675 it had attained the remarkable level of 75,000 members, out of a total population that may have been less than twice that). The two differing facades, overlooking Calle dei Carmini and Campo dei Carmini, are attributed to Baldassarre Longhena (1668) and served to complete the building designed by Franco Cantello (1627).
The interior still features the original arrangement of rooms on two stories, with lavish ceilings, carved wooden altar frontals, and many major paintings from the 17th and 18th c. Note nine canvases by G.B. Tiepolo (1739-44), notable works from the peak of the artist's career, adorning the sumptuous panels in the ceiling of the upstairs hall (Salone Superiore; note in particular, at the center, the *Madonna del Carmelo** giving a scapular to the blessed Simon Stock). A masterpiece from the height of the career of G.B. Piazzetta, *Judith and Holofernes*, hangs in the corridor between the Sala dell'Archivio and the Sala dell'Albergo.

Carmini* (S. Maria del Carmelo; 4 D-E5). Founded as a convent church, the Carmini displays an overlap of sections and styles that correspond to the various enlargements and renovations that occurred from the 14th c. onward. The campanile dates from the 17th c.
On the interior, with its basilican plan, the simple original features of the 14th-c. structure (monolithic columns, wooden chains, a wooden Crucifix hanging from the arch of the presbytery) coexist in the nave with lavish 17th-/18th-c. decoration (gilt facings and sculpture, framing 24 paintings depicting episodes from the history of the Carmelite order); the later decoration does nothing to alter the original perspectival effect tending toward the luminous apse. Among the many paintings and sculptures, we should make special mention of: the altar piece by Cima da Conegliano (ca. 1509) depicting the *Adoration of the Shepherds with Saints Helena and Catherine, Tobiolo, and the Guardian Angel** (right aisle, 2nd altar, restored in 1991-92); the *Deposition**, a bronze bas-relief by Francesco di Giorgio Martini (ca. 1474, right apsidal chapel, left wall of the altar), with portraits of the dukes of Urbino Federico da Montefeltro and Battista Sforza; *St. Nicholas Between St. John the Baptist, St. Lucy, and Angels**, a painting by Lorenzo Lotto (1529, left aisle, 2nd altar).
The main facade of the church overlooks the little *Campo dei Carmini*, alongside the Rio di S. Margherita: adjoining the church is the entrance of the former *monastery* (now Istituto Statale d'Arte, a state art school) founded in the 14th c. and later rebuilt, with a handsome 16th-c. cloister. Across the "rio" stands the immense *Palazzo Foscarini*, somewhat run down, with huge, walled up Serlian windows, built in the second half of the 16th c., and once famous for its great and lavish luxury, the vast rear garden (now partly occupied by buildings), and the library that was collected there by Marco Foscarini, an illustrious man of letters and a doge from 1762 to 1763.

Palazzo Zenobio (4 E4). Since 1850 this palazzo has been the home of the *Collegio Armeno dei Padri Mechitaristi*; it is one of the most interesting examples of Baroque architecture in Venice. Built at the end of the 17th c. by Antonio Gaspari, it still has an unusual structure: note the influence of Borromini in the facade with a curved pediment, and in the central body extended by two wings toward the garden. There are also spectacular halls on the interior: the *ballroom*, with stuccoes and period furnishings and frescoes by Louis Dorigny, and the "portego" with *landscapes* by Luca Carlevarijs.

Fondamenta di Lizza Fusina (4 E3). The earlier name of this quayside – Fondamenta del Traghetto di Lizza Fusina – is a reminder that this was the terminus (moved in the 19th c. to S. Basilio) of the ferryboat that ran from the westernmost edge of the island to the lagoon shore at Fusina.

Campo S. Nicolò dei Mendìcoli (4 E3). This small open "campo," surrounded by water, with a flagstaff and a column topped by a 17th-c. winged lion, maintains the flavor of the original lagoon-side settlement. It lies in the heart of one of the earliest parishes (according to tradition, it dates from the 7th c.), as well as one of the poorest: *mendicoli* (mendicants) was a term applied to the earliest inhabitants, who comprised the fiercely proud community of the Nicolotti, and who enjoyed the privilege of electing a "gastaldo," also known as the "doge dei Nicolotti." Overlooking this "campo" are a little 18th-c. oratory and the church, with its square Venetian-Byzantine campanile (12th c.); across the "rio," note the high wall of the former Cotonificio Veneziano.

S. Nicolò dei Mendìcoli (4 E3). This church, partially rebuilt over the years (the left side has an 18th-c. elevation), still preserves the Venetian-Byzantine basilican layout of the 13th c., and is built on a previously existing foundation (uncovered during the restoration done between 1971 and 1977, confirming its 7th-c. origins): note the typical portico extending before the facade, common in ancient Venetian churches as a haven for the poor.
The basilican three-aisle interior features structural sections from the 14th c. (the columns) and 15th c. (two pointed arches in the transept), and, a spectacular wooden decoration overall (16th c.) with statues of Apostles along the nave, ending in an iconostasis with statues from the school of Girolamo Campagna. Set on an impressive wooden chancel are the *Miracles of St. Martha*, a series of canvases by Carletto Caliari.

S. Nicolò dei Mendìcoli: interior

From here, take the Fondamenta dell'Arziere and you will reach the *Fondamenta delle Procuratie* (4 D3-4), which, with the parallel *Fondamenta dei Cereri*, to the south, encloses a 16th-c. neighborhood, exemplary of a distinctly Venetian phenomenon: ever since the 16th c. it had become common practice to erect buildings with rental apartments, generally funded by private bequests (though sometimes by gifts from convents or "Scuole") and administered by the Procuratori della Repubblica (hence the name of the "fondamenta"). The same building might have aristocratic apartments, usually at the head, and other, more humble dwellings.

Quartiere di S. Marta (4 E1-2). Enclosed by a high wall, this working-class neighborhood was built between 1924 and 1931, resulting in the total transformation of the westernmost section of Venice. Of the homes of the poor people, fishermen, and "remurchianti" (boatmen) of the Arzere di S. Marta, or beach along the southern edge of this section, nothing survives: all that stands of the 15th-c. church of S. Marta is an empty shell, embedded in the surrounding port structures. All the same, this quarter has an eerie charm, conveyed by the distinctly Venetian houses, in long identical rows, the absence of waterways, and the general sense of isolation; this is a fine example of proto-industrial urban outskirts.

Angelo Raffaele (4 E4). Traditionally said to be one of the eight churches founded in the 7th c. by Magnus, the bishop of Oderzo, it has the appearance given it during the reconstruction done by Francesco Contino between 1618 and 1639. Although three facades were planned, only the facade overlooking the "rio," at an angle, was built (1735). The interior, built to a Greek-cross plan, and strangely tall, has a prevalently 18th-c. flavor, though there are many 16th- and 17th-c. artworks Exceptionally fine are the *Stories of Tobiolo** (above the main entrance, on the parapet of the 18th-c. organ), 5 panels painted by Giovanni Antonio Guardi (1750-53) or, according to some, by his brother Francesco.

S. Sebastiano* (4 E4). Rebuilt between 1505 and 1548, possibly by Scarpagnino, in elegant Renaissance style, the church is rendered particularly noteworthy by the immense decorative display created by Paolo Veronese between 1555 and 1565.
The interior, with a single aisle, is arranged in an intriguing array of spaces, revolving around the "barco," or hanging choir: on the ceiling, on the walls of the nave and the presbytery, in the "barco" and in the sacristy, note the splendid array of canvases and frescoes by Paolo Veronese. The artist is buried in this church (in front of the left chapel of the presbytery, while a bust of Veronese, by Mattia Cornero, stands next to the organ) and, it is said (though history does not bear this story out), lived as a prisoner for a certain period in the adjoining convent. Note the three exquisite canvases* in the ceiling of the nave, *Esther Led Before Ahasuerus*, *Esther Crowned by Ahasuerus*, *Triumph of Mordecai* and, among the altar pieces, *Virgin Mary in Glory and Saints* on the main altar, executed to designs by Veronese. Note the remarkable *organ*, also designed by Paolo Veronese, who painted the doors and parapet with episodes from the life of Jesus. Note the *St. Nicholas*, by Titian, on the altar of the vestibule, beneath the choir. In the chapel to the left of the main altar, note the original pavement glazed terracotta (1510); nor is it easy to miss, after the 3rd chapel on the right, the enormous sepulcher built by Jacopo Sansovino (1555-56) for Livio Podocattaro, who was the archbishop of Cyprus.
Extending alongside the church is the former *convent* of S. Sebastiano, rebuilt in 1851, and now part of the university: note the refined renovation done by Carlo Scarpa for the entrance (1979-80).

Zattere al Ponte Lungo (4 F5). This is the westernmost stretch of the Fondamenta delle Zattere, which begins at the Punta della Dogana, and is lined with trees. There are not many cafes: one can be found on the ground floor of the former Scuola dei Luganegheri (guild of the sausage makers; 17th c.), heavily renovated (n. 1473). Palazzetti in Neo-Gothic and Neo Renaissance style, once connected with the nearby Stazione Marittima, and older palazzi (15th/16th c.) make this a quiet and secluded neighborhood, a favorite strolling place for mothers and children. Across the Canale della Giudecca, note the immense silhouette of the Mulino Stucky.
At the end of this stretch is the Ponte Lungo (8 C6), over the Rio di S. Trovaso, with a view of the "squero," leading into the lively and social Fondamenta delle Zattere ai Gesuati.

5 Cannaregio

The entire northwest section of Venice, between the Grand Canal and the lagoon, is occupied by the Sestiere di Cannaregio, the second-largest "sestiere" in the city (about 157 hectares). The name may refer to the reedbeds ("canneti") that once grew abundantly in the area; the name may also refer to the presence of a particularly long canal here, second only to the Grand Canal, and therefore called the Canal Regio (Royal Canal). This was once the most important channel of communication with the mainland, until the 19th c., when a railroad bridge was built across the lagoon. We know that along this broad and well-lit canal, as early as the Gothic era, but especially in the 17th and 18th c., there were major aristocratic palazzi with spacious gardens, alongside working-class housing.

Not far from the central area of Rialto and in the strip of buildings close to the Grand Canal, is the area with the earliest structures standing in this "sestiere"; even now you can see how densely packed the buildings are, gathered around the lovely courtyards of Byzantine origin, among them the Corte del Milion, the Corte del Leon Bianco, and the Corte del Remer.

The northern section of this "sestiere" was shaped in the Gothic period, revolving around existing convents. The neighborhood grew through successive reclamation projects of sandbars and shoals in the lagoon, giving it a distinctive plan made up of parallel "insule," or "blocks," overlooking straight canals, lined by "fondamenta," embankments, open to the south, surrounded by enclosure walls, within which are large open areas containing gardens and vegetable patches. On the edge of this area, following the decision of the Maggior Consiglio to confine the Jewish community of Venice to a certain part of the city, a Jewish quarter was established in the 16th c., one of the best preserved Ghettoes still surviving. Toward the end of the 16th c., the construction of the Fondamenta Nuove established the northernmost boundary of the city of Venice, extending from the Sestiere di Cannaregio to the Sestiere di Castello. Completed in 1589, the construction of the Fondamenta Nuove marked an end to the centuries-long project of reclamation of the sandbars, which had done so much to form the blocks of buildings of this quarter.

Around 1850, the construction of the railroad bridge over the lagoon brought about a massive renovation of the buildings and urban plan of Cannaregio. The demolition of major convent complexes made way for the construction, in 1860, of the new train station; near the train station, major industrial facilities were built, such as the Macello Comunale, or municipal slaughterhouse, and industrial buildings, such as the Saffa factory, especially in the westernmost section. In this same part of town, abandoned churches and convents were reconverted into homes and factories.

Linking the new bridgehead with the center of Rialto, between 1868 and 1871, a new pedestrian thoroughfare was built between S. Fosca and Ss. Apostoli. This route, straight as an arrow, was built by tearing through considerable sections of historic parts of the city, and is entirely alien to the spirit of Venice; it has always been called the Strada Nuova, significantly, instead of the official name, Via Vittorio Emanuele II at first, and later Calle XXVIII Aprile.

Between the end of the 19th c. and the turn of the 20th c., many public works were undertaken, with new residential quarters being built; recently, the architect Vittorio Gregotti built a new section of working-class housing in the Area Ex Saffa.

5.1 From Santa Lucia to Rialto

This route runs from west to east, the length of the "sestiere," following a straight line as far as the Campo Ss. Apostoli from the train station to the center of Rialto, a route that was created in the second half of the 19th c. by filling in canals and tearing through the heart of the historical center. It runs past major religious centers, through lively sections of town, and across enchanting "campi." From Campo Ss. Apostoli, where a number of different thoroughfares converge, the route continues in the direction of Salizzada S. Giovanni Crisostomo, through a compact urban neighborhood, distinguished by the presence of numerous Byzantine courtyards (Corte del Leon Bianco, Corte del Remer), and intact and charming corners of a lesser known Venice.

Stazione Ferroviaria (1 E4). The railroad station was rebuilt in the Rationalist style in 1954; this was the last step in the series of major transformations that had affected this extreme westernmost tip of the "sestiere" since 1841, the year in which construction began on the railroad bridge across the lagoon. The construction of the railroad, shortly followed by the building of the first Ponte degli Scalzi (1858) and, after the demolition of all the existing structures (including the convent complexes of Corpus Domini and S. Lucia), the construction of the first station (1860), marked the definitive transfer of the main mode of entry to Venice from the Bacino di S. Marco (which was thereafter relegated to a purely ceremonial function) to the NW head of the Grand Canal.

Gli Scalzi* (S. Maria di Nazareth; 1 E4-5). Built to plans by Baldassarre Longhena after 1654 for a community of Carmelitani Scalzi (Barefoot Carmelites) who had moved here from Rome just a few years previous, this church clearly shows the influence of the Roman Baroque style in its floor plan and in the lavish decorations, by the express wishes of the clients and future occupants. The facade, by Giuseppe Sardi (1672-80), is the only one in all Venice made of Carrara marble. The interior, designed by Baldassarre Longhena, has a single aisle and three chapels on either side; note the lavish array of polychrome marble, sculptures, and gilding, done under the supervision of the Carmelite Giuseppe Pozzo. In this church are preserved the ashes of Ludovico Manin, the last doge of the Venetian Republic. The enormous canvas set in the vault dates from 1934 (E. Tito) and replaces the notable ceiling decorations by G.B. Tiepolo, badly damaged by an Austrian bomb in 1915. Other frescoes by Tiepolo decorate the vaults of the 2nd chapel on the right (St. Theresa in Glory; 1720-25) and the 1st chapel on the left.

Rio Terrà Lista di Spagna (1 D-E5). This broad and lively pedestrian shopping street, now popular with tourists, was built in 1844 following the filling in of the Rio dei Sabbioni.

Campo di S. Geremia (1 D6). One of the largest "campi" in Venice, and once the scene of popular festivals and spectacular bull-baiting, it is enclosed on the southern and eastern sides by the landward facades of Palazzo Labia and the church of S. Geremia. Rebuilt in 1753-60 to plans by the abbot Carlo Corbellini with a Greek cross floor plan, the church contains the Cappella di S. Lucia, with the relics of St. Lucy, a martyr from Siracusa in Sicily. The long facade overlooking the Rio di Cannaregio was built in 1871 and still features a Romanesque terracotta bell tower from the 13th c.

Palazzo Labia* (1 D6). This is one of the most sumptuous aristocratic homes of 17th-/18th-c. Venice, with splendid rooms frescoed in 1746-47 by G.B. Tiepolo. Now the Venetian headquarters of RAI television, it

S. Geremia and Palazzo Labia from the Riva di Biasio

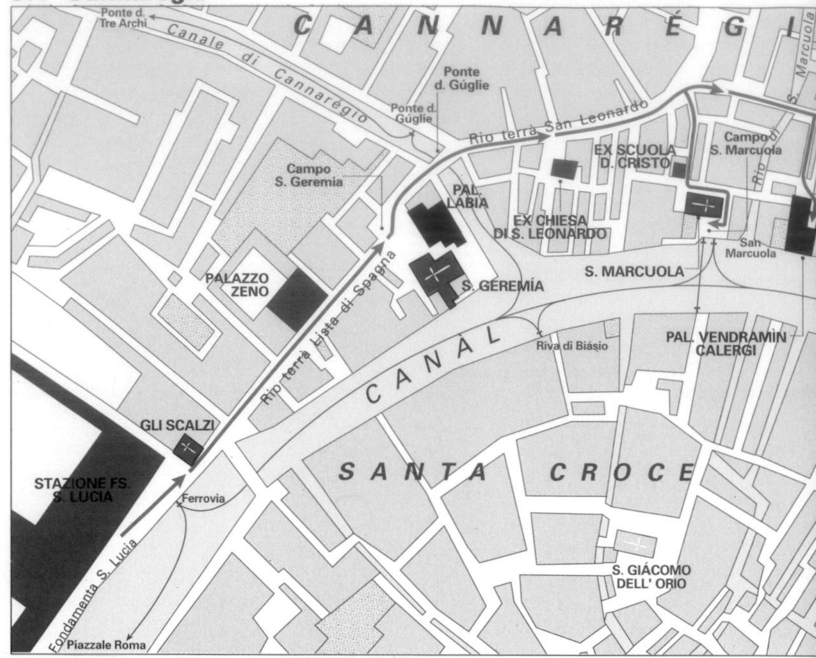

was built to plans attributed variously to A. Cominelli and A. Tremignon, immediately following the drafting into the Venetian aristocracy of the Labia family, originally from Catalonia (1646). In the monumental salone* – a great hall that is entirely frescoed, amidst false perspectives and architecture, largely by G. Mengozzi Colonna – note the *Banquet of Antony and Cleopatra* and the *Embarkation of Cleopatra*, masterpieces of G.B. Tiepolo.

Ponte delle Guglie (1 D6). Literally "Bridge of Spires," it is named for the four obelisks set on its railing; it was built – with a daring single-arch approach – in a strategic location over the Canale di Cannaregio, in 1580. The bridge became even more important following the construction of the railroad and the station, and the reconstruction of the busy route between it and Rialto; that route is always thriving, in part because of its many shops and the daily fish and vegetable market of Rio Terrà S. Leonardo (2 D1-2).

S. Marcuola (Ss. Ermagora e Fortunato; 2 D2). On the Campo S. Marcuola, one of the few "campi" to open directly onto the Grand Canal, note the broad unfinished facade; first built in an early period (9th/10th c.), it was rebuilt by A. Gaspari and G. Massari between 1728 and 1736. Note the remarkable 18th-c. statues by G.M. Morlaiter on the altar of the twin chapels set at the corners of the interior square hall, and the splendid *Last Supper** by Jacopo Tintoretto on the left wall of the presbytery. Behind the church, at the corner of Rio Terrà del Cristo, note the former *Scuola del Cristo* (2 D2), now the headquarters of a religious cultural center, built in 1644 for the Confraternita della Buona Morte, whose members had the task of burying those who had died by drowning.

Corte del Volto Santo (2 D2). The image of the Volto Santo (Holy Face; symbol of the Silk Guild), carved into the architrave of the "sottoportego" and on the 14th-c. well head, is a reminder that this was once a neighborhood occupied by silk-workers, established by political refugees from the city of Lucca around 1360.

Palazzo Vendramin Calergi* (2 D2). One of the most sumptuous aristocratic homes on the Grand Canal, the palazzo was commissioned by the Loredan family, and was designed and built by Mauro Codussi in 1481. The facade overlooking the canal, which reveals a new classical style in the marble facing with exquisite polychrome inlay, and in the subordination of decorative elements to architectural scheme, is a masterpiece of Renaissance architecture in Venice. The interior, where Richard Wagn-

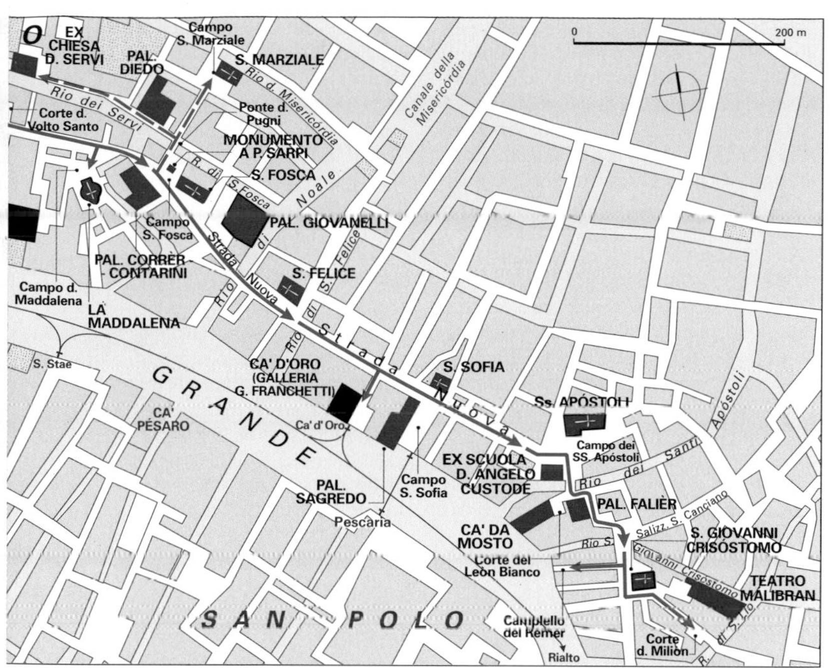

er lived, and died on 13 February 1883, is the winter site of the Casinò Municipale, or town casino, and occasionally hosts art exhibitions.

Campo della Maddalena (2 D3). This intimate and secluded little "campo" – though the busy foot traffic of the Rio Terrà della Maddalena runs right past it – is an urban setting of exquisite beauty, bounded by an interesting array of lesser buildings, with houses whose facades jut forward on buttresses, surmounted by impressive round chimneys. Fitting perfectly into the "campo" is the little church of *S. Maria Maddalena*, with a circular plan, topped by a dome; it was built between 1760 and 1789 by Tommaso Temanza, in a rigorous blend of Palladian tradition and Neoclassical innovation.

Campo S. Fosca (2 D3). This "campo" takes its name from the church of S. Fosca, founded in the 10th c. and rebuilt around 1679; note the simple facade (1741). At the center of the "campo" is a bronze *monument to Paolo Sarpi* (1892), by Emilio Marsili; the Venetian priest, champion of Venice in the dispute with Pope Paul V over Roman intrusion into Venetian religious affairs, at the time of the Interdict (1606), was attacked and wounded near the bridge on the evening of 8 October 1607, by assassins who may have been sent from Rome. Across from the "campo," overlooking the Salizzada S. Fosca, is the interesting *Palazzo Correr*, now used as an auction house; the palazzo comprises two 15th-c. Gothic buildings; in the 18th c. a radical renovation was undertaken, but was limited to only one of the two buildings.

From the *Ponte di S. Fosca* (the four footholds in the Istrian stone show where the traditional "fist fight" between the opposing factions was held), a short detour will allow you to tour the interesting landmarks in the interior zone.
Follow the *Fondamenta Diedo* (2 D3) to the Palazzo Diedo (n. 2386), built to plans by Andrea Tirali between 1710 and 1720, now a government office building. According to the lore of the 18th c., the building was built to its remarkable height in order to cast a spiteful shadow on the nearby *Palazzo Grimani* (n. 2381-83).
If you return to the Ponte S. Fosca and you follow the Calle Zancani, you will reach the church of *S. Marziale* (2 D3-4), rebuilt between 1693 and 1721. The modest architectural appearance of the facade contrasts with the Baroque splendor of the single-aisle interior, with its elaborate carved gilt ceiling, which contains major canvases by Sebastiano Ricci (1700-1705).

Strada Nuova (2 E4). On 2 September 1871 the new thoroughfare that provided a direct link between the railroad station and Rialto was inaugurated. This thoroughfare, the Strada Nuova, had required ripping through the ancient urban setting between S. Fosca

and Campo Ss. Apostoli, aligning and unifying the facades of the buildings. The incongruity of this road in the Venetian setting is quite evident to anyone who walks along it: 10 m. in width, and running in two, arrow-straight lengths, its SW side is bounded by the rear of the row of palazzi overlooking the Grand Canal. The ancient pharmacy, or *Farmacia S. Fosca* (n. 2233) preserves the original 17th-c. furnishings, and Venetian vases and majolica from the 18th c.; a little further along (n. 2292) is the *Palazzo Giovanelli*, headquarters of an auction house; this notable Gothic building was heavily renovated in 1847 by G.B. Meduna, who built, among other things, the octagonal staircase terminating in a skylight in a refined Neo-Gothic style.
On a line with the *Campo S. Felice* (2 E4) is the left side of the church of S. Felice, in a simple Renaissance style, rebuilt in 1531-56, possibly by Sante Lombardo, with an interior on a Greek-cross plan, set in a square structure, with a high cupola.

Ca' d'Oro* (2 E4). One of the largest and most important collections of art in Venice can be seen in this palazzo, renowned for its elegant and elaborate facade overlooking the Grand Canal, with marble fretwork and polychrome marble inlay, once covered with gilding – hence the name (Palace of Gold). Built in the Gothic style between 1422 and 1440 for the Procurator Marino Contarini, by M. Raverti and G. and B. Bon, and renovated repeatedly over the centuries, the building developed around a lovely courtyard with a covered stairway (Raverti) and a *well head* with allegorical figures, a masterpiece by Bartolomeo Bon (1427). In 1916 the Turinese musician and collector Giorgio Franchetti, who had purchased the palazzo in 1895, gave it to the Italian State, along with his considerable collection, the nucleus of the **Galleria Giorgio Franchetti***, which is still installed in this palazzo and in the adjoining Palazzo Giusti. The collection includes Italian and foreign paintings, marble, bronzes, and Venetian ceramics, primarily from the 15th/18th c.
In the halls on the two main floors, on either side of the two large "porteghi," with loggias overlooking the Grand Canal, aside from the splendid *St. Sebastian**, painted by Andrea Mantegna around 1506 for Sigismondo Cardinal Gonzaga, note paintings by Antonio Vivarini (*Passion of Christ**), V. Carpaccio (*Annunciation and Transit of the Virgin*), Giovanni da Rimini (*St. Christopher*), G. Ferrari, L. Signorelli, B. Diana, Andrea di Bartolo, Jacopo del Sellaio, and others. Among the sculpture: *Apollo* by P.J. Alari known as the Antico (1498) and *Pair of Youths**, a masterpiece by Tullio Lombardo. A carved 15th-c. stairway leads up to the third floor, where you can see major works by Titian (*Venus at the Mirror*), Tintoretto (*Portrait of Niccolò Priuli*), H. Van Eyck (*Crucifixion*), Flemish and Dutch paintings, *Views of Venice* by F. Guardi, Flemish tapestries from the 16th c., sketches by Gian Lorenzo Bernini, frescoes by Pordenone, and Venetian ceramics, dating back as far as the 12th c.

The Ca' d'Oro with its marble facade

Campo S. Sofia (2 E4). The thriving activity of the Strada Nuova merges here with the traffic from the markets of Rialto, directly opposite, across the Grand Canal, linked with the "campo" by gondola service. At n. 4199 is the landward entrance of the Gothic *Palazzo Sagredo*, the interior of which was rebuilt entirely in the 18th c.; among the additions were an immense stairway attributed to Andrea Tirali, with walls and vault frescoed by Pietro Longhi (1734). On a line with the Campo S. Sofia, directly behind an anonymous 19th-c. building facing the Strada Nuova, is the church of *Santa Sofia*, founded around the year 1000, repeatedly renovated and finally rebuilt entirely at the end of the 17th c., to plans by Antonio Gaspari; the interior has a basilican floor plan, and is split up into three aisles by high round arches atop Renaissance columns.

Campo Ss. Apostoli (2 F5). This square became a crowded crossroads after the inauguration of the Strada Nuova; it is a major intersection where many pedestrian thoroughfares converge like spokes to the hub of a wheel, leading to Rialto and the northern sector of the "sestiere." The square is broken up into a number of smaller spaces by the volume of the church, alongside of which stand a number of other buildings, from different periods and serving various functions; among them note the tall bell-tower, rebuilt in 1672, with an elegant classical-style belfry added in the early-18th c. by Andrea Tirali.
On the southern side of the "campo" is the *Scuola dell'Angelo Custode* (now a Lutheran Evangelical church), built after 1713 to plans by Andrea Tirali; it stands alone beside the bridge, which is believed to have been lined with shops on the right (Canaletto depicted it this way in an 18th-c. engraving). This creates an element of continuity between the "campo" and the porticoes of the 13th-c. Palazzo Falier, its facade decorated by handsome Venetian-Byzantine *paterae*.

Ss. Apostoli (2 E-F5). Rebuilt in 1575, possibly by Alessandro Vittoria, this church preserves the elegant late-15th-c. Cappella Corner, attributed to Mauro Codussi, with remarkable carvings, possibly by Tullio Lombardo, and a refined altar piece by G.B. Tiepolo depicting the *Communion of St. Lucy* (ca. 1748). In the chapel to the right of the presbytery, note the rare fragments of 14th-c. Byzantine-style frescoes, and, in the chapel to the left, by Francesco Maffei, *The Guardian Angel*.

If you turn to the right, after the bridge, you will enter the *Corte del Leon Bianco* (2 F5), named after the famous Albergo del Leon Bianco; this hotel was installed, from the 16th to the 18th c., in the Venetian-Byzantine "casa-fondaco" of the *Ca' Da Mosto* (2 F5), a rare example of the earliest merchant's homes built along the Grand Canal.

Campiello del Remer (2 F5). Looking out over the Grand Canal is a small and charming little square, of Byzantine origin, bounded by the remains of the 13th-c. *Palazzo Lion-Morosini* with an exterior stairway (rebuilt), a portal, and handsome two-light mullioned windows with basket arches. Also, the square well head is Byzantine, made of red Verona marble.

S. Giovanni Crisostomo (2 F5). An elegant campanile (1532-90) dominates the church's simple Renaissance facade with curving crown, rebuilt by Mauro Codussi between 1497 and 1504. The proportions and the organization of the interior to a Greek-cross floor plan, punctuated in neat geometric modules, blend the Byzantine tradition with a classical approach typical of the Renaissance. Since 1977, this church has also had the status of sanctuary of the Madonna delle Grazie, due to the presence of an image of the Virgin Mary that is particularly venerated by the Venetians. There are numerous art works here, some of them of considerable importance, such as the masterpiece of Giovanni Bellini's old age, a painting depicting the *Saints Christopher, Jerome, and Augustine** (or St. Louis of Toulouse; 1513), on the 1st altar on the right; a celebrated altar piece by Sebastiano del Piombo, *St. John Chrysostom and Saints* (1509 c.) on the main altar, and a marble altar piece by Tullio Lombardo, *Coronation of Mary and Apostles** dated 1500-1502, and set on the altar of the chapel in the left arm of the transept.

Corte del Milion (2 F5). The area directly behind the church of S. Giovanni Crisostomo, Byzantine in its grid, is articulated into courtyards, among which is the Corte Seconda del Milion, so called because it is the site (n. 5845) of what is believed to be the *house of Marco Polo* (Polo wrote an account of his travels, the earliest first-hand European account of Asia, which in Italian, or Venetian dialect, was called, variously, Il Milione, or "Divisament dou Monde," known in English as the "Book of Marco Polo").
Also overlooking this courtyard are notable buildings with architectural elements dating from various eras. In the nearby *Corte del Teatro* note the entrance to the *Teatro Malibran*, open in 1678 and rebuilt in the early-20th c.; the name of the theater, dedicated in 1835, honored the famous Spanish mezzo-soprano Maria de la Felicidad Malibran. Currently closed, renovation works will commence shortly.

The Salizzada di S. Giovanni Crisostomo (2 F5) leads directly to the Market of Rialto.

5.2 From the Ponte delle Guglie to the Ghetto

The route runs along the broad Canale di Cannaregio, an important waterway used by public transportation running around the edges of town. As you walk along the SW edge of this area, you will reach a fairly built-up area that was once the site of much manufacturing, as well as the Macello Comunale, or municipal slaughterhouse, now badly neglected, despite its remarkable location on the Laguna Nord, or northern lagoon. Passing over the Ponte dei Tre Archi along the opposite quay, or Fondamenta di Cannaregio, bounded by impressive country homes, the route runs along the Calle Ferraù, and reaches the area of S. Girolamo, with sections that were recently built up, including the Sacca S. Girolamo, which opens out onto the broad expanse of lagoon water. From here the route winds through the three parallel "insule" in the NW section of the "sestiere," distinguished by specific urban organization.
From the Ghetto – where for centuries the Jews of Venice were forced to establish their residence, one of the most picturesque and unusual areas in Venice, distinguished by tall tower-houses and exquisite synagogues – you will return to the Fondamenta di Cannaregio, not far from the Ponte delle Guglie.

Fondamenta Venier-Savorgnan (1 C5-D6). This quay runs along the broad and sunny Canale di Cannaregio; at the beginning is the *Palazzo Priuli-Manfrin*, formerly Palazzo Venier, a rigorous, nearly Neoclassical structure (Andrea Tirali, 1734), and the *Palazzo Savorgnan*, built at the end of the 17th c. to plans by Giuseppe Sardi, with luxuriant gardens (a typical feature in this area because of the ample supply of land, on the outskirts of Venice) that have now been unified and opened to the public. At n. 469 a gate marks the entrance to a vast area known as Saffa, from the name of one of the many industrial factories set up here after 1868; the area is now occupied by a newly built working-class residential neighborhood, designed by the architect Vittorio Gregotti, and the subject of much criticism. On a line with the *Campo S. Giobbe* you can cross over to the opposite "fondamenta" by the Ponte dei Tre Archi.

S. Giobbe* (1 C4). Through the generosity of the doge Cristoforo Moro, who is buried here, what was originally a modest monastery attained great prestige around the 16th c. The church, rebuilt by Antonio Gambello in the Gothic style (after 1450) and completed by Pietro and Tullio Lombardo in the Renaissance style, is particularly notable for the exquisite architectural and sculptural decoration of the portal (Pietro Lombardo, late-15th c.) and the interior arcades which frame the chapels looking out onto the single broad nave.
In the 2nd chapel on the left, built for the Martini, a family of silk merchants who moved to Venice from Lucca in the 14th c., the influence of Tuscan art clearly predominates; note the *altar piece* by Antonio Rossellino and the splendid *ceiling*, sheathed with polychrome glazed terracotta, the sole example in Venice of the art of the Della Robbia family. There is a small Lombard-style masterpiece: the *tombstone of the doge Cristoforo Moro and his wife Cristina Sanudo**, set in the floor, on a line with the presbytery. After 1810, the adjoining convent was almost entirely demolished (with the exception of a wing of the first of the two cloisters) and was replaced by a Botanical Garden.

Ex Macello Comunale (1 B3). Named for the former Municipal Slaughterhouse, this area has always featured manufacturing and industry. With facades overlooking both the Canale di Cannaregio and the Laguna Nord, or Northern Lagoon, stands the Neoclassical complex of the Ex Macello Comunale, built between 1841 and 1843 to plans by G. Salvadori and G.B. Meduna, with the aim of consolidating all slaughterhouse activity in Venice into a single, well equipped area on the outskirts of town. Once the project by Le Corbusier for a new hospital (1964) was ruled out, the area of the Macello became the domain of athletic associations, and it has long awaited proper reconversion.

Ponte dei Tre Archi (1 B4). Designed by Andrea Tirali in 1688 with a three-arch structure, this bridge is the only one of its kind in Venice, and was originally built without parapets.

Fondamenta di Cannaregio (1 B4-C5). This quay runs along the Canale di Cannaregio, past the bridge. Among the more significant pieces of architecture here, note the imposing, theatrical facade of *Palazzo Surian* (n. 967), begun by Giuseppe Sardi around the middle of the 17th c.; it was used in the 18th c. as the French Embassy, when the secretary to the ambassador was none other than Jean Jacques Rousseau. On the final stretch of the "fondamenta," note the complex of *S. Maria delle Penitenti* (now the Pensionato S. Giobbe), built to plans by Giorgio Massari between 1730 and 1740, to house "repentant fallen women."

S. Girolamo (1 A4-B6). This area on the outskirts of Venice is now a working-class neighborhood; in the past it had some importance due to the presence of the complex of the convent of the Cappuccine, built at the beginning of the 17th c. (all that survives of that complex is the church of the Cappuccine; 1 B5), and, on the other side of the "rio," the *Convent of S. Girolamo* (1 B6), founded in the 14th c. The church of S. Girolamo, rebuilt at the beginning of the 18th c. to plans by Domenico Rossi, was restored for worship in 1952; from 1840 until 1885, it housed a steam-driven mill, and was later used as a glucose factory. Adjoining the church of the Cappuccine is the notable aristocratic palazzo of the Grimani family (n. 3023), which dates from the end of the 16th c., a fine indicator of the importance that this area once had.
Following the First World War, it became necessary to deal with the problem of housing in Venice; the result was a series of major construction projects in this pristine area on the outskirts of the city.

Fondamenta della Sensa (2 B2). The long extension of the Rio della Sensa and the orderly succession in parallel zones of the various urban features (canals, "fondamenta," or quays, buildings, rear gardens) create remarkable, entrancing perspectival views. The favorable southern exposure, the quiet that reigns over all, the vast green areas – all have made this an ideal area for the construction of aristocratic palazzi and princely dwellings, a number of interesting examples of which survive, among them the 16th-c. *Palazzo Michiel* (n. 3218), whose facade was once decorated with frescoes by Andrea Schiavone.

Campo S. Alvise (2 B2). In this section of the city, characterized by long "fondamenta," there are no large "campi," and community life is largely oriented along the canalside. Campo S. Alvise, in fact, is a solitary churchyard/courtyard, partly tree-lined, and bounded by low brick walls; note the adjoining religious settlement of S. Alvise: the convent, arranged around two cloisters; the small, former *Scuola di S. Alvise* (to the left of the church), built in 1402, where only the original inhabitants – already a shrinking minority – could worship; and the church itself.

S. Alvise (2 B2). Built in 1388, supposedly at the behest of a young aristocratic woman of the Venier family who was particularly devoted to St. Louis, bishop of Toulouse (Alvise is the Venetian dialect form of Louis), this church has a special charm that derives from the contrast between its

5.2 Cannarégio

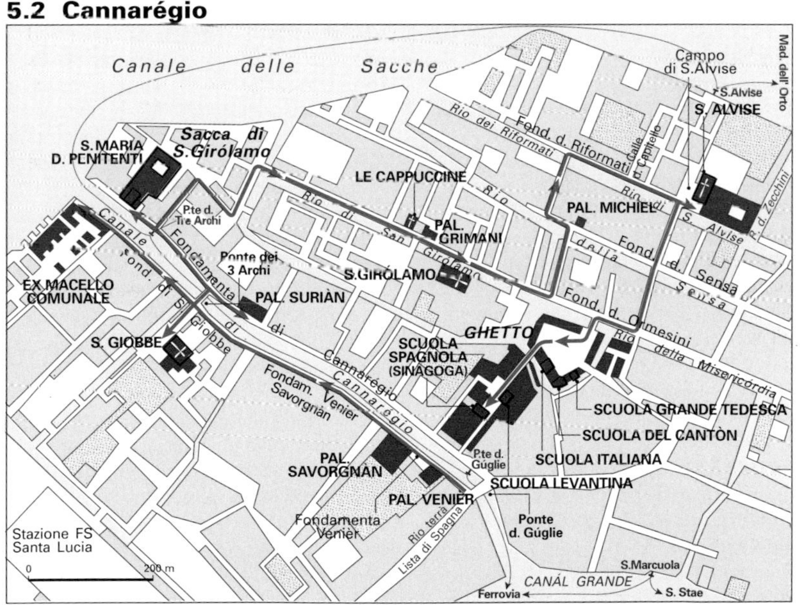

Characteristic houses in the Ghetto

setting on the outskirts of Venice and the exquisite decoration of the interior, with major paintings by G.B. Tiepolo, including the splendid *Climb up to Calvary** (1743) on the right wall of the presbytery. The nave, rebuilt in the 17th c., preserves from the original structure one of the earliest examples of a "barco" (hanging choir) supported by columns, used by the nuns to enter the church directly from their convent.

Behind the line of buildings that bounds the nearby *Fondamenta dei Riformati* (2 A1-B2) extends a verdant stretch of orchards and gardens, stretching to the edge of the lagoon and dotted with industrial sheds, storehouses, and laying-up yards. What remains is the luxuriant garden (now public) of the long-demolished Palazzo Donà, with an entrance in Calle del Capitello (2 A-B2).

Fondamenta degli Ormesini (2 B1-C2). Ormesin, the Italian name for a cloth that was originally imported from Hormuz, on the Persian Gulf, was woven in a number of manufactories once located here. Also overlooking this quay is the facade of a typical rental residential complex of the 17th c.

Ghetto (2 C1). You can detect something odd and very special as you enter the Campo del Ghetto Nuovo, built in one of the areas that made up the Venetian Ghetto, where for almost three centuries (from 1516 to 1797) Jews were forced to establish their residence. The center of a small "insula," entirely surrounded by a ring of water, rendering it particularly easy to oversee (note the absence of doors giving onto the water), what is most striking about this area is the closed structure of the buildings, which were built particularly tall in order to make the most of the limited area available. From this early core, as the population of the thriving Jewish community continued to grow, the Ghetto developed, after 1541, into the area that extends to the Rio di Cannaregio (Ghetto Vecchio) and, after 1633, in the small annex of the Ghetto Nuovissimo. The existence in the area of cannon foundries, where the operation of the "ghetto" or "getto" was performed (literally, casting of metal), gave the area its name, later used throughout Europe to designate the areas set aside for the enclosure of the Jewish population. In the dense urban structure, the emergence of little domes, without any clear connection to the underlying architecture, marks the presence of synagogues (also called Scuole, or Schools, for the array of functions that they served), which were established in existing buildings, and can be identified by the series of tall windows on the top floor. The considerable number of synagogues (in all, there are five) is a result of the specific way in which life was organized in the Jewish community, split up into "tribes," each with its own rites and charitable and educational institutions. The oldest ones, the *Scuola Grande Tedesca* (founded in 1528-29 and rebuilt in the 18th c.), the *Scuola Canton* (1531-32) and the *Scuola Italiana* (1575, rebuilt between the end of the 18th c. and the beginning of the 19th c.), stand in the Campo del Ghetto Nuovo, set above little porticoes with columns, where the crafts workshops and the pawn shops were, such as the Banco Rosso (n. 2911). In the nearby *Museo d'Arte Ebraica* are collections of objects, sacred furnishings, tapestries, codices, and other interesting examples of Venetian Jewish art from the 17th to the 19th c. The most spectacular one – and the only one not incorporated into an existing building – is the *Scuola Levantina*, which dominates the *Campiello delle Scuole* in the Ghetto Vecchio, founded in 1538 and rebuilt in the 17th c., possibly to plans by B. Longhena, with remarkable structures and decorations by A. Brustolon. Longhena, or his pupil A. Gaspari, also oversaw the renovation of the 16th-c. *Scuola Spagnola*, which still preserves on the ground floor the 18th-c. hall of the Talmud-Torah, a place for children's religious study.

5.3 From the Madonna dell'Orto to the Gesuiti

The route winds through the NE sectors of the "sestiere," in secluded areas on the outskirts of Venice, charming places where you can clearly sense the nearby vastness of the lagoon. From the Ponte delle Guglie, the n. 5 vaporetto line will take you to the vaporetto stop of "Madonna dell'Orto": from the secluded and lovely little "campo" before the church, the route winds along the well-lit "fondamenta" and arrow-straight canals that distinguish the northern sections of the "sestiere," crossed by major waterways linking the Laguna Nord, or northern lagoon, with the center of Rialto. The close urban array of buildings, marked by splendid landmarks of art history, suddenly opens out with a panoramic view that includes the islands of S. Michele and Murano. Following the first stretch of the Fondamenta Nuove, which marks the northernmost point of the city of Venice, you will pass the landing stages for the vaporettos heading for the islands in the northern lagoon and the center of town, and you will then enter the Calle del Fumo, which leads to Rialto.

Campo della Madonna dell'Orto (2 B3-4). In a quiet and secluded area, the small, charming "campo"- cum-church courtyard, with the original terracotta pavement broken up by strips of stone, is a remarkably lovely setting dominated by the exquisite facade of the church of the Madonna dell'Orto.

Madonna dell'Orto* (2 B3-4). Originally dedicated to S. Cristoforo (St. Christopher), it was given its present name after a statue of the Virgin Mary with Christ Child ("Madonna col Bambino"), traditionally said to have been found in a nearby garden ("orto"), was brought here in the late-14th c. The original 14th-c. church was rebuilt, or more likely renovated, in the 15th c.; the magnificent terracotta facade is decorated with statues and a rich portal. Behind it stands the 15th-c. bell tower, topped by a small onion dome, added in 1503 by Bartolomeo Bon.
The interior, flooded with a diffuse light pouring down from the upper windows, has a basilican floor plan, with three aisles ending in apses. In the chapel to the right of the main chapel, Jacopo Tintoretto is buried; he lived for many years in the nearby Fondamenta dei Mori. This church has many major paintings by the renowned painter, including the large canvases on the side walls of the presbytery depicting the *Last Judgement** and the *Adoration of the Golden Calf While Moses Receives the Ten Commandments** (ca. 1546) and, over the door of the Cappella di S. Mauro (right aisle), the *Presentation of Mary at the Temple** painted in 1552. In the same chapel, note the *Virgin Mary with Christ Child*, a large 14th-c. sculpture, from which the church takes its name. Other major works of art adorn the chapels along the sides of the church, which belong to venerable Venetian families, including the painting of *St. Agnes Reviving Licinius*, also by Jacopo Tintoretto (ca. 1579), in the Cappella Contarini (the 4th chapel in the left aisle) and a *Virgin Mary with Christ Child* by Giovanni Bellini (1478) which once hung in the first chapel on the left, but was stolen in 1993. On the first altar of the right aisle there is a noteworthy canvas by Cima da Conegliano, painted around 1493, depicting *St. John the Baptist between St. Peter, St. Mark, St. Jerome, and St. Paul**.

The "fondamenta" to the right of the "campo" was named after Gasparo Cardinal Contarini, a diplomat and a man of letters, who ordered the construction, in the first half of the 16th c., of the *Palazzo Contarini dal Zaffo* (n. 3539; 2 C4), with an enormous and renowned garden, which extends all the way to the lagoon. Isolated, set in a splendid location between the Sacca della Misericordia and the Laguna Nord, or northern lagoon, the *Casino degli Spiriti* (2 B4), an annexe of the palazzo, was a celebrated drawing room for writers, scholars, and artists in the 16th c. At n. 3536, along the same "fondamenta," you will find the *Palazzo Minelli-Spada* (2 C4), built in the second half of the 17th c., with an asymmetrical facade in the style of Longhena.

From the bridge to the end of the "fondamenta," you overlook the *Sacca della Misericordia* (2 C4-

5.3 Cannarégio

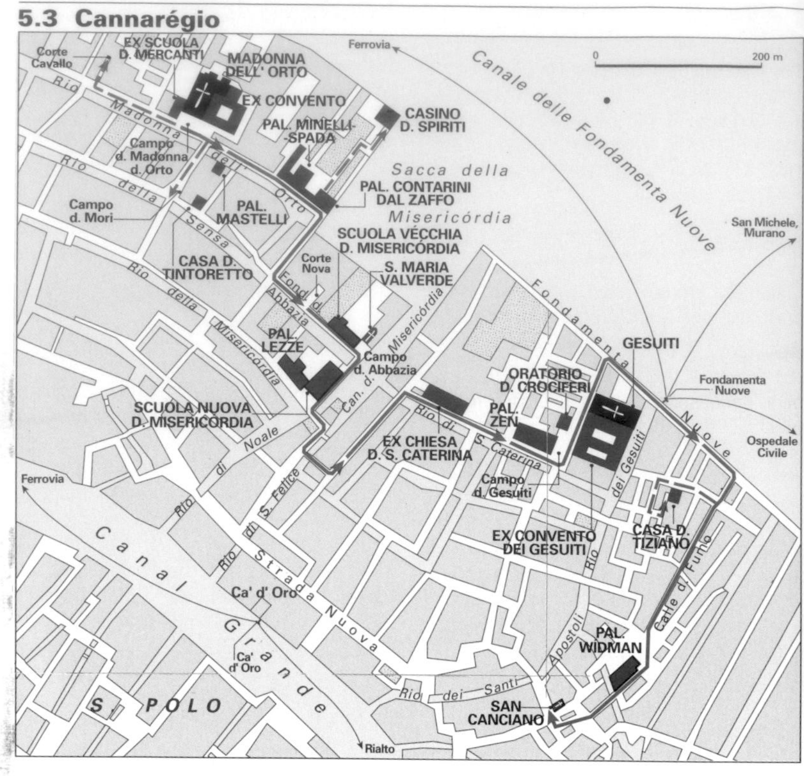

5), a broad inlet, where lumber floated down from the Cadore was originally brought ashore.

Across the Rio della Madonna dell'Orto is the *Palazzo Mastelli* (2 C4), also known as the Palazzo del Cammello, or Palace of the Camel, after the high relief to the right of the balcony; this is a 15th-/16th-c. reconstruction of a building founded in the 12th c. by the brothers Mastelli, wealthy merchants from Morea, supposedly depicted in the curious figures with turbans on the facades along the Campo dei Mori and the Fondamenta dei Mori (2 C3). To the right of the fourth statue (n. 3399 in the Fondamenta dei Mori) is the house where Jacopo Tintoretto lived until his death, on 31 May 1594.

S. Maria della Misericordia (S. Maria Valverde; 2 D4). Follow the *Fondamenta dell'Abbazia* and you will reach the tranquil and secluded *Campo dell'Abbazia*. Standing at the intersection of Rio della Sensa and Rio di Noale, and bounded by the facades of the church and the former Scuola di S. Maria della Misericordia, the little church-courtyard with original terracotta paving still preserves all its antique charm. The *church*, founded with the adjoining abbey in the 10th c., was rebuilt in the 13th c., and later renovated more than once. At an angle with the Baroque facade, built between 1651 and 1659 by Clemente Moli, stands the 15th-c. facade of the *Scuola Vecchia di S. Maria della Misericordia*, one of the "Scuole Grandi" of Venice, built in 1310 with the permission of the friars of the abbey, and repeatedly enlarged onto land owned by them. The two angels holding scrolls on the architrave of the portal are all that survives of the relief depicting the "Madonna della Misericordia Worshipped by the Confreres," by Bartolomeo Bon; the relief was dismantled in 1612, and is now at the Victoria and Albert Museum in London. After the confraternity moved to a new building on the other side of the "rio," the Scuola Vecchia was put to other uses.

Scuola Nuova di Santa Maria della Misericordia (2 D4). The building is distinguished by the imposing mass of brick of the unfinished facades, and was designed by Jacopo Sansovino and built between 1534 and 1583 to give a new and adequate headquarters to the rapidly growing Confraternita della Misericordia. The interior preserves the appearance and structure of the Scuole di Devozione (Schools of Devotion) with an enormous ground-floor hall, split up into three aisles by twin columns, and the enormous *Salone Superiore*, or upstairs hall, with fre-

soes from the school of Veronese, in very poor condition.
The Campo della Misericordia is bounded on the west by the side of the *Palazzo Lezze*, a noteworthy stucture by Baldassarre Longhena, dating from the period between 1645 and 1670.

Fondamenta di S. Caterina (2 D5). This quay takes its name from the *church* of S. Caterina, which was founded, with the adjoining convent, between the 11th and 12th c., and was rebuilt around the middle of the 15th c.; it overlooks the quay with its right wall. Damaged in 1977 by fire, it has been deconsecrated, and is closed to the public. The last section of the "fondamenta" is bounded by the long facade of the *Palazzo Zen*, built around 1534, possibly with the assistance of Sebastiano Serlio; the building is a mixture of Renaissance and Byzantine motifs, at the wishes of the patron of the arts and owner Francesco Zen.

Campo dei Gesuiti (2 D5-6). This "campo" has an unusual elongated shape, and is largely a thoroughfare for foot traffic to and from the Fondamenta Nuove, marked to the east by the long elevation of the former *Convento dei Gesuiti*. Founded, with the adjacent church, in the 12th c. by the order of the Crociferi, and rebuilt following a fire in 1514 (work continued throughout the 17th c.), the convent was taken over by the Jesuits in 1657, when the order was allowed to return to Venice, after its banishment for political reasons in 1606. In this area there were other buildings that once belonged to the order of the Crociferi; all that survives today, in the building with tall chimneys on the far side of the "campo," is the *Oratorio dei Crociferi*, renovated at the end of the 16th c.; note the series of paintings by Palma the Younger, executed between 1583 and 1591.

I Gesuiti* (S. Maria Assunta; 2 D6). The original church of the Crociferi ("crucifers," or cross-bearers in a procession), passed in 1657 under the ownership of the Company of Jesus (or Jesuits), and was rebuilt between 1715 and 1730 by Domenico Rossi, in conformity with the Jesuit models of church building, and with a vast Baroque facade, clearly in imitation of its Roman counterparts. The remarkable quality of the new church, however, is chiefly to be found in the lavish virtuoso decoration of the interior, which breaks up the broad space of the nave, covering every available surface: from the white-and-green marble intarsias, imitating damask upholstery and covering pillars and columns, to the white-and-gold stuccoes on the vault and the exquisite white-and-green marble decorations on the floor. Further enhancing the prestige of this church are such major paintings as the *Martyrdom of St. Lawrence** by Titian (1588), on the 1st altar on the left, and *Our Lady of the Assumption* by Jacopo Tintoretto at the altar of the left transept.

Fondamenta Nuove (2 C5-D6). Despite the notable view over the great expanse of water and the nearest islands in the northern lagoon (Laguna Nord; namely S. Michele and Murano), this long "fondamenta" (nearly 1 km. in length), which runs from the Sacca della Misericordia to the Rio di S. Giustina, has maintained over the years the character of a thoroughfare, rather than of a place where people stroll or spend leisure time; the reason is that it has a northern exposure, and is therefore swept by the cold "tramontane" winds; it links the northern areas of the Sestiere di Cannaregio and the Sestiere di Castello, serving as a major artery between the islands of the northern lagoon and the center of Venice. Completed in the late-16th c., the construction of this quay involved centuries of reclamation of the mudbanks to the north; palazzi and aristocratic homes were built here from the 17th c. onward, and yet it remained primarily an area filled with warehouses, workshops, and storage yards (wood-working was a major industry here, and later, marble-cutting became important as well, due to the proximity of the cemetery of the island of S. Michele).

Take *Calle del Fumo* (2 E6) and, turning right, you will enter *Campo Tiziano* in which stands the dignified home (n. 5182-83), built in 1527, where the painter Titian lived for 45 years, dying in 1576. Continue along the Calle del Fumo, and then along the *Calle Widman* and, at n. 5403, you will see the *Palazzo Widman*, later Palazzo Rezzonico Foscari (2 E-F6), a youthful project by Baldassarre Longhena (ca. 1625-30) with interiors richly decorated with stuccoes and frescoes. Overlooking the next "campo" is the church of **S. Canciano** (2 F5), dedicated to the brothers Canzio, Canziano, and Canzianilla, martyrs from Aquileia. Founded in ancient times (A.D. 864), it was given its modern appearance in 1550, and was partly renovated by Giorgio Massari around 1760. To the left of the facade, built by A. Gaspari (1705-1706), is the bell tower, rebuilt in 1532.

6 Castello

Castello – whose name probably derives from the presence of a fortress on the island of S. Pietro, possibly dating back as early as late-Roman times – occupies the entire eastern section of the city, roughly 186 hectares to the east of S. Marco and Cannaregio. Bounded on its other sides by the Lagoon and the Bacino di S. Marco, this is the most extensive "sestiere" in Venice, and it is made up of well-defined sections of the city, strongly shaded and flavored by the presence of the Arsenale, which sent forth the glorious fleets of fighting galleys of the Repubblica Serenissima. This enormous architectural complex created a sharp rift in the urban terrain, so to speak. The area to the west, closer to the economic and political focus of Rialto-S. Marco, densely built-up and developed around parishes dating back to the earliest foundation of the city, now has its chief commercial activities in connection with the development of tourism. In the other direction, an area extends, reaching to the easternmost fringes – S. Pietro and S. Elena, overlooking the broad spaces of the lagoon. Here are the largest public gardens in Venice, extending around a working-class neighborhood, which still has some of the lively social interaction that elsewhere in Venice has been irremediably lost. Along the south side, the two sections are linked by the Riva degli Schiavoni, which – with its various extensions – constitutes a splendid stroll along the Bacino di S. Marco.

Of fundamental importance in the context of the urbanistic and social development of the "sestiere" was the settlement, from the 12th c. onward – on part of the so-called Isole Gemine – of the economic and manufacturing center of the Arsenale. Its presence conditioned in a decisive manner the development of the adjacent urban sector; here skilled workers had their homes, service buildings were erected (granaries, ovens, and so on) along with other "allied industries," of which testimony can be found in the place names: Calle del Piombo (street of lead), Calle della Pégola (street of tar), Calle delle Vele (street of sails), and Calle delle Ancore (street of anchors).

The urban development of the "sestiere" continued throughout the Gothic era, along the courses of the main canals, where sizable Byzantine and Gothic courtyards were built. In the northernmost area, which expanded between the 13th and 16th c. on a series of reclaimed areas, large monastic compexes were built here by the orders of the Mendicant Friars, beginning around the middle of the 13th c. (the Dominican order of Ss. Giovanni e Paolo, i.e., Saints John and Paul, and the Franciscan order of S. Francesco della Vigna); they attracted a number of charitable institutions, giving the area a major religious and charitable imprint. The easternmost portion of the "sestiere" is strongly characterized by the great green patch of the Giardini Pubblici, the largest parkland in the city. In a sense these public gardens can be considered to be the most significant urbanistic creation of the Napoleonic era. The gardens were built at the orders of Napoleon in 1807, requiring the reclamation of the marshy Paludo S. Antonio and the demolition of a densely packed section of town. The new and spectacular route linking the Riva and the Giardini Pubblici

Rio Terrà Garibaldi lies at the heart of a lively neighborhood

led, moreover, to the creation of a new and ample artery, now the Via (or Rio) Terrà Garibaldi. The Napoleonic project of continuing the Riva along the Canale di S. Marco was not achieved until 1936, with the creation of the Riva dell'Impero – a Fascist name, referring to Italy's recent African conquests – now Riva dei Sette Martiri (Seven Martyrs; victims of a Nazi firing squad).
The outlying location of the "sestiere," which made it possible to clean up areas and to have new areas available for development and building, caused extensive construction of working-class housing, from the late 19th c. on; the most notable examples are – besides the enormous section of S. Elena – the sections of Via Garibaldi and Quintavalle (1909-10), the Celestia (1938-39), and lastly, the most recent constructions of S. Pietro di Castello (1961).

6.1 From Rialto to St. Mark's

From the area around the Ponte di Rialto you will pass through the Insula di S. Lio, following the busy Salizzada di S. Lio. At the mouth of that thoroughfare lies the small but popular Campo Sagrato di S. Lio, a church courtyard and square in one. From here, turn to the right, and you quickly come to the handsome 18th-c. church of the Fava. Nearly at the end of the Salizzada di S. Lio, the Gothic Calle del Paradiso leads to the enormous and active Campo di S. Maria Formosa, bounded by major monumental buildings. From this "campo," short side-trips will allow you to tour two noteworthy 16th-c. palazzi: Palazzo Grimani in Ruga Giuffa and Palazzo Querini-Stampalia, with its major collection of paintings. The main route leads on to Campo S. Marina and Fondamenta Sanudo. After the magnificent Renaissance creation of the church of S. Maria dei Miracoli, you will reach the area of Ss. Giovanni e Paolo, with its rich trove of religious and civic monuments. This "insula" (meaning "block," but also "island" originally) revolves around the huge "campo"; running through the center of the "insula" is the long pedestrian thoroughfare of Barbaria delle Tole, splitting the area in two; the area to the south tends to cluster around Byzantine courtyards, such as the charming Corte Botera. The area to the north, which developed between the 13th and 16th c., remains today the enormous complex of religious and charitable institutions that it was in origin: note the presence of the Ospedale Civile (city hospital) and the Casa di Riposo dell'Ospedaletto (a rest home). You will then follow a route that takes you past a number of Byzantine-Gothic centers (S. Giustina, S. Lorenzo, S. Severo, S. Giovanni in Oleo); then you will find yourself quite close to Piazza San Marco. Here you may choose to tour the former convent of S. Apollonia, the Lapidario Marciano (collection of inscriptions and epigraphs), or the noteworthy Museo Diocesano di Arte Sacra (collection of religious art).

Salizzada S. Lio (6 C2). This major thoroughfare is lined with shops; note, at numbers 5662 and 5691, two interesting 13th-c. Byzantine structures: double tower-houses with an arch linking them. At the mouth of the Salizzada lies the little *Campo S. Lio* (6 C2), where there is often a flower market, with the charming backdrop of the facade of the church of S. Lio, a 9th-c. *church* dedicated to St. Leo I the Great, a 5th-c. Latin Father ("Lio" is the Venetian version of his name). A late-16th-c. portal leads inside; the interior was rebuilt in 1619. Note the single central aisle, ending in three apsidal chapels; in the chapel on the right (*Cappella Gussoni*) there are exquisite Renaissance decorations by Pietro Lombardo and assistants. Luminous *frescoes* by Giandomenico Tiepolo (1783) decorate the flat ceiling; among the more notable paintings is the *St. James the Apostle** by Titian (1st altar on the left).

From Salizzada S. Lio you can easily reach the *Campo della Fava* (6 C2), bounded by the unfinished facade of the church of *S. Maria della Consolazione*, also known as *S. Maria della Fava*, begun to plans by A. Gaspari (1705-1715) and completed by G. Massari (1740-1753); Massari was also responsible for the design of the decorations and furnishings. At the various altars that punctuate the interior, note major paintings, such as *The Education of the Virgin*, a youthful work by G.B. Tiepolo, prior to 1733 (1st altar on the right) and an altar piece by G.B. Piazzetta depicting *The Virgin Mary and St. Philip Neri* (1727; 2nd altar on the left).
Facing the church you will see, across the "rio," the monumental late-Gothic *Palazzo Giustinian Faccanon* (ca. 1460; 6 C1), surmounted by a balustrade and grotesque statues, added in the 18th c.

Calle del Paradiso* (6 C2). Lined by two series of row-houses, with shops on the ground floor, and overhanging upper stories set on wooden buttresses, this street offers an interesting example of Gothic working-class architecture (beginning of the 15th c.,

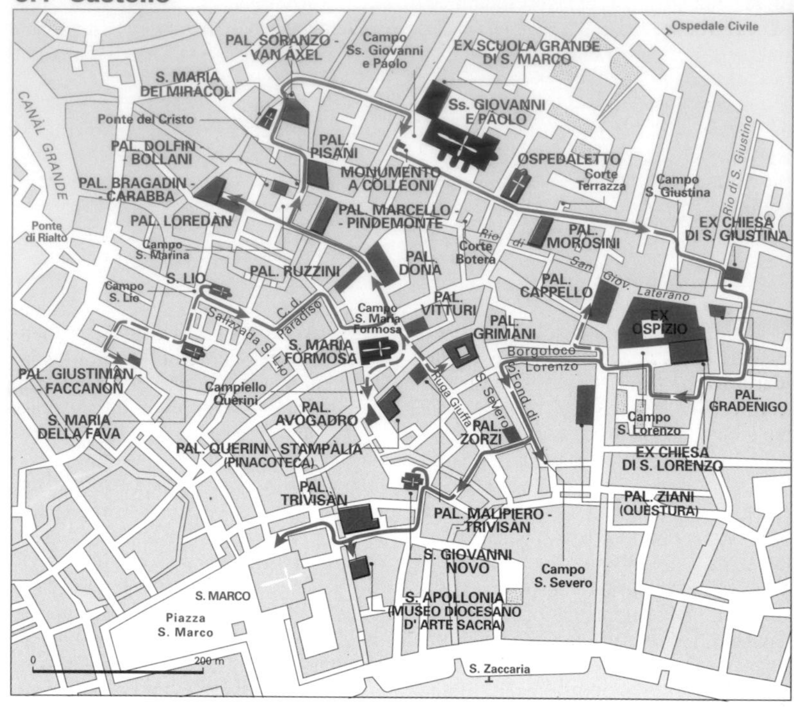

renovated in later centuries). Both ends of the street are crowned with Gothic arches: toward the Rio di S. Maria Formosa is the so-called *Arco del Paradiso*.

Campo S. Maria Formosa (6 C3). One of the largest and most charming squares in Venice, this "campo" was once the setting of renowned feasts and entertainments, bull-baiting, and theatrical performances; this was the civic center of an ancient quarter (founded in the 7th c.). It is still the site of a fine little market, and boasts crowded cafes. This plaza is broken into an interesting array of spaces by the unusual placement of the church; it is lined with noteworthy palazzi from various eras.

S. Maria Formosa* (6 C3). Traditionally said to have been founded in A.D. 639 by St. Magnus, bishop of Oderzo, to whom the Virgin appeared in the form of a beautiful woman (Latin, "formosa"); the church was rebuilt in 1175, and then rebuilt again, after 1492, by Mauro Codussi. Between the facade by Sansovino, overlooking the "rio," and the facade overlooking the "campo," both built between 1542 and 1604, at the personal expense of the Cappello family, note the Baroque bell tower, built between 1678 and 1688 to plans by Francesco Zucconi. Of particular interest is the cusp, which resembles a lighted candle dripping wax.

The interior, damaged by an Austrian bomb in 1916, was restored to the appearance given it by Codussi; this architect succeeded in interpreting the original, expansive Byzantine concept of space, in new, Renaissance terms of pure reason. Among the many artworks: note a remarkable *triptych* by Bartolomeo Vivarini (1473) in the 1st chapel on the right, and a polyptych by Palma the Elder, depicting *St. Barbara Surrounded by Saints* (ca. 1509), in the Cappella della Scuola dei Bombardieri.

Palazzo Grimani (Ruga Giuffa 4854; 6 C3). This palazzo is the result of thirty years' worth of work; completed in 1569, it was once renowned for the collections of art and archeology assembled there by Giovanni Cardinal Grimani, the patriarch of Aquileia, and by his heirs. Among these collections, the Greco-Roman collection, bequeathed to the Republic of Venice in 1593, was the core of the Museo Archeologico. The portal – attributed to Sanmicheli, and decorated with busts from the Roman era – leads into the monumental courtyard, in the traditional Central Italian style.

Palazzo Querini-Stampalia* (6 C3). Set in

the small and charming Campiello Querini-Stampalia along the Rio di S. Maria Formosa is the principal facade of the palazzo, following the curving line of the canal. Built around 1528 by the Querini family (the second name comes from the Greek island of Stampalia, which they held in fief from 1207 until 1522), the building has been the headquarters of the Fondazione Querini Stampalia (with a fine public Library and a noteworthy collection of art, or Pinacoteca). The foundation was established by a bequest by Count Giovanni Querini-Stampalia, the last surviving heir to the family. You enter the *Library* (2nd floor) across a slender metal bridge designed by the late Carlo Scarpa; this architect also brilliantly renovated the ground floor and garden (1959-63). The 3rd floor, lavishly decorated with stuccoes showing a transitional style from Rococo to Empire, and notable 18th-c. furnishings, houses the **Pinacoteca**, with a fine collection of paintings from the 14th to 18th c., by such artists as Catarino and Donato Veneziano, Palma the Younger, Luca Giordano, Giovanni Bellini, and Pietro Longhi.

Campo S. Marina (6 B2). Ever since the ancient church of S. Marina was demolished in 1820, this "campo" has been a purely residential space, with relatively unassuming buildings and architecture.

Continuing along the relatively short Ramo Bragadin you will reach the 15th-c. **Palazzo Bragadin Carabba**, restored by Michele Sanmicheli around 1542; note the facade overlooking the Rio dei Miracoli, visible from the Ponte del Teatro, with its Gothic-Renaissance transitional style.

From the Ponte del Cristo over the Rio di S. Marina (6 B2), part of a major waterway linking the Rialto area with the Arsenale, note the remarkable flamboyant Gothic structure of *Palazzo Pisani* (ca. 1460; 6 B2), in which the elements added in the 16th/17th c. (balconies, water gates, etc.) harmonize nicely with the overall Gothic structure. Facing this palazzo, at an angle, is the Baroque facade of *Palazzo Marcello-Pindemonte* (6 B2; entrance on Calle di Borgoloco).

Palazzo Soranzo Van Axel (6 B2). This late-Gothic palazzo was built in 1473-79, so as to create two independent aristocratic homes, with a double entrance, both from land and from the water, and two interior courtyards, each with an exterior stairway, well head, portico, and storehouse. The portal giving onto Fondamenta Sanudo is the only one in Venice that still has its original wooden doors and the 15th-c. door knocker. The Van Axel family were Flemish merchants originally from Axel near Ghent; they were made Venetian nobles in 1665.

S. Maria dei Miracoli* (6 B2). In the narrow Campo dei Miracoli, this small and isolated church, one of the first and most successful examples of Renaissance architecture in Venice, seems like a little jewel box, encrusted with exquisite polychrome marble. Built between 1481 and 1489 by Pietro Lombardo, with assistance from his sons, the church was meant to hold an image of the Virgin Mary painted in 1408, an image which in time had become an object of great veneration.
Inside, the same elegance can be seen in the marble facing, the barrel vault ceiling, with exquisite wooden coffering, painted by P.M. Pennacchi and assistants (1528), in the raised apse enclosed by a balustrade, adorned with sculptures by Tullio Lombardo. Above the entrance, note the "barco" (hanging choir), decorated with a *Virgin and Child* by Palma the Younger.

Campo of Ss. Giovanni e Paolo* (6 B3). The presence of the major Dominican structure of the church and convent of S. Zanipòlo (Venetian dialect for the proper Italian name, meaning Saints John and Paul) and the adjoining Scuola Grande di S. Marco, make this "campo" one of the most significant sites in Venice, in both social and architectural terms. It revolves around a central pivot: the bronze **equestrian monument to Bartolomeo Colleoni***, who was for 21 years a condottiere at the service of the Venetian Republic. This impressive Renaissance sculpture was modelled by Andrea Verrocchio (1481-1488) and cast, after Verrocchio's death, by Alessandro Leopardi, who also designed the tall marble pedestal. The statue stands in this "campo" because of the exceedingly loose interpretation that the Venetian Senate gave to the conditions of Colleoni's last will and testament. The condottiere had bequeathed his estate to the Serenissima providing that a statue of him be placed – contrary to Venetian law – "before St. Mark's." The well head dating from the early-16th c. in the center of the "campo" is another, lesser masterpiece of sculpture. Facing the southern facade of the church, note the 17th-c. *Palazzo Dandolo* (n. 6826) and a late-16th-c. *Palazzo Grimani* (numbers 6775-81).

The Campo of Ss. Giovanni e Paolo

Basilica dei Ss. Giovanni e Paolo* (S. Zanipòlo; 6 B3). From the middle of the 15th c., this church was the site of the solemn funerals of the doges; with the church of the Frari, it ranks as the most spectacular example of Venetian Gothic architecture, a Pantheon of Venice's greatest glory. Built by the Dominican order between 1246 and 1430, the church has an impressive terracotta facade, with a 14th-c. lower section, deep blind arcades containing burial urns, and a majestic portal with a pointed-arch arcade set on columns of Greek marble from Torcello, by Bartolomeo Bon (1459-1461). On the right side, note the protruding shapes of the numerous chapels that run up to the transept; at the end of the transept, with its huge Gothic window, stands the former Scuola di S. Orsola (it was for this institution that Vittore Carpaccio painted his famous series of nine canvases, depicting the life of St. Ursula, now in the Gallerie dell'Accademia. Note the splendid polygonal **apses***, with their tall trilobate windows, one of the most remarkable pieces of late-Gothic architecture from the mid-15th c.

The interior is surprisingly large (over 100 m. in length, and 32 m. in height); equally astonishing is the flood of light that culminates in the virtually transparent appearance of the main apse; there are three aisles, divided by round pillars. There are five apsidal chapels giving onto the transept. On the walls are a series of sepulchers, some of them of great artistic worth; for instance, note the *Monument to the Doge Pietro Mocenigo** (died 1476), by Pietro Lombardo (1476-81; counter-facade) and the *Monument to the Doge Andrea Vendramin** (died 1478), by Pietro and Tullio Lombardo, on the left wall of the presbytery. On the same wall, the Gothic *Monument to the Doge Marco Corner** (died 1368), is decorated with statues of Virgin Mary and Saints, by Giovanni Pisano. In the left aisle, note, among others, the *Monument to the Doge Tomaso Mocenigo* (died 1423), by Tuscan artists; also the *Monument to the Doge Nicolò Marcello* (died 1474), by Pietro Lombardo. Among the many chapels that line the right aisle, note the Gothic Cappella dell'Addolorata, to which lavish Baroque decoration was added around 1639; also, just before the transept, note the impressive Cappella di S. Domenico, by Andrea Tirali (1690-1716). On its carved gilt ceiling is the spectacular *St. Dominick in Glory**, a masterpiece by G.B. Piazzetta (1725-27). The large *window* with Gothic perforated fretwork in the right transept features exquisite stained glass, with figures of saints; among the artists who worked on this stained glass were G.A. Licinio, B. Vivarini, Cima da Conegliano, and G. Mocetto. From the left section you enter the Cappella del Rosario. A fire broke out in 1867 here, almost entirely destroying the impressive structure, which was built between 1582 and 1608 to plans by Alessandro Vittoria; it was restored in 1913 with major **canvases*** by Paolo Veronese, which were restored in 1992. Among the many paintings in this church, note: the polyptych of *St. Vin-*

*cent Ferrer**, a youthful work by Giovanni Bellini (ca. 1465), with the original wooden frame (2nd altar on the right); *Charity of St. Antony*, altar piece by Lorenzo Lotto (1542), set on the far wall of the right transept; and a *triptych* by Bartolomeo Vivarini (1473), beneath the 18th-c. organ by Gaetano Callido, in the left aisle.

Scuola Grande di S. Marco* (6 B3). Headquarters of the Confraternity of St. Mark, this structure was built by Pietro Lombardo, with assistance from his sons Antonio and Tullio, as well as from Giovanni Buora (1487-90); it was completed by Mauro Codussi (1490-95), who designed the unusual curving crown of the facade. The elegant marble facade is one of the most superb creations of the Venetian Renaissance; note the fine carving, the rhythmic composition of the circular fronts, and the interesting optical illusions of the false perspective in the four panels alongside the two doors, by P. and T. Lombardo. The portal is adorned with a rich porch, enclosing a lunette by Bartolomeo Bon (*St. Mark Venerated by His Confreres*, 1445). In the huge upper hall and in the adjoining Sala dell'Albergo (now a library, the Biblioteca dell'Ospedale), with a spectacular carved dark blue and gold coffered ceiling, by F. and B. da Faenza (1504), note works by Palma the Younger, D. Tintoretto, and G. Mansueti.

From the large ground-floor hall of the Scuola, you enter – through the far door – the *Ex-Convento dei Domenicani dei Ss. Giovanni e Paolo* (now the Ospedale Civile, or municipal hospital), rebuilt by Baldassare Longhena between 1660 and 1675, while maintaining the original floor plan of the 13th c., structured around two cloisters and a courtyard. In the long side of the former monastic dormitory, you can tour the Library, or Biblioteca, also built by Longhena (1670-74); note the carved wooden ceiling, by Giacomo Piazzetta (1682), decorated with three paintings by Federico Cervelli.

From the Campo Ss. Giovanni e Paolo, take Calle Bressana and Fondamenta Felzi (6 B3) to reach the small and charming **Corte Botera**; note the handsome Venetian-Byzantine portal with a carved arch illustrated with stories, Carolingian in style, as well as a portico, exterior staircase, and well head, typical features of private Venetian courtyards.

Barbaria delle Tole (6 B4). This is a long and lively thoroughfare linking the center of Venice with the easternmost sections of town; note the Baroque facade of the church of the Ospedaletto. A little further along, on the left, a "sotoportego" leads into the shady *Corte della Terrazza*, with the ruins of the Renaissance *Palazzo Magno* and a handsome well head, with mascarons and shields, from about 1480.

Ospedaletto (6 B4). The smallest of the four main Venetian hospitals was founded in 1527, following a very serious famine, to accommodate poor and elderly patients (it is still a rest home for the elderly). What survives of the original structure, aside from the church, includes the Sala da Musica, or music room, frescoed in 1776 by J. Guarana and A. Mengozzi-Colonna, where the young girls who lived in the institute would hold concerts. Overlooking the Barbaria delle Tole is the Baroque facade of the church of *S. Maria dei Derelitti* by Baldassare Longhena (1668-74), conceived as an impressive cenotaph for the client, Bartolomeo Carnioni, fairly dripping with decorative sculpture and architectural overhangs, sharply foreshortened to fit into the narrow "calle." The interior, rebuilt after 1662 under the supervision of Giuseppe Sardi and, later, by Longhena himself, has a single hall with a flat ceiling, frescoed by Giuseppe Cherubini (1907), containing numerous canvases from the Venetian early-17th and 18th c.

Campo S. Giustina (6 C5). This square lies at the intersection of two major waterways linking different sections of the city. Alongside the public bridges, a number of private bridges lead to important aristocratic palazzi located across the canals, such as the 17th-c. *Palazzo Gradenigo* (n. 2838); inside are 18th-/19th-c. stuccoes and decorations. The northern side of the "campo" is bounded by the facade of the former church of *S. Giustina*, repeatedly rebuilt and renovated between 1636 and 1640 by Baldassare Longhena; the notable facade survives, although it has been stripped of its sculptural decoration and top. Suppressed as a church in 1807, it now houses a high school, the Liceo Scientifico Benedetti.

Campo S. Lorenzo (6 C4). When the wing of the monastery that closed off this "campo" from the canal was demolished, it lost its quality of a secluded courtyard-"campo," dominated by the broad unfinished terracotta facade of the *church* of S. Lorenzo. Rebuilt between 1592 and 1602 to plans by Simone Sorella, the church in question has an intriguing structure: it is a large cubic space divided down the middle into two parts (one for the faithful and one for nuns) by three large arcades, with the central arcade filled by the colossal main altar with a double facade, a masterpiece by Girolamo Campagna (1615-18).

From the Ponte di S. Lorenzo you climb down into *Borgoloco S. Lorenzo* (6 C3-4), lined by interesting 17th-c. buildings.

Fondamenta S. Severo and Campo S. Severo (6 C3-4). Beyond the "rio" are the facades of such major monumental buildings as the Palazzo Grimani, mentioned above (6 C3), the Gothic *Palazzo Zorzi-Bon* and the Renaissance *Palazzo Zorzi* (6 C4), attributed to Mauro Codussi (ca. 1480). In the Campo S. Severo note the building of the Prigioni, a prison for political offenders, which remained in use until 1926; it is built on the site of a church demolished in 1829. At n. 4999 is the monumental entrance to the *Palazzo Priuli all'Osmarin* (6 D4), a noteworthy example of a late-14th-c. Gothic residence, with a line of windows and corner mullioned windows in the facade overlooking the Fondamenta dell'Osmarin.

S. Giovanni Novo, or S. Giovanni in Oleo (6 D3). Founded in 968 and rebuilt more than once, this church was given its current structure during the renovation done between 1751 and 1762 by Matteo Lucchesi, possibly to plans by Giorgio Massari. The interior, with two chapels on either side, has for some years had a permanent exhibit of paintings by Virgilio Guidi.

Museo Diocesano d'Arte Sacra, or Diocesan Museum of Religious Art (6 D3). Located in the former Benedictine convent of S. Apollonia (12th/13th c.), arranged around a small but lovely Romanesque cloister, this building was the subject of a thorough restoration in the Sixties; it now houses the Diocesan Museum, an Ecclesiastical Tribunal, and the *Lapidario Marciano*, with a major collection of architectural fragments of Roman and Byzantine origin, which were largely ornaments of the original Basilica di S. Marco (St. Mark's Cathedral); they were installed on the walls of the cloister in 1969. On the 2nd floor, the Diocesan Museum displays paintings, artistic objects, and religious furnishing, generally taken from churches in Venice no longer used for worship.

In Fondamenta S. Apollonia, the building at n. 4310, now the offices of the Jesurum company, which makes lace and embroideries, was the church of Ss. Filippo, Giacomo, e Apollonia, until 1806; inside – though it has been divided into two stories – it still has the original late-Gothic structure, with three aisles and apses. From the nearby Ponte della Canonica, you can admire the sumptuous Renaissance facade of *Palazzo Trevisan-Cappello* (6 D3), attributed to Bartolomeo Bon (early-15th c.).

6.2 The Rive, or Shoreside Quays, as far as Sant'Elena

From Piazza San Marco all the way to the great green patch of the Giardini Pubblici, you will walk through the full length of this "sestiere," skirting its southern boundary, the Riva degli Schiavoni, and the extensions of that "riva." This lengthy walk (1.5 km.), with fine panoramic views of the Bacino di S. Marco and the islands in the lagoon, which you can pick out one by one to the south, passes major architectural landmarks. From the "riva," two brief side-trips lead into the old quarters of S. Zaccaria and S. Giovanni in Bràgora, charming and secluded sections of the city. Continuing along the broad Riva dei Sette Martiri, where large ships often moor, you will reach the Giardini Pubblici, where the Venice Biennale (Biennale Internazionale d'Arte) is located. The Giardini Pubblici, or Public Gardens, are an interesting piece of urban renewal from Napoleonic times; they offer a chance to relax in a remarkably fine setting. The stroll then continues through the large Parco della Rimembranza (Memorial Park) on the Island of Sant'Elena, as far as the convent that once occupied a little islet all its own.

Riva degli Schiavoni* (6 E3-4-5). This is the most admirable stroll that you can take if you are interested in savoring the enchanting atmosphere of the lagoon without leaving the city; it runs along the "riva" – meaning 'shore' or 'embankment' – that, under different names, links San Marco with the Giardini Pubblici. This broad and lively route, jammed with the stands of souvenir vendors and with the easels of painters daubing stereotypical Venetian lagoonscapes, takes its name from the sailors of "Schiavonia," or "Slavonia," which corresponds to modern-day Dalmatia; those sailors would sell and buy, load and unload their cargo on this quay. Lined with the numerous landing-stages of the maritime public transportation that serves the city, islands, and the littoral strips, and dotted with major hotels and crowded cafes, the Riva degli Schiavoni is unquestionably a tourist attraction, especially the section closest to St. Mark's Square. The row of palazzi that overlooks it, even today, has a prevalently 19th-c. appearance, alongside a few major landmarks from earlier periods. From St. Mark's Square, after crossing the Ponte della Paglia (6 E3; here ships would unload the straw – "paglia" – used in the prisons and in the stables of Palazzo Ducale), from which you can see the famous Ponte dei Sospiri, or Bridge of Sighs, you will pass in front of the massive structure in Istrian stone of the *Palazzo delle Prigioni* (6 E3), the centuries-old prison of Venice, with a noble facade in the classical style, built between the second half of the 16th c. and the start of the 17th c. (A. Da Ponte and A. and T. Contin). Used as a prison until 1919, it now houses offices and an Artist's Association. Alongside it stands a massive, questionable building designed and built by the architect Vallot in 1947-48, an annex of the Hotel Danieli, one of the most prestigious in Venice. The Hotel Danieli proper occupies the building next door, the 15th-c. *Palazzo Dandolo* (6 E3) with interesting neo-Gothic interiors. In the next stretch of "riva," running in front of the 19th-c. Hotel Londra Palace, stands the impressive equestrian statue of Victor Emmanuel II (Ettore Ferrari; 1887). After the church of the Pietà (see below) and the Rio della Pietà, on the wall of the Gothic *Casa Navagero* (n. 4146; 6 E4) is a plaque commemorating the stays here of Petrarch and Boccaccio; actually, both stayed in Palazzo Molin dalle Due Torri, which was later incorporated into the adjoining Monastero del Santo Sepolcro. This monastery, established in 1475 near a hospice for pilgrims on their way to the Holy Land, was enlarged in the early-16th c., and then suppressed in 1806; it is now the headquarters of the Presidio Militare; it features a long and unadorned elevation, with an elegant central portal, by Jacopo Sansovino (1570). Shortly thereafter, at n. 4110, stands *Palazzo Gabrielli* (now Hotel Gabrielli-Sandwirth; 6 E5), dating from the late-14th c.

Short detours from the main route will take you to areas of considerable historic and artistic interest: the former convent complex of S. Zaccaria and the church of S. Giovanni in Bràgora on the Campo (for both, see below).

S. Maria della Visitazione or S. Maria della Pietà (6 E4). This church is part of the hospital of the Pietà, which was famous for the musical activity of the patients, under the direction of such great musicians as Antonio Vivaldi (known as the "Red Priest," for the color of his hair). Built between 1745 and 1760 to plans by Giorgio Massari, who also furnished the interior, the church comprises an elegant oval hall, conceived as a concert hall, with the ceiling decorated by a luminous fresco by G.B. Tiepolo (*Coronation of the Virgin Mary*, 1754-55) and a large entry atrium, which blocks off outside noise.

Campo S. Zaccaria (6 D3). Secluded and comfortably small, this "campo" was originally a private square that belonged to the convent of S. Zaccaria, served by one of two entryways, closed by large doors. The main entrance, from Campo S. Provolo, is marked by a lavish flamboyant-Gothic portal, with an exquisite high-relief carving in the lunette, (*Virgin Mary Enthroned, with Christ Child and Saints*, 1430) possibly by a Tuscan artist. The "campo" is dominated by the imposing facade of the church. To the north, it is closed off by elegant late-15th-c. arches, which once bounded the convent cemetery. A 16th-c. portal (n. 4693) marks the entrance to a former convent, the *Ex Monasterò delle Benedettine*, one of the richest and most prestigious in all Venice, where young women from the leading Venetian families, whose conduct was deemed to be unseemly, were persuaded to renounce the things of this world. The immense complex, now used as a barracks by the Carabinieri, still preserves the layout of the late-15th and early-16th c.

S. Zaccaria* (6 D4). The reconstruction of the existing Romanesque church (12th c.), begun by Antonio Gambello around 1440 with the new version of the apsidal area in flamboyant Gothic, was completed between 1483 and 1490 by Mauro Codussi, in distinctly Renaissance style. Codussi himself designed and built – on the polychrome marble base by Gambello, decorated with busts of Prophets (1470) – a new facade in white stone, surrounded by an arched triple crowning, typical of his architectural style. The interior, too, divided into three aisles by columns set on exceedingly tall plinths, is a fascinating blend of styles: the polygonal Gothic apse, and ambulatory with radiating

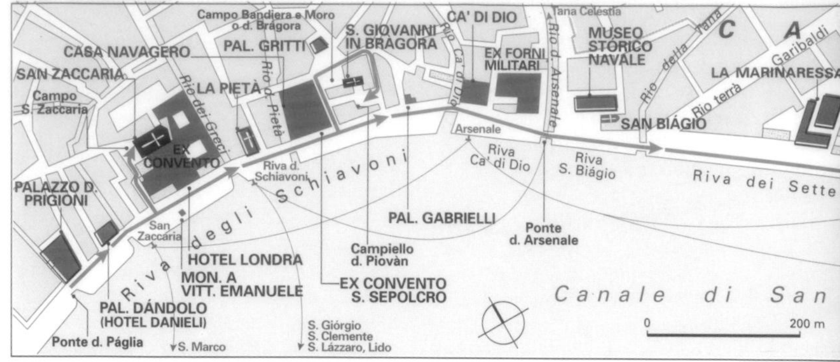

semicircular chapels, is adjoined harmoniously by the cross-vault ceilings, with hemispheric cupola and little domes along the ambulatory, typical signs of the work of Codussi. Covering the walls of the side-aisles are large 17th-c. canvases, recently cleaned and restored, but the most noteworthy painting is *The Virgin Mary, Enthroned, with Christ Child, an Angel Playing a Musical Instrument, and Saints**, an immense and renowned altar piece by Giovanni Bellini, dated 1505 (2nd altar on the left). From the left aisle, you enter the late-Renaissance Cappella di S. Atanasio, built from the nave of the original Gothic church, with paintings by J. Tintoretto (*Birth of John the Baptist*) and G.D. Tiepolo, and the rich carved and inlaid stalls of the choir of the nuns (1455-64). From the adjoining Cappella dell'Addolorata, you enter the Cappella di S. Tarasio, once part of the apsidal area of the Gothic church; note the *frescoed vaults** by Andrea del Castagno and Francesco da Faenza (1442), with three fine Gothic *polyptychs** by Antonio Vivarini and Giovanni d'Alemagna (1443).

The Church of S. Zaccaria

Campo Bandiera e Moro or Campo della Bràgora (6 D5). Situated at the edge of the busy pedestrian thoroughfares, partly lined with trees, and dotted with benches, this square offers a restful place to stop amidst a lovely city setting. This "campo" was the center of a settlement dating back before Venice was ruled by a doge. Alongside the church stands the former *Scuola di S. Giovanni Battista*, an elegant Baroque building dating from 1716. The northern side of the "campo" is dominated by the Gothic facade of *Palazzo Gritti*, later Palazzo Morosini e Badoer, built at the end of the 14th c., with a five-light mullioned window encrusted with polychrome marble and with broad stretches of wall that were once covered with frescoes.

S. Giovanni in Bràgora* (6 D-E5). The existing structure dates from the reconstruction done between 1475 and 1505. On the late-Gothic facade, in brick, note a plaque that commemorates the baptism here in 1678 of Antonio Vivaldi. A restoration in 1925 returned the interior – which had been rebuilt in the 18th c. – to the original Gothic style and the three-aisle structure, covered by a wooden truss roof, ending in apsidal chapels. The central apsidal chapel, with vault decorated with stuccoes by Alessandro Vittoria (1596), features an exquisite panel by Cima da Conegliano depicting the *Baptism of Jesus** (1494); on the right wall, *Last Supper* by Paris Bordon. Two major triptychs: *Saints Andrew, Jerome, and Martin* by F. Bissolo and *Virgin Mary Enthroned, between St. Andrew and St. John the Baptist** by Bartolomeo Vivarini (1478; undergoing restoration) are located in the

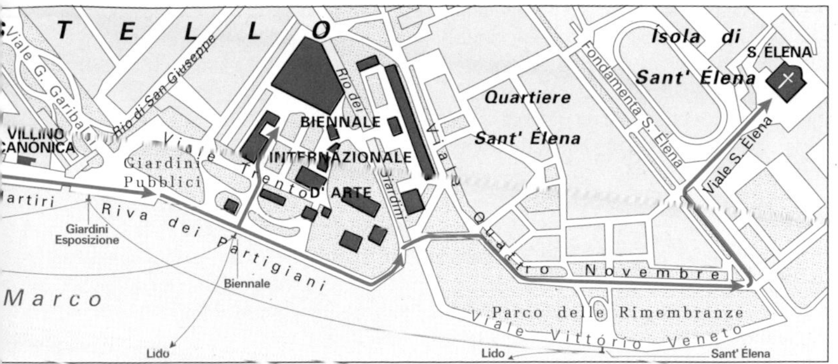

right aisle. On the walls of the same aisle, also note various paintings by Alvise Vivarini: *Head of the Redeemer* (1493) and *Virgin Mary, Praying, with the Christ Child* (1490) in the left aisle; *Christ Risen** in the right aisle. In the same aisle, note another painting by Cima da Conegliano, depicting *Helena and Constantine* (1502).

Between the Campo della Bràgora and the lively Riva degli Schiavoni, the tranquil and distinctive *Campiello del Piovan* is bounded by a group of 16th-c. row houses (n. 3752-56) and by the late-17th-c. *Palazzo Tamagnini-Massari*, where the architect Giorgio Massari lived (and died, in 1766). In the recess facing the side entrance to the church, note the 16th-c. well head, with an uncommon square shape, and with an image in relief of the saint.

Riva Ca' di Dio (6 E5). This embankment takes its name from the enormous building of the Ca' di Dio, built in the 13th c. as a hospice for pilgrims, and later as a refuge for women fallen into poverty; it was rebuilt after 1545 under the supervision of J. Sansovino with subsequent interventions by B. Longhena and B. Maccaruzzi. The complex, now used as a home for the elderly, features a notable elevation overlooking the Rio di S. Martino, punctuated by tall chimneys.
In the interior church, note fine 17th-/18th-c. canvases.
A little further along, two buildings overlook the "riva" (n. 2181 and n. 2178-80) once the site of the Military Bread Ovens and Bread Storehouse for the Venetian Fleet: the ovens (Forni Militari) date from 1473, and have a handsome portal, a terracotta frieze, and dense crenelation; the storehouse (Deposito), rebuilt in 1596, has a portal decorated with a pediment with the crest of the doge Marino Grimani, surmounted by a figure of Justice.

Riva San Biagio (6 F6). From the Ponte dell'Arsenale, built in 1936 to replace the 19th-c. iron bridge, you can walk down into the *Campo S. Biagio*, bounded to the north by the ancient Granai (Granaries), now the Museo Storico Navale (see below) and, to the east, by the church of *S. Biagio ai Forni* (6 F6). Founded in 1052, this church was given its present structure – with a single rectangular nave and square presbytery – in the reconstruction in 1749-54, to plans attributed variously to F. Bognolo and F. Rossi. The building was then placed in a block of residential buildings; thus, the unfinished facade has an unusual feature: four stories of windows. Note the Cappella della Marina Militare (1817).

Museo Storico Navale (6 F6). Set up in a fairly bare building dating from the end of the 16th c., which was once used as a granary for the Venetian Republic and as a storehouse for hardtack for the Navy, this historical naval museum has a huge collection of memorabilia, models, trophies, engravings, and relief maps, concerning navies of bygone times (especially the Venetian Navy), and the Italian Navy, or Marina Militare Italiana. In the many halls are displayed, among other items, the model of the Bucintoro (hall 17), the splendid galley used by the doge during the ceremony of the Wedding with the Sea, which took place on the day of the Feast of the Ascension, a large model of a 16th-c. Venetian galeass (hall 15), models of Venetian frigates and ships of the 18th c., as well as models of various sorts of boats used in fishing and shipping in the Venetian Lagoon, and insignia, standard, banners, and pilot's books.

In the nearby Fondamenta della Madonna (6 E6), the Sala Navi, a separate section of the Museo Storico Navale, is a rare and fascinating museum of real historic vessels (see Arsenale).

Riva dei Sette Martiri (11 B-C1-2). The seven martyrs of the name were Venetians, shot by Nazi soldiers in 1944. The broad quay, built in 1936 by covering over an area that for centuries had been used for "squeri," is now used for the docking of large cargo ships. Overlooking it is the interesting complex of the *Marinaressa*, containing working-class homes, assigned free of charge to sailors who had performed conspicuous services to the Venetian Republic. The central building, erected in 1645, is marked by large vaults in line with the inland "calli," running along the three rear buildings, which date from the late-15th c. A short way further along (n. 1364 A) the Neo-Renaissance *Villino Canonica* has a refined elevation, covered with a minute decoration in polychrome marble and terracotta. It was built in 1911 by the sculptor Pietro Canonica, as a home-qua-museum, and later donated to the Consiglio Nazionale delle Ricerche (National Research Council).

Giardini Pubblici (11 C2-3; D2-3). The only city-sized park in Venice was built under Napoleon, to plans by Giannantonio Selva, and involved the demolition of a crowded complex of religious buildings as well as the filling in and covering over of a good stretch of the Rio di Castello, now called the Rio Terrà Garibaldi, to create the new and spectacular route linking the "riva" and the gardens themselves. All that survives of the original Neo-Classical Italian-style gardens is the layout of the main walkways: the entire park was renovated around the mid-19th c., and was transformed into an English-style garden, better suited to the Romantic sensibility. At the end of the 19th c. the structure of the Biennale d'Arte was erected. Among the greenery, note the numerous 18th-c. garden statues and the elegant 16th-c. arch, which once marked the entrance to the Cappella Lando in the church of S. Antonio Abate; it was destroyed to make way for the gardens. Of the many

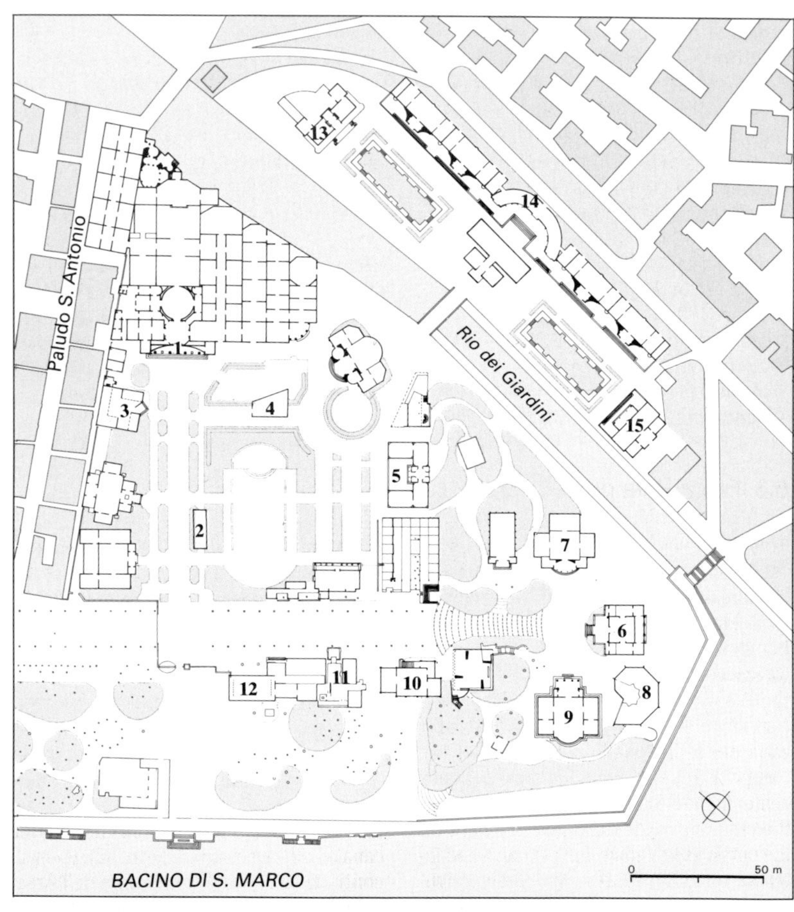

Giardini Pubblici: Pavilions of the Biennale

commemorative monuments present in this area, the most noteworthy one is certainly the *Monumento alla Partigiana Veneta*, a monument to the Venetian Female Resistance Fighter, designed by Carlo Scarpa, with a bronze statue by Augusto Murer, half submerged in the waters of the lagoon, along the Riva dei Partigiani.

Biennale Internazionale d'Arte (11 D3). Established in 1895 by the mayor of Venice, Riccardo Selvatico, this world-renowned biennial festival of painting, sculpture, graphics, and the decorative arts enjoys the participation of artists from many nations. Inside the main entrance gate (C. Scarpa, 1952) a tree-lined boulevard leads to the Italian Pavilion, or *Padiglione Italia* (map on page 92; 1), the first to be built, enlarged repeatedly over time (it is slated for demolition; a new pavilion is to be designed and built). Along the boulevard, among other pavilions, is the new *Padiglione del Libro* (2), or Pavilion of Books, by J. Stirling (1991), which takes its inspiration from shipbuilding, and the *Padiglione di Olanda* (Dutch Pavilion; G.T. Rietveld 1954; 3) and *Padiglione di Finlandia* (Finnish Pavilion; A. Aalto, 1956; 4). To the right, set somewhat back, is the Neo-Classical *Padiglione USA* (American Pavilion; 5) by W.A. Delano and C.H. Aldrich (1930). Along a second avenue, which ends with the *Padiglione della Gran Bretagna* (6), or Pavilion of Great Britain, by E.A. Rickards (1909), are the pavilions of *France* (7) by F. Finzi (1912); *Canada* (8), designed in 1957-58 by the Gruppo BBPR of Milan, *Germany* (9), rebuilt in 1937-38 by E. Halger; *USSR* (10) by A. Scusev (1914); *Venezuela* (11) by C. Scarpa (1954-56), and *Switzerland* (12) by Bruno Giacometti (1952). In the area located on the other side of the Rio dei Giardini are the pavilions of: *Austria* (13), by J. Hoffmann and R. Kramreiter (1933-34), with a courtyard enlarged by Hoffmann in 1954; *Venice, Poland, Egypt, Yugoslavia, Romania* (Brenno Del Giudice, 1931-32; 14), and *Greece* (Papandreou, 1934; 15).

Isola di Sant'Elena (11 D-F6). Until the last quarter of the 19th c., this was nothing but a small islet, entirely occupied by a church and convent, separated from the city by a broad arm of the Lagoon.

The modern-day size and shape are the result of a major reclamation project undertaken from 1923, with the construction of the Quarter of Sant'Elena and the vast Parco delle Rimembranze, which marks the lagoon shore, facing the Giardini. The church of *S. Elena* (11 E6), founded in 1175 and rebuilt after 1439, became property of the state in 1806 and was transformed into a military granary and mill; rescued by the Servi di Maria and restored, it was reopened as a house of worship in 1929, the parish church of the new quarter. The terracotta facade is decorated with a Renaissance portal with a *sculptural group* by Antonio Rizzo (ca. 1470). Near the apsidal area, note the outsized campanile, built by Ferdinando Forlati in 1958 to replace the 16th-c. bell tower, which had been demolished. In the stark nave, ending in a polygonal apse with tall Gothic windows, note on the right the chapels of S. Elena and Giustinian (St. Helena and Justinian), in late-Gothic style, from the mid-15th c., and, on the left of the main altar, the Renaissance chapel of S. Francesca Romana, from the late-15th c.

The adjacent convent still preserves a charming cloister (15th c.).

6.3 From Riva degli Schiavoni to San Giuseppe di Castello

This route runs from west to east across the "sestiere," through the inland quarters usually forsaken by tourists. In the area closest to S. Marco you will find two neighborhoods with historic ties to the two largest foreign communities in Renaissance Venice: the "Greci" (or Greeks) and the "Schiavoni" (or Slavs). Take Calle dei Furlani and Salizzada de le Gate, and you will reach the Campo di S. Francesco della Vigna, a major center in the Renaissance reconstruction of the city. The route runs through areas on the outskirts of Venice, full of charm and interest, once the centers of a lively neighborhood that grew up around the Arsenale, with all the various allied industries and services, and the homes of the workers in the shipyards. After running past the church of S. Martino, the route skirts the high walls, surrounded by canals, that gird the enormous ancient shipyards, from which the mighty fleets of the Venetian Republic once sailed out to rule the Mediterranean.

After the Campo dell'Arsenale, onto which the imposing entrance portal opens (though the Arsenale is closed to the public, and you can only see a part of it from the interior canale with the circular line n. 52), you will continue along the Fondamenta dell'Arsenale and then along the Campo della Tana and the Fondamenta della Tana, bounded

6.3 Castello

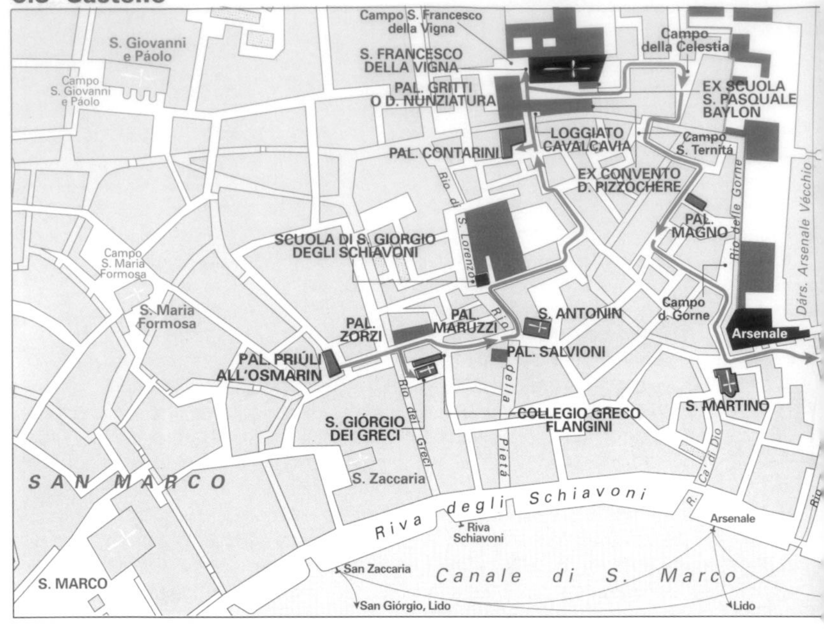

by the long elevation of the Corderie. Rio Terrà Garibaldi, built under Napoleon when a stretch of the Rio di Castello was filled in and covered over, is the center of a lively and sociable working-class quarter. From here, cross the lovely Campo Ruga, and you will reach the easternmost section of the "sestiere," the lovely and quiet Isola di S. Pietro, considered to be the original center of Venice before the doges. Turning onto Fondamenta S. Anna and continuing through the 16th-c. section of Secco Marina and the convent complex of S. Giuseppe, you will reach the Riva dei Partigiani; from here, you can take public transportation back into the city center.

S. Giorgio dei Greci (6 D4). A fretwork architectural screen stands between the "rio" and the complex of the Greek-Orthodox community of Venice, the largest community of outsiders in Venice during the Renaissance. The land was purchased in 1526; the first building to be erected was, in the 16th c., the church (by S. Lombardo and G.A. Chiona), a harmonious and majestic rectangular hall, richly adorned with paintings and Byzantine icons, separated from the three-apse presbytery by a marble iconostasis, adorned with late-Byzantine paintings with gold backgrounds. Alongside the graceful facade, in the style of Sansovino, stands an elegant campanile, which has begun to lean considerably since its construction (by Bernardo Ongarin under the supervision of Simone Sorella; 1587-92). The other buildings in the community, built in the second half of the 17th c. under the supervision of Baldassarre Longhena, now contain such cultural institutions as the Istituto Ellenico di Studi Bizantini e Postbizantini (Hellenic Institute of Byzantine and Post-Byzantine Studies), in the Collegio Flangini (n. 3412) and, in the Scuola di S. Nicolò dei Greci, the *Museo dei Dipinti Sacri Bizantini*, with collections of Byzantine and post-Byzantine icons, sacred furnishings, and other religious objects; on the right of the church is the *Scuoletta Greca*, a small, elegant building, also by Longhena.

S. Antonin (6 D5). Closed as a house of worship for many years and now undergoing restoration, this church was founded in the 7th c. and rebuilt by Baldassarre Longhena between 1637 and 1680, with the transformation of the existing three-aisle structure (12th/13th c.) into a single-aisle structure, while preserving the 16th-c. Cappella di S. Saba. The unfinished facade, also by Longhena, is flanked by an 18th-c. bell tower.

Scuola di S. Giorgio degli Schiavoni* (6 C5). The Confraternita dei Dalmati (Schiavoni; a confraternity originally from Dalmatia, or Slovenia) founded this institution in the 15th c., dedicating it to St. George and

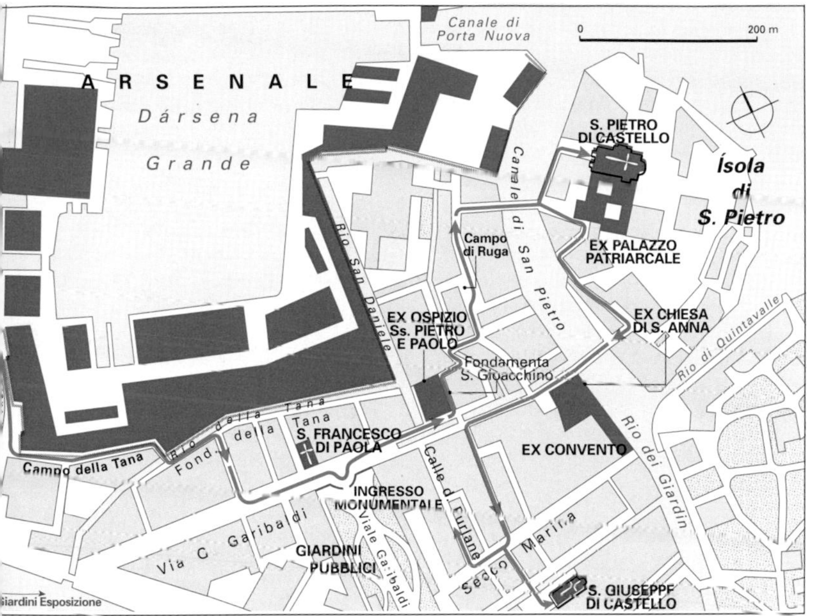

St. Trifone; it marks the end of the Fondamenta dei Furlani with its lively facade inspired by the style of Sansovino (1551). In a special exception to the Napoleonic decree of suppression, this was one of the few religious institutions allowed to preserve its artistic estate, comprising, among other things, a major series of paintings by Vittore Carpaccio, done between 1501 and 1511, including an exquisite *St. George Killing the Dragon**, the *Vocation of St. Matthew** and the *Vision of St. Augustine**; this last painting is of particular interest because it offers a detailed depiction of the interior of a 15th-c. study. On the upper floor, the Sala dell'Albergo is decorated with wooden altar frontals and paintings from the first half of the 17th c.

To the right of the Scuola lies the *Corte di S. Giovanni di Malta*, a courtyard bounded by the former hospital of S. Caterina and the church of S. Giovanni dei Cavalleri di Malta (St. John of the Knights of Malta), a complex founded between the 11th and 12th c., enlarged in the 14th c., and rebuilt between 1565 and the end of the 16th c.

Palazzo Contarini della Porta di Ferro (6 C5). A *Virgin Mary with Christ Child* by Giuseppe Torretti (1716) marks the corner of the wall enclosing this palazzo, whose name recalls the decorations in wrought iron (removed in 1839) that once adorned the doors in the main entrance ("Porta di Ferro" means "iron door"). From the portal, surmounted by a splendid Venetian-Byzantine lunette (first half of the 13th c.) which encloses a majestic 14th-c. Angel Bearing a Scroll, you can enter the charming inner courtyard where you can still see the open-air staircase, in poor condition, similar to the stairway in the Ca' d'Oro, and like that staircase, attributed to Matteo Raverti (1st half of the 15th c.).

Campo S. Francesco della Vigna (6 B5). This articulated urban space, dominated by the 16th-c. church, took on its current conformation in the 2nd quarter of the 16th c., in conjunction with the rebuilding of Piazza S. Marco. The same doge promoted both projects (Andrea Gritti); the same architect worked on both (Jacopo Sansovino); and both sites are linked to the cult of the city's patron saint (in fact, according to an exceedingly ancient tradition, St. Mark landed here, on his way back from Aquileia, and was greeted by the angel with the words *Pax tibi Marce Evangelista meus*). The "campo" is entirely bounded by buildings of particular architectural and historical interest: the *Convento dei Minori Osservanti* (to the left of the church), largely dates from around 1450. On the opposite front, note the former *Palazzo della Nunziatura*, possibly built by the Scarpagnino for the Doge Gritti; in 1586 it was purchased by the Venetian

Republic and donated to Pope Sixtus V as a residence for the apostolic legate or nuncio. A monumental 19th-c. loggia-overpass (A. Pigazzi) joins the palazzo with the Ex-Convento delle Pizzocchere, founded in the 15th c. Lastly, at the corner of the church, is the simple but elegant 17th-c. elevation of the former *Scuola di S. Pasquale Baylon*.

S. Francesco della Vigna* (6 C5). The name comes from the enormous vineyard ("vigna"), bequeathed in 1253 by Marco Ziani (son of the doge Pietro), where the early-Gothic church of the Franciscans was built in 1300, by Marino da Pisa. With the patronage of the doge Andrea Gritti and under the supervision of the priest Francesco Zorzi, the church was rebuilt after 1534 to plans by Jacopo Sansovino, and completed by Andrea Palladio. The enormous facade was designed and built by Palladio between 1564 and 1570. Behind it stands the cusped campanile, similar to the bell tower of St. Mark, and one of the tallest in Venice, under construction as early as 1543. The interior, built to a Latin-cross plan, with a single large nave, side chapels, and a deep presbytery, preserves the classical flavor of the original design by Sansovino, who uses an austere Tuscan style here. The Cappella Giustiniani, to the left of the presbytery, is decorated with a major series of sculptures by Pietro Lombardo and pupils (1495-1510); in the presbytery, note the *funerary monuments of the Doge Andrea Gritti* and members of his entourage, pieces of elegant and sober architectural composition (possibly by Jacopo Sansovino), clear indications of the way in which this church had become a dogal ("ducal" i.e., of the doge) pantheon. The church also contains other major paintings, including the large panel by Fra' Antonio da Negroponte (ca. 1470) depicting the *Virgin Mary Enthroned, Adoring the Christ Child and Glorifying Angels** (1st altar in the right transept) and a *Sacred Conversation* by Paolo Veronese (ca. 1551) in the 5th chapel on the left. From the left transept, you can enter the Cappella Santa, on the altar of which is a notable panel by Giovanni Bellini depicting the *Virgin Mary with Christ Child and Saints** (1507).

Campo della Celestia and Campo di S. Ternità (6 C6). Set on the outskirts of town, and fairly secluded, this area is charming, though it has lost the lively social atmosphere it must once have had.
Overlooking the Campo della Celestia is the former *Convento delle Monache Cistercensi* (n. 2737 F), or Convent of the Cistercian Nuns, in a state of sad neglect; the building is structured around a porticoed cloister that clearly shows the influence of Palladio. The complex is now occupied by private homes and the Archivio Storico Comunale (the Venetian historical archives, with considerable documentation on the history of the city from the beginning of the 19th c).
The neighboring Campo S. Ternità is still quite charming, though it has lost its main landmarks (the ancient church and the Venetian-Byzantine bell tower), demolished in the 19th c.

Casa Magno (6 C6). A wall with Gothic crenelation surrounds the courtyard, with its distinctive exterior staircase and well head; this is one of the most interesting and complete examples of an aristocratic Venetian-Gothic home of the second half of the 14th c., although it has been somewhat modified.

Campo delle Gorne (6 D6). Silent and secluded, this elongated triangular "campo" has the Rio delle Gorne running along its longest side.

S. Martino (6 D-E6; 7 D-E1). What you now see is the reconstruction begun around 1540 by Jacopo Sansovino, with a square central space, surrounded on all sides by short architectural arms, and by the somewhat deeper presbytery. The facade, rebuilt in the 19th c., preserves the original portal by Sansovino; nearby, note the lion's-mouth slot in which letters could be placed, denouncing blasphemers. To the right, note the early-15th-c. bas-relief depicting *St. Martin and the Poor Man*.
The interior, with simple Renaissance lines, and with Baroque and late-Baroque decorations, is made to seem more spacious by the remarkable ceiling fresco by Jacopo Guarana (*Glory of St. Martin*), with perspective by Domenico Bruni.

Arsenale (7 D1). A high walled perimeter surrounded by natural and manmade canals marks this enormous complex of shipyards, workshops, and storehouses; here, Venice built and maintained its fleet, the foundation of the wealth, power, and military might of the Serenissima. From the earliest nucleus, established in 1104 (or, according to the most recent studies, at the beginning of the 13th c.), through a process of development that lasted for centuries, the complex grew to occupy some 46 hectares of the eastern sector of the city. Now underuti-

lized by the Marina Militare, or Italian navy, and largely in a sad state of neglect, the complex has been awaiting a new function for years.
The public is not admitted, and only part of this area can be seen at all, by taking the Circular Line n. 52, a vaporetto that runs around Venice.
The landward entrance is marked by the splendid *portal** built in 1460 (map on page 96; 1), considered to be the earliest piece of Renaissance architecture in Venice, designed as a triumphal arch with an attic decorated with a mighty Lion of St. Mark, attributed to Bartolomeo Bon. In 1692-94 the little entry bridge was transformed by Alessandro Tremignon into a terrace surrounded by an iron fence, and dotted with Baroque allegorical statues, and on either side (1692) two colossal marble lions, taken as booty in war by Francesco Morosini: the one on the left comes from the Piraeus, and bears legends engraved in runes; of the two other, smaller lions, the one on the left, from the island of Delos, seems to be an archaic Greek sculpture from the 6th c. B.C. The repoussé bronze doors were made in 1694 to commemorate the victories of Francesco Morosini; also erected in his honor is the flagstaff in the center of the "campo," cast in bronze by Giovanni Francesco Alberghetti (1693). To the right of the portal, note the bronze bust of Dante Alighieri, which commemorates the visit that the great poet paid to the Arsenale as an envoy of Guido da Polenta; Dante immortalized that visit in the Canto XXI of *Inferno*, referring to the "sticky pitch boiled in the Venetian Arsenale."
The watergate is flanked by towers (2), built in 1686. The area of the original structure, called the Arsenale Vecchio, features – along the Darsena and its extension, the Rio delle Galeazze – buildings of considerable historical and architectural interest; you can see them by taking the Linea Circolare of the vaporetto n. 52: the building of the Bucintoro (16th c.; 3), where the doge's spectacular galley was stored (only the "arsenalotti," or workers in the Arsenale, could row the galley, or Bucintoro, during public cerimonies); two fine and well-preserved boat-houses (1560) and the long building of the Squadratori (4), by Giovanni Scalfarotto (1st half of the 18th c.), used in the shaping of the ship's ribbing. On either side of the large opening made in 1964 to allow public water transportation to pass through, note the great 16th-c. sheds erected for the construction of galleasses (5), large three-masted, lateen rigged fighting galleys, used in the Mediterranean from

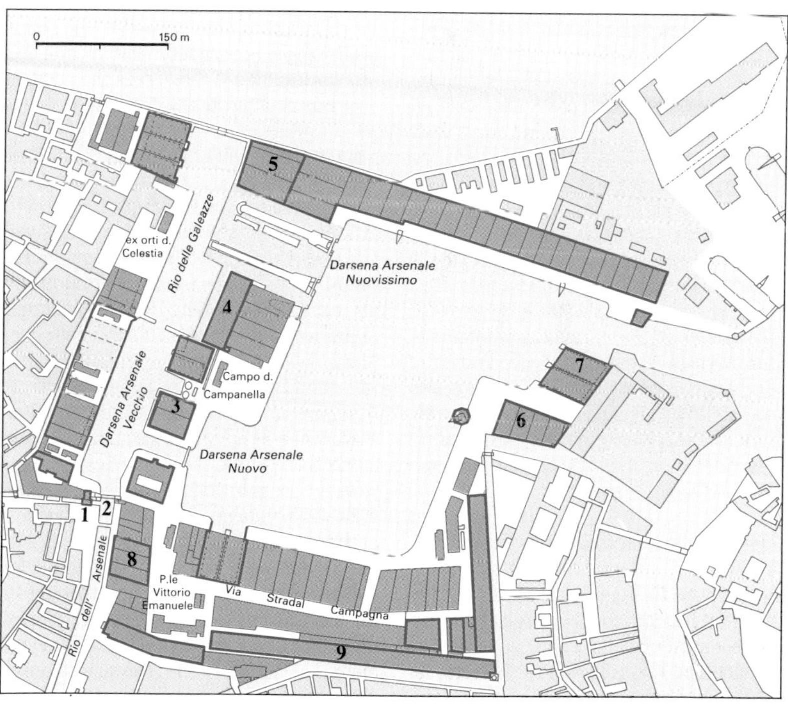

The Arsenale: plan

The Porta dell'Arsenale

the 15th to the 18th c. In the area around the Darsena Grande (Arsenale Nuovo and Arsenale Nuovissimo; this was the area dating from the 14th-/15th-c. expansion), note the major 16th-c. buildings (6), including two enormous wet-docks called the Gaggiandre (7), built in 1568-73 to plans attributed to Jacopo Sansovino. The Officina Remi (8) has for the past several years had an interesting collection of historic ships, a detached section of the Museo Storico Navale; note the remarkable interiors of the three huge 16th-c. sheds. Along the south side of the area, the Corderie della Tana (9) extend over a length of 316 m.; they were built in 1303 and rebuilt from 1579 to 1585 by Antonio Da Ponte. Used as storehouses for the hemp used in the manufacture of ropes, hawsers, and cables (Italian, "gòmene"), they take their name from the city of Tana on the river Tanai, now the Don, in Russia, whence hemp was imported. There is a separate entrance from Campo della Tana (n. 2196 C); they are now used for temporary exhibitions.

Campo and Fondamenta della Tana (7 E2-3; 11 B1-2). The entire left side of the "campo" is enclosed by the long structures of the Fonderie and the Corderie, while on the right a portal (n. 2157) with the Cicogna crest (the family name literally means "stork") and the date 1589 marks the entrance to the former *Casa dei Visdomini alla Tana* (magistrates). Next, you will reach the Fondamenta della Tana, a lovely part of Venice, with the long line of the "rio" bounded by the side of the Corderie and the massive structures of the towers that stand at the foot and the head of that canal.

Via Garibaldi (7 F2-3; 11 B1-2). At the heart of a working-class quarter that maintains intact its lively social fabric, this is the largest thoroughfare in all of Venice, and is always crowded, due to the presence of a popular neighborhood market. It was built in 1808 by covering over part of the Rio di Castello, so as to create a new and impressive pedestrian walkway leading to the Napoleonic Giardini Pubblici (public gardens), with a monumental entrance designed by Giannantonio Selva. Note the *monument to Garibaldi* (A. Benvenuti, 1885). Almost directly across from the entrance to the Giardini Pubblici is the church of *S. Francesco di Paola*, built by the Frati Minimi from 1588 on; the interior, heavily renovated in the 18th c., has a rectangular hall, with a noteworthy "barco" (hanging choir chancel) which stretches from the interior elevation of the facade along the sides of the church, extending over the side chapels. In this church, note paintings by Palma the

Younger, G. Contarini, J. Marieschi, and others.
Extending along the route of the "rio terrà," the easternmost stretch of the Rio di Castello (now Rio di S. Anna) is still uncovered, flanked by the Fondamenta di S. Anna (on the right) and the Fondamenta di S. Gioacchino (on the left). Overlooking this quay is, at n. 452-54, the entrance to the former *Ospizio dei Ss. Pietro e Paolo*, with a portal with 14th-c. relief, in the nearby Calle S. Gioacchino.

Campo di Ruga S. Lorenzo Giustiniani (11 A3). Center of a neighborhood founded in early times (10th c.), this lovely square is bounded by interesting examples of lesser architecture; note the two small 17th-c. "palazzetti" that echo the design of the aristocratic homes.

Isola di San Pietro (11 A 4-5). Secluded and charming, at the easternmost extremity of the city, this island was almost certainly the first part of the entire city to be inhabited (possibly at the end of the 6th c.). In ancient times it was called Olivolo (either for its olive-like shape, or else for the presence of an olive grove); it was most likely the site, in late-Roman times, of a fortress or castle (in Italian, "castello"; hence the name of the "sestiere"). Between the 8th c. and 1807 this was the center of religious power in Venice. The *campo*, looking out over the broad Canale di S. Pietro and covered with grass, is a silent and timeless corner of the city, lying in the shadow of the solitary, slightly leaning Renaissance bell tower, rebuilt by Mauro Codussi between 1482 and 1490. Alongside the badly run-down former Palazzo Patriarcale (late-16th c.), now subdivided into homes, stands the church of **S. Pietro di Castello** (11 A4), the bishopric from A.D. 775 until 1451, and then the patriarchate until 1807, when power and prestige shifted to the Basilica di S. Marco (St. Mark's cathedral). Built at the turn of the 11th c. and repeatedly rebuilt in later centuries, it was given its current appearance between the end of the 16th c. and the beginning of the 17th c., when the monumental facade was also built (1594-96), the execution of an earlier design by Andrea Palladio. In the vast and well-lit interior – which was rebuilt in mannered Palladian style by Girolamo Grapiglia by 1619 and 1621 – note the Baroque Cappella Vendramin, built by Baldassarre Longhena in 1663 (left transept) and the Cappella Lando, a pointed-arch construction (1425), part of the existing church.

Sant'Anna (11 B3). Since 1867 this former convent has housed the Ospedale della Marina Militare (navy hospital), and is now in a state of acute neglect; the entire complex was recently deeded to the city government. In accordance with a project to use it for living quarters and other services for the quarter, in the near future, the former convent and the 17th-c. church (F. Contin), now used as a warehouse, should be restored.

Secco Marina (11 C3). This quarter, configured in parallel blocks separated by "calli-corti," is one of the most notable examples of 16th-c. Venetian urban planning. In the nearby *Calle delle Furlane*, the massive chimney pots that distinguish the low 17th-c. houses may derive from the architectural traditions of the Friulians, who originally lived in this area.

S. Giuseppe di Castello (11 C3). Set at an angle between the picturesque Rio di S. Giuseppe and the little church-courtyard ("campo sagrato"), this church, founded by decree of the Senato in 1512, has a simple facade adorned by a noteworthy portal, with a relief by Giulio del Moro (*Adoration of the Magi*; 2nd half of the 16th c.). The interior has a rectangular nave, with a presbytery flanked by two chapels, and a broad flat ceiling decorated with frescoes by Pietro Ricchi depicting *St. Joseph in Glory* (prior to 1664) amidst architectural perspectives with colonnades, by Antonio Torri.

7 The Islands

Venice was not the first. The flat expanse of sand bars and islands that constitutes the delicate ecosystem of the lagoon was home to other cities, earlier peoples, prior civilizations. Now the names, and in some cases the stones, survive; there were many islands, inhabited by man in long-forgotten times, which the ingenuity of their inhabitants was unable to save. Eraclea once stood amidst water in the long-silted up lagoon of Oderzo; Malamocco was swallowed up by the sea; Ammiana, once the burial ground of the doges, extended over numerous islands, and has now worn away to a patch of earth; Costanziaca met the same fate but left not a trace; Torcello, which still floats, unreal, on the wavering horizon. Little is known about these early settlements, or even about the configuration of the land that in time became Venice and the other island towns. We can say with certainty that the lagoon was shaped by a delta system in which a number of river branches emptied into the sea. Much more land rose above the water in the form of islands than is now the case, and the boundaries between the lagoon and the mainland remains fairly unclear. Without a doubt, the decline and death of so many island-towns must have sounded a grim note of alarm to the Venetians, who soon understood the importance of working tirelessly to safeguard their lagoon.

A view of the Canale della Giudecca

The lagoon is 50 km. in length, ranges from 8 to 14 km. in width, and has a surface area of a little more than 550 sq. km.; it is a small inland sea of brackish and salt water, at once formed and threatened by the confluence of sea waves and rivers' flow. The area is normally covered by the waters of the canals or the marshlands (shallow bodies of water, whose beds – or "velme" – sometimes appear at low tide); it is enriched by the flow ("sevente") and ebb ("dosana") of sea water. The other half of this vast expanse is constituted by land emerging from the water, islands used as farmland or built up into villages and towns, "barene," or shoals (spits or strips of land that are sometimes covered at high tide), and by the "valli di pesca chiuse" (sections of the lagoon with bodies of water and sand bars or shoals; used primarily for fish-farming), bounded by embankments, barriers to the flow of water, impregnable to the tides.

The landscape of the lagoon is unique: the dry land and the bodies of water are braided together, crisscrossed by the networks of canals that, in a clear hierarchy, run out from the mouths of the harbors, and like capillaries extend throughout the three great basins. The largest canals are those that extend from the ancient river beds out into the sea; the rivers were deviated centuries ago so that they now pour into the sea outside of the lagoon. They are still in communication with the lagoon through a network of locks, constituting – for the various towns on the lagoon – links with the hinterland and with the sea. To prevent the continual silting caused by the rivers, the government of the Venetian Republic undertook major projects of hydraulic engineering such as the "tagli," literally, cuts. These cuts were deviations of the flow of a river, sometimes for dozens of kilometers; thus

the Brenta, the Sile, and Bacchiglione were rerouted into the sea (15th/17th c.). In order to protect the lagoon from the fury of the sea, the "murazzi" were built in the 18th c., massive embankments of boulders, running some 20 km. between the mouth of the port of Lido and the mouth of the port of Chioggia, two of the three outlets linking the lagoon and the Adriatic Sea (the third is that of Malamocco). In more recent years, these harbor mouths were shielded by breakwaters and moles, designed to give some protection to a delicate and unstable equilibrium, in an environment that – with the dissolution of any sense of proportion between Venice and its lagoon – has been subjected over the past 150 years to all sorts of mistreatment and decay.
And yet, even today, understanding and studying the islands of the Venetian lagoon will allow you better to understand Venice itself. What is more, it allows you to discover a world without equals, a watery universe that is still splendid, even though it has been seriously compromised by industrial, urban, and agricultural pollution. The routes through the lagoon and its islands offer therefore a great many points of interest, intricately bound up with the history of Venice and its possessions, from the earliest times to the modern day. First and foremost, of course, are the links of art and architecture, of which there is a great treasury scattered throughout the islands of the Venetian lagoon. The best known of the inhabited islands are certainly Giudecca and Murano. Giudecca is clearly visible from the Zattere, part of the central Bacino di S. Marco (Basin of St. Mark's). Murano is the center of the fine glass industry, overlooking the northern edge of the Fondamenta Nuove. Both Giudecca and Murano were once used by the Venetian aristocracy as holiday retreats, until the Renaissance; later, they were used for manufactories. Burano, Mazzorbo e Torcello all have the allure of relics of a renowned urban past, set in a world of water and land, light and color, with vague and elusive boundaries. Rising between the old centers of S. Nicolò and Malamocco, the Lido forms part of the multi-centered lagoon system, and rose in the last century to glory as the capital of international vacationers, interested in healthful bathing: it is to Lido that the gondola is cutting through the water, "black, as only coffins are black in this world," transporting Aschenbach to his *Death in Venice*. It was the center of a cosmopolitan society that is perfectly reflected in the eclectic Moorish style of the great hotels and in the Art-Nouveau architecture of the little homes and beach villas. Other islands feature hospitals or cultural activities; they thus maintain the intermediary role traditionally played by the monasteries. Founded as hospices for pilgrims on their way back from the Holy Land, they later served as the site of Venetian hospitality to important rulers and celebrities who were guests of the Venetian Republic. Foremost among them was the island of S. Giorgio Maggiore, coddled by the Signory, renovated under the supervision of the leading architects, Buora, Palladio, and now with only minimal monastic activity, but serving as the headquarters of the prestigious cultural organization, the Fondazione Giorgio Cini.
The islands of S. Francesco del Deserto and S. Lazzaro degli Armeni are still monastic centers, although they have other activities as well. Both communities date from the earliest years of the 13th c. and work hard to preserve their heritage – historical, environmental, spiritual – of great and intense beauty.
S. Andrea is one great fortress guarding the port, now undergoing a difficult restoration, made necessary by the damage caused by the sea. La Grazia, San Clemente, and San Sèrvolo, all are the sites of exquisite monasteries now used as hospitals, and are being adapted to many different activities. Lastly, in the heart of the lagoon, is the last home of the Venetians: S. Michele and S. Cristoforo della Pace, now united in a single island, constitute the cemetery of Venice. There are many great non-Venetian artists buried here, in the city they inhabited during their lives. Nor should it be thought strange to consider an unusual route through the lagoon, stopping at S. Ariano, an unsettling and verdant island-ossuary; and the little Camposanto di Mazzorbo, a meadow surrounded by water; and the Jewish *Beth-Chaim* S. Nicolò, one of the oldest and saddest cemeteries in the world.

7.1 The Island of the Giudecca and San Giorgio Maggiore

Once known as Spinalonga ("Long Spine"), this long, narrow, and long-uninhabited island is thought by some to have received the name of Giudecca because of the settlement of Jews ("Giudei") here, possibly during the Middle Ages; others think that the name came from the term "giudicato," (*zudegà* in Venetian dialect), referring to the judgements whereby, during the 9th c., the government of the Venetian Republic gave

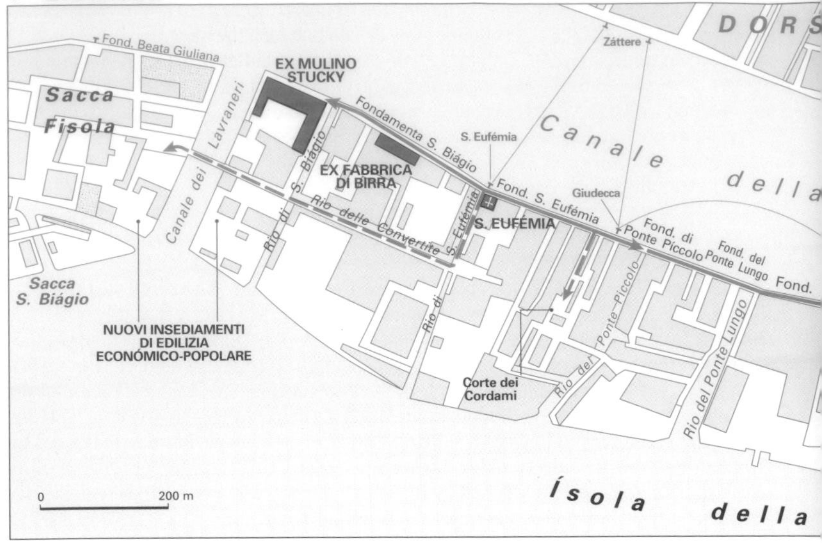

lands here to exiled noble families.

In that period, the island covered only the ground extending from the church of S. Eufemia and the Rio di Ponte Lungo, but with a series of reclamation projects, it attained its present size as early as the 16th c.; it was then that, due to its location far from the center, but still well within the Bacino di S. Marco (it extends between the Canale di S. Marco and the Laguna Sud, or southern lagoon), it became a holiday and leisure spot, where aristocratic homes alternated with orchards, gardens, and monasteries, as well as storehouses for materials both from the mainland and from the Porto di Malamocco. This island was the site of intense social life, but was also considered the appropriate setting in which to build, at the end of the 16th c., the votive church of the Redentore, erected by the government of the Venetian Republic in grateful recognition of the victory over the Turkish fleet at the battle of Lepanto (1571).

It was during the 19th c. – after the fall of the Serenissima, the decline of the aristocracy, the suppression of the convents – that this island progressively became a place of barracks, prisons, factories, and working-class residential neighborhoods.

The island of S. Giorgio has a different origin; as early as the 9th c. it was already a religious and cultural center with its own special role as a political drawing room (among the guests of Venice to stay here were, in 1232, Frederick II of Swabia, and in 1433, Cosimo de' Medici); when the Republic fell, the island lost its status and much of its wealth. It regained its standing as a cultural center in 1951 as the headquarters of the Fondazione Giorgio Cini.

The route, which begins at the landing jetty near the church of S. Eufemia, extends along the "fondamenta," or quay, which runs, with different names, around the entire island, offering a splendid view of the Canale della Giudecca, and past such notable monuments as the church of the Redentore and the Complex of the Zitelle. Short detours allow you to see charming and little-known areas, and to see the southern lagoon.

A natural conclusion of this tour, which can be reached by boat, is the Palladian architecture of S. Giorgio Maggiore.

The two islands can be reached from Venice by taking the vaporetto lines 5 and 8.

Fondamenta di S. Eufemia (8 D5-6). This stretch of quay takes its name from the nearby church, once bounded by the Rio di Ponte Lungo. Lining it are various palazzi; behind them is the dense architectural network of an old working-class neighborhood. The *Accademia dei Nobili* (n. 607-608) was founded in 1619, and occupied an existing 16th-c. building; it housed young nobles from families that had fallen on hard times.

A short distance away, note the Sottoportego dei Nicoli and the Calle dei Nicoli, which lead to the elongated *Corte dei Cordami* (8 E6), where the hawsers of ships were braided: overlooking this courtyard is a row house, possibly from the 17th c., with impressive chimneys.

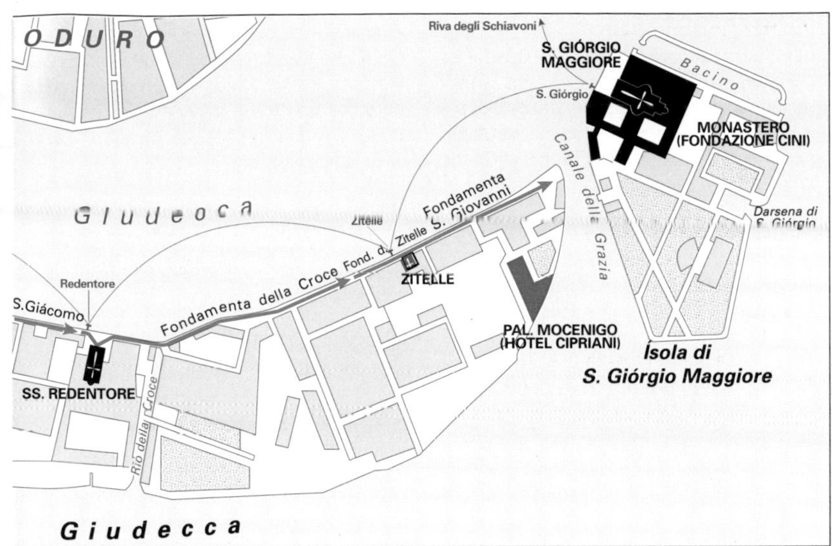

S. Eufemia (8 D5). At the confluence of the Rio di S. Eufemia, which the facade of this church overlooks, and the Canale della Giudecca; it is said that the church was founded in the 9th c., and it has preserved over time the simple barn-structure that dates from the 11th c., left intact despite the renovations done in the 18th and 19th c., when the exterior portico was added (the 16th-c. columns come from the church of Ss. Biagio e Cataldo, demolished to build the Mulino Stucky).

The three aisles, dating from the 11th c. and built to a Venetian-Byzantine plan, co-exist with the sumptuous 18th-c. decorations on the ceilings and walls; on the 1st altar on the right, note a *St. Rocco and Angel*, and in the lunette above it, a *Virgin Mary with Christ Child*, the central section of a triptych signed by Bartolomeo Vivarini and dated 1480.

To the right of the church, the "fondamenta" reaches *Campo S. Cosmo* (8 E5), dominated by the former church of *Ss. Cosma e Damiano* (transformed by the faithful into Cosmo), from the late-15th c.; in 1886 it was transformed into a factory, the Opificio Herion, which was in operation until the 1960s: the bell tower was transformed into a smokestack.

Another building that has been through an improbable succession of uses is the 16th-c. *Ex-Convento delle Convertite* (across the Rio delle Convertite, along the Fondamenta delle Convertite, at n. 712; 8 E4), once a home for repentant former prostitutes; after 1857, a women's penitentiary. After you cross the Rio di S. Biagio from the Fondamenta delle Convertite, you will see the Mulino Stucky on your right and the working-class residential complex designed by Gino Valle (1987) on your left; then cross the Canale dei Lavraneri, and you will reach the much-debated working-class neighborhood of *Sacca Fìsola* (1956; 8 C-D 1-3): stroll on through the greenery of the embankments, and you will see the unsettling, fascinating industrial structures of Marghera.

Fondamenta S. Biagio (8 C-D 4-5). This far-westernmost extremity of the long quay that bounds the Giudecca – lined with small palazzi built from the 15th c. until the end of the Venetian Republic – was consolidated and reinforced, at the end of the 19th c., to allow large ships to dock; at the same time, industrial buildings were erected here, radically changing the area. At n. 797 stand the tall crenelated walls (1902) of the former *Fabbrica di Birra e Liquori*, or beer and liquor brewery and distillery, which has since been adapted for other uses; it almost seems an architectural harbinger of the nearby Mulino Stucky; at n. 805 stands the *Fabbrica di Tessuti Fortuny*, a cloth manufactory that is still active, built in 1919.

The "fondamenta" comes to an end at a metal bridge that has long since closed; in a setting that is reminiscent of the docks of fog-bound harbors of northern Europe, beyond the Rio stands the imposing Hanoverian Gothic bulk of the **Mulino Stucky** (8 C-D4), built among much controversy, to plans by the German architect Ernest Wullekopf (1896) at the behest of the Swiss businessman Giovanni Stucky. It was Stucky who defended to the last the style of his building, going so far as to threaten to shut down his business if the city of Venice refused to accept that style willingly. This harshness of character may perhaps be associated with the violent death that Stucky met; he was in fact murdered by one of his workers in 1910. No decision has yet been made as to what is to be done with the now-decrepit Mulino.

Fondamenta S. Giacomo (9 E2-3). This quay runs from the Ponte Lungo (1340) along the Giudecca "Nuova," formed through reclamation projects from the 14th c. on: here, as early as the end of the 15th c., the Visconti family, former rulers of Milan, had established a vacation home, the *Rocca Bianca* (n. 218-224), whose one-time vast and splendid gardens are now occupied by the former *Cantieri Navali Officine Meccaniche di Venezia*, or naval metalworking shops.

Walk through the successive Campo S. Giacomo, take a short detour along the Calle S. Giacomo, and then the Calle dei Frati, and you will reach a small public garden overlooking the southern lagoon (Laguna Sud).

Il Redentore* (9 E-F3). Designed as the terminus of the procession held on the day of the "Redentore," or "savior," this masterpiece was begun by Palladio in 1577 and completed by Antonio Da Ponte in 1592; it appears in all its glory to those who arrive by boat. The church was built to fulfill a vow taken by the Venetian Senato during an outbreak of the plague that ended in 1577; by 1578 it was already the destination of a procession headed by the doge, who walked to the church over a bridge of boats from the opposite quay, or Fondamenta delle Zattere.
You can sense the horizontal extent of the church on the interior as well, designed to accommodate the final phases of the procession, all the way up to the transept, where there are spaces where the doge and other dignitaries would sit. The pictorial and sculptural decorations follow an iconographic scheme based on the idea of redemption, for which Jesus suffering on the Cross was the intermediary (the "redeemer," as in the name of the church). On the counter-facade, note the gilded plaque, with the vow taken by the doge on 8 September 1576, in hopes of stilling the raging pestilence. On the left wall of the presbytery, the 1st altar holds an *Ascension* by Jacopo Tintoretto and assistants; on the 2nd altar is a *Resurrection* by Francesco Bassano, and, on the 3rd altar, a *Deposition* by Jacopo Palma the Younger. In the sacristy is a notable *Virgin Mary with Christ Child and Angels* by Alvise Vivarini, and a *Baptism of Jesus Christ* by Paolo Veronese; note the unsettling wax sculptures (late-17th c.), which are casts of the faces of several Capuchin saints.

From the adjoining Convento dei Cappuccini you can enter the church of *S. Maria degli Angeli* and the Renaissance funerary chapel of the Stravazino family, dedicated to *S. Giovanni Battista* (St. John the Baptist).

Fondamenta della Croce, Fondamenta delle Zitelle, and Fondamenta di S. Giovanni (9 D-E 4-6). This long "fondamenta," or quay, which runs along the easternmost "insula," beyond the Rio della Croce, takes its various names from the 16th-c. Monastero della Croce, a monastery that is now incorporated into the "Casa di Lavoro Maschile" (men's prison), from the complex of the Zitelle, and from the Monastero di S. Giovanni (no longer in existence). Note the large, several-story buildings that were once grain siloes, a building with three enormous and curious windows, and the Casa dei Tre Oci (a piece of Neo-Gothic architecture designed by the painter Mario De Maria; on the interior of this house, the film *Anonimo Veneziano* was made) – all preceding the long facade of the Zitelle.

Zitelle (S. Maria della Presentazione; 9 D-E 5-6). Established by the church and adjoining hospice for poor young women, the complex was built between 1579 and 1586 to plans reliably attributed to Andrea Palladio; he established a typology that later became quite common in buildings of this sort. Two symmetrical wings containing the hospice enclose the church, which on its interior appears as an enormous hall with semicircular side windows, serving as chancels or choirs. The building has been restored, and is now used as a conference center.

San Giorgio Maggiore* (10 D-F 4-5). From the landing jetty, or Pontile delle Zitelle, you can take the vaporetto line 82 to the island of San Giorgio Maggiore, renowned for the enormous Benedictine convent of San Giorgio Maggiore. The construction of the **church**, a masterpiece designed by Andrea Palladio, was begun by him in 1566 and brought to completion in the first half of the 17th c., following his death (1580); the new church replaced a very old one on the same site (11th c.), which had already been rebuilt once: dedicated to St. George, and later to

St. Stephen as well (1109); it was under the special protection of the Signoria (Seigneury) that each year a great feast was held on Christmas Eve.
The marble facade, with a pediment front and side wings corresponding to the side-aisles, allows one to see the two broad brick apses (the rest of the church, which extends in considerable length, punctuated by dome and bell towers, can be seen only from the opposite shores, or from the Bacino di S. Marco). The statues of saints Stephen and George, in niches, and the aedicules with busts of the doges Tribuno Memmo and Sebastiano Ziani, recall the origins of the complex. The interior clearly indicates the enormous length of the building, in the sequence of aisle, presbytery, and monk's choir, punctuated by the dome set at the intersection with the very broad transept, and broken by the columns that divide the choir.
The decorative aspect of this church, which is fairly bare and arranged with rigorous simplicity, includes a number of masterpieces: on the altar in the chapel to the right of the presbytery, *Virgin Mary, Enthroned, with Saints* by Sebastiano Ricci (1708); in the presbytery, two paintings by Jacopo Tintoretto, *Last Supper** (right wall) and *Gathering the Manna* (left wall), which may have been his last painting (1594); in the choir of the monks, behind the colonnade, note the magnificent *wooden choir** (carved by A. Van der Brulle and G. Gatti); at the altar of the winter choir (or Sala del Conclave, named for the conclave held here in the year 1800 to elect Pope Pius VII Chiaramonti) note the canvas *St. George Killing the Dragon** by Vittore Carpaccio (1516; visible only by advance request).
The **monastery**, now the headquarters of the Fondazione Giorgio Cini, is a complex array of spaces and rooms, of remarkable architectural value, with work by some of the finest architects between the end of the 15th c. and the middle of the 17th c. The building is occupied by the cultural and social activities of the Fondazione Giorgio Cini, as well as by a small community of monks, founded by the Benedictine order at the end of the 10th c. The monastery was rebuilt following an earthquake in 1223, and again completely rebuilt after the late-15th c., resulting in its present form.

The Church of S. Giorgio Maggiore, a masterpiece by A. Palladio

Andrea Palladio designed the *Chiostro Palladiano**, a perfectly proportioned cloister (formerly the Chiostro dei Cipressi), begun in 1579 (completed by another architect in 1646) and the *refectory* (or Cenacolo), with a monumental entrance, composed of three particularly tall halls (on the far wall, note the *Wedding of the Virgin* by Jacopo Tintoretto). The second cloister, the *Chiostro dei Cipressi* (confusingly, this cloister was formerly known as the Chiostro degli Allori), is an elegant piece of early-Renaissance architecture (1516-1540), by Giovanni Buora and his son, Andrea. The latest creations in this complex (1643-44) are by Baldassarre Longhena: the monumental *stairway* that leads up to the 1st floor, the *Foresteria Piccola* (or Foresteria degli Abati), and the sumptuous *Biblioteca* (set between the two cloisters, this operating library now possesses 100,000 volumes of art his-

tory), decorated with imposing bookcases (carved by Franz Pauc but designed by Longhena) and two *globes* by Vincenzo Coronelli.
At the end of the 2nd cloister stands the *dormitorium*, the so-called "long sleeve," for its remarkable extension of 128 m., punctuated by the shafts of light pouring in from above (this too is by Giovanni and Andrea Buora, and was built between 1494 and 1533).

Outside of the convent complex, the north side of the island is marked by the basin enclosed by a breakwater, and flanked by two lighthouse-towers, built, along with the adjoining storehouse and customs buildings, in the 19th c., when this island was a free port. At about the middle of this structure stands the 16th-c. *facade* of the Dormitorium, with lunettes, mullioned windows, and a relief of *St. George on Horseback* by G.B. and L. Bregno (1508). Lastly, we suggest climbing the 75-m.-tall campanile (built in 1791 to replace the 15th-c. bell tower), from which you can enjoy a remarkable view of Venice.

To complete the tour of the island, you must first obtain authorization from the Direzione della Fondazione (directors of the foundation).

7.2 The Lido di Venezia

This route covers the entire island of Lido (which, with its approximately 12 km. of extension, separates the lagoon from the open sea, along with the island of Pellestrina and the peninsula of Cavallino), beginning at eration, namely the fortresses set at the harbor mouth. Lastly, it completes the historic panorama of lagoon settlements, with the ancient islands of San Nicolò and Malamocco.

The dining hall of the Grand Hotel Des Bains, built in 1900

the Piazzale S. Maria Elisabetta, where you will leave water transportation to make your way by land (we strongly suggest at this point renting a bicycle); this will take you to a beach resort that was once famed and worldly, with a handsome beach, large hotels, and villas, a Casino, and the modern Mostra del Cinema (Venice Film Festival); it is now far less opulent, and largely residential.
This route will also allow you to grasp the other features that provide equilibrium to the lagoon system, the barriers built by the Venetian Republic; both the physical breakwaters, or Murazzi, still functioning, and the military barriers, no longer in op-

Pontile del Lido (landing point at Lido, A2). This landing jetty overlooks the Piazzale S. Maria Elisabetta, the terminus of the Gran Viale S. Maria Elisabetta, the center of the urban structure of the modern center of Lido. Lido abounds in hotels and neighborhoods of small mansions in the Art Nouveau (in Italian, "Liberty"), Art Déco, and (occasional) Rationalist styles.

At a distance of 500 m. from Lido, you can clearly see the island of **S. Lazzaro degli Armeni** (C1), the headquarters and cultural center of the monastic congregation of the Padri Mechitaristi, who settled in 1717 on the ruins of the hospital/leper colony of S. Lazzaro (12th c.). The convent is surrounded by a lush garden, and hous-

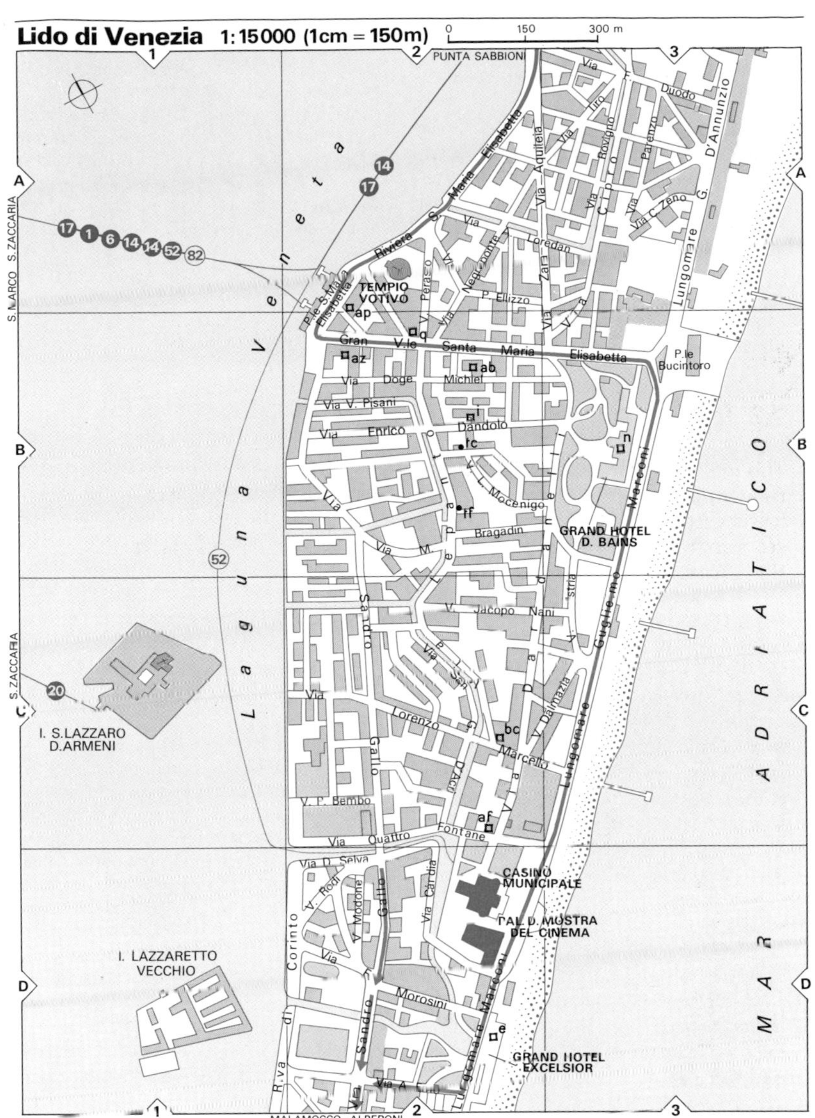

es a library, a renowned multilingual press, a museum (paintings, archeological objects, including a mummy from the 15th c. B.C., memorabilia of all sorts, and a priceless collection of over 2,000 Armenian manuscripts).
The island can be reached from Venice with the vaporetto n. 20.

Lido (A-B2-3). The urban grid runs along either side of the Gran Viale S. Maria Elisabetta: toward the NE is the Lungomare Gabriele d'Annunzio, which ends opposite the Ospedale al Mare; to the SW runs the Lungomare Guglielmo Marconi, which extends to the better-known and more prestigious resort area, with the *Grand Hotel des Bains* (1900, architect Francesco Marsich), known to the general public through the book "*Death in Venice*" by Thomas Mann, as well as through the film version made by Luchino Visconti (1971); the *Casinò* (1936-38, architect Eugenio Miozzi), in "Littorio" style, typical of the Fascist regime; the *Palazzo della Mostra del Cinema* and the *Grand Hotel Excelsior* (1898-1908, designed by Giovanni Sardi), in the eccentric but by now familiar Moorish style. The residential area that developed in the early-20th c. is organized largely along streets running parallel to the Gran Viale, and features no particularly noteworthy architectural or functional structures; rather homogeneous, this zone is characterized by an eclectic

The Island of Pellestrina

19th-/20th-c. architecture, Neo-Gothic and Neo-Byzantine, or else Art Nouveau and Art Déco, arranged along tree-lined lanes that are often flanked by canals and dotted with verdant gardens and parks: this array of structures results in a decorous and comfortable city setting, sadly blemished by many constructions of the post-war period.

Antico Cimitero Israelitico (A2, off map). Along the Riviera S. Nicolò, this is one of the oldest Jewish cemeteries in Europe, established in 1389. It preserves tombs and funerary steles from the 14th to the 17th c. To find the custodian, you must go to the *Nuovo Cimitero Israelitico* (along Via Cipro, after the Catholic cemetery) founded in the 18th c.; note the entrance structure, built in 1911 by Guido Sullam.

San Nicolò (A2, off map). This ancient settlement lies at the NE extremity of the island of Lido. It served as a major stronghold securing the mouth of the port of Lido, Venice's chief outlet to the sea; note the ruins of the 16th-/17th-c. Forte di S. Nicolò (or Forte Castel Vecio), and, on the opposite shore, the *Forte di S. Andrea* (or Castel Nuovo) alle Vignole, a magnificent structure designed by Michele Sanmicheli and built between 1545 and 1550, now being restored; a chain was extended between the two fortresses to prevent ships from entering. In these waters, beginning in 1177, the Doge in the ducal galley, the Bucintoro, would sail out to the Peatone del Patriarca, and perform the ceremony of wedding Venice to the sea, by tossing a golden ring into the sea, *in signum veri perpetuique dominii* – in Latin, "as a sign of true and perpetual dominion". The ceremony, which begins in Piazza S. Marco with a spectacular procession, ends with a Mass held at the church of S. Nicolò di Lido. And it was around this church, and a convent founded by Benedictine monks in the mid-11th c., repeatedly renovated and restructured since, that the settlement of Lido grew up. Today the church has 17th-c. style architecture. The interior, with a single aisle, features – in the counter-facade – a fresco by Girolamo Pellegrini, *Allegory of Venice at the Feet of St. Nicholas*, and, in the apse, a *choir*, made of walnut, with carvings of scenes from the life of St. Nicholas, for whom of course the church is named, carried out in 1635 by Giovanni da Crema.

Along the Canale di Treporti, not far from the mouth of the port of Lido, testing is underway of the controversial MOSE (Modulo Sperimentale Elettromeccanico; literally, electromechanical experimental module, but commonly called Mosè, Italian for Moses, a prophet who knew something about controlling water), a prototype of a hydraulic breakwater, meant to control the tides of the Adriatic Sea; it is hoped that this will solve the problem of "acqua alta," or high water.

Malamocco (D2, off map). This small town, in the southern section of the island, was heir to one of the earliest lagoon settlements, destroyed by the great tidal wave of 1106-07 (the place name derives from *Medoacus*, which later became *Methamaucus*, one of the branches of the river Brenta), and developed from the 14th c. on, preserving a clear herring-bone structure, organized along the actual Rio Terrà (and originally a canal-harbor), and the parallel Mercerie, which extend from Piazza della Chiesa to Piazza delle Erbe.
Between the lagoon shore and the Piazza della Chiesa, note the *Palazzo del Podestà* (15th c.); in the church of *S. Maria Assunta* (also dating from the 15th c.; renovated), there is an interesting votive painting by Girolamo Forabosco (*A Family Rescued from Shipwreck*, left wall of the presbytery) and, in the sacristy, an *altar frontal* (16th c.).

Alberoni (D2, off map). A small resort and residential area, at the edge of the littoral strip of Lido, at the mouth of the Porto di Malamocco: the broad beach and the dunes with little groves behind them are worth a stroll; a golf course surrounds the ruins of the former *Forte della Punta*, a presidio at the mouth of the harbor. On the other side of the canal is the shore of the island of **Pellestrina**, with the small towns of S. Piero in Volta (possibly ancient Albiola) and Pellestrina, a small town traditionally inhabited by fishermen, extending along the shore of the lagoon; on the sea shore extend the embankments, or *murazzi*: the massive breakwater, built between 1774 and 1782 to plans by the famous cosmographer Vincenzo Coronelli, protects the island throughout its length (about 11 km.; a further stretch of about 6 km. extends around the southern end of the island of Lido, and was badly damaged by the ferocious storms of 4 November 1966; it was further reinforced in the Seventies).

7.3 San Michele and Murano

The two islands were once linked by their names, as well: S. Michele in Paluo (meaning "palude," or "marsh") was, in fact, known as Cavana de Muran; it was probably uninhabited, and constituted a natural haven for vessels caught in this section of the lagoon by sudden storms. In the 13th c., the history of the two islands was suddenly altered: Camaldolite monks inhabited S. Michele from 1212 until 1810, making it a major religious and cultural center, with a notable library. On 13 July 1819 (the convent had been transformed into a prison, in which the Italian writer and patriot Silvio Pellico was held, along with Maroncelli and Arrivabene) this library collapsed during a bad storm.

Murano, on the other hand, already independent and prosperous around the year 1000, became home to all the glass makers in Venice, according to a law passed by the Maggior Consiglio in 1291, out of fear of fires, particularly dangerous to a city then built almost entirely out of wood.

The Island of Murano can be reached directly with lines 23 (seasonal) and 52, setting out from the Fondamenta Nuove, not far from the church of the Gesuiti.

San Michele (3 A-B-C4-5-6). The island was

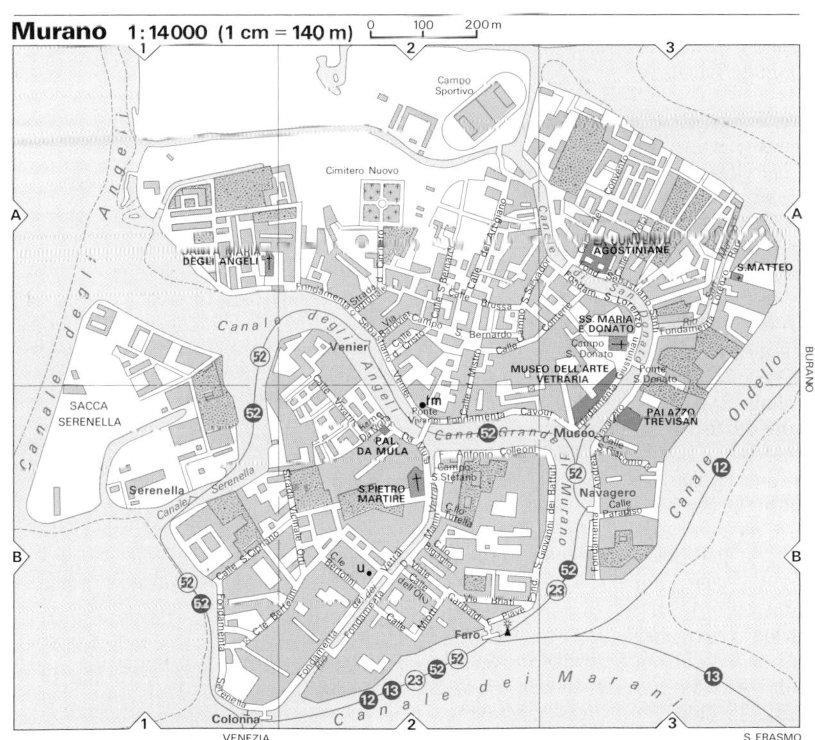

Glass objects manufactured in Murano

destined for its present function in 1837, when it was joined to the adjacent island of S. Cristoforo della Pace, selected in 1807 by Napoleon as the municipal cemetery of Venice. The landing plaza is bounded by the facades of the church and the adjacent convent of *S. Michele in Isola*. Built by Mauro Codussi (1469-78) with an elegant Renaissance facade in Istria stone, the **church** features a handsome, three-aisle interior with a lacunar ceiling and a "barco." Buried here, in the pavement facing the door, are the ashes of Fra' Paolo Sarpi, a Venetian historian, theologian, and patriot; until 1828 they lay in the church of the Servi in Venice, which was suppressed in that year. Among the many Renaissance plaques in the aisles, note the inscription honoring the monk Eusebio Ispano (left aisle) dictated by the Humanist and publisher Aldo Manuzio (Aldus Manutius) in 1502. Lastly, note the lovely Cappella Emiliani, which makes its mark even on the exterior of the left side of the church, a delicate Renaissance creation by Guglielmo Bergamasco.

Lines of identical white crosses, the occasional monument, black cypresses, and many many flowers: in this, the *cemetery* of Venice, rest the mortal remains of Diaghilev, Stravinsky, Pound, and other adoptive Venetians.

Murano (map on page 117). Its name is a synonym for glass: Murano – more than 6,000 inhabitants, 70 factories, some of them world famous, its own Grand Canal, palazzi and houses that are comfortably built to a human dimension – is both independent of, and an imitation of Venice. An ironic twist of history is responsible for this island's age-old prosperity: in 1291 the government of the Venetian Republic ordered by decree that all glass factories be moved to Murano, to reduce the danger of fires. Strict laws and special privileges (Venetian aristocrats were allowed to marry the daughters of master glassblowers without blemishing in any way their nobility) led the way to the island's development.
The settlement covers five main islands, and is split in two by the so-called Canal Grande, a meandering waterway crossed by only one bridge; joining it are the Canale di S. Donato (to the north) and the Rio dei Vetrai (to the south), which both flow into the lagoon. As is the case in Venice, the historic structures cluster along the canals and the "calli" that run perpendicular to those canals; they comprise palazzi where the Venetian aristocracy once took its holidays, alternating with "palazzetti" of the mercantile middle class, and, without any clear rules or patterns, rows of modest and undistinguished homes.
In the image that Murano now presents, very little survives of the palazzi and gardens that once made it famous, while the rips and tears in the urban fabric, so to speak, the variety and hodge-podge of the buildings, certain conditions of breakdown and abandonment, and the incursions of commercial architecture, all offer a complex and contradictory account of the enormous changes that have resulted from the vigor and capacity for innovation of the age-old glass-making industry. It is along the shorefront overlooking the lagoon, where the winds blow hardest, that the rears of the glass factories can be seen, part of them still in use and part of them empty and abandoned; in the complex of the former Cristallerie Veneziane, note the *Casino Mocenigo*, a house dedicated to lettered leisure and aristocratic pursuits, built between 1591 and 1617, either by a student of Palladio or by Scamozzi.
On the *Fondamenta Giustinian* the vaporetto docks just in front of the **Museo dell'Arte Vetraria***, or museum of the glassmaker's art, founded by the Abbot Vincenzo Zanetti, and enriched with the glass collections of the Civico Museo Correr; this museum has been housed since 1861 in the halls of *Palazzo Giustinian* (A-B3), built in 1680 at the behest of Bishop Marco Giustinian, who decided to transfer the bishopric there from its former site on Torcello.

The craft of glass-making at Murano (the earliest surviving document to speak of the glass industry there dates from A.D. 982) developed especially after 1291, when a decree by the government of the Venetian Republic ordered the wholesale transfer of all glass kilns out of the city of

Venice, to prevent fires. Even then the glass and glass objects manufactured in Murano were being exported through the Mediterranean basin, and later to countries beyond the Alps, often with the master glass-blowers themselves, despite strict laws passed by the Venetian Republic to prevent this early "brain drain." After a decline following the end of the Republic, glass-making resumed and flourished from the 1850s on.

The museum – aside from the ground floor, where there are archeological finds, including glass from the 2nd c. B.C. to the 2nd c. A.D., from the necropolis of Enona, – is organized chronologically, assembling in the various halls of the 2nd and 3rd floors glass dating from as early as the 15th c. up to more recent times. There are examples of the various techniques (milk glass, filigree, and other more exotic types). Note the priceless Coppa Barovier*, an exceptional piece of the glassmaker's art from the 15th c., in dark-blue glass with portraits of the bride and groom for whose wedding it was made.

On the opposite shore, note the *Palazzo Trevisan* (B3), built in 1557, with an innovative façade, possibly the result of the learned discussions of the intellectuals, – A. Palladio, P. Veronese, A. Vittoria – who met in the refectories of Murano.

Not far from the museum, at the end of the "fondamenta," note the splendid apse of the cathedral of **Ss. Maria e Donato*** (A3), overlooking the canal. The church building, founded as early as the 7th c. and rebuilt in the 12th c., along with the bell tower, is one of the most notable pieces of Venetian-Byzantine architecture in the lagoon.

The interior, built to a basilican plan, with three aisles divided by columns made of Greek marble, with rare Venetian capitals, presents a remarkable mosaic floor dating from 1140, depicting a fantastic and intricate bestiary. Between the second and the third column, note the depiction of two roosters carrying a fox that has been captured and bound to a pole, clearly influenced by the mosaic from the same period in S. Marco, symbolizing the victory of vigilance over cleverness. From the gold background of the vault of the apse emerges the hieratic figure of the *Mother of God** (1st half of the 13th c.). Also note the wooden altar piece depicting *St. Donato*, dating from 1310, by Paolo Veneziano (left aisle) and, in the lunette over the door leading into the baptistery, *Virgin Mary with Christ Child and Saints* by Lazzaro Bastiani (1484).

From Campo S. Donato continue straight until you reach the *Calle Conterie* (A2-3), whose name hearkens back to a distinctive type of glass-manufacturing, that of beads: the Italian term "conterie" supposedly derives either from the Latin *comptus*, meaning "ornament," or from the even more interesting concept of "accounting," with reference to the use of beads as a form of primitive trading currency by Europeans in the new colonies. The manufacturing of beads was chiefly done by women, who would string them (these were the famous *impiraresse*). **Ponte Vivarini** (or Ponte Lungo; B2), built in 1866, and made of iron to replace an earlier stone bridge, is the only bridge over the Canal Grande di Murano. It

Murano: the Church of Ss. Maria e Donato

runs to the *Fondamenta Da Mula* (B2), named for the 15th-c. Palazzo Da Mula (on the right; note, in the courtyard, the remains of the portico with twin-light mullioned windows, and the monumental Venetian-Byzantine arch from the 12th/13th c.).

The parish church of **S. Pietro Martire** (B2), rebuilt between the 15th and 16th c. (but originally founded in 1363), contains works of art from churches and convents suppressed under Napoleonic rule, replacing the original furnishings of the church, which have since been lost. Note *Our Lady of the Assumption and Saints* (1510-13: undergoing restoration) and the *Virgin Mary with Christ Child, Enthroned, with Angels and Saints* (1488: both on the right wall) by Giovanni Bellini; *St. Jerome in the Desert* by Paolo Veronese (ca. 1566) over the door of the sacristy, where the furnishings of the Scuola di S. Giovanni dei Battuti, demolished, were assembled (note the wooden altar-frontals).

The **Fondamenta dei Vetrai** (B2), along with the opposite Fondamenta Manin, is where the first glass-making furnaces were built, hence the simple structural unity, with buildings that combine home, furnace and workshop, and storehouse.

7.4 Burano and Torcello

Colorful and cheerful, Burano lies at the heart of the Laguna Nord (or northern lagoon), although the pillars of its economy are no longer fishing and the art of lace-making, as in the past; Torcello is an entrancing and quiet island (though not on weekends!), and in the 7th c. it was a major power on the lagoon: in that era, it had a population of 20,000. This was the cradle of Venetian civilization: in A.D. 639, driven before the relentless onslaught of barbarian hordes, the cathedral of Altino, the main city in this region, was transferred to the island of Torcello; the Porta Boreana of Altino was the source of the name of Burano. It is likely that classical columns and ornaments that were re-used in the buildings on these islands originally came from Altino. And Mazzorbo, the island of *Majorbum* that appears in the poetry of the ancient Roman poet Martial, now has little more than vegetable patches surrounding its old church and a small and unusual working-class neighborhood (1987; architect De Carlo); in ancient times, it was a vacation spot for the Romans of Altino. Forty minutes by vaporetto – line n. 12 – separate Burano and Torcello from Murano, but that is nothing compared with the gulf of historical time across which you will seem to move: on the island of Torcello, now familiar to tourists, Hemingway sought the silence and inspiration he needed to write *Across the River and Into the Trees* (1950).

Burano (map on page 121). Beyond Mazzorbo, the landing jetty stands in an open lagoon landscape, along the Canale di Burano: in the distance you can see the tall silhouette of the church and bell tower of Torcello, while all around stretch sandbanks crisscrossed by canals, leading to the lagoon fish-breeding areas. It is here that fishing once thrived, the mainstay of the people of this island, the "Buranelli," but now a forgotten trade; fishing built this town, and a long stroll around the interior "fondamenta," or quays, will give you a taste of the working-class personality of Burano, sheltered from wind and waves (here too, as on Murano, the rears of the houses overlook the lagoon). The *Fondamenta Cavanelle, Fondamenta Cao* and *Fondamenta della Pescheria* (E-F2), surround a typical block, comprising a succession of houses overlooking the "fondamenta," which is an extension of that block, as well as a public space at the service of both the individual houses and the canal; the different colors on the exteriors clearly distinguish the various properties. *Piazza Baldassarre Galuppi* (E-F3), a strangely large space that is named for the Burano-born light-operatic composer (1706-1785), lies at the end of the Via B. Galuppi (built in the 19th c. by filling in the the eastern stretch of the Rio di Mezzo); on the north side of the square stand two Gothic buildings, one of them the former town hall(once known as the Palazzo del Podestà), the other now serving as the *Museo del Merletto* (E3), or Lace Museum.

The making of lace with sewing needles developed here at the turn of the 16th c., and was encouraged by Venetian noblewomen, such as the Dogaressa Morosina Morosini, wife of Marino Grimani; declining by the end of the 18th c., the crafts industry was given a new lease on life by Paolo Fambri and the Contessa Adriana Marcello, who founded (1872) the school and workshop that are still operating.

On the south side of the square, note the church of *S. Martino* (F3), a parish church

Burano and Torcello 1:10000 (1 cm = 100 m)

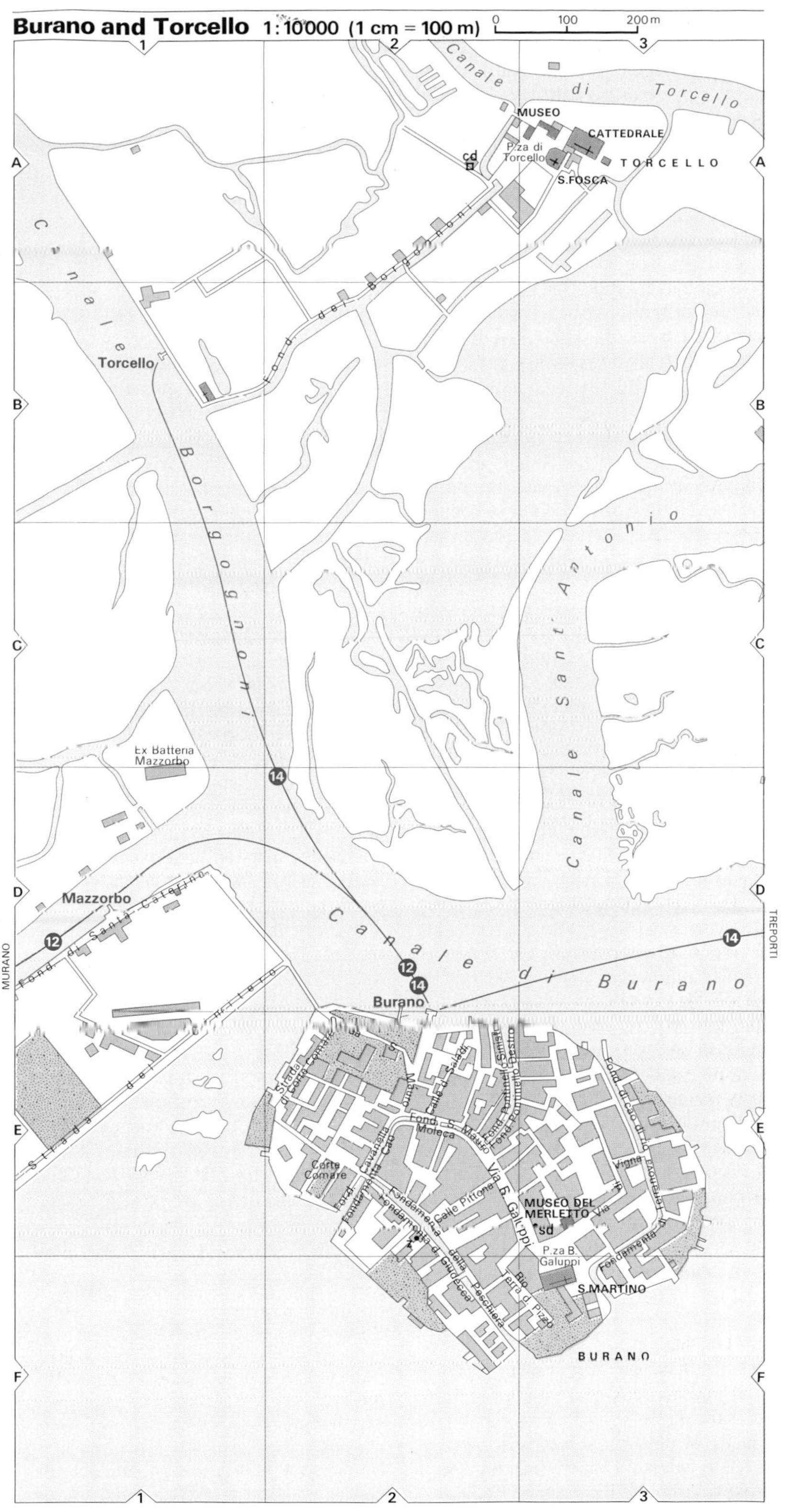

founded and built in the 16th c., with an 18th-c. bell tower, by Andrea Tirali. The interior has three aisles, and a number of anonymous paintings; note the exceptional *Crucifixion* by G.B. Tiepolo (ca. 1725, wall of the left side-aisle); also an intriguing view painting, *Procession of the Patron Saints of Burano*, from the Venetian school, between the 17th and 18th c. (on the wall of the chapel to the left of the main chapel).

Torcello* (map on page 121). On the Canale di Borgognoni (once a major channel connecting the hinterland with the sea, running through the lagoon), amidst sandbanks and marshes, the landing jetty stands in a handsome landscape dotted with gardens and orchards: of the town center – which flourished from the 5th to the 10th c., and was progressively abandoned due to the silting up of this section of the lagoon, becoming a quarry for the monuments of Venice, then under construction – the monumental center still, miraculously, survives. You will reach it by following a road that runs along the Canale di Torcello, in a green landscape dotted with tamarisks, within sight of the bell tower of the cathedral.

Cross that bridge and you can follow a trail through the greenery, a brief detour through the many relics of the agrarian past, within sight of monumental architecture shrouded in silence.

You will thus reach the grassy plaza around which are arranged – forming the central square of a town that no longer exists – the buildings that speak eloquently of the wealth and artistry of this first settlement in the Venetian lagoon: to the right, linked by a portico, the Cattedrale, or cathedral, the ruins of the Battistero, or baptistery, and the church of S. Fosca; opposite, on the left, the Palazzo dell'Archivio and the Palazzo del Consiglio; at the center of the little plaza, the so-called *throne of Attila*, a stone chair probably used by the Roman tribunes when administering justice.
The existing structure of the cathedral, dedicated to **S. Maria Assunta*** (Our Lady of the Assumption; A3), dates from the first enlargements (824) and partial reconstruction (1008) of the early church, built here in A.D. 639 to accommodate the diocese of Altino. Before it, stand the remains of the baptistery (7th c.) and a narthex begun in the 9th c. but enlarged in the 14th/15th c. On the left side is an apsidal structure (15th c.); on the rear, note the handsome forms of the apses (the central apse belongs to the original 7th-c. structure, the side apses date from the enlargements done in the 9th c.); alongside stands the *campanile* (11th c.), one of the tallest in the lagoon.
The interior, with a three-aisle basilican plan, has a solemn array of decoration and iconography, remarkably consistent in style, dating back to the period from the 11th to the 13th c.: from the marble in the floor, columns, and capitals (11th c.), to the remarkable mosaics of the counterfacade, entirely covered with the painting of the *Last Judgement** (12th/13th c.), and the vault of the main chapel, with the **Virgin Mary with Christ Child*** (13th c.), the chapel to the right of the main chapel, and the iconostasis with marble plutei (or dwarf walls connecting columns) with bas-reliefs (10th/11th c.). To the left of the altar, note an original incription commemorating the foundation of the church (A.D. 639), the oldest surviving document of Venetian history.
Linked to the cathedral by a narthex is the church of **S. Fosca** (A3). Note the complex volumes culminating in the round tambour, linked to a pentagonal portico, possibly hearkening back to the floor-plan of a 7th-c. *martyrium*; this church was built around the year 1100; the interior shows the same rich articulation of spaces and volumes that you can sense on the outside, with the Greek-cross plan that is merged with the presbytery.
In the space before the churches, you will also find the 14th-c. *Palazzo dell'Archivio* and the *Palazzo del Consiglio*, where the *Museo di Torcello* is located (established in 1870: A2-3), with archeological finds from the lagoon in general and from Torcello in particular.

8 The Riviera del Brenta

The Riviera del Brenta means, literally, the banks of the river Brenta; as the word "riviera" suggests, however, it has long been an attraction, as well as one of the routes linking Padua and Venice. It does not actually correspond to the banks of the natural watercourse, but rather to a manmade canal running off from it, the "Naviglio di Brenta," or the "Brenta Vecchia," which runs from Stra to Fusina on the banks of the Venetian lagoon. The Naviglio corresponds roughly to the course of one of the older branches of the river Brenta, the *Medoacus Major*, which dried up sometime around the 5th c., and was "brought back to life" by the Paduans in 1142, by isolating it from the Medoacus Minor, a longer and winding river, less well suited for river shipping. After Venice conquered Padua and its territory in 1405, the Venetians undertook a vast series of projects to make the Naviglio more navigable and to limit the silting up of the lagoon.
Following the Venetian conquest, the Naviglio also became the site of the construction of villas, meant for the owners or overseers of new landholdings acquired by the Venetian nobility, often through simple expropriation from the previous Paduan owners. The villas became so numerous that between the 16th and 18th c., the appearance of the Riviera del Brenta changed radically, coming to resemble a sort of continuation of the Grand Canal. In effect, the splendid villas, the creations of an organic architectural culture, certainly hearkened back to the palazzi of Venice, with the addition of structures vital to agrarian needs ("barchesse," dovecotes); the principal facade overlooked the canal, where all trading and pleasure vessels would sail by or dock. The pleasures of living out of town were at first a secondary consideration; the main purpose of these villas was to oversee the considerable investments in land and agriculture. In time, and increasingly over the decades, the villa became a holiday retreat, as well as a status symbol. Holidays in one's villa – usually from mid-June to late-July, and from early-October to mid-November – took on a social significance for the nobility and the well-to-do bourgeoisie of Venice. All this was nicely portrayed, and neatly ridiculed, by Carlo Goldoni in his trilogy of plays on the subject of the "smanie per la villeggiatura" (or "frenzy for country holidays"). The Burchiello – a large and comfortable vessel, driven by oars or pulled by another vessel, or else towed by horses on towpaths – passed along the Naviglio on a daily basis, providing regular communications with Padua and Venice. During the trip, one could enjoy lovely views, and there were numerous and very pleasant stopovers: along the bank there were craftsmen's workshops, taverns, and restaurants. Once the Republic fell, the society of the villas and the villas themselves rapidly declined; during the 19th c. they were largely abandoned, or transformed for other uses, or in some cases actually demolished by owners no longer willing to pay the taxes on luxury homes introduced by the Italian government after unification (1866). Thereafter, a new economic system developed along the Riviera, with different buildings and different methods of transportation – no longer on water, but by land – especially after the inauguration of the railroad between Marghera and Padua.

From Stra to Venice

The route described here runs entirely along the river, and offers, to the extent that it is still possible, a sense of the landscape and architecture that has largely been lost. Still, tourists should be aware that along this river – now that the factors no longer hold which once, in the 16th and 17th c., so closely bound the surrounding hinterland with the Naviglio, or canal, and the entire route with Venice itself – you will find residential areas and structures that clash sharply, even glaringly. Along this waterway there is a new Burchiello, running from Padua to Venice and back ever since 1960, through the good offices of the Ente Provinciale per il Turismo (Tourism Office) of Padua. Service generally runs from late March to late October: Wednesday, Friday, and Sunday departing from Padua (Stra); Tuesday, Thursday, and Saturday departing from Venice. The outing – which takes a full day – is organized by SIAMIC EXPRESS of Padua (tel. 049/660944); you may contact them to make the necessary reservations, or you make them through a travel agency (during the busy seasons, you should make reservations well ahead). The Burchiello generally leaves

Riviera del Brenta

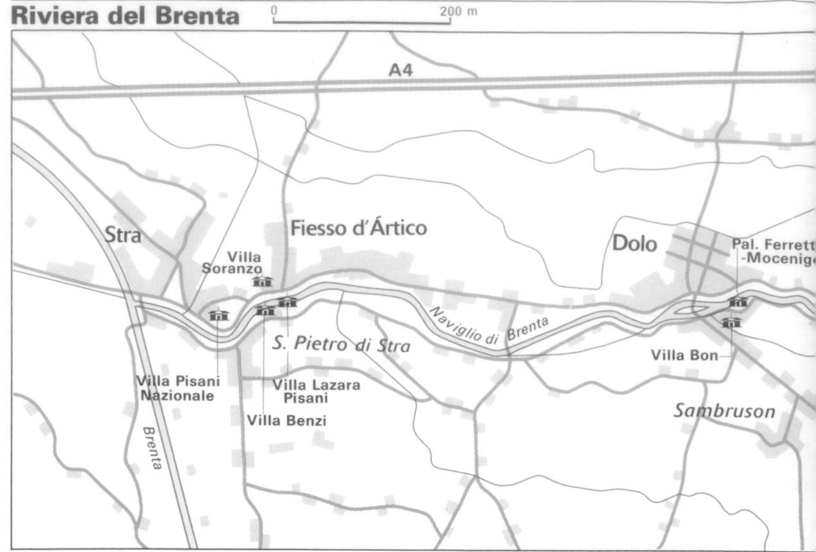

from Stra following a guided tour of Villa Pisani (you can get here from Venice, Piazzale Roma, with public transportation), stopping at Villa Wildmann (Mira Porte) and Villa Foscari (Malcontenta), and arriving in Venice at the landing jetty, or Pontile Giardinetti di S. Marco.

Stra. This prosperous manufacturing town (footwear), through which the Via Emilia Altinate ran in Roman times (it would seem that the name of the town derives from a shortened version of the Italian word "strada," meaning "road"), was fortified in the Middle Ages, and was later dotted with numerous handsome villas. Its chief claim to fame, however, comes from the immense **Villa Pisani*** (now Villa Nazionale), the last major structure to emerge from the "cultura di villa," a princely home built in full Venetian decline.

The Pisani family already possessed a small building on this land, which extended over roughly 11 hectares, and decided to build a villa that would adequately reflect the wealth and power it had accumulated in Venice. We are not certain just when work began, though it appears that when Alvise Pisani was elected doge, in 1735, the walls and all masonry had been completed. The project was at first entrusted to the Paduan architect Girolamo Frigimelica, who built the stables and other structures in the garden; then the job was taken over by Francesco Maria Preti, who modified the existing plans for the villa, while basically remaining faithful to the ideas of his predecessor.

After the fall of Venice in 1797, as the riches of the family dwindled, Alvise and Francesco Pisani sold the villa for a large sum of money, on 8 June 1807, to Napoleon Bonaparte, who made a gift of it to the Viceroy of Italy Eugène Beauharnais (hence the name of Villa Eugenia, by which it is also known); in 1814 it became a possession of the Emperor of Austria, and finally, in 1866, it passed to the house of Savoy, kings of Italy. In 1882 it was given to the local government, which in turn leased it in 1911 to the Centro di Ricerche Idrotecniche, an irrigation-research center, which built the large wading pool in the park. On 14 July 1934, grim history was made here; Mussolini and Hitler met for the first time. Now it belongs to the Italian state.

Of the splendid furniture with which the wealthy family of the Pisani had decorated their sumptuous villa, almost nothing remains; there are just a few items still adorning the countless cold and empty rooms: virtually the only ornaments that remain are the frescoes, done by the best known Venetian artists of the 18th c.

The facade overlooking the Brenta, more magnificent than the facade overlooking the park, has a central structure with caryatids on the ground floor, supporting the broad balcony; from that balcony rise large Corinthian semi-columns, surmounted by an ornate cornice and a triangular pediment adorned with statues; two long wings, punctuated by Ionic pilaster strips and crowned by a balustrade with statues, terminate in the lesser facades, with triangular pediments. To the left and right, note the

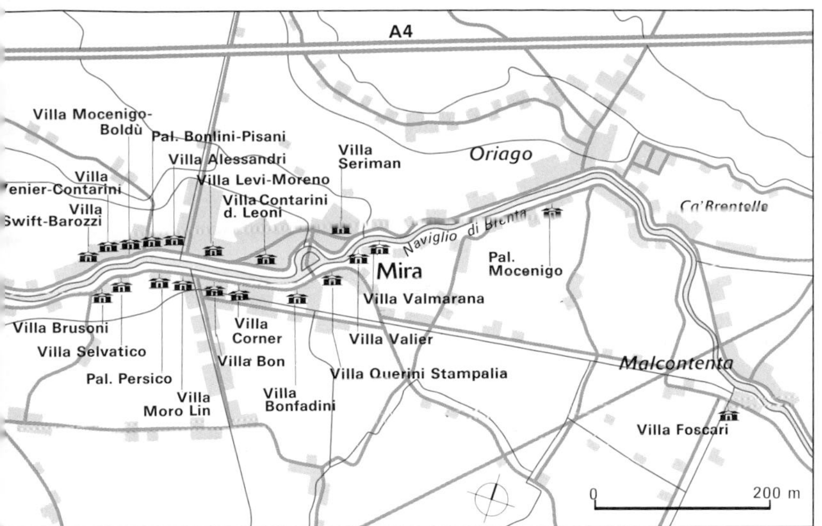

two splendid portals leading into the grounds, with handsome wrought-iron gates. The complex, which still has the stately grandeur of an 18th-c. palace, despite all the plundering it has suffered, is periodically subjected to restoration, so that from time to time both the villa and its grounds may be closed. The tour may therefore vary in the features visited. Hours: 9-1:30, closed Monday; the grounds are open until 4 in the winter and until 6 in the summer.

On the interior, the central building contains an entrance hall on the ground floor, and the ball room on the second floor; this latter is twice the height of a normal story, and is flanked by two smaller halls (overlooking the river Brenta and overlooking the grounds); the two side wings, arranged around interior courtyards, feature the various services on the ground floor, and the master apartments and guest rooms on the second floor. The only existing bathroom was built for Napoleon, next to his bedroom, set at the far east end of the building, toward the Brenta.

You will enter through the atrium, with rusticated columns; the atrium extends the length of the building all the way to the garden; this atrium is flanked by two porticoed courtyards, decorated with monochrome frescoes. A stairway with a frescoed tondo, by Jacopo Guarana, leads up to the main floor. Of the many richly frescoed rooms, the one that sticks in the memory is the majestic ball room, two stories tall, with a gallery. At the doorways, note two gilded brass gateways. The painted archi-

The Villa Pisani at Stra

tecture seems to make the hall larger, and serves as a frame for the ceiling fresco* by G.B. Tiepolo; painted between 1760 and 1762, it was Tiepolo's farewell to his birthplace, before he left for Spain. The theme is the glory of the Pisani family. The monochromatic scenes above the gallery, where the orchestra played, are by his son, Gian Domenico Tiepolo.
The immense grounds, renovated in the 19th c. and impoverished by the cutting of valuable plants following WWII, still have iment and attic, also lined with statues, and lateral structures, with 24 enclosures for horses, each adorned with a slender column supporting a small wooden horse, rearing up. You then walk through the woods and, skirting the fence, along a boulevard lined with hornbeam trees, where you will reach the *belvedere*, a monumental gate flanked by two columns; each column has a spiral staircase that leads up to a terrace; from here, you can enjoy a splendid view of the park and the banks of the canal.

A drawing room in Villa Pisani at Stra

the flavor of the 18th-c. design. They contain a number of buildings dating from the 18th c., designed by Girolamo Frigimelica.
Take the large avenue to your right and then, as you turn to your left, you will reach the *labyrinth* (described by Gabriele d'Annunzio in '*Il Fuoco*'), formed by little twisting lanes of boxwood; after twisting and turning through the maze for awhile, you will reach the central tower, with two spiral staircases; climb to the top. Then you will encounter the *exedra*, a remarkable panoptical structure built to frame a view of the farthest reaches of the park, but also the sky (which appears, from this viewpoint, to be framed by a dome that is open above, around which is a terrace with a balustrade and a line of statues. A little further along, a small lane left ends not far from a moat surrounding a hillock, atop which stands a rectangular pavilion (once used as an ice house). At the end of the walkway, a gate and a fence separate the park from the *serre*, or greenhouses, and from the *aranciera*, or "orangerie," which is still dotted with 18th-c. statues. Then you will reach the *stables*, an elegant building with a central pronaos with Ionic columns and a ped-

Also in the town proper, beyond the Baroque *Palazzo Cappello* which once belonged to the nearby Villa Pisani, along the segment of the state road 11 (running toward Padua) known as the "Strada del Capriccio" – a reference to the intense social activity that went on here during the height of the Serenissima – are a series of notable villas. On the right is the *Villa Badoer-Draghi*, a late-15th-c. building with a central portico with three arches, twin-light and single-light mullioned windows with round arches, and traces of exterior painted decorations. Next comes the *Villa Zanetti*, built in the 17th c. and enlarged in 1768, decorated on the interior with perspectival paintings, decorations, and landscapes (1768). Last, also on the right, is *Villa Gritti*, from the 16th c., with a large "barchessa," and a handsome park.
Beyond the oxbow curve in the river Brenta that encloses the Villa Pisani, on the right is the 17th-c. *Villa Benzi*. To the left, across the road, is the early-16th-c. *Villa Soranzo*, frescoed on the elevation overlooking the water with *mythological episodes* attributed to Benedetto Caliari, and, on the western elevation, with architectural motifs.

On the opposite bank, note the long facade of the **Villa Lazara Pisani**, an imposing complex with horizontal orientation, known as *La Barbariga* because it was the home of Chiara Barbarigo Pisani. It has a central Baroque building with symmetrical wings added at the end of the 18th c.; the facade overlooking the water is simpler than the inner elevation, with elegant porticoes.
In the English-style garden (18th/19th c.), note the *Torre dell'Orologio*, an early-18th-c. clock tower.
Between Fiesso d'Àrtico and Dolo the villas become less frequent, and the river Brenta runs over the locks that recall the verses by Goldoni: "D'acque sonanti un mormorio si sente; / Esco all'aperto e riconosco Dolo" – "I hear a murmur of rushing waters; / I come out on deck and I see Dolo."

Dolo. The name is linked to the Paduan family of Dauli, which once had immense landholdings here; the town began to grow in size and importance from the end of the 15th c. It was then that the "conca" was built (now covered) around which it expanded. Here mills were built (one of which is still operating) as well as the only "squero" (16th c.) along the entire Naviglio, still standing not far from the late-16th-c. *Villa Bon* and not far from Palazzo Ferretti Mocenigo (now a school) designed in 1596 by Vincenzo Scamozzi.

As you sail toward Mira Vecchia note the growing number of villas, which form an almost unbroken succession, with the houses of the surrounding villages.

Mira. This scattered township comprises various villages, including Mira Vecchia (or Piazza Vecchia), Mira Taglio, and Mira Porte; some say that the name comes from the cult of S. Nicolò (St. Nicholas) bishop di Myra, an ancient city in Lycia (now Turkey); this cult spread through the proselytizing done by a local land-owning family that supposedly helped to transport that saint's remains to Bari in the 11th c.
In the great curve in the river just before *Mira Vecchia*, on the right stands the *Villa Brusoni*, probably built in the late-17th c. but rebuilt in the 19th c., with the Romantic park attributed to Giuseppe Jappelli. On the left is the 18th-c. *Villa Swift-Barozzi*, with an elevation in 19th-c. style, decorated with frescoes; on the right, with a landing jetty, note the *Villa Selvatico*, built between the end of the 17th c. and the beginning of the 18th c., and later renovated. At the curve in the Naviglio, on the left bank, surrounded by gardens, stands the *Villa Venier-Contarini*, first built in the late-16th c.; in the 17th c., guest-houses were added, along with an oratory, rebuilt in 1752.
Along the left bank, note the series of villas: the *Villa Mocenigo-Boldù*, possibly built in the 17th c., but heavily renovated since; the late-16th-c. or early-17th-c. *Palazzo Bonlini-Pisani*, with grounds and outlying buildings; the **Villa Alessandri**, composed of a cube-shaped 16th-c. "palazzetto" and a Baroque guest-house in the style of Longhena.
At this point you are in Mira Taglio, which takes its name from the "taglio," or "cut," meaning the Canale di Mirano, built in 1595 to link the river Brenta with Mirano, center of the scattered township of Mira.
Overlooking the bridge over the Canale di Mirano is the 17th-c. *Palazzo Persico*, with 19th-c. additions (balustrade); next, at the confluence with the Canale Nuovissimo (or Taglio di Brenta) – which was excavated in 1621 in order to shift the course of the river Brenta away from the Venetian lagoon, so that some of the water emptied south of Chioggia – is the *Villa Moro Lin*, which was rebuilt in the 20th c. After the Piazza del Municipio, a town square built on the site of the dry river basin that was shut down in the 19th c., you will see on your left the 17th-c. *Villa Levi-Moreno*, with a large park. On the other bank, beyond the 18th-c. *Villa Bon*, with frescoes on the interior by Costantino Cedini, is the *Villa Corner*, renovated in the 19th c., with a park and a little chapel. Facing it is the *Villa Contarini dei Leoni*, now owned by the city, a compact cubic structure built in 1558 by the Procurator Federico Contarini, and once decorated with frescoes by Giambattista Tiepolo (1754); the frescoes depict a stay in the villa by Henry III of France, who visited here in 1574: those frescoes were detached in 1893 and sold abroad; they are now in the Musée Jacquemart-André in Paris.
The economy here is for the most part industrial: on the site where the Villa Contarini dalle Torri, by Longhena, once stood, you will now see the enormous industrial complex of the Mira Lanza company, one of the largest manufacturers in Italy of soaps and detergents. The nucleus of this structure was a candle factory built around 1838, with the demolition of the 17th-c. architecture.
As you leave Mira Taglio, on a line with the 18th-c. *Villa Bonfadini*, you will see that the Naviglio splits in two; the original course turns off to the left, running through the town of *Mira Porte*, where the locks once

stood (filled in in 1936). After another set of locks and a bridge over the right-hand branch of the Naviglio, you will see on the right bank the *Villa Querini Stampalia*, a building dating from the early-16th c., with a large central structure and lateral "barchesse"; on the inside, note the remarkable 16th-c. frescoes, some of which are attributed to Bonifacio de' Pitati and Andrea Schiavone. Next you will see what survives of the *Villa Valier*, known as *La Chitarra*, after the subject of one of the frescoes that once adorned the facade, partly detached and now preserved in the Gallerie dell'Accademia, in Venice.

The Naviglio enters *Riscossa*, a town named after the fact that the Venetian tithes were collected here ("riscossa" means "tax collection"). On the left bank, note the **Villa Seriman**, later the *Villa Widmann-Rezzonico-Foscari*, now property of the Venetian Provincial Government. Built in 1719 along with the "barchessa" and the oratory, attributed to Andrea Tirali, it was given its present appearance through a renovation done in the second half of the 18th c., to adapt it to the Rococo tastes of the owners of the time. Open: 9-7; closed Monday.

In the central hall, set in lavish cornices in false stucco, note the series of frescoes attributed to Giuseppe Angeli: in the ceiling, *Glory of the Widmann family*; on the walls, *Abduction of Helen* and the *Sacrifice of Iphigenia* (perhaps done with the assistance of students). In the garden, note the numerous 18th-c. statues, many of which come from villas that have been demolished.

Across from the Villa Seriman, on the right bank, you can see the 17th-c. "barchesse" of the *Villa Valmarana*, whose main structure was demolished in 1908 to avoid the taxes on luxury homes; the building on the right, once a guest-house, contains rooms with late-18th-c. frescoes.

Oriago. After you cross the swing bridge and sail under the railroad bridge, the Naviglio continues straight as an arrow, lined by the occasional villa, running through Oriago, which existed in Roman times; until 1405 Oriago was a border outpost between the territories of Padua and Venice. On the right bank, note the *Palazzo Gradenigo*, built at the end of the 16th c., with fragments of frescoes still adorning the facade. Next comes the imposing facade of the 18th-c. *Palazzo Mocenigo* (now a school building), with a curving pediment which surmounts the slightly jutting central structure. On the left bank, after the swing walkway, note the parish church of *S. Maria Maddalena*, rebuilt in 1515, with a 15th-c. campanile with a conical cusp (on the main altar, note the two marble *angels* by Giulio del Moro). Next to it stands the heavily renovated *Palazzo Querini Moro*, built at the end of the 16th c. (though some say a century earlier); note the plaque engraved with the verses from Dante's Divine Comedy (Purgatorio V, 64-84) describing the death of Jacopo del Cassero, murdered here in 1298 at the orders of Azzo VIII d'Este.

As it leaves Oriago, the Naviglio runs past the *Villa Allegri*, on the left, note a composite construction dating from the second half of the 18th c., and (walled into the corner of a modern building) a cusped aedicule boundary stone, erected in 1375 to mark the boundaries of the Dogado. The buildings begin to become more scattered: you will sail along for a good distance before seeing, on the left, the *Villa Priuli*, an elegant building comprising an original nucleus dating from the 16th c.; in the 17th c., a three-arched loggia was added. After you cross the aqueduct over the Statale Romea (state road), in a curve of the river, on the right, you will see through the trees the lovely shape of the **Villa Foscari*** known as **La Malcontenta** from a legend that it was the country "exile" of a woman from the Foscari family who was caught in adultery. Built by Andrea Palladio around 1555 for Nicola and Alvise Foscari, a three-story building with smooth ashlars, presenting different facades toward the river Brenta and toward the countryside.

On the river side, note the majestic Ionic loggia set on a high base, surmounted by a pediment and flanked by two handsome staircases, laying open the main floor to the surrounding countryside. On the other side, the facade is quite compact, with a slightly jutting central structure (which features a flattened version of the relief on the loggia) with a pediment, enlivened by a large central thermal window. On the roof, note the four sophisticated round chimneys. Open: from 1 May to 31 October: Tuesday, Saturday, and the first Sunday of the month, 9-12.

The arrangement of rooms and halls on the interior revolves around the large hall with a Greek-cross plan on the main floor ("piano nobile"), around which open four rooms and two small cubicles. The frescoes decorating the various rooms, completed by 1561, are chiefly by G.B. Zelotti, who replaced Battista Franco; it is likely that some work was also done by B. India. The hall, entirely frescoed by Zelotti, is stylistically consistent, within the architectural and

The Palazzo Mocenigo at Oriago

decorative framework: in the ceiling vault, surrounding the central hexagon with the *Virtues and Evils of the Earth*, note four ovals with *Astraea Showing Zeus the Pleasures of the Earth; Midas on His Throne with Envy, Discord, and a Troop of Evils; Two Women Offering Incense to Janus* and *Zeus and Hermes Descending to Earth*. In the lunettes, *Banquet of Philemon and Baucis; The Gods Watch the Murder of a Wayfarer;* and *Zeus and Hermes Return to the Heavens After Thanking Philemon and Baucis for Their Hospitality*; the other lunettes depict *Astrology, Poetry, Music* and *Strategy*. Toward the corners of the cross vault that leads to the two square rooms, note the *Four Seasons* (yellow monochromes) and, above the corbels, *Busts of Roman Emperors* (mono chromes in chiaroscuro). In the two small cubicles, note landscapes and grotesques, probably by Bernardino India. In the four halls ("Stanze") on either side of the cross vault, note frescoes by Zelotti (rooms of Bacchus and Venus, Aurora, and Cacus and Prometheus) and, by B. Franco (*Fall of the Giants*); in the Stanza dell'Aurora, note the *Woman Entering Through a Door*, identified as the "Malcontenta" of legend.

The Naviglio flows into the lagoon. The Palladian villa certainly marks the climax of this route; it then approaches the lagoon in a somewhat damaged environmental setting. Following the village of *Malcontenta*, which extends along the river, on either bank, both sides being linked by a swing bridge (the name of the town, documented as early as the 14th c., supposedly comes from the suffering inflicted upon the population by the flooding that was triggered by the Paduans, who turned the river out of its course in order to harm the Venetians), the dominant element in the landscape is constituted by the looming industrial plants of Porto Marghera. You will pass a last set of locks, built in the 18th c., at *Moranzani*; this was the location of the "palada," i.e., the toll and customs station, named after the docking poles, which marked the terminus of the Seriola, the 16th-c. aqueduct of Venice; the Seriola deviated the flow of water upstream from the Naviglio and purified it along its long course, ending in a series of pools for final decantation. The last town before you enter the lagoon is *Fusina*, which takes its name from the presence, in the Middle Ages, of "fucine," a term that was used to describe forges or smithies, or, in that period, the dye-works that had been installed here. In the 19th c., prior to the construction of the bridge across the lagoon, this was the terminus of the tramway to Padua; the vaporetto to Venice also docked here. All that survives of the settlement that sprang up on the bank around these structures are a small and ancient chapel, and a tavern, founded in the 16th c. By this point, you are in the lagoon, the horizon spreads out and in the distance you can see the skyline of Venice; toward which you head, and finally arrive at the landing jetty of St. Mark's (Pontile di S. Marco).

Information for Travellers: Hotels, Restaurants, Places of interest

Sestiere by sestiere, this list includes hotels, with an indication of their official classification, expressed by number of stars, in compliance with the Italian law (from ★★★★L to ★). All restaurants listed are classified with the "fork" simbols that TCI has long used to indicate level of overall quality (from 🍴🍴🍴 to 🍴). This is not an official classification, only an indicative ranking, indicating the levels of quality, comfort, setting and price.
Hotels and restaurants are followed by a capital letter and number (E5) followed by one (or two) bold letters (**ab**) which should refer you to its location on the maps, identified by a number.
As of 18th December 1998 each location's telephone code must also be dialled for local calls, indicated in the following list next to the symbol ☎. For those calling from abroad, the local code (including the 0) must be dialled after the international code for Italy, followed by the subscriber's number. The following information has been carefully checked before going to press. We would, however, advise readers to confirm certain data which is susceptible to change, before departure. All observations and suggestions are gratefully accepted.

Venice

✉ 30100 ☎ 041

Tourist information offices, page 20

San Marco

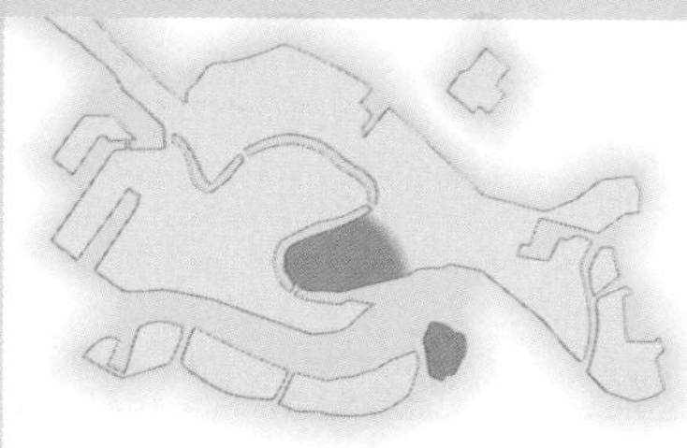

This is the official drawing room of Venice, the historical, political, and monumental nucleus of the city over the centuries. Surrounding the square is a "sestiere" with a rich array of hotels, fine restaurants, and a vast shopping section. From the countless museums to the churches, theaters, and movie house (almost all of the cinemas in Venice are concentrated in San Marco), the only problem is picking and choosing.

Hotels

★★★★L **Gritti Palace ITT Sheraton.** Campo S. Maria del Giglio 2647, tel. 794611, fax 5200942; 93 rooms, all with baths or showers. Restaurant. Access for the disabled. Private beach, swimming pool, and tennis courts at Lido. A 15th-c. palazzo on the Grand Canal, renovated and furnished with fine antiques. (5 F3, **f**).

★★★★ **Bauer Grünwald.** Campo S. Moisè 1459, tel. 5207022, fax 5207557, tlx 410075 Baveve I; 214 rooms, all with baths or showers. Restaurant. Access for the disabled. (5 E4, **a**).

★★★★ **Cavalletto & Doge Orseolo.** Calle del Cavalletto 1107, tel. 5200955, fax 5238184; 95 rooms, all with baths or showers. Restaurant. (5 D5, **l**).

★★★★ **Concordia.** Calle Larga S. Marco 367, tel. 5206866, fax 5206775, tlx 411069 Concor I; 57 rooms, all with baths or showers. No restaurant. (5 D6, **m**).

★★★★ **Europa & Regina Cigahotel.** Corte Barozzi 2159, tel. 5200477, fax 5231533; 185 rooms, all with baths or showers. Restaurant. Private beach, pool, and tennis courts at Lido; garage in Piazzale Roma. (5 E4, **d**).

★★★★ **Luna Hotel Baglioni.** Calle Larga de l'Ascension 1243, tel. 5289840, fax 5287160, tlx 410236 Lunave; 117 rooms, all with baths or showers. Restaurant. (5 E5, **ab**).

★★★★ **Saturnia & International.** Calle Larga XXII Marzo 2398, tel. 5208377, fax 5207131-5205858; 95 rooms, all with baths or showers. Restaurant. (5 E4, **ag**).

★★★★ **Starhotel Splendid Suisse.** S. Marco Mercerie 760, tel. 5200755, fax 5286498, tlx 410590 Hosple; 166 rooms, all with baths or showers. Restaurant. (5 C5, **ah**).

★★★ **Ala.** Campo Santa Maria del Giglio 2494, tel. 5208333, fax 5206390, tlx 410275 Alavce; 85 rooms, all with baths or showers. No restaurant. (5 E3, **al**).

★★★ **Bonvecchiati.** Calle Goldoni 4488, tel. 5285017, fax 5285230; 95 rooms, all with baths or showers. Restaurant. (5 D4-5, **aq**).

★★★ **Do Pozzi.** Corte dei Do Pozzi 2373, tel. 5207855, fax 5229413; 29 rooms, all with baths or showers. No restaurant. (5 E4, **av**).

★★★ **Flora.** Calle dei Bergamaschi 2283/A, tel. 520584 4, fax 5228217; 44 rooms, all with baths or showers. No restaurant. Special access for the handicapped. (5 E4, **aw**).

★★★ **La Fenice et Des Artistes.** Campiello Marinoni or Campiello della Fenice 1936, tel. 5232333, fax 5203721; 69 rooms, 67 of which have either bath or shower. No restaurant. (5 D-E3, **bb**).

★★★ **Rialto.** Pescaria S. Bartolomeo 5149, tel. 5209166, fax 5238958, tlx 420809 Rialbe I; 77 rooms, all with baths or showers. Restaurant. (5 B-C4-5, **bg**).

★★★ **San Moisè.** Piscina S. Moisè 2058, tel. 5203755, fax 5210670; 16 rooms, all with baths or showers. No restaurant. (5 E4, **bi**).

★★ **San Fantin.** Campiello Marinoni or Campiello della Fenice 1930/A, tel. and fax 5231401; 14 rooms, 10 of which have either bath or shower. No restaurant. (5 D3, **by**).

★★ **San Zulian.** Calle S. Zulian 535, tel. 5225872, fax 5232265; 22 rooms, all with baths or showers. No restaurant. (5 C5, **bz**).

Restaurants

Antico Martini. Campo S. Fantin 1983, tel. 5224121. Closed Tuesday and Wednesday lunch. International menu. (5 E4, **rt**).

Harry's Bar. Calle Vallaresso 1323, tel. 5285777, fax 5208822. (5 F5, **sl**).

Alla Colomba. Piscina di Frezzeria 1665, tel. 5221175, fax 5221468. Closed Wednesday. Venetian cooking. (5 D4, **rf**).

La Caravella. Calle Larga XXII Marzo 2397/2402, tel. 5208901-5208938. Closed Wednesday. Venetian cooking, primarily seafood. (5 E4, **so**).

Taverna La Fenice. Campiello della Fenice 1938, tel. 5223856. Closed Sunday and Monday lunch. International menu. (5 E3-4, **ta**).

Al Graspo de Ua. Calle dei Bombaseri 5094, tel. 5200150-5223647, fax 5233917. Closed Monday. (5 C5, **rb**).

Da Raffaele. Ponte delle Ostreghe 2347, tel. 5232317-5289940, fax 5229413. Closed Thursday. Seafood especially. (5 E3-4, **sc**).

Do Forni. Calle degli Specchieri 457/468, tel. 5230663. Closed Thursday in low season. Venetian cooking. (5 D6, **se**).

Antica Carbonera. Calle Bembo 4648, tel. 5225479. Closed Tuesday and Sunday. Traditional cooking. (5 C4, **rp**).

Bàcari

Agli Assassini. Rio Terrà dei Assassini 3695, tel. 5287986. Closed Sunday and Saturday lunch. Near Campo S. Angelo. Excellent wine; try the grilled vegetables (5 D4, **s**).

Al Bacareto. Calle de le Boteghe 3447, tel. 5289336. Closed Saturday evening and Sunday. Try the "*cichéti al bruco*". International clientele. (5 D2, **x**).

Al Volto. Calle Cavalli 4081, tel. 5228945. Closed Sunday and Saturday lunch. Near the Municipio. It is especially renowned for its wine list, with 1,300 varieties (5 C4, **rn**).

Vino Vino. Calle del Cafetièr 2007/A, tel. 5237027. Closed Tuesday. This is a pleasant place for a quick meal. There are traditional Venetian dishes and a good selection of wines (5 E4, **td**).

Cafes and pastry shops

Caffè Florian. Piazza S. Marco 56, tel. 5285338. Closed Wednesday. Since 1720 this cafe has been famous throughout Europe, and it is one of the symbols of the city: this was the office of the newspaper, the Gazzetta Veneta, and it witnessed the uprisings of 1848. It has always been a gathering place for intellectuals, Venetian and from elsewhere (ranging from such historic Italian authors as Gozzi and Parini, to Goethe and George Sand, and such latter-day figures as Piovene and Guttuso); today it is as lively as ever, and the coffee is always first-rate.

Gran Caffè Quadri. Piazza S. Marco 120, tel. 5289299-5222105, fax 5208041. Closed Monday. This 19th-c. cafe has a little restaurant upstairs, and is a well estalished rival to Caffè Florian. Both places claim to have been the first to serve Turkish coffee in Venice.

Le Bistrot de Venise. Calle dei Fabbri 4685, tel. 5236651. Closed Tuesday. Breton crepés, Venetian specialities.

Marchini. Calle del Spezier 2769, tel. 5229109-5287507. Closed Tuesday. Excellent pastry shop not far from Campo S. Stefano. Marzipan, fruit tarts, and traditional pastries.

Rosa Salva A. Campo S. Luca 4589, tel. 5225385. Closed Sunday. Rosa Salva E. Calle Fiubera 951, tel. 5210544. Closed Sunday. Rosa Salva E. Mercerie S. Salvador 5020, tel. 5227934. Closed Sunday. A family of pastry chefs in the Sestiere di S. Marco; they also supply hotels and restaurants, and cater meals and parties. Renowned for its Venetian-style semolina pudding, with raisins.

Zorzi. Calle dei Fuseri 4357, tel. 5225350. Closed Sunday morning. This is a traditional dairy bar, nicely renewed. Try the excellent whipped cream and crème caramel.

Museums and cultural institutions

Campanile di S. Giorgio Maggiore. Isola di S. Giorgio Maggiore, tel. 5227827 (switchboard). *Weekdays, weekends and holidays: 10-12:30; 2:30-4:30.*

Campanile di S. Marco. Tel. 5224064. *Weekdays, weekends and holidays: 9:30-4.*

Gallerie Basilica di S. Marco. Tel. 5225205. *Weekdays, weekends and holidays: 9:30-4:30.*

Museo Archeologico. Piazza S. Marco 52, tel. 5225978. *Weekdays, weekends and holidays 9-2.*

Museo Civico Correr. Piazza S. Marco 52, tel. 5225625. *Weekdays, weekends and holidays 9-5.*

Museo & Centro di Documentazione di Palazzo Fortuny. San Beneto 3780, tel. 5200995. Closed for restoration.

Pala d'Oro & Treasure of San Marco. Basilica di S. Marco, tel. 5225697. *Weekdays and Saturday 9:30-5; Sunday and holidays 1-4:30.*

Palazzo Ducale. Piazzetta S. Marco, tel. 5224951. *Weekdays, weekends and holidays 8:30-5.*

Torre dell'Orologio. Mercerie dell'Orologio, tel. 5231879. Closed for restoration.

Ateneo Veneto (Venice University). Campo S. Fantin 1897, tel. 5224459, fax 5200487.

Biblioteca Nazionale Marciana (Library). Piazzetta S. Marco 7, tel. 5208788 (switchboard). Open by reservation; *Weekdays 9-7; Saturday 9-1:30.* Closed Sunday.

Centro Internazionale della Grafica. Campo S. Maurizio 2670, tel. 5221825-5235707.

Conservatorio di Musica Benedetto Marcello (Conservatory). Campiello Pisani 2810, tel. 5225604 (secretariat).

Dipartimento di Studi Storici (Università degli Studi; Historical Institute). Calle del Piovan 2546, tel. 2704811.

Fondazione Bevilacqua La Masa (Foundation). Piazza S. Marco 71/c, tel. 5208955-5208879-5237819.

Fondazione Giorgio Cini (Foundation). Isola di S. Giorgio Maggiore, tel. 5289900.

Fondazione Levi (Foundation). Calle Giustinian 2893, tel. 786711.

Gran Teatro La Fenice (Independent Org.). Palazzo Franchetti, San Marco 2847, tel. 786511, 5210161 (box office CA.RI.VE), 5204010 (Tronchetto), fax 5209986.

Istituto Veneto di Scienze, Lettere ed Arti (Institute for Science, Literature, and Arts). Campiello S. Stefano 2945, tel. 5210177 (Library).

Palazzo Grassi. Campo S. Samuele 3231, tel. 5231680 (switchboard) – 5286722 (cultural activities) – 5221375 (press office), fax 5286218.

Comune di Venezia. (Ca' Farsetti) city hall and administrative offices. Riva del Carbon 4136, tel. 2708111 (switchboard).

World Monuments Fund Venice Committee. Piazza San Marco 63, tel. 5237614.

Churches

Basilica di S. Marco. Tel. 5225697. *Open: summer 9:45-5; Sunday 2-5; winter 10-4; Sunday 2-4.*

S. Moisè. Tel. 5285840. *Open: 3:30-7.*

S. Salvador. Tel. 5236717. *Open: 10-12; 5-7.*

S. Zulian. Tel. 5235383. *Open: 8:45-12; 4-7.*

S. Stefano. Tel. 5222362. *Open: 8-12; 4-7.*

Santa Maria del Giglio. Tel. 5225739. *Open: 9-12; 3:15-6:30 (winter: 3:30-5:30).*

S. Maurizio. Tel. 5222294. *Open: 7-12.*

S. Giorgio. Tel. 5289900. *Open: 9-12:30; 2-5.*

S. Fantin. Tel. 5235236. *Open: 9-12; 4-6:30.*

S. Luca. Tel. 5229566. *Open: 8-12; 4:30-6:30.*

Entertainment

Cinema Centrale. Piscina di Frezzeria 1659, tel. 5228201.

Cinema Olimpia. Campo S. Gallo 1094, tel. 5205439.

Cinema Ritz. Calle dei Segretari 617, tel. 5204429.

Cinema Rossini. Salizada del Teatro 3988, tel. 5230322.

Sala Concerti del Circolo Artistico (Concert hall). Palazzo delle Prigioni, tel. 5225707.

Teatro Goldoni. Calle del Teatro or Calle de la Comedia 4650/B, tel. 5205422 (switchboard) – 5207583 (ticket window).

In Campo S. Maurizio, on Christmas, Easter, and during the Regata storica, there is a very nice antiques market, the **Mercatino dell'Antiquariato**.

Sports

Compagnia della Vela (Sailing). Molo S. Marco (secretariat), tel. 5222593. Darsena Grande S. Giorgio. Isola di S. Giorgio Maggiore, tel. 5210723.

Shops, crafts, and fine art

Bottega Veneta. Calle Vallaresso 1337, tel. 5228489. Accessories in leather; colorful, high quality.

Franz. Calle del Spezier 2770/A, tel. 5285408. Refined clothing and linen, and especially items in silk. Near Campo S. Stefano.

Franz Baby. Calle S. Luca 4578/A, tel. 5227846. **Franz** for children: elegant clothing, with a slightly old-fashioned style.

Olbi. Calle della Mandola 3653, tel. 5285025. Marbled paper, created with an age-old technique.

Piazzesi. Campiello della Feltrina 2511, tel. 5221202. Refined tradition, with 18th-c. prints, located between Santa Maria del Giglio and S. Maurizio.

Bohm. Salizzada S. Moisè 1349/1350, tel. 5222255. Prints from the 18th and 19th c., modern lithographs, and a handsome edition of photographs from the Naya archives.

Galleria d'Arte Del Cavallino. Frezzeria 1725, tel. 5210488. Founded by Carlo Cardazzo, this is one of the historic private art galleries of Venice. It now works mainly with English and American painters.

Galleria d'Arte Il Capricorno. Calle Drio la Chiesa 1994, tel. 5206920. Between S. Fantin and Piscina di Frezzeria. This gallery has begun to work with the European Transavanguardia.

Galleria d'Arte Il Traghetto. Campo S. Maria del Giglio 2460, tel. 5221188. From Guidi to Santomaso, from Vedova to Saetti.

Galleria d'Arte Ravagnan. Piazza S. Marco 50/a, tel. 5203021. In the "high-society drawing room" of Venice, with works by De Luigi, Memo, Pagnacco.

Galleria d'Arte Santo Stefano. Campo S. Stefano 2953, tel. 5234518. This was Giorgio de Chirico's favorite art gallery in Venice.

Studio d'Arte Barnabò. Calle Malipiero 3074, tel. 5200673. Near Palazzo Grassi, with special attention to new talents.

Codognato. Calle Seconda de l'Ascension 1295, tel. 5225042. For generations, a solid assurance of quality: antique and modern jewelry, Art Nouveau.

Herriz. Calle Larga XXII Marzo 2381, tel. 5204276. Jewelry for collectors (especially from the Twenties and Thirties).

Missaglia. Piazza S. Marco 125, tel. 5224464. A Venetian institution for nearly 150 years. Creations in gold and precious stones, entirely handcrafted.

Nardi. Piazza S. Marco 69, tel. 5225733-5232150. Under the Sign of the Moors ("Il Segno dei Mori"), brooches, rings, bracelets, and necklaces.

Cassini. Calle Larga XXII Marzo 2424, tel. 5231815. The oldest of Venice's antiquarian bookshops.

Fantoni. Salizzada S. Luca 4121, tel. 5220700. The art bookshop with the largest selection in the historical center.

Il Fontego. Calle del Fontego dei Tedeschi 5361, tel. 5200470. A small bookshop with a wide selection, of magazines as well.

Valese. Calle Fiubera 793, tel. 5227282. From the most respected foundry in Venice, fine Venetian masks in brass.

De Marchi. Salizzada S. Samuele 3157, tel. 5285694. A world of wooden sculptures, some of them life-size, ranging from everyday implements to carved animals, startlingly real.

"M" Oggetti d'Arte. Frezzeria 1691, tel. 5235666. Jewelry inspired by the Art Nouveau style, clothing and fabrics for home furnishing, printed in the old style.

Stuffi. Calle Fiubera 815, tel. 5226610. Restoration of antique fans.

Zanin. Salizzada S. Samuele 3337, tel. 5285346. Restoration, gilding, and lacquering of statues, furniture, and frames. Stefano Zanin does the most delicate restorations, such as that of *boiseries* and the gilding of the Accademia Militare in the Palazzo Ducale of Modena.

Rubelli. Campo S. Gallo 1089 (exhibition), tel. 5236110. Fabrics for home furnishings, famous throughout the world: "soprarizzi" in velvet, silk brocades, motifs taken from designs by contemporary artists.

Trois. Campo S. Maurizio 2666, tel. 5222905. You can still find Fortuny fabrics, produced according to the original methods of dyeing and printing.

Archimede Seguso. Piazza S. Marco 61, tel. 5289041. Designer glass: a revolution of styles and techniques.

Venini. Piazzetta dei Leoncini 314 (retail outlet), tel. 5224045. Designer glass, famous throughout the world.

San Polo

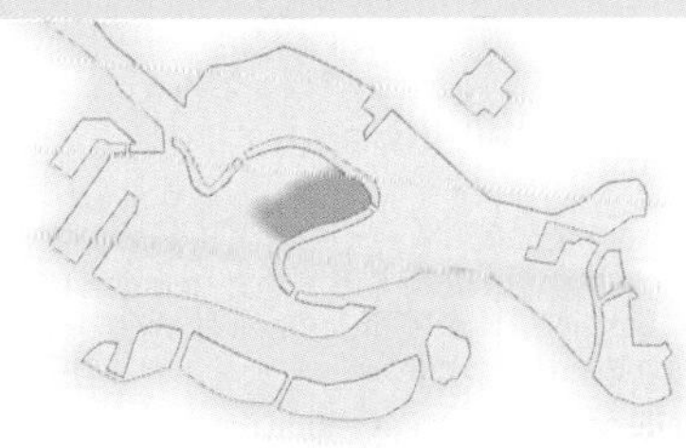

This is the smallest sestiere in Venice: it doesn't offer much in the field of hotels in the strict sense, but you can sample some of the finest restaurants, trattorias, and bàcari in the historical center. Among the shops, there are some excellent craftsmen and some real collectors' items.

Hotels

★★★ **Carpaccio.** Ramo Pisani e Barbarigo 2765, tel. 5235946, fax 5242134; 17 rooms, 14 of which have either bath or shower. No restaurant. (5 B2, **ar**).

★★★ **Marconi.** Riva del Vin 729, tel. 5222068, fax 5229700; 26 rooms, all with baths or showers. No restaurant. (5 B4, **be**).

★★ **Iris.** Calle del Cristo 2910/A, tel. and fax 5222882; 29 rooms, 15 of which have either bath or shower. Restaurant. (5 C1, **bt**).

Restaurants

🍴🍴🍴 **Antica Trattoria ae Poste Vecie.** Rialto Pescheria 1608, tel. and fax 721822. Closed Tuesday and Monday evening. Primarily seafood. (2 F4, **rr**).

🍴🍴🍴 **Da Fiore.** Calle del Scaletèr 2202, tel. 721308. Closed Sunday and Monday. Primarily seafood, Venetian style. (2 F2, **rz**).

🍴🍴 **Agli Amici.** Calle dei Botteri 1544, tel. 5241309. Closed Wednesday. Venetian cooking. (2 F3, **r**).

🍴🍴 **Carampane.** Rio Terrà de le Carampane 1911, tel. 5240165. Closed Sunday evening and Monday. Venetian cooking. (2 F3, **ri**).

🍴 **Trattoria alla Madonna.** Calle della Madonna 594, tel. 5223824. Closed Wednesday. Venetian cooking, especially seafood. (5 B4, **rg**).

Bàcari

Antico Dolo. Ruga Vecchia S. Giovanni – Calle del Fighèr 778, tel. 5226546. Closed Sunday. An old Venetian "tripperia," or tripe shop, slightly renovated. Vast selection of "primi," or pasta dishes (all first rate) and "baccalà," or dried cod. Clean and friendly (5 B4, **rs**).

Da Pinto. Campo delle Beccarie 367, tel. 5224599. Closed Monday. The most venerable bàcaro in the Market, for the past century. Hot "cotechino" sausage, "mantecato" dried cod, and good wine (2 F4, **ts**).

Do Mori. Calle dei Do Mori 429, tel. 5225401. Closed Wednesday afternoon and Sunday. One of the best-known bàcari (and one of the oldest: some say it dates from the 15th c.) in Venice: an incredible array of wines and *cichéti*, which you consume standing (2 F4, **sf**).

Do Spade. Calle Do Spade 860, tel. 5210574. Closed Thursday afternoon and Sunday. Casanova may have eaten here. Unlike the Do Mori, here – if you can find a chair – you can eat sitting down: some pasta dishes, fish sandwiches, and *cichéti* of wild game in spicy sauce (2 F4, **sh**).

Museums and cultural institutions

Archivio di Stato. Campo dei Frari 3002, tel. 5222281 (switchboard).

Casa Goldoni (Museum and Library). Calle dei Nomboli 2793, tel. 5236353. Closed for restoration (Library is open).

Scuola Grande di S. Giovanni Evangelista. Campiello della Scuola 2454, tel. 718158.

Scuola Grande di S. Rocco. Campo di S. Rocco 3054, tel. 5234864. *Weekdays, weekends and holidays 10-4.*

Churches

S. Polo. Tel. 5237631. *Open: 8-12; 4-6.*

Santa Maria Gloriosa dei Frari. Tel. 5222637. *Open: weekdays and Saturday 9-11:45/3-6; Sunday and holidays 3-6.*

Shops, crafts, and fine art

Balocoloc. Calle del Scaletèr 2235, tel. 5240551. Hats for all tastes: from the Venetian three-cornered tricorne to straw hats. Strictly handmade.

Cicogna. Campo S. Tomà 2867, tel. 5227678. A historic family of restorers and gilders of wood, in the third generation.

Il Forziere di Rita. Calle dei Saoneri 2720, tel. 5210042. Elegant evening wear; custom made, if you have the patience.

La Bottega di Cenerentola. Calle dei Saoneri 2721, tel. 5232006. A spectacular array of antique lace: handmade, for collectors and others.

Penso. Campo S. Tomà 2916/A, tel. 719706. One of the finest antiquarian bookshops in Venice.

Polliero. Campo dei Frari 2995, tel. 5285130. An authentic Venetian bindery, with all the allure of tradition. Especially popular with Venetians.

Santa Croce

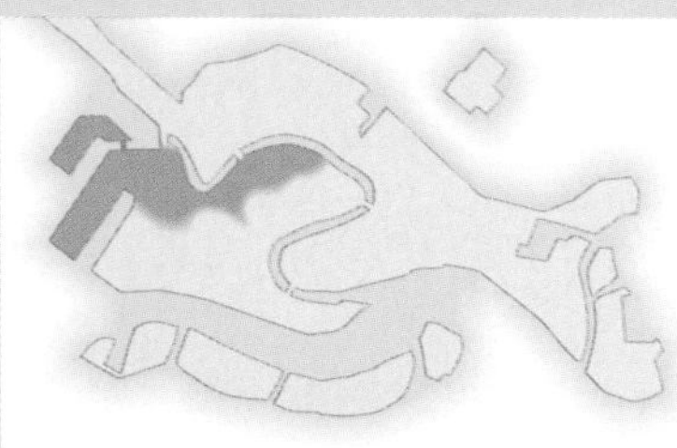

This is a "sestiere" with more than one soul: the automobile terminal in Piazzale Roma and the routes mostly overlooked by tourists, profound urban changes that have partly scrambled the layout, cutting off aristocratic palazzi of enormous beauty. The hotel facilities, for all tastes and for all pocketbooks, is quite similar: from the rebuilt hotel, which you can reach by car, all the way to the little jewel tucked away along the Grand Canal. There are not many restaurants in the area, but those few boast fine menus and service.

Hotels

★★★★ **Carlton Executive.** Fondamenta di S. Simeone Piccolo 578, tel. 718488, fax 719061, tlx 410070 Chcve I; 136 rooms, all with baths or showers. Restaurant. Special access for the handicapped. (1 E4, **j**).

★★★★ **Sofitel Venezia.** Giardino Papadopoli 245, tel. 716077, fax 710394, tlx 410310 Sofive; 97 rooms, all with baths or showers. Restaurant. Transportation service is provided for guests. (4 B4-5, **ae**).

★★★ **Al Sole Palace.** Fondamenta Minotto 136, tel. 710844, fax 719061, tlx 410070 Chcve I; 79 rooms, all with baths or showers. Restaurant. (4 C5, **am**).

★★★ **Basilea.** S. Croce, Rio Marin 817, tel. 718477, fax 720851, tlx 420320 Basel I; 30 rooms, all with baths or showers. No restaurant. (1 F6, **ao**).

★★★ **Gardena.** Fondamenta dei Tolentini 239, tel. 5235549, fax 5220782, tlx 410070 Chcve I; 22 rooms, all with baths or showers. No restaurant. (1 F4, **ax**).

★★★ **San Cassiano – Ca' Favretto.** Calle del Rosa 2232, tel. 5241768, fax 721033, tlx 420810 Scasve I; 35 rooms, all with baths or showers. No restaurant. (2 E3, **bh**).

★★★ **Santa Chiara.** Fondamenta di Santa Chiara 548, tel. 5206955, fax 5228799, tlx 420690 Chiara I; 28 rooms, all with baths or showers. No restaurant. (1 F3-4, **bj**).

★★ **Falier.** Salizzada S. Pantalon 130, tel. 710882, fax 5206554; 19 rooms, all with baths or showers. No restaurant. (4 C5, **bs**).

Restaurants

Antica Besseta. Salizzada de Ca' Zusto 1395, tel. 721687. Closed Tuesday and Wednesday. Classical Venetian cooking. (1 E6, **ro**).

Dalla Zanze. Fondamenta dei Tolentini 231, tel. 5223555. Closed Sunday. Venetian cooking. (1 F4, **sa**).

Ae Oche. Calle del Tintor 1552/A, tel. 5241161. Closed Monday. Traditional Venetian cooking and pizza. (2 F2, **rj**).

Alla Zucca. Ramo del Megio 1762, tel. 5241570. Closed Sunday. Vegetarian cooking. (2 E2, **ss**).

Bàcari

La Rivetta. Fondamenta Secchére 637, tel.

718111. Closed Sunday. The last old "bàcaro" in the "sestiere" (1 D5, **sr**).

Cafes and pastry shops

Gilda Vio. Fondamenta dei Garzoti 890, tel. 718523. Closed Wednesday. Try the fruit tarts and the tiramisù.

Museums and cultural institutions

Galleria d'Arte Moderna di Ca' Pesaro. Fondamenta di Ca' Pesaro 2076, tel. 721127. Closed for restoration.

Museo di Storia Naturale. Salizzada del Fontego dei Turchi 1730, tel. 5240885. Closed for restoration.

Museo Orientale. Fondamenta di Ca' Pesaro 2076, tel. 5241173. Closed Monday. *Weekdays, weekends and holidays 9-2.*

Archivio Storico delle Arti Contemporanee. Calle de Ca' Corner 2214, tel. 5218711, fax 5240817. Closed Friday afternoon and weekends. *Weekdays 9-5:30.*

Istituto Universitario di Architettura. Campazzo dei Tolentini 191, tel. 2571111 (switchboard).

Palazzo Mocenigo. San Stae 1992, tel. 721798. Closed Monday. *Weekdays 8:30-1, Saturday and Sunday 10-4.*

Centro Studi di Storia del Tessuto e Costume. Library: *Tuesday and Thursday 10-4.*

Scuola Internazionale di Grafica. Calle de Ca' Corner 2213, tel. 721950.

Churches

S. Giacomo dell'Orio. Tel. 5240672. *Open: 8-10; 5-7.* Closed Saturday afternoon and Sunday.

S. Nicola da Tolentino. Tel. 5225806. *Open: 9-11:30; 5-6:30.*

S. Simeone Grande. Open: 8-12; 5:30-7:15.

Shops, crafts, and fine art

There are few crafts workshops worthy of note:

Bevilacqua. Campiello de la Comare 1320, tel. 721566, fax 5242302. Production of Venetian fabrics for home furnishing.

Colore Veneziano. S. Croce 111, tel. 710688. Production and restoration of artistic stained glass and mosaics.

Dorsoduro

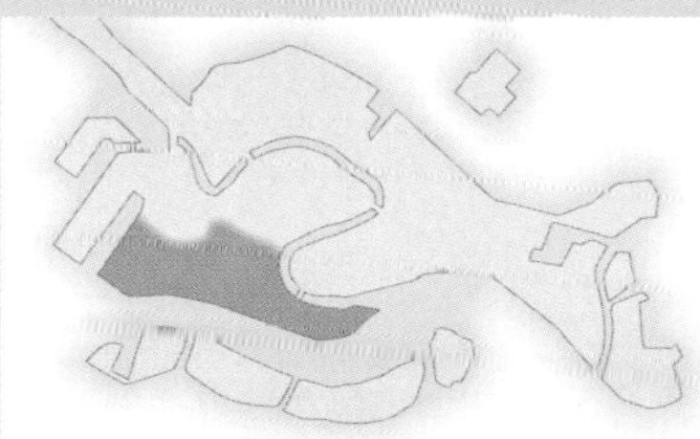

This is an intellectual "sestiere" par excellence (it contains museums and private and public collections, foundations, and many university buildings), and it remains extraneous to the network of hotels and luxury hotels. Despite this, the hotels (from "three stars" down) all have the benefit of a strongly Venetian connotation, and are exceedingly quiet. The same should be said of the trattorias and the "bàcari", frequented chiefly by "natives" and by students.

Hotels

★★★ **Accademia Villa Maravege.** Fondamenta Bollani 1058, tel. 5210188, fax 5239152; 27 rooms, 25 of which have either bath or shower. No restaurant. Interior garden. (5 E1, **aj**).

★★★ **American.** Fondamenta Bragadin 628 (S. Vio), tel. 5204733, fax 5204048; 29 rooms. No restaurant. (9 B-C2, **an**).

★★★ **La Calcina.** Zattere 780, tel. 5206466, fax 5227045; 30 rooms, 27 of which have either bath or shower. No restaurant. (9 C2, **bu**).

★★★ **Pausania.** Fondamenta Gherardini 2824, tel. 5222083, fax 5222989, tlx 420178 Pauvce; 26 rooms, all with baths or showers. No restaurant. (4 E5, **bf**)

★★ **Agli Alboretti.** Rio Terrà A. Foscarini 884, tel. 5230058, fax 5210158; 20 rooms, all with baths or showers. Restaurant. (5 F2, **bo**).

★★ **Seguso.** Zattere 779, tel. 5286858, fax 5222340; 36 rooms, 27 of which have either bath or shower. Elevator. Restaurant. (9 C2, **ca**).

★ **Antica Locanda Montin.** Fondamenta di Borgo 1147, tel. 5227151, 9 rooms, 4 with bath or shower. Renowned restaurant. (4 F6, **cc**).

Restaurants

🍴🍴 **Antica Locanda Montin.** Fondamenta di Borgo 1147, tel. 5227151-5223307, fax 5200255. Closed Tuesday evening and Wednesday. Traditional cooking. (4 F6, **cc**).

🍴 **Ai Cugnai.** Piscina del Forner 857, tel. 5289238. Closed Monday. (5 F2, **v**).

🍴 **Dona Onesta.** Ponte de la Dona Onesta 3922, tel. 710586. Traditional cooking. (4 C-D6, **sg**).

🍴 **La Furatola.** Calle Longa S. Barnaba 2870/A, tel. 5208594. Closed Thursday. Traditional cooking. (4 E5, **sq**).

Bàcari

Cantinone "già Schiavi". Fondamenta Nani 992, tel. 5230034. Closed Sunday afternoon. Not far from S. Trovaso, ideal for the extensive selection of wines and for the sandwiches, which you eat standing up (4 F6, **tc**).

Da Codroma. Ponte del Soccorso 2540, tel. 5246798. Closed Thursday. Across from the Collegio Armeno, you can enjoy wine and *cichéti* here until one in the morning, often to the tune of good jazz (4 E4, **ry**).

Linea d'Ombra. Zattere 19 (Ponte dell'Umiltà), tel. 5285259-5204720. Closed Wednesday and Sunday evening. More than a bàcaro, this is a full-fledged piano bar, within sight of the Punta della Dogana (9 C4, **sv**).

Cafes and pastry shops

Al Caffè. Campo S. Margherita 2963, tel. 5287998. Closed Sunday. An old-fashioned pastry shop, with marble counters, and mirrors on the walls, in the heart of the Sestiere di Dorsoduro.

Gelateria Nico. Zattere ai Gesuati 922, tel. 5225293. Closed Thursday. This ice cream shop is one of the most popular places in Venice on sunny days; note the terrace overlooking the Canale della Giudecca and its "panna in ghiaccio."

Vio alla Toletta. Calle Seconda de la Toletta 1192, tel. 5227451. Closed Tuesday. Traditional Venetian pastry shop, not far from the Accademia.

Museums and cultural institutions

Gallerie dell'Accademia. Campo della Carità 1050, tel. 5222247. *Weekdays and Saturday 9-7; Sunday and holidays 9-2.*

Museo del Settecento Veneziano. Ca' Rezzonico, S. Barnaba 3136, tel. 2410100. Closed Friday. *Weekdays, weekends and holidays 10-4.*

Collezione Peggy Guggenheim. Calle S. Gregorio 701, tel. 5206288. Closed Tuesday. *Weekdays, weekends and holidays 11-6.*

Collezione Vittorio Cini. Piscina del Forner 864 (S. Vio), tel. 5210755. Open in the summer months.

Pinacoteca Manfrediniana. Seminario Patriarcale. Campo della Salute 1, tel. 5225558. *Open by reservation.*

Scuola dei Carmini. Campo dei Carmini, tel. 5289420. *Weekdays 9-12; 3-6.* Closed Sunday.

Accademia di Belle Arti. Campo de la Carità 1050, tel. 5225396.

Ca' Foscari – Università degli Studi. Calle de Ca' Foscari 3246, tel. 2578111 (switchboard). Aula Magna di Ca' Dolfin, Calle de la Saoneria 3825/E, tel. 5204680.

Collegio Armeno Moorat Raphael. Fondamenta del Soccorso 2596, tel. 5228770-5239837.

Fondazione Angelo Masieri. Calle del Remer 3900, tel. 5226875.

Churches

Gesuati. Tel. 5230625. *Open: 8-12; 5-7.*

S. Maria del Carmelo (Carmini). Tel. 5226553. *Open: 7:30-12; 4:30-7.*

S. Maria della Salute. Tel. 5225558. *Open: 8:30-12; 3-6:30.*

S. Nicolò dei Mendicoli. Tel. 5285952. *Open: 10-12; 4-6.*

S. Pantalon. Tel. 5235893. *Open: 7:45-11:30; 4:30-7.* Closed Sunday morning.

S. Raffaele Arcangelo. Tel. 5228548. *Open: 7:30-12; 4-6.* Closed Sunday morning.

S. Sebastiano. Tel. 5282487. Undergoing restoration, no tours allowed.

S. Trovaso. Tel. 5222133. *Open: 8-11; 3-5.* Closed Sunday.

Entertainment

Although it is lacking in movie houses, the Sestiere di Dorsoduro does have the Teatro a l'Avogaria (its Compagnia Stabile taught the world to love the Commedia dell'Arte).

Teatro a l'Avogaria. Calle dell'Avogaria 1617, tel. 5206130.

Scuola Regionale Biennale di Teatro Giovanni Poli. Dorsoduro 1540, tel. 5204651.

Cinema Accademia. Calle Contarini Corfù 1019, tel. 5287706.

Sport

Canottieri Bucintoro (rowing). Fondamenta de la Dogana a la Salute 15, tel. 5205630-5222055 (secreteriat).

Shops, crafts, and fine art

With a rich array of curiosities and craftsmanship, here is the panorama of "botteghe" in Dorsoduro.

Canestrelli. Campiello Barbaro 364, tel. 5227072. One of the best-known *marangoni da soasa* (frame-makers) in Venice, specialized in restoring antique frames.

Imagine Venezia London. Calle de la Dona Onesta 3921, tel. 5239298. Antique silver, jewelry, and prints.

Libreria San Pantalon. Crosera San Pantalon 3950, tel. 5224436. Specializing in children's books, graphics, and texts of musicology.

Mondo Novo. Rio Terrà Canal 3063, tel. 5287344. From theatrical gadgets to the finest masks for the Venetian Carnevale. The workshop is also in Rio Terrà Canal, at number 3120, tel. 5231607.

Signor Blum. Fondamenta Gherardini 2830, tel. 5226367. Everything in wood: colored Venetian images, miniature facades of palazzi, conversation pieces, and puzzles.

Totem – Il Canale. Ponte dell'Accademia 878B, tel. 5223641. A gallery of unconventional art: note African jewelry, but also exhibits by new young artists (especially applied arts).

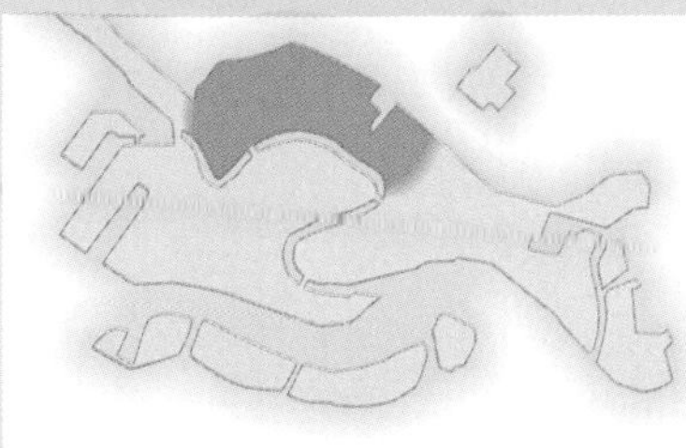

This is the pounding heart of the most authentic Venice: an area of shopping and craftsmanship, one of the most densely populated "sestieri." The hotels – because of the presence of the Santa Lucia train station – are numerous. The restaurants include many trattorias and plenty of bàcari.

Hotels

★★★★ **Amadeus.** Lista di Spagna 227, tel. 715300, fax 5240841, tlx 420374 Amave; 63 rooms, all with baths or showers. Restaurant. Interior garden. (1 D5, **g**).

★★★★ **Bellini.** Lista di Spagna 116/A, tel. 5242488, fax 715193, tlx 420374 Boscol; 67 rooms, all with baths or showers. (1 E5, **h**).

★★★ **Continental.** Lista di Spagna 166, tel. 715122, fax 5242432, tlx 410286 Contel I; 93 rooms, all with baths or showers. Restaurant. (1 D5, **at**).

★★★ **Corso.** Lista di Spagna 119, tel. 716422, fax 715193, tlx 420374 Boscol I; 24 rooms, all with baths or showers. No restaurant. Garden. (1 D-E5, **au**).

★★★ **Giorgione.** Calle Larga dei Proverbi 4587, tel. 5225810, fax 5239092; 70 rooms, all with baths or showers. No restaurant. (2 E5, **ay**).

★★★ **Malibran.** Corte del Milion 5864, tel. 5228028, fax 5239243, tlx 420337 Malibr; 29 rooms, all with baths or showers. Restaurant. (2 F5, **bd**).

★★ **La Forcola.** Volto Santo 2356, tel. 5241484; 22 rooms, 20 of which have either bath or shower. No restaurant. (2 C-D2-3, **bv**).

Restaurants

A la Vecia Cavana. Rio Terrà dei Franceschi 4624, tel. 5238644-5287106. Closed Thursday. Traditional Venetian cooking. (2 E5, **w**).

Fiaschetteria Toscana. Salizzada S. Giovanni Crisostomo 5719, tel. 5285281. Closed Tuesday. Traditional cooking. (2 F5, **sj**).

Antica Mola. Fondamenta degli Ormesini 2800, tel. 717492. Venetian cooking. (2 B-C2, **rq**).

Antiche Cantine Ardlenghi. Calle della Testa 6369, tel. 5237691-5274245. Closed Sunday. *Open only in the evenings.* (3 F3, **rv**).

Il Paradiso Perduto. Fondamenta della Misericordia 2540, tel. 720581. Closed Wednesday. Traditional cooking. (2 C3, **sn**).

Da Bes - Tre Spledi. Salizzada S. Canzian 5906, tel. 5208035. Closed Sunday lunch and Monday. Venetian cuisine, especially fish. (2 F5, **tl**).

Gam - Gam. Sottoportego del Ghetto Vecchio 1122, tel. 717538. Closed Friday evening, Saturday and Jewish holidays. Italian Jewish, Israelian and Ashkenazi cuisine. (2 C1, **ai**).

Iguana. Fondamenta della Misericordia 2515, tel. 713561. Closed Tuesday. Mexican restaurant. (2 C3, **cb**).

Sahara. Fondamenta della Misericordia 2519, tel. 721077. Closed Monday. Arabic restaurant. (2 D4, **cm**).

Bàcari

Alla Bomba. Calle dell'Oca 4297, tel. 5237452. Closed Wednesday. Behind the Strada Nova: a true bàcaro, completely unpretentious, but very popular (2 E5, **rc**).

All'Antica Adelaide. Calle Priuli 3728, tel. 5203451. Closed Monday. Fine wine in the homeland of *cichéti* (2 E4, **rd**).

Da Alberto. Calle Giacinto Gallina 5401, tel. 5238153. Closed Sunday. The best fried sardines, end also baccalà (dried cod) with polenta and "musetto" (3 F2, **cd**).

Da Andrea. Calleselle 1423, tel. 716269. Closed Sunday. Marinated anchovies and bass cooked in orange (2 C2, **ce**).

Cantina Vecia Carbonera. Ponte Sant'Antonio 2392, tel. 710376. Closed Monday. Recently opened, and a must of Cannaregio Bàcari tour (2 D3, **cu**).

Ca' d'Oro. Ramo Ca' d'Oro 3912, tel. 5285324. Closed Thursday and Sunday morning. A deluxe bàcaro, nicely renovated. Try the "fritto di verdura," or mixed fried vegetables and – in the evening – the pasta (2 E4, **rw**).

Enoteca Boldrin. Salizzada S. Canzian 5550, tel. 5237859. Closed Sunday. Popular with Venetians at lunchtime, especially for the pasta and the wine (2 F5, **si**).

Vini da Gigio. Fondamenta San Felice 3628/a, tel. 5258140. Closed Sunday evening and Monday. Traditional cuisine and an interesting wine list (2 D4, **cu**).

Cafes and pastry shops

Costarica. Rio Terrà S. Leonardo 321, tel. 716371. Closed Sunday. This cafe roasts its own coffee beans, and serves some of the finest espresso in Venice. A must.

Dal Mas. Lista di Spagna 150/A, tel. 715101.

Closed Tuesday. A memorable breakfast.

Museums and cultural institutions

Ca' d'Oro – Galleria Franchetti. Calle Ca' d'Oro 3933, tel. 5238790. *Weekdays and holidays 9-2.*

Museo Comunità Ebraica. Campo di Ghetto Novo 2902/B, tel. 715359. Closed Saturday and Jewish holidays. *Weekdays and holidays 10-4:30. Guided tours of the Synagogues every 30 minutes from 10:30 until 3:30.*

Istituto Gramsci Veneto. Calle Longo 2593, tel. 720510-717940 (Foundation)

RAI. Regional offices for the Veneto. Palazzo Labia, Campo S. Geremia 275, tel. 781111.

Salone del Tiepolo. Tel. 5242812. *Visits on request Wednesday-Friday 3-4.*

Churches

Gesuiti. Tel. 5286579. *Open: 10-12; 5-6:30.*

Madonna dell'Orto. Tel. 719933. *Open: 9:30-12; 4:30-6:30.*

SS. Geremia e Lucia. Tel. 716181. *Open: 7:30-12; 3-7.*

S. Giobbe. Tel. 5241889. *Open: 10-11:30; 4:30-5:30.*

S. Giovanni Crisostomo. Tel. 5227155. *Open: 8-12; 4-7.*

S. Maria dei Miracoli. Tel. 5235293. Currently undergoing restoration.

S. Maria di Nazareth. Tel. 715115. *Open: 6:30-12: 3:30-7.*

Ss. Apostoli. Tel. 5238297. *Open: 7:30-11:30; 5-7.*

Sinagoghe. Tel. 715359, fax 723007. Daily tours of the Ghetto.

Entertainment

Cannaregio offers virtually nothing in this field, but it does have the winter location of the Casinò Municipale.

Casinò Municipale. Ca' Vendramin Calergi, Campiello Vendramin 2040, tel. 5297111.

Shops, crafts, and fine art

Cannaregio is especially famous for its fine craftsmen: goldsmiths and silversmiths, mosaicists, and violinmakers.

Fecchio. Sottoportego Bragadin 2258. You can get here from the Strada Nova, just before Santa Fosca. This silversmith is one of the finest in Venice, and does engraving and repoussé.

Fusetti & Mariani. Ghetto Vecchio 1219, tel. 720092. A shop specializing in Jewish craft work. Note the objects in silver filigree and the goblets in Murano glass.

Semenzato. Strada Nova 2217, tel. 721811. In Palazzo Giovannelli, the only auction house in Venice, dealing in fine antiques, from Europe and Asia.

Venturini. Sottoportego de le Colonnette 2147. Behind the church of the Maddalena, Venturini makes violas, violins, cellos, and double-basses, in limited editions.

Castello

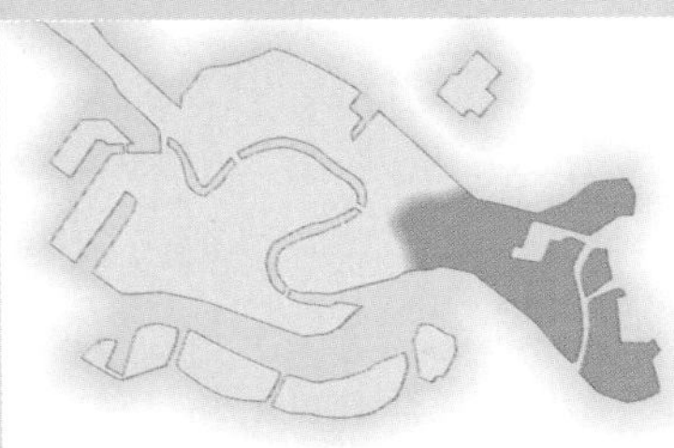

This is the largest "sestiere" in Venice, and there is no end of surprises in its versatile universe: major cultural events in reasonably isolated areas, athletic facilities with no other surrounding services, and so on. Despite all that, the charm of this part of the city – an authentic working-class Venice, untouched by the crowds of tourists during much of the year – is only enriched by these contradictions. The array of hotels here offers a variety of solutions, ranging from the luxury hotel to the "pensione," while the restaurants scattered throughout the "sestiere" (refined dining spots and fashionable trattorias) offer excellent assurances of quality and service.

Hotels

★★★★L **Danieli.** Riva degli Schiavoni 4196, tel. 5226480, fax 5200208, tlx 410077 Danive I; 231 rooms, all with baths or showers. Restaurant. Access for the disabled. Transportation service for guests: pool, tennis courts, and private beach at Lido di Venezia. (6 E3, **c**).

★★★★ **Gabrielli Sandwirth.** Riva degli Schiavoni 4110, tel. 5231580, fax 5209455; 100 rooms, all with baths or showers. Restaurant. Interior garden. (6 E5, **o**).

★★★★ **Londra Palace.** Riva degli Schiavoni 4171, tel. 5200533, fax 5225032; 53 rooms, all with baths or showers. Restaurant. Special access for the handicapped. (6 D-E4, **aa**).

★★★★ **Metropole.** Riva degli Schiavoni 4149, tel. 5205044, fax 5223679, tlx 410340 Hotmet; 76 rooms, all with baths or showers. Restaurant. Garden. (6 E4, **ac**).

★★★ **Bisanzio.** Calle della Pietà 3651, tel. 5203100, fax 5204114, tlx 420099 Bistel I; 39 rooms, all with baths or showers. No restaurant. (6 D4, **p**).

★★★ **Castello.** Calle del Fighèr 4365, tel. 5230217, fax 5211023, tlx 420659 Frama; 26 rooms, all with baths or showers. No restaurant. (5 D6, **as**).

★★★ **Santa Marina.** Campo S. Marina 6068, tel.

5239202, fax 5200907; 20 rooms, all with baths or showers. No restaurant. (5 B6, **bl**).

★★★ **Savoia & Jolanda.** Riva degli Schiavoni 4187, tel. 5206644, fax 5207494; 79 rooms, all with baths or showers. Restaurant. (6 D-E3, **bm**).

★★★ **Scandinavia.** Campo S. Maria Formosa 5240, tel. 5223507, fax 5235232, tlx 420359 Tnchtl; 34 rooms, all with baths or showers. No restaurant. (5 C6, **bn**).

★★ **Al Nuovo Teson.** Calle de la Pescaria 3980, tel. 5205555, fax 5285335; 30 rooms, all with baths or showers. No restaurant. (6 E5, **bp**).

★★ **Canada.** Campo S. Lio 5659, tel. 5229912, fax 5235852; 25 rooms, all with baths or showers. No restaurant. (5 B-C5, **bq**).

★★ **La Residenza.** Campo Bandiera e Moro 3608, tel. 5285315, fax 5238859; 16 rooms, 15 of which have either bath or shower. No restaurant. (6 D5, **bw**).

★★ **Paganelli.** Riva degli Schiavoni 4182, tel. 5224324, fax 5239267; 15 rooms, 13 of which have either bath or shower (annex in Campo S. Zaccaria 4687, tel. 5224324, fax 5239267; 6 rooms with bath or shower). (6 E4, **bx**).

Restaurants

Danieli Terrace. Riva degli Schiavoni 4196 (at Hotel Danieli), tel. 5226480. Open 24 hours a day. International cooking. (6 E3, **c**).

Ai Barbacani. Calle del Paradiso 5746, tel. 5210234, fax 5204691. Closed Monday. Refined cooking. (5 C6, **t**).

Corte Sconta. Calle del Pestrin 3886, tel. 5227024. Closed Sunday and Monday. Venetian cooking, primarily seafood. (6 D5, **rx**).

Do Leoni. Riva degli Schiavoni 4174 (restaurant of the Hotel Londra Palace), tel. 5200533, fax 5225032. Closed at midday and on Tuesday. Traditional cooking. (6 D-E4, **aa**).

Al Giardinetto da Severino. Calle Rotta 4928, tel. 5285332. Closed Thursday. Traditional cooking. (6 C-D3, **ra**).

Alla Rivetta – da Lino. Ponte di S. Provolo 4625, tel. 5287302. Closed Monday. Home-style cooking. (6 D3, **sz**).

Bàcari

Al Mascaron. Calle Lunga Santa Maria Formosa 5525, tel. 5225995. Closed Sunday. Nicely renovated and a bit touristy (there is even a piano). The cooking is quite good, and there is a fine array of wines (6 C3, **rl**).

Alle Testiere. Calle del Mondo Novo 5801, tel. 5227220. Closed Sunday. On the road to Santa Maria Formosa. There is not much space, but it is used ingeniously. The cooking offers variations on Venetian tradition, enriched with some new ideas. Try the entrees ("secondi") (5 C6, **su**).

Dal Pampo. Calle Chinotto 24, tel. 5208419. Closed Friday. Speciality: fish pie (11 E4, **cx**).

Cafes and pastry shops

Didovich. Campo Santa Marina 5909, tel. 5230017. Closed Sunday. This remarkable pastry shop has its own pastry chefs working on the premises. It has the full array of traditional pastries, with something extra.

Museums and cultural institutions

Museo dei Dipinti Sacri Bizantini. Ponte dei Greci 3412, tel. 5226581. A museum of Byzantine icons and religious paintings. *Weekdays and Saturday 9-1; 2-4:30.*

Museo Diocesano di Arte Sacra. Ponte della Canonica 4312 (Chiostro di Santa Apollonia), tel. 5229166. Religious art. Closed Sunday. *Weekdays, Saturday and holidays 10:30-12:30.*

Museo Storico Navale. Campo S. Biagio 2148, tel. 5200276. Naval history. Closed Sunday and holidays. *Weekdays and Saturday 9-1.*

Pinacoteca Querini Stampalia. Campiello Querini Stampalia 4778, tel. 5225235. Closed Monday. *Tuesday-Thursday and Sunday 10-1, 3-6; Friday and Saturday 10-1, 3-10pm.* Library, tel. 2711411. *Weekdays 4-11:30 pm; Saturday 2:30-11:30 pm; Sunday 3-7.*

Scuola di S. Giorgio degli Schiavoni. Ponte dei Greci, tel. 5228828. Closed Monday. *Weekdays and Saturday 10-12:30 and 3-6; Sunday and holidays 10-12:30.*

Biennale (Esposizione Internazionale di Arte ai Giardini di Castello; biennial exhibition of avant-garde art), tel. 5218711.

Istituto Ellenico di Studi Bizantini e Post-bizantini. Ponte dei Greci 3412, tel. 5226581. Hellenic studies.

Churches

Pietà. tel. 5204431. Tours: in the winter, by appointment; *summer 9:30-12:30; 3-6; all day when there are concerts.*

S. Francesco della Vigna. tel. 5206102. *Open: 8-12; 3:30-7.*

S. Giorgio dei Greci. tel. 5225446. *Open: weekdays 9-1; 2-5; holidays 9-12.*

S. Giovanni in Bragora. tel. 5205906. *Open: 8-11; 5-7. Saturday 8-11.*

S. Martino. tel. 5230487. *Open: 11-12; 5-6. Sunday 10-12.*

S. Pietro di Castello. tel. 5235137. *Open: 8-12; 3:30-7.*

S. Zaccaria. tel. 5221257. *Open: 10-12; 4-6.*

S. Maria Formosa. tel. 5234645. *Open: 8:30-12:30; 5-7.*

Ss. Giovanni e Paolo. tel. 5237510. *Open: 7:30-12:30; 3:30-7.*

Sport

Canottieri Querini. Fondamenta Nuove 6576/e, tel. 5222039. Rowing.

Lega Navale Italiana. Fondamenta de Fazza l'Arsenal, tel. 5289294.

Palasport Arsenale. Calle S. Biagio 2132, tel. 5207899-5204205. Sports.

Diporto Velico Veneziano. S. Elena, tel. 5231927. Sailing.

Healthcare facilities

Ospedale Civile. Campo Ss. Giovanni e Paolo. Switchboard tel. 5294111;
Emergency service tel. 5294517;
Water ambulance tel. 5230000.

Shops, crafts, and fine art

The panorama of crafts activities here reflects the great diversity of the "sestiere" the largest and more versatile.

Carli. Corte Rotta 4725, tel. 5224155. A great carver of the "forcola," the elaborate oarlock of the gondola.

Filippi. Calle del Paradiso 5763, tel. 5235635. Publisher-bookseller, who has been reprinting for decades texts that make up the history of Venetian traditions: the *Storia di Venezia* by Romanin, for example, or the *Curiosità Veneziane* by Giuseppe Tassini.

Laboratorio Artigiano Maschere. Barbarìa delle Tole 6657, tel. 5223110. The rebirth of the tradition of Venetian masks began here. Restoration and manufacture, with remarkable techniques.

Giudecca

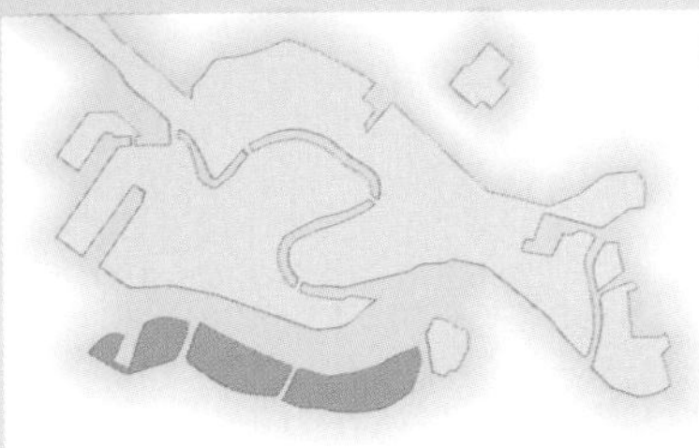

This island, which is technically part of the Sestiere di Dorsoduro, has an unusual feature: it is both an outlying area and an elite center. There may not be many shops or restaurants or bars; but there is a luxury hotel and an exclusive hotel. The island even has a youth hostel.

Hotels

★★★ **Cipriani.** Fondamenta S. Giovanni 10, tel. 5207744, fax 5203930; 104 rooms, all with baths and showers. Restaurant. Special access for the handicapped. Swimming pool with sea water, tennis courts, marina, and a splendid garden. (9 E6, **b**).

Hostel

Ostello della Gioventù. Fondamenta Zitelle 86, tel. 5238211, fax 5235689; 60 camere, with a total of 260 beds and 40 baths. Closed from 16/1 to 1/2. Opens at 6 pm. In the summer you should make reservations: this is the only youth hostel in Venice (9 D-E5, **cs**).

Restaurants

All'Altanella. Calle delle Erbe 268, tel. 5227780. Closed Monday and Tuesday. Traditional cooking. (9 E2, **rc**).

Harry's Dolci. Fondamenta S. Biagio 773, tel. 5224844-5208337. Closed Tuesday. (8 D5, **sm**).

Entertainment

Centro Teatrale di Ricerca C.T.R. Fondamenta S. Giacomo 211/A (ex-Cantieri Navali NOMV; experimental theater), tel. 5231039.

Churches

Il Redentore. Tel. 5231415. *Open: 8-12; 3-6:30.*

Sport

Piscina Comunale di Sacca Fisola, tel. 5285430. Swimming pool.

Murano

✉ 30121 ☎ 041

Page 117

Murano is the island of glass, but as far as hotels and tourist services, it offers little or nothing.

Restaurants

Valmarana. Fondamenta Navagero 31, tel. 739313. Closed Wednesday.

Bàcari

Ai Cacciatori. Fondamenta dei Vetrai 69. No telephone. Closed Sunday. The only real "bàcaro" on Murano. (pg. 117, B2, **u**).

Museums and cultural institutions

Museo dell'Arte Vetraria. Fondamenta M. Giustinian 8, tel. 739586. Closed Wednesday. Glassmaking museum. *Weekdays and holidays 10-4.*

Churches

Basilica dei Ss. Maria e Donato. Tel. 739056. *Open: 8-12; 4-6:30.*

S. Fosca. Tel. 730084. *Open: 10-12:30; 2-6:30; from October to March 2-5.*

Shops, crafts, and fine art

Barovier & Toso. Fondamenta dei Vetrai 28, tel. 739049, fax 5274385, tlx 411084 Bartos I. Since 1324, a dynasty founded on glass.

Carlo Moretti. Fondamenta Manin 3, tel. 739217-736588, fax 736282. Chiefly household glass, in the modern style.

Ercole Moretti. Fondamenta Navagero 42, tel. 739083. The finest "murrine" (glass jewelry), beads, and buttons in Murano glass.

Seguso Vetri d'Arte. Ponte Vicarini 138, tel. 739423. From the tradition of Flavio Poli to the "sanded" glass of today.

Venini. Fondamenta dei Vetrai 50, tel. 739955, fax 739369, tlx 420095 Venini. A name known throughout the world of fine glass.

Burano ⊠ 30012 ☎ 041

Page 120

Lace and fine seafood: thesere are two fundamental attractions of the island of Burano.

Restaurants

🍴 **Al Gatto Nero.** Via Giudecca 88, tel. 730120, fax 735570. Closed Monday. Traditional cooking. (pg. 121, E-F2, **z**).

🍴 **Da Romano.** Piazza Galuppi 221, tel. 730030. Closed Tuesday. Traditional cooking. (pg. 121, E3 **sd**).

Museums and cultural institutions

Consorzio Merletti di Burano (Museum and School of Lacemaking). Piazza Galuppi, tel. 730034. Closed Monday. *Weekdays and Saturday 9-6.*

Torcello ⊠ 30121 ☎ 041

Page 122

Torcello, in long-ago times was a flourishing and crowded town; it is now almost uninhabited. There are still historic and artistic monuments of inestimable worth, and few services, including a renowned inn, or locanda.

Restaurants

🍴🍴 **Locanda Cipriani.** Piazza Santa Fosca 29, tel. 730150, fax 735433. Closed Tuesday. Restaurant with refined Venetian cooking. (pg. 121, A2, **cd**).

Museums and cultural institutions

Museo di Torcello. Piazza Santa Fosca, tel. 730761. Closed Monday and holidays. *Weekdays and Weekends 10:30-12:30; 2-4.*

Churches

Cattedrale di S. Maria Assunta. Tel. 730084. *Weekdays, weekends and holidays 10-12:30; 2-5.*

Lido di Venezia

Page 114

Once the beach of the elite, now somewhat come down in the world, the island maintains a solid hotel infrastructure and has recreational fine activities. A less cheerful note comes from the restaurants: there really aren't very many places worth pointing out. The Lido is not distinguished by the presence of any specific noteworthy crafts activities.

Hotels

★★★★L **Excelsior.** Lungomare Marconi 41, tel. 5260201, fax 5267276, tlx 410023 Exceve I; 193 rooms, all with baths or showers. Seasonal. Restaurant. Access for the disabled. Transportation service for guests, parking lot with attendant and garage, a private beach, swimming pool. (pg. 115, D2, **e**).

★★★★ **Biasutti (Adria-Urania-Villa Nora).** Via Enrico Dandolo 27/29, tel. 5260120, fax 5261259; 70 rooms, all with baths or showers. Restaurant, garden, and use of a private beach. (pg. 115, B2, **i**).

★★★★ **Des Bains ITT Sheraton.** Lungomare Marconi 17, tel. 5265921, fax 5260113, tlx 410142 Bains; 191 rooms, all with baths or showers. Restaurant. Transportation service for guests. Private beach, tennis courts, and swimming pool on the grounds. (pg. 115, B3, **n**).

★★★★ **Le Boulevard.** Gran Viale S. Maria Elisabetta 41, tel. 5261990, fax 5261917, tlx 410185 Boulve I; 45 rooms, all with baths or showers. Restaurant. Garden. Transportation offered to guests and parking lot with attendant. (pg. 115, A-B2, **q**).

★★★★ **Quattro Fontane.** Via delle Quattro Fontane 16, tel. 5260227, fax 5260726; 62 rooms, all with baths or showers. Restaurant. Parking lot with attendant. Garden and tennis courts. (pg. 115, C2, **af**).

★★★★ **Villa Mabapa.** Riviera S. Nicolò 16, tel. 5260590, fax 5269441; 62 rooms, all with baths or showers. Restaurant. Parking with attendant, special terms for garage, garden, private beach. (*off the map*).

★★★ **Belvedere.** Via Cerigo 1/D, tel. 5260115-5260164, fax 5261486; 27 rooms, all with baths or showers. Restaurant, parking lot with attendant, and private beach. (pg. 115, A2, **ap**).

★★★ **Helvetia.** Gran Viale S. Maria Elisabetta 4/6, tel. 5260105-5268403, fax 5268903, tlx 420045 Helve; 50 rooms, all with baths or showers. No restaurant. Special access for the handicapped. Garden, private beach. (pg. 115, B2, **az**).

★★★ **Hungaria.** Gran Viale S. Maria Elisabetta 28, tel. 5261212, fax 5267619, tlx 410393 Hungar I; 66 rooms, 60 of which have either bath or shower. Restaurant and garden. (pg. 115, B2, **ba**).

★★★ **La Meridiana.** Via Lepanto 45, tel. 5260343, fax 5269240; 33 rooms, all with baths or showers. No restaurant. Parking lot with attendant, garden, and private beach. (pg. 115, C2, **bc**).

★★ **Vianello.** Via Ca' Rossa 10-14 Alberoni, tel. and fax 731072; 22 rooms, 13 of which have either bath or shower. No dining facilities. Garden. (off map).

Restaurants

🍴🍴 **Andri.** Via Lepanto 21, tel. 5265482. Closed Monday. Traditional cooking. (pg. 115, **tf**).

🍴 **Africa.** Via Lazzaro Mocenigo 9, tel. 5260186. Closed Tuesday. A lively "trattoria" offering only seafood menu. (pg. 115, **te**).

🍴 **Da Ciccio.** Via Sandro Gallo 241, tel. 5265489-5260649. Closed Tuesday. Traditional cooking. (pg. 115, **tg**).

Churches

S. Lazzaro degli Armeni. Monastero Mechitarista. tel. 5260104. Guided visits. *Open: 3:20-5.* Linee ACTV 10-20 from San Zaccaria, every 2:55.

Santa Maria Elisabetta. tel. 5260072. *Open: 7-12; 4-6:30.* Closed Sunday morning.

S. Nicolò. tel. 5260241. *Open: 9-12; 3:15-7:15; Sunday 8:15-12; 3:15-7:15.*

Entertainment

Casinò Municipale – Summer location. Lungomare Marconi 4, tel. 5267054.

Cinema Astra. Via Corfù 9, tel. 5260289.

Biennale – Festival del Cinema (film festival). Palazzo del Cinema, Lungomare Marconi, tel. 2726511. August-September.

Sport

Circolo Ippico Veneziano (horse-racing). Ca' Bianca, tel. 5261820-5265162.

Golf Lido di Venezia. Via Alberoni, tel. 731333, fax 731339.

Healthcare facilities

Ospedale al Mare. Lungomare D'Annunzio 1, tel. 5294111 (centr.); 5261750-5295234 (pronto soccorso).

Mestre ✉ 30170 ☎ 041

Map on the right
ℹ *Nuova Rotatoria Autostrada*, tel. 937764.

Hotels

★★★ **Alexander.** Via Forte Marghera 193/C, tel. 5318288, fax 5318283; 61 rooms, all with baths or showers. Restaurant. Parking lot with attendant and garage. (B5, **cg**).

★★★ **Ambasciatori.** Corso del Popolo 221, tel. 5310699, fax 5310074, tlx 410445 Ambhtl; 95 rooms, all with baths or showers. Restaurant, parking lot with attendant. (B-C4, **ch**).

★★★ **Bologna & Stazione.** Via Piave 214, tel. 931000, fax 931095; 130 rooms, all with baths or showers. Restaurant, garage. (C3, **ci**).

★★★ **Michelangelo.** Via Forte Marghera 69, tel. 986600-986664, fax 986052, tlx 420288 Michel I; 51 rooms, all with baths or showers. No restaurant. Garage and garden. (B4, **cj**).

★★★ **Plaza.** Viale Stazione 36, tel. 929388, fax 928385, tlx 410490 Plazav I; 221 rooms, all with baths or showers. Restaurant. Special terms for garage. (C3, **cl**).

★★★ **Sirio.** Via Circonvallazione 109, tel. 984022, fax 984024, tlx 410626 Sirio I; 103 rooms, all with baths or showers. Restaurant. Parking lot with attendant. (A3, **cn**).

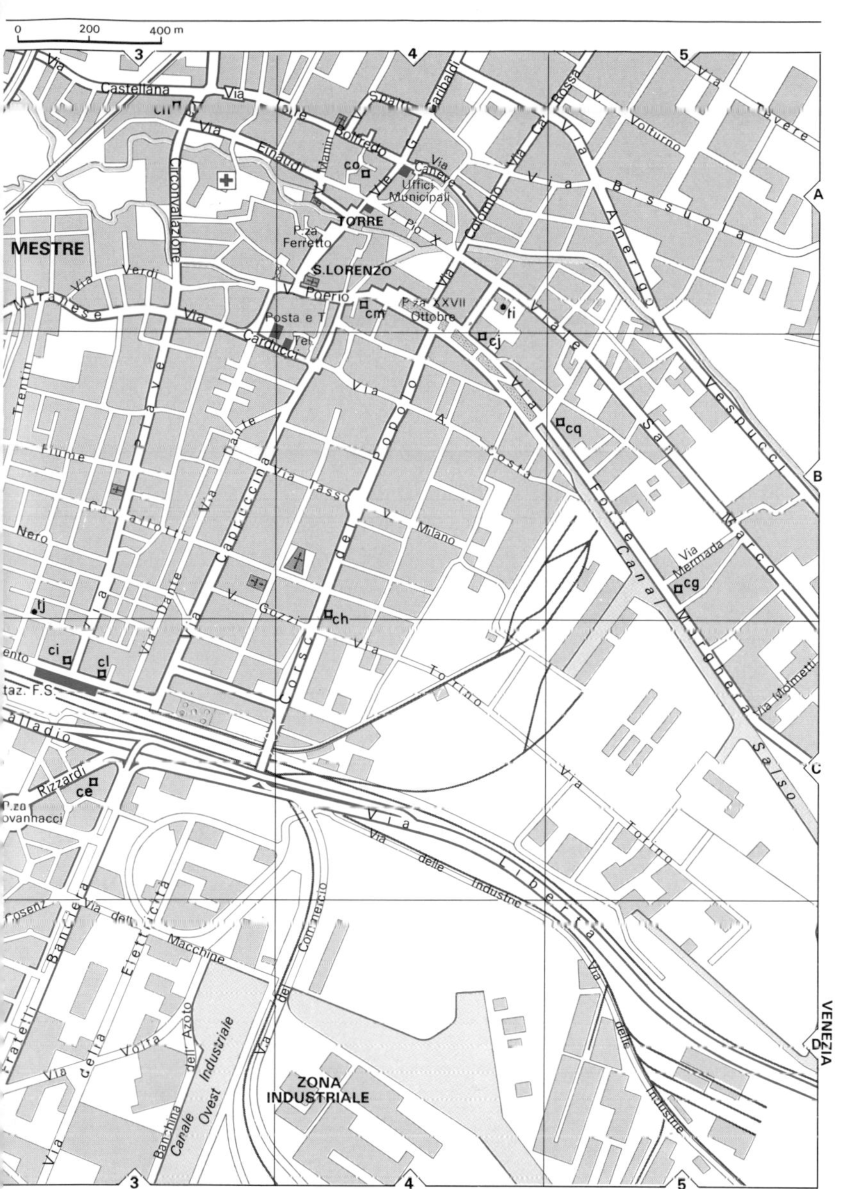

★★★ **Ai Pini.** Via Miranese 176, tel. 917722, fax 912390; 16 rooms, all with baths or showers. No restaurant. Special access for the handicapped. Transportation service and parking lot with attendant. Large garden. (B1, ***cr***).

★★★ **Clubhotel.** Via Villafranca 1, tel. 957722, fax 983990; 30 rooms, all with baths or showers. No restaurant. Special access for the handicapped. Garden and parking lot with attendant. (A1-2, **cp**).

★★★ **President.** Via Forte Marghera 99/A, tel. and fax 985655; 51 rooms, all with baths or showers. No restaurant. Garden, garage and parking lot with attendant. (B5, **cq**).

★★ **Delle Rose.** Via Millosevich 46, tel. 5317711, fax 5317433; 26 rooms, all with baths or showers. No dining facilities. Parking with attendant. (B-C5, **co**).

Camping

★★★★ **Alba d'Oro.** Via Triestina 214/B – Ca' Noghera, tel. and fax 5415102.

★★ **Fusina.** Via Moranzani 79 – Fusina, tel. 5470055, fax 5470050.

★★ **Serenissima.** Via Padana 334/A – Oriago, tel. and fax 920286.

★★ **Venezia**. Via Orlanda 8 – Campalto, tel. and fax 5312828.

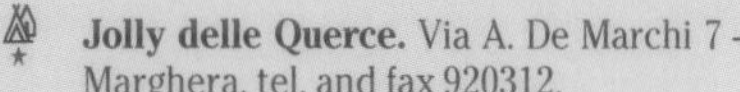

Jolly delle Querce. Via A. De Marchi 7 – Marghera, tel. and fax 920312.

Marco Polo. Via Triestina 167 – Tessera, tel. 5416033, fax 5415346.

Rialto. Via Orlanda 16 – Campalto, tel. 900785.

Restaurants

Dall'Amelia. Via Miranese 113, tel. 913955, fax 5441111. Closed Wednesday. Refined restaurant with many cultural events. (B1, **th**).

Marco Polo. Via Forte Marghera 67, tel. 989855. Closed Sunday. International menu. (A4, **ti**).

Valeriano. Via Col di Lana 18, tel. 926474-926457. Closed Sunday evening and Monday. Classical cooking. (B-C3, **tj**).

Marghera

✉ 30175 ☎ 041

Map on page 142-143

Hotels

★★★★ **Forte Agip.** Rotatoria di Marghera 1, tel. 936900, fax 936960, tlx 411418 Afve; 188 rooms, all with baths or showers. Restaurant. Special access for the handicapped. (D1, **cf**).

★★★★ **Lugano Torretta.** Via Rizzardi 11, tel. 936777, fax 921979; 62 rooms, all with baths or showers. Restaurant. Swimming pool. In a strategic location, along the road to Venice. (C3, **ce**).

Alphabetical Listing of Hotels, by Category

Venice (including the Lido)

★★★★★L

Danieli (Castello)
Excelsior (Lido)
Gritti Palace ITT Sheraton (S. Marco)

★★★★

Amadeus (Cannaregio)
Bauer Grünwald (S. Marco)
Bellini (Cannaregio)
Biasutti (Adria - Urania - Villa Nora) (Lido)
Carlton Executive (S. Croce)
Cavalletto e Doge Orseolo (S. Marco)
Cipriani (Giudecca)
Concordia (S. Marco)
Des Bains ITT Sheraton (Lido)
Europa e Regina Cigahotel (S. Marco)
Gabrielli Sandwirth (Castello)
Le Boulevard (Lido)
Londra Palace (Castello)
Luna Hotel Baglioni (S. Marco)
Metropole (Castello)
Quattro Fontane (Lido)
Saturnia e International (S. Marco)
Sofitel Venezia (S. Croce)
Starhotel Splendid Suisse (S. Marco)
Villa Mapaba (Lido)

★★★

Accademia Villa Maravege (Dorsoduro)
Ala (S. Marco)
Al Sole (S. Croce)
American (Dorsoduro)
Basilea (S. Croce)
Belvedere (Lido)
Bisanzio (Castello)
Bonvecchiati (S. Marco)
Carpaccio (S. Polo)
Castello (Castello)
Continental (Cannaregio)
Corso (Cannaregio)
Do Pozzi (S. Marco)
Flora (S. Marco)
Gardena (S. Croce)
Giorgione (Cannaregio)
Helvetia (Lido)
Hungaria (Lido)
La Calcina (Dorsoduro)
La Fenice et Des Artistes (S. Marco)
La Meridiana (Lido)
Malibran (Cannaregio)
Marconi (S. Polo)
Pausania (Dorsoduro)
Rialto (S. Marco)
San Cassiano - Ca' Favretto (S. Croce)
San Moisè (S. Marco)
Santa Chiara (S. Croce)
Santa Marina (Castello)
Savoia & Jolanda (Castello)
Scandinavia (Castello)

★★

Agli Alboretti (Dorsoduro)
Al Nuovo Teson (Castello)
Canada (Castello)
Falier (S. Croce)
Iris (S. Polo)
La Forcola (Cannaregio)
La Residenza (Castello)
Paganelli (Castello)
San Fantin (S. Marco)
San Zulian (S. Marco)
Seguso (Dorsoduro)
Vianello (Lido)

★

Antica Locanda Montin (Dorsoduro)

Marghera

★★★★

Forte Agip; Lugano Torretta

Mestre

★★★★

Alexander; Ambasciatori; Bologna & Stazione; Michelangelo; Plaza; Sirio

★★★

Ai Pini; Clubhotel; President;

★★

Delle Rose

Alphabetical Listing of Restaurants and “Bàcari”

Venice and islands

Africa (Lido)
Agli Amici (S. Polo)
Agli Assassini (S. Marco)
Ai Barbacani (Castello)
Ai Cacciatori (Murano)
Ai Cugnai (Dorsoduro)
Ai Gondolieri (Dorsoduro)
Ai Nouboli (S. Paolo)
A la Vecia Cavana (Cannaregio)
Al Bacareto (S. Marco)
Al Gatto Nero (Burano)
Al Giardinetto (Castello)
Al Graspo de Ua (S. Marco)
All’Altanella (Giudecca)
All’Antica Adelaide (Cannaregio)
Alla Bomba (Cannaregio)
Alla Colomba (S. Marco)
Alla Patatina (S. Polo)
Alla Rivetta da Lino (Castello)
Alle Oche (S. Croce)
Alle Testiere (Castello)
Al Mascaron (Castello)
Al Volto (S. Marco)
Andri (Lido)
Antica Besseta (S. Croce)
Antica Carbonera (S. Marco)
Antica Locanda Montin (Dorsoduro)
Antica Mola (Cannaregio)
Antica Trattoria Poste Vecie (S. Polo)
Antiche Cantine Ardenghi (Dorsoduro)
Antico Dolo (S. Polo)
Antico Martini (S. Marco)
Ca’ d’Oro (Cannaregio)
Cantina Vecia Carbonera (Cannaregio)
Cantinone (Dorsoduro)
Carampane (S. Polo)
Corte Sconta (Castello)
Da Alberto (Cannaregio)
Da Andrea (Cannaregio)
Da Codroma (Dorsoduro)
Da Fiore (S. Polo)
Dal Pampo (Castello)
Dalla Zanze (S. Croce)
Danieli Terrace (Castello)
Da Pinto (S. Polo)
Da Raffaele (S. Marco)
Da Romano (Burano)
Do Forni (S. Marco)
Do Leoni (Castello)
Do Mori (S. Polo)
Dona Onesta (Dorsoduro)
Do Spade (S. Polo)
Enoteca Boldrin (Cannaregio)
Fiaschetteria Toscana (Cannaregio)
Gam Gam (Cannaregio)
Harry’s Bar (S. Marco)
Harry’s Dolci (Giudecca)
Iguana (Cannaregio)
Il Paradiso perduto (Cannaregio)
La Caravella (S. Marco)
La Frasca (Cannaregio)
La Furatola (Dorsoduro)
La Rivetta (S. Croce)
La Zucca (S. Croce)
Linea d’Ombra (Dorsoduro)
Locanda Cipriani (Torcello)
Sahara (Cannaregio)
Shri Ganesh (S. Polo)
Taverna La Fenice (S. Marco)
Trattoria alla Madonna (S. Polo)
Tre Spiedi (Cannaregio)
Valmarana (Murano)
Vecio Fritoin (S. Croce)
Vini da Gigio (Cannaregio)
Vino Vino (S. Marco)

Mestre

Dall’Amelia
Marco Polo
Valeriano

Index of Places and Things

The city of Venice

Lagoon and the Riviera del Brenta

Venice Atlas

City key map

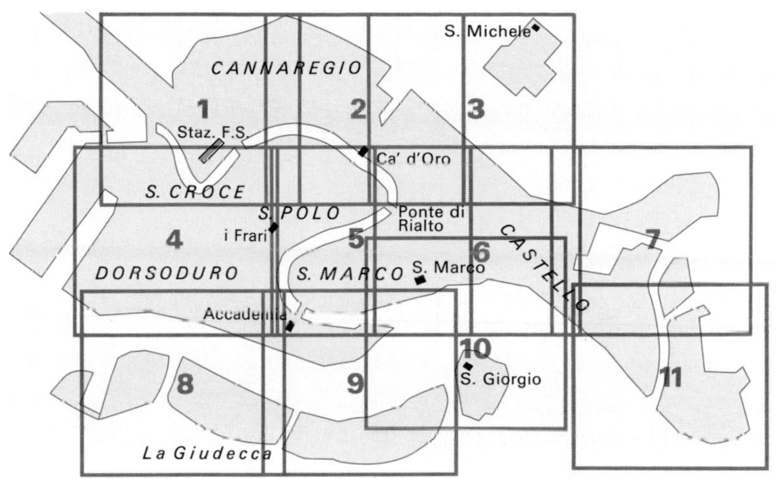

Conventional signs

	Palazzi, public buildings		State access road
	Churches		Railroads
	Convents, former houses of worship		Urban and other lagoon transportation lines
	Synagogues		Summer lagoon transportation lines
	Working class housing		Lagoon transportation lines with ferry service
	Private and public gardens		Ferry gondolas for pedestrians (Grand Canal)
	Cemeteries		Hotels; restaurants or "bàcari"
	Jewish Cemetery	0 100 200m	1:6000 (1 cm.=60 m.)

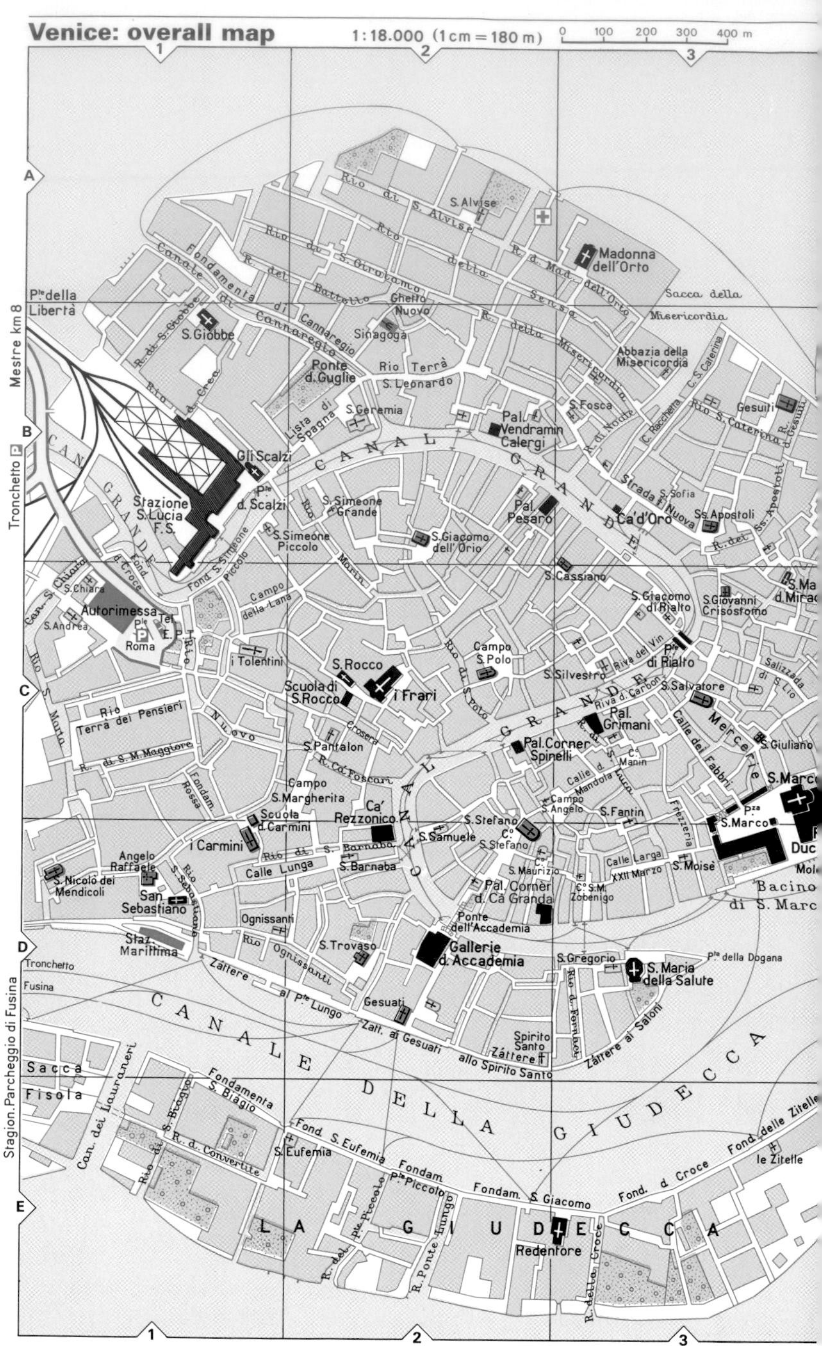
Venice: overall map
1:18.000 (1 cm = 180 m)
0 100 200 300 400 m
Madonna dell'Orto
Sacca della Misericordia
Abbazia della Misericordia
Gesuiti
S. Alvise
Ghetto Nuovo
Sinagoga
S. Giobbe
Ponte d. Guglie
S. Geremia
Pal. Vendramin Calergi
Gli Scalzi
Stazione S. Lucia F.S.
CANAL GRANDE
Ca' d'Oro
Ss. Apostoli
S. Simeone Grande
S. Simeone Piccolo
S. Giacomo dell'Orio
Pal. Pesaro
S. Cassiano
S. Chiara
Autorimessa
P.le Roma
S. Andrea
i Tolentini
S. Rocco
Scuola di S. Rocco
i Frari
Campo S. Polo
S. Silvestro
P.te di Rialto
S. Giacomo di Rialto
S. Giovanni Crisostomo
S. Salvatore
Pal. Grimani
Mercerie
S. Giuliano
S. Pantalon
Pal. Corner Spinelli
Campo S. Margherita
Ca' Rezzonico
Scuola d. Carmini
i Carmini
S. Samuele
S. Stefano
S. Fantin
S. Marco
P.za S. Marco
Angelo Raffaele
S. Nicolò dei Mendicoli
San Sebastiano
S. Barnaba
Calle Lunga
Pal. Corner d. Cà Granda
S. Moisè
Bacino di S. Marco
Staz. Marittima
Ognissanti
S. Trovaso
Ponte dell'Accademia
Gallerie d. Accademia
S. Gregorio
S. Maria della Salute
P.ta della Dogana
Zattere
Gesuati
Spirito Santo
CANALE DELLA GIUDECCA
Sacca Fisola
S. Eufemia
le Zitelle
Fondam. S. Giacomo
LA GIUDECCA
Redentore
Mestre km 8
Tronchetto
Stagion. Parcheggio di Fusina

S.Michele
Ss.Giovanni e Paolo
S.M. Formosa
Sc. di S.Giorgio d. Schiavoni
S.Zaccaria
S.Giovanni in Bragora
Riva degli Schiavoni
Darsena Grande
Torri d. Arsenale
Museo Navale
Via Garibaldi
S. Pietro di Castello
Isola di S.Pietro
CANALE DI S. MARCO
S. Giorgio Maggiore
Isola di S.Giorgio Maggiore
Teatro Verde
Esposizione Internazionale d'Arte Moderna
Giardini Pubblici
Isola di S. Elena
S.Elena
Campo Sportivo

0 60 120 m
Ponte della Libertà
Canale Colambola
Ex Macello Comunale
C.llo del Beccari
Calle delle Beccarie
C. d. Scarlatto
C. dei Tintor
C. dei Col
C. Biscotella
Calle della Cereria
Rio della Crea
Rio
TRONCHETTO
MERCATO ITTICO
CAPITANERIA DI PORTO
EX CONVENTO DI S. CHIARA
Fondamenta di S. Chiara
S. NOME DI GESÙ
P.le Roma
Calle Volto
STAZIONE MARITTIMA (MERCI)
Campo S. Andrea
EX CHIESA DI S. ANDREA
GARAGE COMUNALE
STAZIONE AUTOBUS
Can. di S. Chiara
S.
C
R

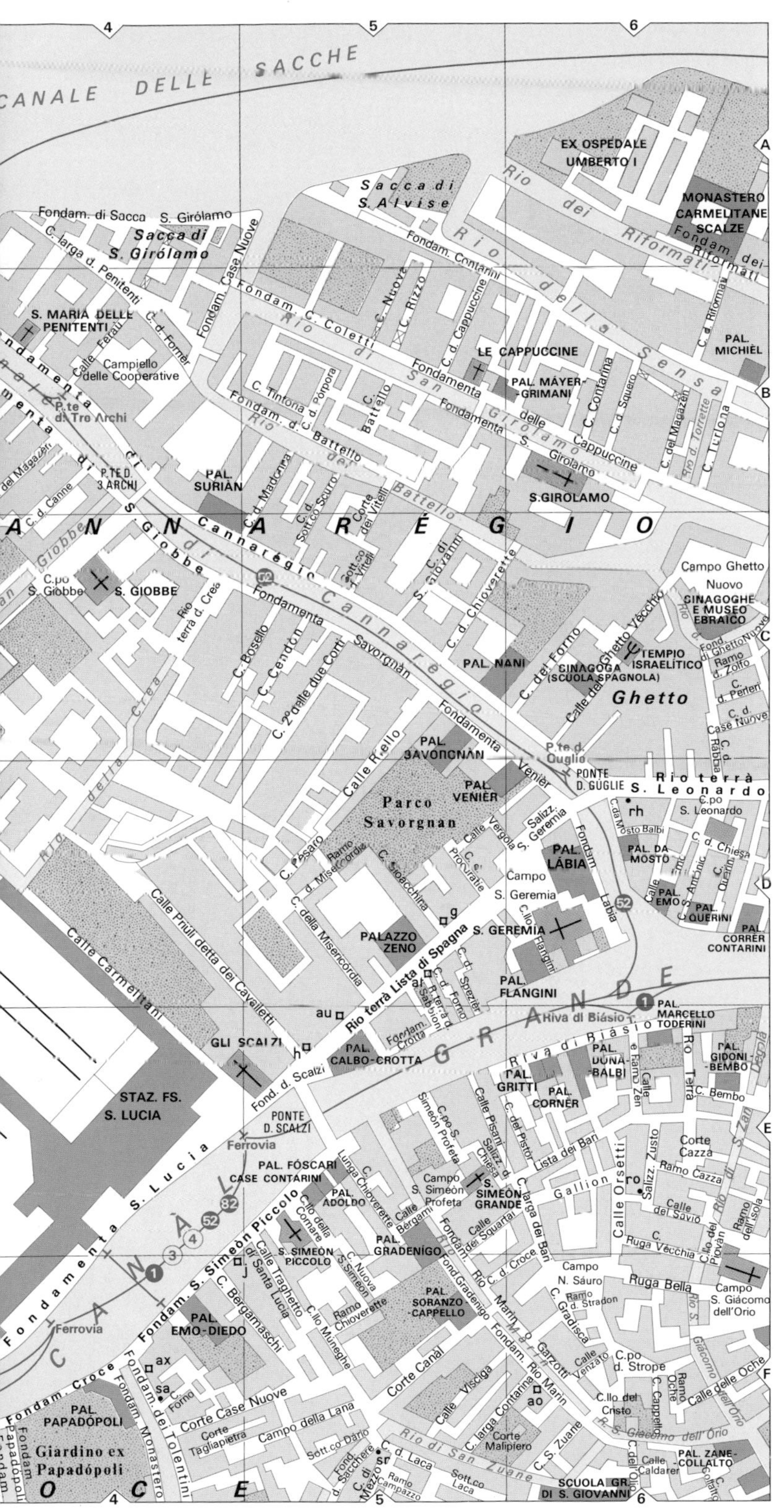
CANALE DELLE SACCHE
EX OSPEDALE UMBERTO I
MONASTERO CARMELITANE SCALZE
Sacca di S. Alvise
Sacca di S. Girólamo
S. MARIA DELLE PENITENTI
LE CAPPUCCINE
PAL. MÁYER-GRIMANI
PAL. MICHIÈL
PAL. SURIÀN
S.GIROLAMO
CANNARÉGIO
S. GIOBBE
Campo Ghetto Nuovo
SINAGOGHE E MUSEO EBRAICO
TEMPIO ISRAELÍTICO
CINAGOGA (SCUOLA SPAGNOLA)
Ghetto
PAL. NANI
PAL. SAVORGNAN
PAL. VENIÈR
Parco Savorgnan
PONTE D. GUGLIE
Rio terrà S. Leonardo
PAL. LÁBIA
PAL. DA MOSTO
PAL. EMO
PAL. QUERINI
PAL. CORRER CONTARINI
Campo S. Geremia
S. GEREMIA
PALAZZO ZENO
PAL. FLANGINI
PAL. MARCELLO TODERINI
Rio terrà Lista di Spagna
GLI SCALZI
PAL. CALBO-CROTTA
PAL. DONÀ-BALBI
PAL. GRITTI
PAL. CORNÈR
PAL. GIDONI-BEMBO
STAZ. FS. S. LUCIA
PONTE D. SCALZI
PAL. FÓSCARI CASE CONTARINI
PAL. ADOLDO
Campo S. Simeòn Profeta
S. SIMEÒN GRANDE
S. SIMEÒN PICCOLO
PAL. GRADENIGO
PAL. SORANZO-CAPPELLO
Campo N. Sáuro
Ruga Bella
Campo S. Giácomo dell'Orio
PAL. EMO-DIEDO
PAL. PAPADÓPOLI
Giardino ex Papadópoli
Corte Case Nuove
Campo della Lana
SCUOLA GR. DI S. GIOVANNI
PAL. ZANE-COLLALTO
CANAL GRANDE
Fondamenta S. Lucia
Fondam. S. Simeòn Piccolo

 1:6000 (1 cm = 60 m)

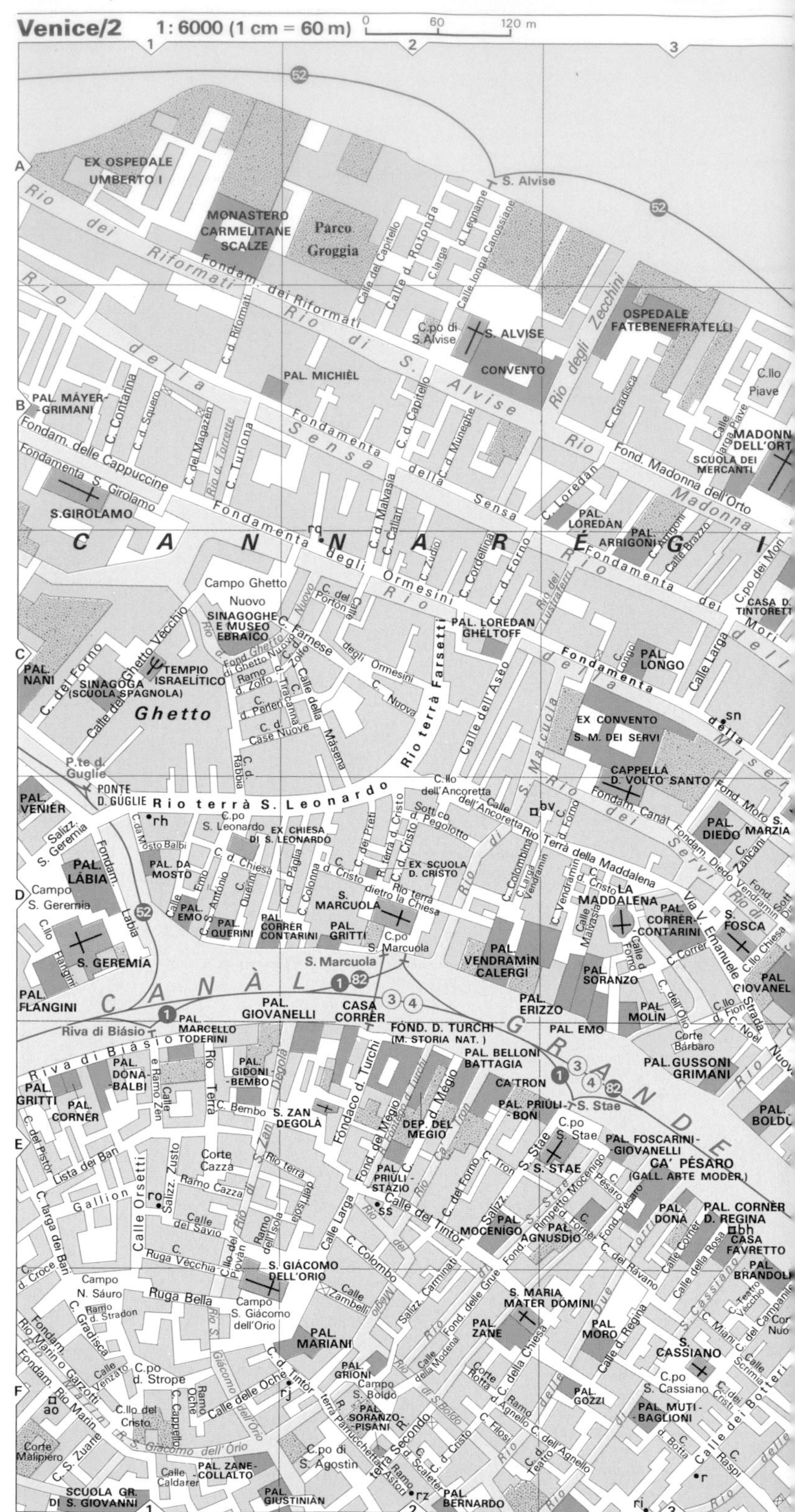

MURANO
Sacca della
Misericórdia
CASINO
D. SPÍRITI
PAL. MINELLI-SPADA
PAL. CONTARINI
D. ZAFFO
SCUOLA VECCHIA
D. MISERICÓRDIA
S. MARIA
VALVERDE
SCUOLA NUOVA
D. MISERICÓRDIA
PAL. LEZZE
PAL. PAPAFAVA
EX CONVENTO E
CHIESA DI S. CATERINA
GESUITI
EX CONVENTO
PAL. DONÀ
PALAZZI ZEN
PAL. SERIMAN
Fond. Nuove
Fondamenta Nuove
Canale della Misericórdia
Calle lunga S. Caterina
Strada Nuova
S. SOFIA
PAL. FONTANA
PAL. SAGREDO
PAL. FÓSCARI
PAL. MICHIEL
D. COLONNE
SCUOLA D.
ANGELO
CUSTODE
PAL. MANGILLI
SS. APÓSTOLI
S. CANCIANO
PAL. WIDMAN
PAL. GRIFALCONI
PESCARIA
CA' DA MOSTO
FÁBBRICHE NUOVE
FÁBBRICHE VECCHIE
PAL. DIECI SAVI
PAL. FALIÈR
S. GIOVANNI CRISÓSTOMO
PAL. CIVRAN
TEATRO MALIBRAN
PAL. BEMBO E BOLDÙ
S. MARIA D. MIRACOLI
PAL. SORANZO-VAN AXEL
PAL. PISANI
C.po S. Giov. e Paolo
Calle larga dei Botteri
Calle del Fumo
Calle Stella
Rio della Panada
Rio dei Mendicanti

Venice/3 1: 6000 (1 cm = 60 m)

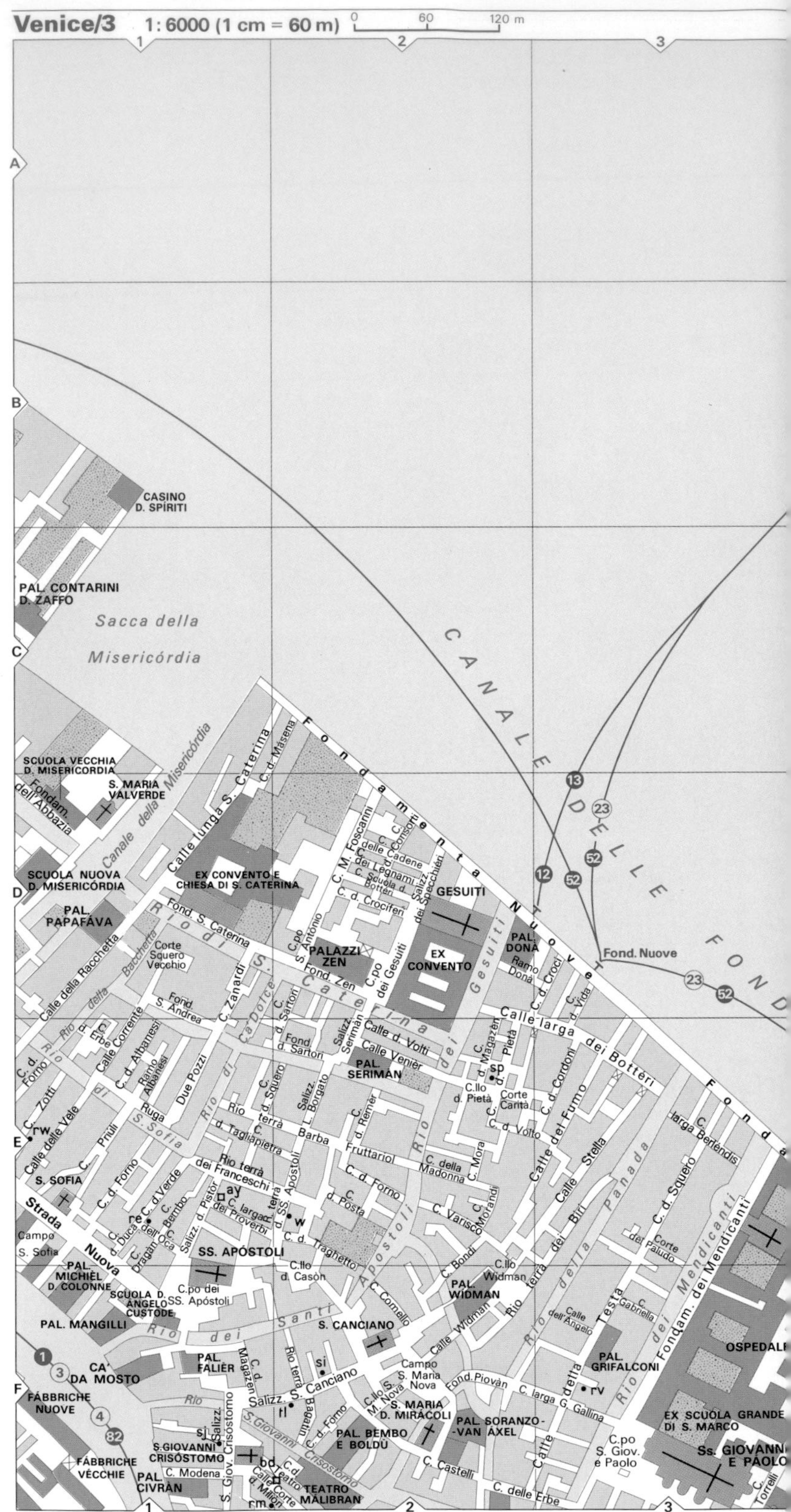

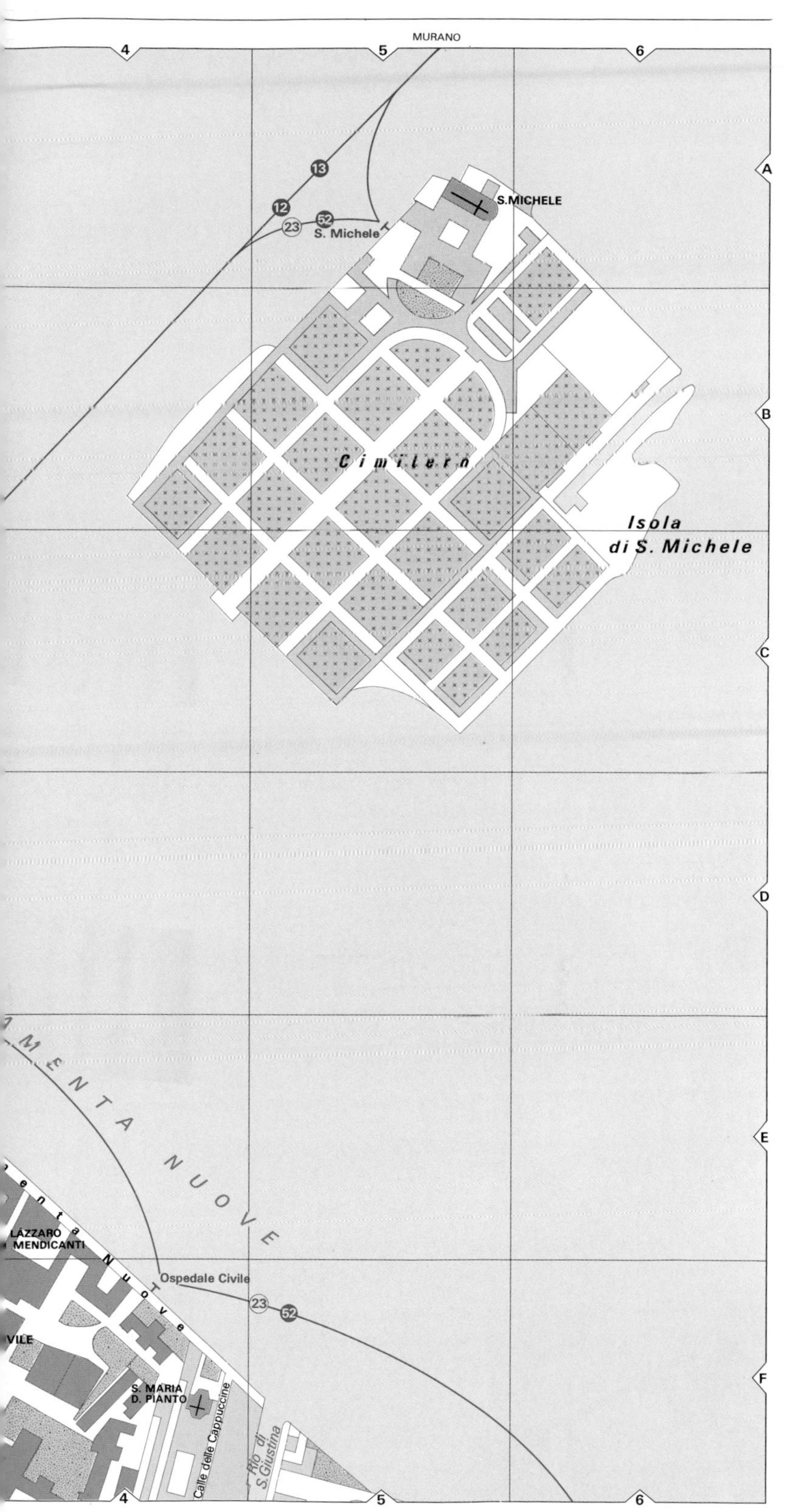
MURANO
S.MICHELE
S. Michele
Cimitero
Isola
di S. Michele
LAZZARO
MENDICANTI
Ospedale Civile
S. MARIA
D. PIANTO
Calle delle Cappuccine
Rio di S.Giustina

1: 6000 (1 cm = 60 m)

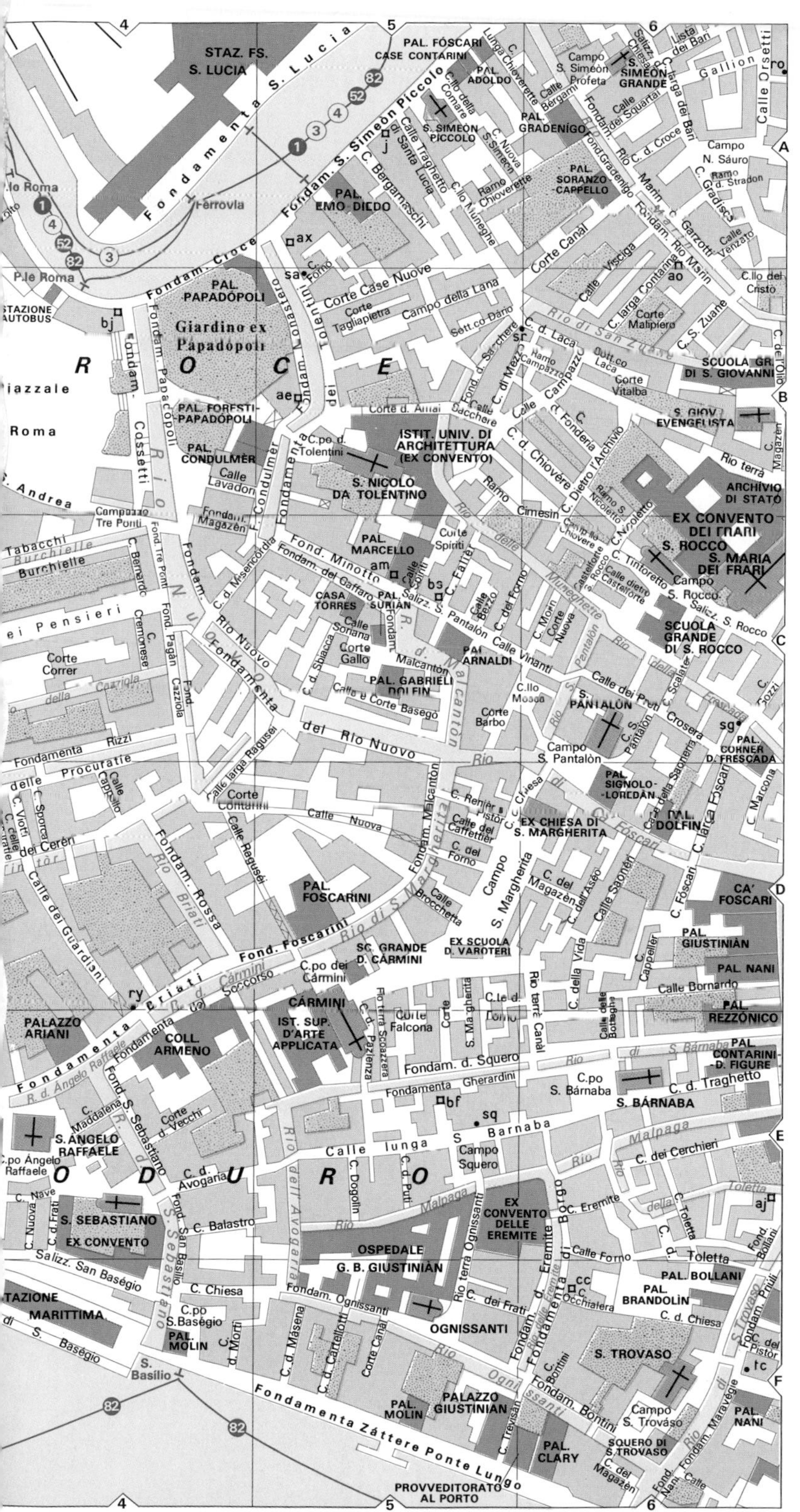
STAZ. FS. S. LUCIA
Fondamenta S. Lucia
Fondam. S. Simeòn Piccolo
S. SIMEÒN PICCOLO
PAL. FÓSCARI
CASE CONTARINI
PAL. ADOLDO
PAL. GRADENÍGO
S. SIMEÒN GRANDE
Campo S. Simeòn Profeta
PAL. SORANZO-CAPPELLO
PAL. EMO-DIEDO
Campo N. Sàuro
Fondam. Croce
PAL. PAPADÓPOLI
Giardino ex Papadópoli
P.le Roma
STAZIONE AUTOBUS
Piazzale Roma
Campo della Lana
Corte Canal
Corte Malipiero
SCUOLA GR. DI S. GIOVANNI
S. GIOV. EVANGELISTA
ISTIT. UNIV. DI ARCHITETTURA (EX CONVENTO)
S. NICOLÒ DA TOLENTINO
PAL. FORESTI-PAPADÓPOLI
PAL. CONDULMÈR
ARCHIVIO DI STATO
EX CONVENTO DEI FRARI
S. ROCCO
S. MARIA DEI FRARI
SCUOLA GRANDE DI S. ROCCO
PAL. MARCELLO
CASA TORRES
PAL. SURIÀN
PAL. ARNALDI
PAL. GABRIELI DOLFIN
S. PANTALÒN
Campo S. Pantalòn
PAL. CORNER D. FRESCADA
PAL. SIGNOLO-LOREDÀN
EX CHIESA DI S. MARGHERITA
PAL. DOLFIN
Rio Nuovo
PAL. FOSCARINI
Campo S. Margherita
CA' FOSCARI
PAL. GIUSTINIÀN
PAL. NANI
SC. GRANDE D. CÀRMINI
EX SCUOLA D. VAROTERI
CÀRMINI
IST. SUP. D'ARTE APPLICATA
PALAZZO ARIANI
COLL. ARMENO
PAL. REZZÓNICO
PAL. CONTARINI-D. FIGURE
S. BÁRNABA
Campo S. Bárnaba
S. ANGELO RAFFAELE
D O R S O D U R O
S. SEBASTIANO
EX CONVENTO
EX CONVENTO DELLE EREMITE
OSPEDALE G. B. GIUSTINIÀN
OGNISSANTI
PAL. BOLLANI
PAL. BRANDOLÌN
S. TROVASO
Campo S. Trovàso
SQUERO DI S.TROVASO
STAZIONE MARITTIMA
PAL. MOLIN
PAL. MOLIN
PALAZZO GIUSTINIAN
PAL. CLARY
PAL. NANI
Fondamenta Zàttere Ponte Lungo
PROVVEDITORATO AL PORTO

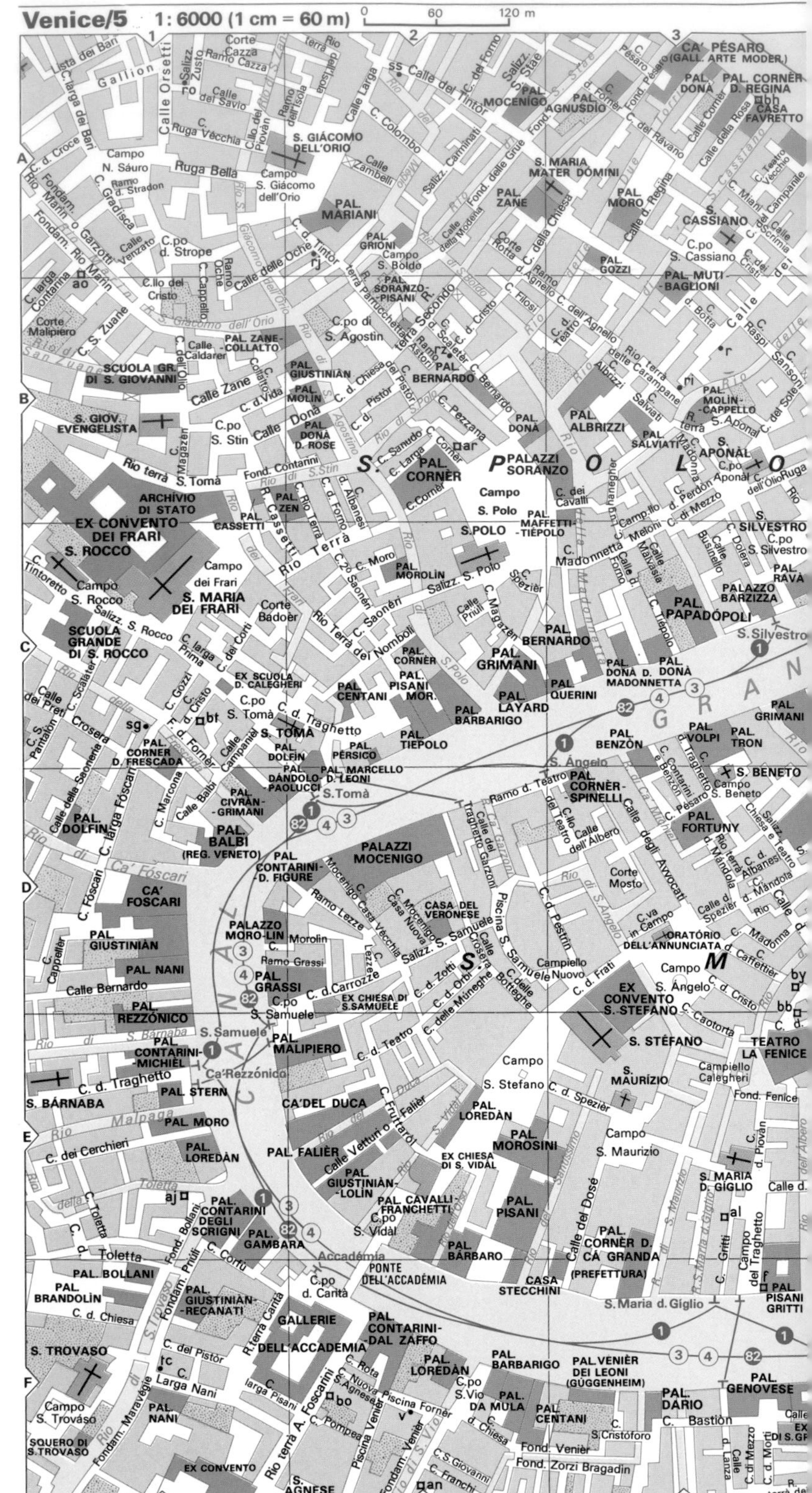
0 60 120 m
CA' PÉSARO (GALL. ARTE MODER.)
PAL. DONÀ
PAL. CORNÈR D. REGINA
CASA FAVRETTO
PAL. MOCENIGO
PAL. AGNUSDIO
S. GIÁCOMO DELL'ORIO
Campo S. Giácomo dell'Orio
S. MARIA MATER DÓMINI
PAL. ZANE
PAL. MORO
PAL. MARIANI
S. CASSIANO
C.po S. Cassiano
PAL. GRIONI
Campo S. Boldo
PAL. SORANZO-PISANI
PAL. GOZZI
PAL. MUTI-BAGLIONI
C.po di S. Agostin
PAL. ZANE-COLLALTO
SCUOLA GR. DI S. GIOVANNI
PAL. GIUSTINIÀN
PAL. MOLIN
PAL. BERNARDO
PAL. MOLIN-CAPPELLO
S. GIOV. EVENGELISTA
C.po S. Stin
PAL. DONÀ D. ROSE
PAL. DONÀ
PAL. ALBRIZZI
PAL. SALVIATI
S. APONÀL
C.po Aponàl
S. POLO
PAL. CORNÈR
PALAZZI SORANZO
Campo S. Polo
PAL. MAFFETTI-TIÉPOLO
ARCHÍVIO DI STATO
EX CONVENTO DEI FRARI
PAL. ZEN
PAL. CASSETTI
S. SILVESTRO
C.po S. Silvestro
PAL. RAVÀ
S. ROCCO
Campo S. Rocco
Campo dei Frari
S. MARIA DEI FRARI
Corte Badoèr
PAL. MOROLIN
PALAZZO BARZIZZA
PAL. PAPADÓPOLI
SCUOLA GRANDE DI S. ROCCO
PAL. BERNARDO
PAL. GRIMANI
S. Silvestro
EX SCUOLA D. CALEGHERI
PAL. CORNÈR
PAL. PISANI MOR.
PAL. CENTANI
PAL. LAYARD
PAL. QUERINI
PAL. DONÀ D. MADONNETTA
PAL. DONÀ
C.po S. Tomà
S. TOMÀ
PAL. BARBARIGO
PAL. TIEPOLO
GRAN
PAL. GRIMANI
PAL. CORNER D. FRESCADA
PAL. PÉRSICO
PAL. DOLFIN
PAL. DÁNDOLO-PAOLUCCI
PAL. MARCELLO D. LEONI
S. Tomà
PAL. BENZÒN
PAL. VOLPI
PAL. TRON
S. Ángelo
PAL. CORNÈR-SPINELLI
S. BENETO
Campo S. Beneto
PAL. CIVRÀN-GRIMANI
PAL. DOLFIN
PAL. BALBI (REG. VENETO)
PAL. FORTUNY
PALAZZI MOCENIGO
PAL. CONTARINI-D. FIGURE
Corte Mosto
CA' FOSCARI
CASA DEL VERONESE
PALAZZO MORO-LIN
PAL. GIUSTINIÀN
PAL. NANI
ORATÓRIO DELL'ANNUNCIATA
Campiello Nuovo
Campo S. Ángelo
PAL. GRASSI
C.po S. Samuele
EX CHIESA DI S. SAMUELE
EX CONVENTO S. STEFANO
PAL. REZZÒNICO
S. Samuele
S. STÉFANO
TEATRO LA FENICE
PAL. CONTARINI-MICHIÈL
PAL. MALIPIERO
Campo S. Stefano
S. MAURÍZIO
Campiello Calegheri
Ca' Rezzónico
S. BÁRNABA
PAL. STERN
CA' DEL DUCA
PAL. LOREDÀN
PAL. MORO
PAL. LOREDÀN
PAL. FALIÈR
EX CHIESA DI S. VIDÀL
PAL. MOROSINI
Campo S. Maurizio
PAL. GIUSTINIÀN-LOLÌN
S. MARIA D. GIGLIO
PAL. CONTARINI DEGLI SCRIGNI
PAL. CAVALLI-FRANCHETTI
C.po S. Vidàl
PAL. PISANI
PAL. GAMBARA
Campo del Traghetto
PAL. CORNÈR D. CÀ GRANDA (PREFETTURA)
Accadémia
PAL. BÁRBARO
PAL. BOLLANI
PONTE DELL'ACCADÉMIA
CASA STECCHINI
PAL. PISANI GRITTI
PAL. BRANDOLÌN
PAL. GIUSTINIÀN-RECANATI
C.po d. Carità
S. Maria d. Giglio
GALLERIE DELL'ACCADEMIA
PAL. CONTARINI-DAL ZAFFO
S. TROVASO
PAL. LOREDÀN
PAL. BARBARIGO
PAL. VENIÈR DEI LEONI (GÜGGENHEIM)
PAL. GENOVESE
C.po S. Vio
PAL. DA MULA
PAL. CENTANI
PAL. DARIO
Campo S. Trováso
PAL. NANI
S. Cristóforo
SQUERO DI S. TROVASO
EX CONVENTO
S. AGNESE
Fond. Venièr
Fond. Zorzi Bragadin
S. POLO
S. MARCO
CANAL GRANDE

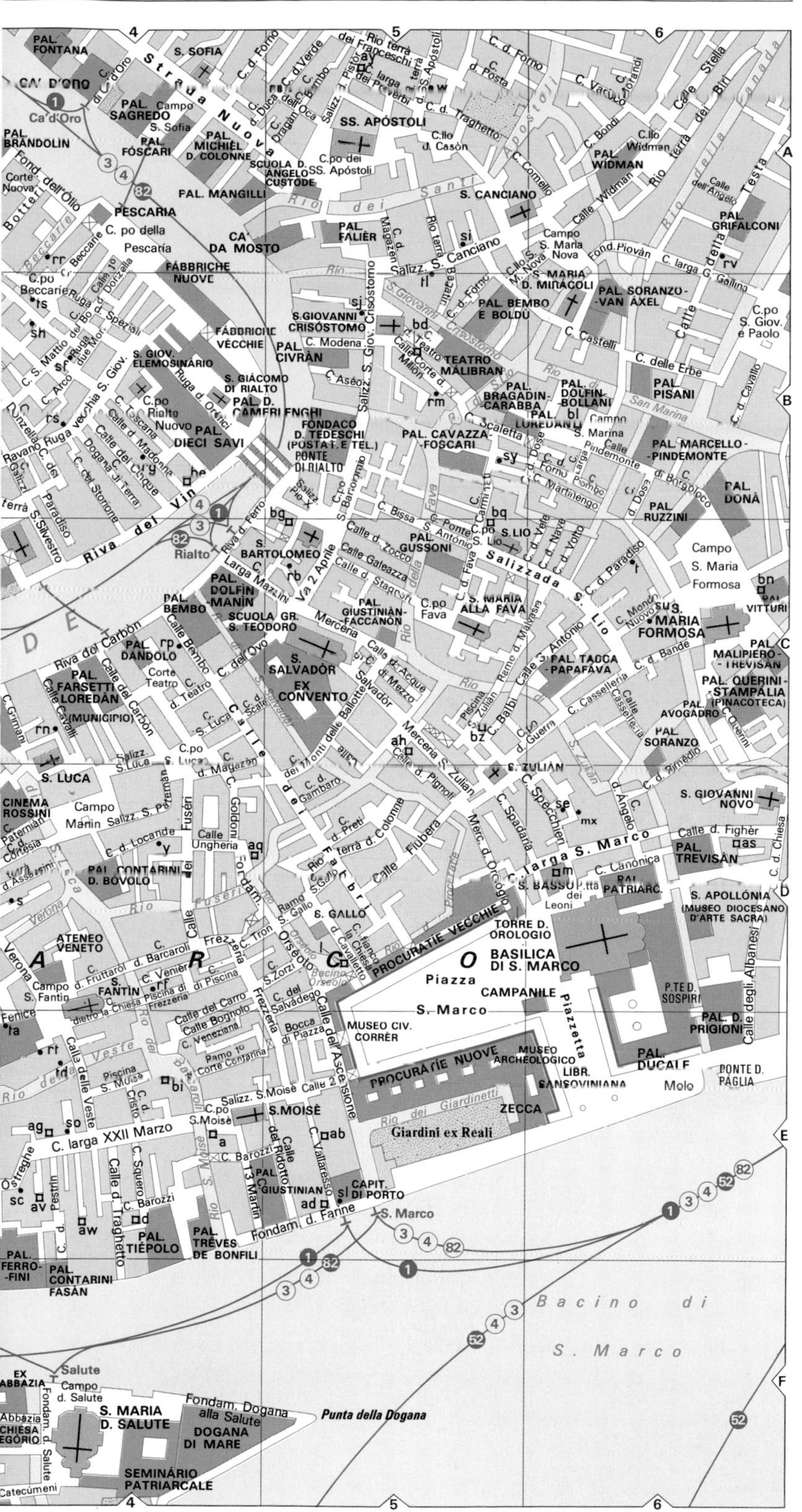

4
5
6
A
B
C
D
E
F
PAL. FONTANA
CA' D'ORO
Ca' d'Oro
S. SOFIA
Strada Nuova
PAL. SAGREDO
Campo S. Sofia
PAL. BRANDOLIN
PAL. FÓSCARI
PAL. MICHIEL D. COLONNE
SCUOLA D. ANGELO CUSTODE
Fond. dell'Olio
Corte Nuova
PAL. MANGILLI
PESCARIA
C. po della Pescaria
CA' DA MOSTO
FÁBBRICHE NUOVE
C.po Beccarie
FÁBBRICHE VÉCCHIE
S. GIOV. ELEMOSINÁRIO
S. GIÁCOMO DI RIALTO
PAL. D. CAMERLENGHI
C.po Rialto Nuovo
PAL. DIECI SAVI
Riva del Vin
Rialto
S. Silvestro
SS. APÓSTOLI
C.po dei SS. Apóstoli
Rio dei Santi Apostoli
PAL. FALIÈR
S. CANCIANO
Salizz. S. Canciano
S.GIOVANNI CRISÓSTOMO
C. Modena
PAL. CIVRAN
TEATRO MALIBRAN
FONDACO D. TEDESCHI (POSTA E TEL.)
PONTE DI RIALTO
PAL. CAVAZZA-FOSCARI
S. BARTOLOMEO
Riva del Ferro
PAL. DOLFIN-MANIN
PAL. BEMBO
SCUOLA GR. S. TEODORO
Riva del Carbon
PAL. DANDOLO
S. SALVADOR EX CONVENTO
Mercerie
PAL. FARSETTI LOREDAN (MUNICIPIO)
PAL. GUSSONI
S. LIO
Salizzada S. Lio
PAL. GIUSTINIAN-FACCANON
C.po Fava
S. MARIA ALLA FAVA
PAL. TAGGA-PAPAFAVA
S. MARIA FORMOSA
Campo S. Maria Formosa
PAL. MALIPIERO-TREVISAN
PAL. QUERINI-STAMPALIA (PINACOTECA)
PAL. AVOGADRO
PAL. SORANZO
PAL. WIDMAN
PAL. GRIFALCONI
S. MARIA D. MIRACOLI
PAL. SORANZO-VAN AXEL
PAL. BEMBO E BOLDÙ
C.po S. Giov. e Paolo
C. delle Erbe
PAL. PISANI
PAL. BRAGADIN-CARABBA
PAL. DOLFIN-BOLLANI
PAL. LOREDAN
Campo S. Marina
PAL. MARCELLO-PINDEMONTE
PAL. DONÀ
PAL. RUZZINI
PAL. VITTURI
S. LUCA
CINEMA ROSSINI
Campo Manin
PAL. CONTARINI D. BOVOLO
Calle Ungheria
S. ZULIAN
S. GIOVANNI NOVO
Calle d. Figher
PAL. TREVISAN
C. larga S. Marco
PAL. PATRIARC.
S. APOLLÓNIA (MUSEO DIOCESANO D'ARTE SACRA)
S. GALLO
Bacino Orseolo
PROCURATIE VECCHIE
TORRE D. OROLOGIO
BASILICA DI S. MARCO
Piazza S. Marco
CAMPANILE
Piazzetta
P.TE D. SOSPIRI
PAL. D. PRIGIONI
PAL. DUCALE
PONTE D. PAGLIA
Molo
ATENEO VENETO
S. FANTIN
Campo S. Fantin
Fenice
MUSEO CIV. CORRER
PROCURATIE NUOVE
MUSEO ARCHEOLOGICO
LIBR. SANSOVINIANA
ZECCA
Giardini ex Reali
S.MOISÈ
C.po S.Moisè
C. larga XXII Marzo
C. Vallaresso
CAPIT. DI PORTO
PAL. C. GIUSTINIAN
Fondam. d. Farine
S. Marco
PAL. TIÉPOLO
PAL. TRÈVES DE BONFILI
PAL. FERRO-FINI
PAL. CONTARINI FASAN
Bacino di S. Marco
Salute
EX ABBAZIA
Campo d. Salute
S. MARIA D. SALUTE
Fondam. Dogana alla Salute
Punta della Dogana
DOGANA DI MARE
SEMINÁRIO PATRIARCALE

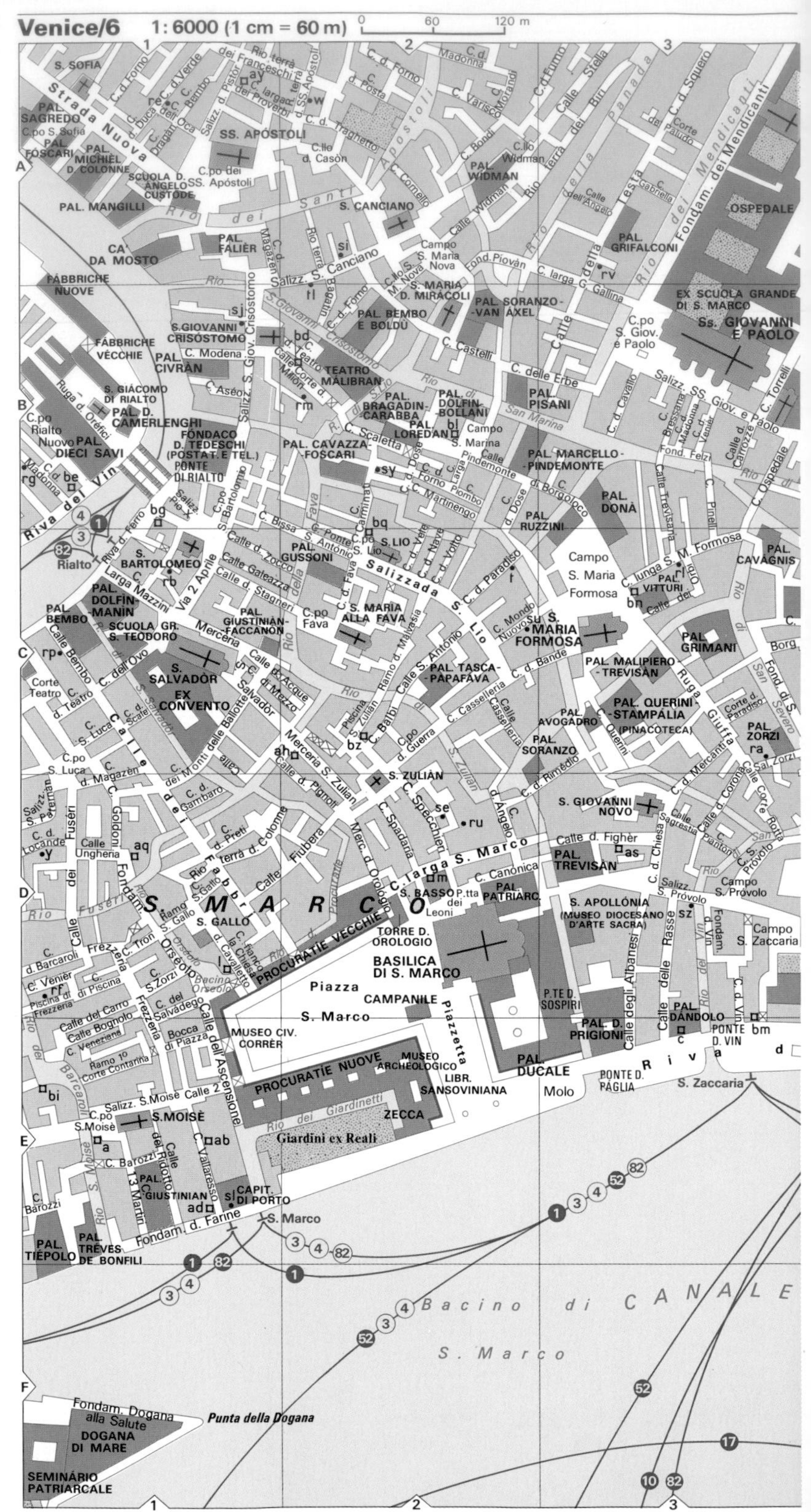
0 60 120 m
Strada Nuova
SS. APÓSTOLI
S. CANCIANO
PAL. WIDMAN
OSPEDALE
PAL. GRIFALCONI
EX SCUOLA GRANDE DI S. MARCO
Ss. GIOVANNI E PAOLO
S. MARIA D. MIRACOLI
PAL. SORANZO-VAN AXEL
S.GIOVANNI CRISÓSTOMO
TEATRO MALIBRAN
PAL. CIVRAN
S. GIÁCOMO DI RIALTO
PAL. D. CAMERLENGHI
PAL. DIECI SAVI
FÓNDACO D. TEDESCHI (POSTAT. E TEL.)
PONTE DI RIALTO
Riva del Vin
PAL. PISANI
PAL. LOREDAN
PAL. MARCELLO-PINDEMONTE
PAL. DONÀ
PAL. RUZZINI
S. LIO
Salizzada S. Lio
Campo S. Maria Formosa
S. MARIA FORMOSA
PAL. GRIMANI
S. BARTOLOMEO
PAL. DOLFIN-MANIN
SCUOLA GR. S. TEODORO
S. SALVADÒR EX CONVENTO
S. MARIA ALLA FAVA
PAL. TASCA-PAPAFAVA
PAL. MALIPIERO-TREVISAN
PAL. QUERINI-STAMPÀLIA (PINACOTECA)
S. ZULIÀN
S. GIOVANNI NOVO
PAL. TREVISAN
S. APOLLÓNIA (MUSEO DIOCESANO D'ARTE SACRA)
S. MARCO
S. GALLO
PROCURATIE VECCHIE
TORRE D. OROLOGIO
BASILICA DI S. MARCO
Piazza S. Marco
CAMPANILE
Piazzetta
MUSEO CIV. CORRÈR
PROCURATIE NUOVE
MUSEO ARCHEOLOGICO
LIBR. SANSOVINIANA
PAL. DUCALE
P.TE D. SOSPIRI
PAL. D. PRIGIONI
PAL. DÀNDOLO
PONTE D. PAGLIA
Riva d
S. Zaccaria
Molo
ZECCA
Giardini ex Reali
S.MOISÈ
CAPIT. DI PORTO
S. Marco
PAL. TIÉPOLO
PAL. TRÈVES DE BONFILI
Bacino di CANALE S. Marco
Punta della Dogana
DOGANA DI MARE
SEMINÁRIO PATRIARCALE

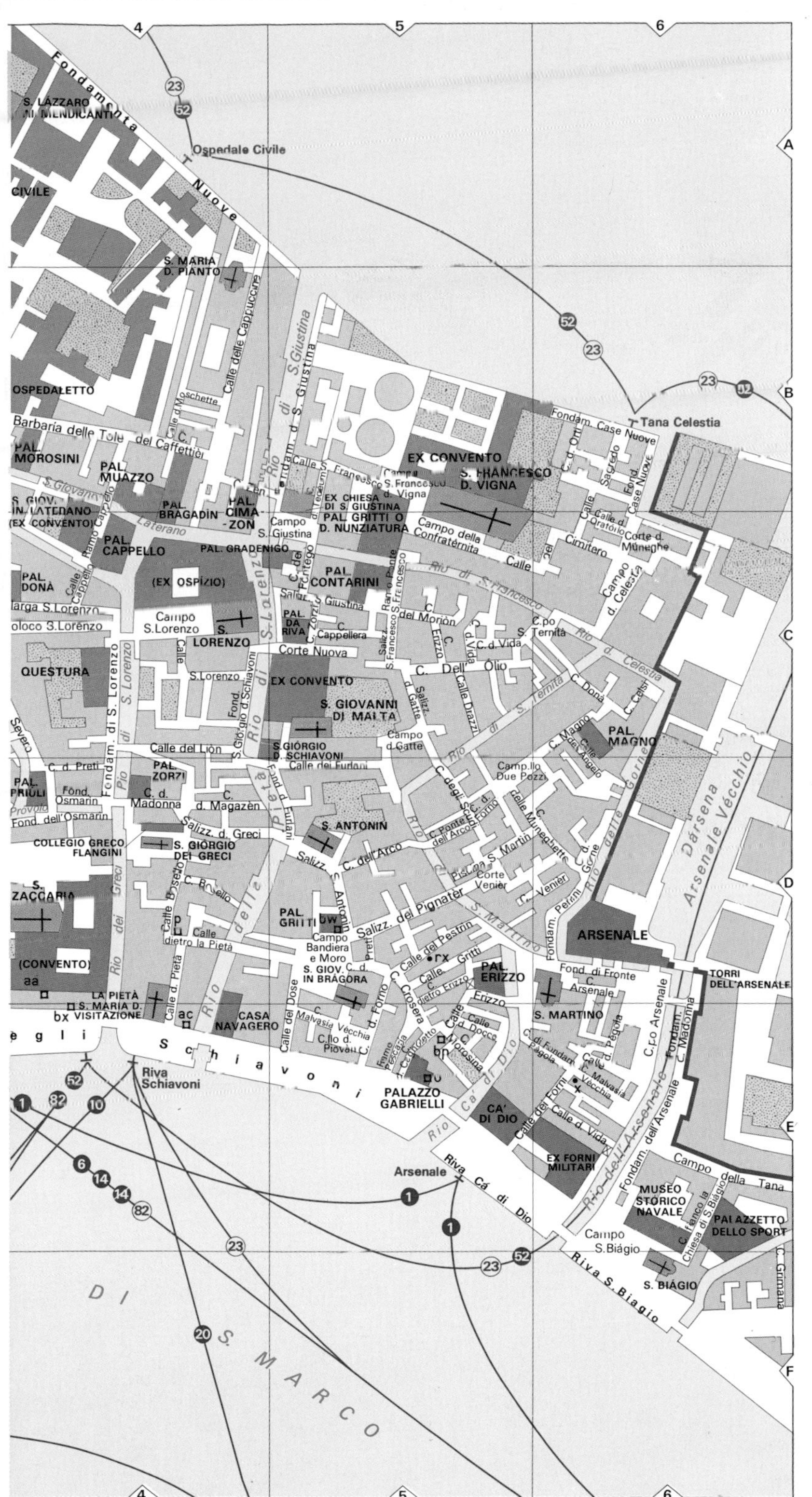
Ospedale Civile
S. LAZZARO DI MENDICANTI
CIVILE
OSPEDALETTO
S. MARIA D. PIANTO
EX CONVENTO S. FRANCESCO D. VIGNA
Tana Celestia
PAL. MOROSINI
PAL. MUAZZO
PAL. BRAGADIN
PAL. CIMA-ZON
PAL. CAPPELLO
PAL. GRADENIGO
PAL. CONTARINI
PAL. DONÀ
(EX OSPIZIO)
S. LORENZO
QUESTURA
EX CONVENTO
S. GIOVANNI DI MALTA
S. GIÒRGIO D. SCHIAVONI
PAL. MAGNO
PAL. ZORZI
PAL. PRIULI
S. ANTONIN
COLLEGIO GRECO FLANGINI
S. GIÒRGIO DEI GRECI
S. ZACCARIA
(CONVENTO)
PAL. GRITTI
ARSENALE
TORRI DELL'ARSENALE
PAL. ERIZZO
S. GIOV. IN BRÀGORA
LA PIETÀ
S. MARIA D. VISITAZIONE
CASA NAVAGERO
S. MARTINO
PALAZZO GABRIELLI
CA' DI DIO
EX FORNI MILITARI
MUSEO STORICO NAVALE
PALAZZETTO DELLO SPORT
S. BIÀGIO
Riva Schiavoni
Arsenale
Riva Cá di Dio
Riva S. Biagio
Dársena Arsenale Vécchio
DI S. MARCO

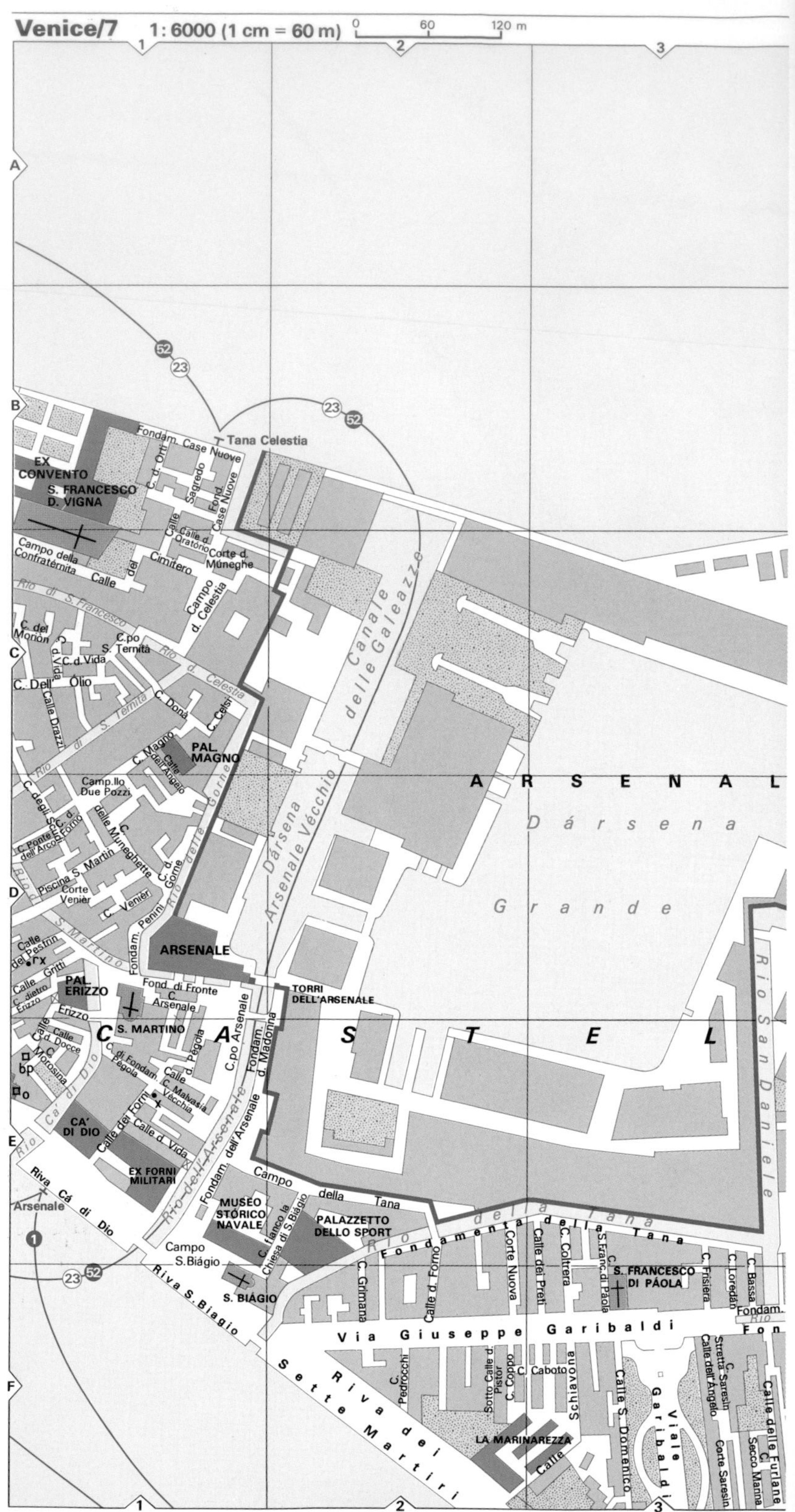
1: 6000 (1 cm = 60 m)
0
60
120 m
Tana Celestia
Fondam. Case Nuove
EX CONVENTO
S. FRANCESCO D. VIGNA
C. d. Orti
Sagredo
Fond. Case Nuove
Calle
Calle d. Oratorio
Corte d. Muneghe
Campo della Confratérnita
Calle del Cimitero
Campo d. Celestia
Rio di S. Francesco
C. del Morion
C. d. Vida
C.po S. Ternità
C. d. Vida
C. Dell Ólio
Calla Drazzi
Rio d. Celestia
C. Donà
C. Celsi
Rio di S. Ternità
PAL. MAGNO
C. Magno
Calle dell'Ángelo
Camp.llo Due Pozzi
C. degli Sti
C. d. Forno
C. Ponte dell'Arco
delle Muneghette
Piscina S. Martin
Corte Venièr
C. Venièr
C. d. Gorne
Rio delle Gorne
Fondam. Penini
Rio di S. Martino
Calle del Pestrin
ARSENALE
PAL. ERIZZO
Calle Gritti
C. dietro Erizzo
Erizzo
Fond. di Fronte
C. Arsenale
S. MARTINO
C.d. Docce
C. Morosina
C. di Fondam. Pegola
C. d. Pegola
C. Malvasia Vécchia
Calle dei Forni
Calle d. Vida
CA' DI DIO
EX FORNI MILITARI
Rio Cá di Dio
Rio dell'Arsenale
Fondam. dell'Arsenale
C.po Arsenale
Fondam. d. Madonna
TORRI DELL'ARSENALE
Canale delle Galeazze
Dársena Arsenale Vécchio
A R S E N A L
Dársena Grande
C A S T E L
Rio San Daniele
Riva Cá di Dio
Arsenale
Campo S. Biágio
Campo della Tana
MUSEO STÓRICO NAVALE
C. franco la Chiesa di S. Biágio
PALAZZETTO DELLO SPORT
Rio della Tana
Fondamenta della Tana
S. BIÁGIO
Riva S. Biagio
C. Grimana
Calle d. Forno
Corte Nuova
Calle dei Preti
C. Coltrera
S. Franc. di Paola
C.
S. FRANCESCO DI PÁOLA
C. Frisiera
C. Loredàn
C. Bassa
Fondam.
Fon
Via Giuseppe Garibaldi
Riva dei Sette Martiri
C. Pedrocchi
Sotto Calle d. Pistor
C. Coppo
C. Caboto
Schiavona
Calle S. Domenico
Viale Garibaldi
C. Stretta Saresin
Calle dell'Ángelo
Corte Saresin
Calle delle Furlane
C. Secco Manna
LA MARINAREZZA
Calle
52
23
1

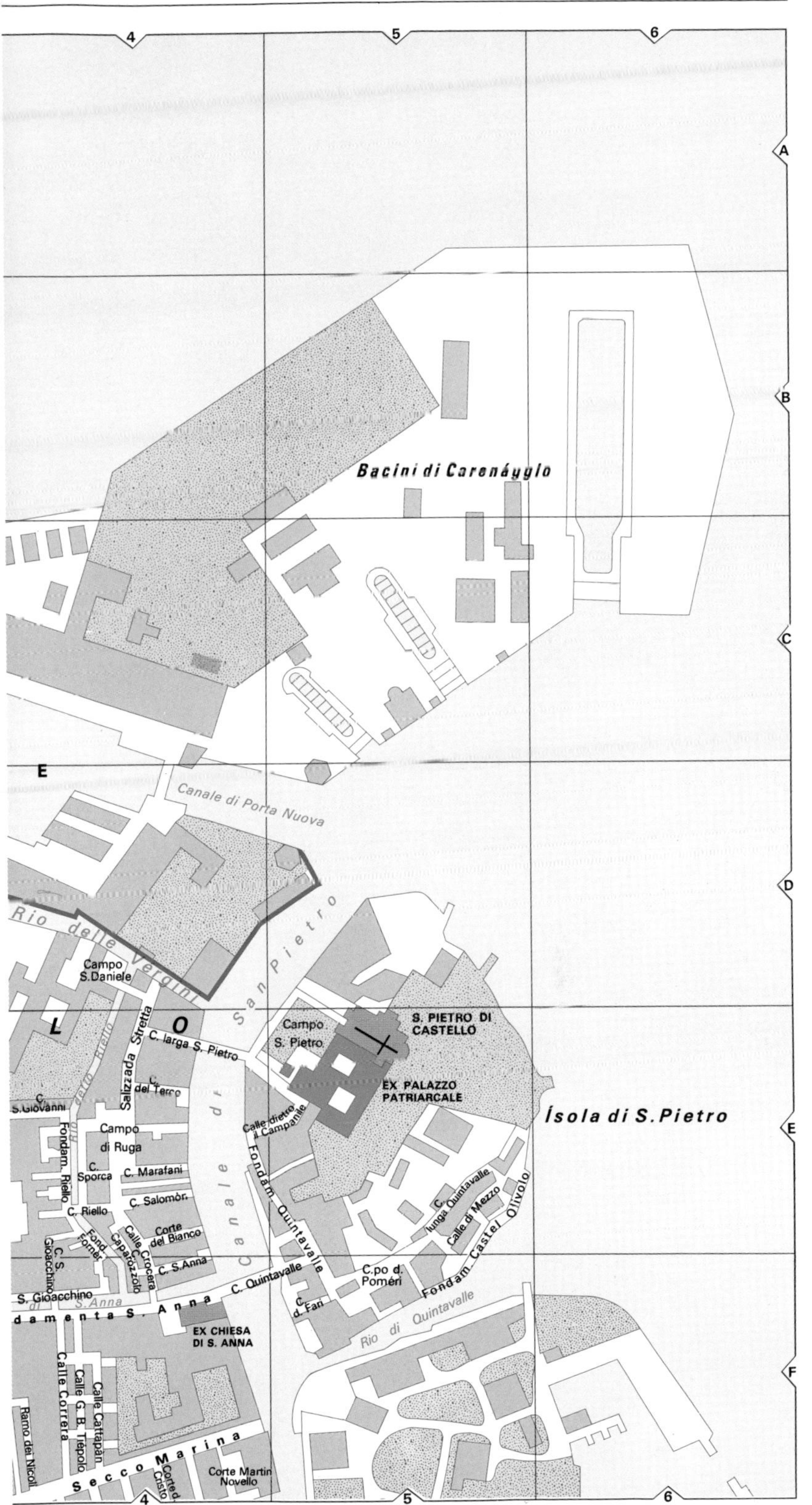

4
5
6
A
B
C
D
E
F
Bacini di Carenáyglo
E
Canale di Porta Nuova
Rio delle Vergini
Canale di San Pietro
Campo S.Daniele
L
O
C. larga S. Pietro
Salizzada Stretta
Campo S. Pietro
S. PIETRO DI CASTELLO
EX PALAZZO PATRIARCALE
Ísola di S.Pietro
C. del Terro
C. S.Giovanni
Campo di Ruga
Fondam. Riello
C. Sporca
C. Marafani
C. Salomòr.
C. Riello
Corte del Bianco
Calle Crocera
Capazzolo
Fond. Fornér.
C. S. Gioacchino
C. S.Anna
S. Gioacchino
C. Quintavalle
Calle dietro il Campanile
Fondam. Quintavalle
C. lunga Quintavalle
Calle di Mezzo
Fondam. Castel Olivolo
C.po d. Poméri
C. d. Fari
Rio di Quintavalle
damenta S. Anna
EX CHIESA DI S. ANNA
Calle Correra
Calle G. B. Tiepolo
Calle Cattapan
Ramo dei Nicoli
Secco Marina
Corte d. Cristo
Corte Martin Novello

 1: 6000 (1 cm = 60 m)

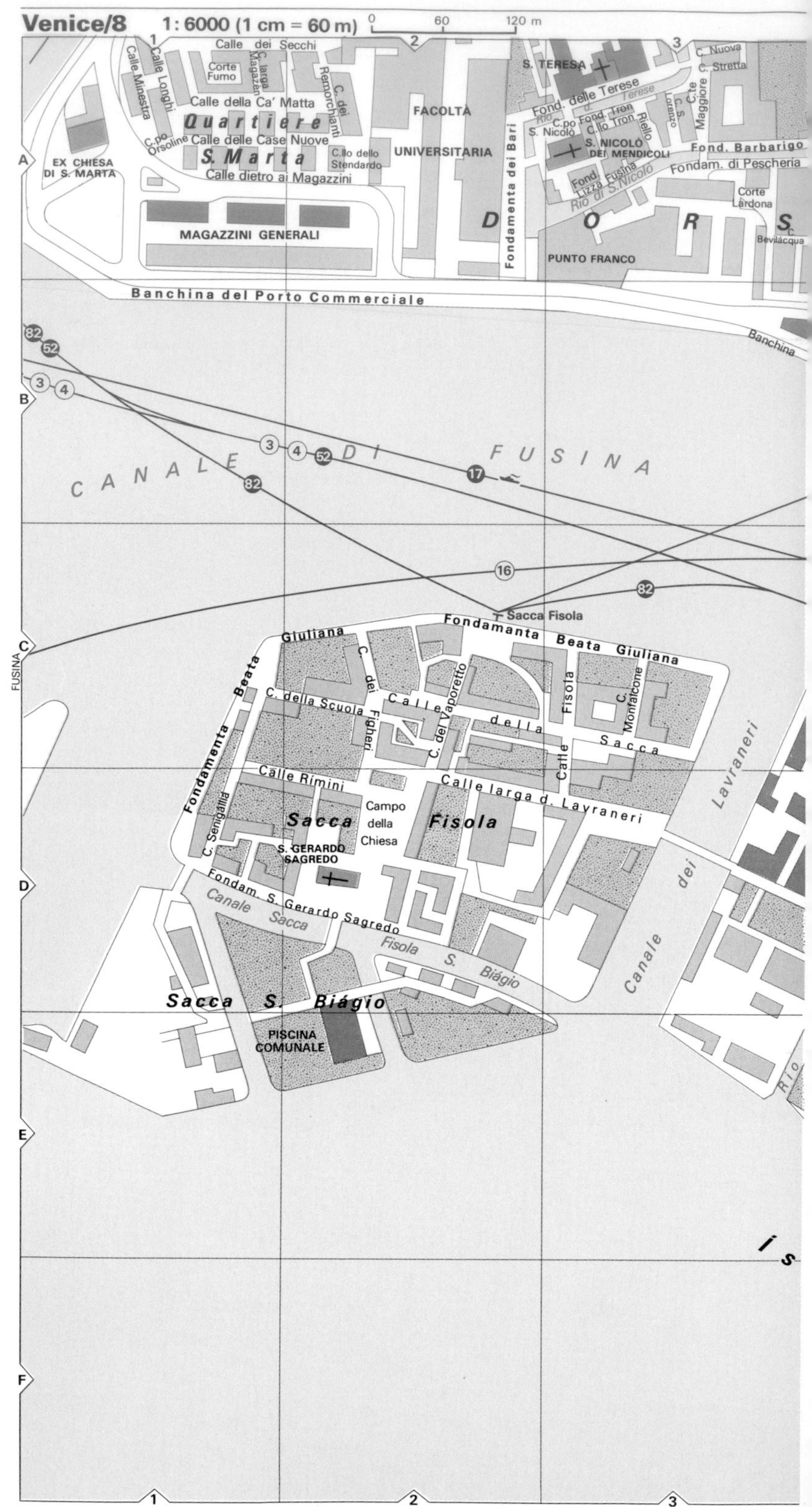

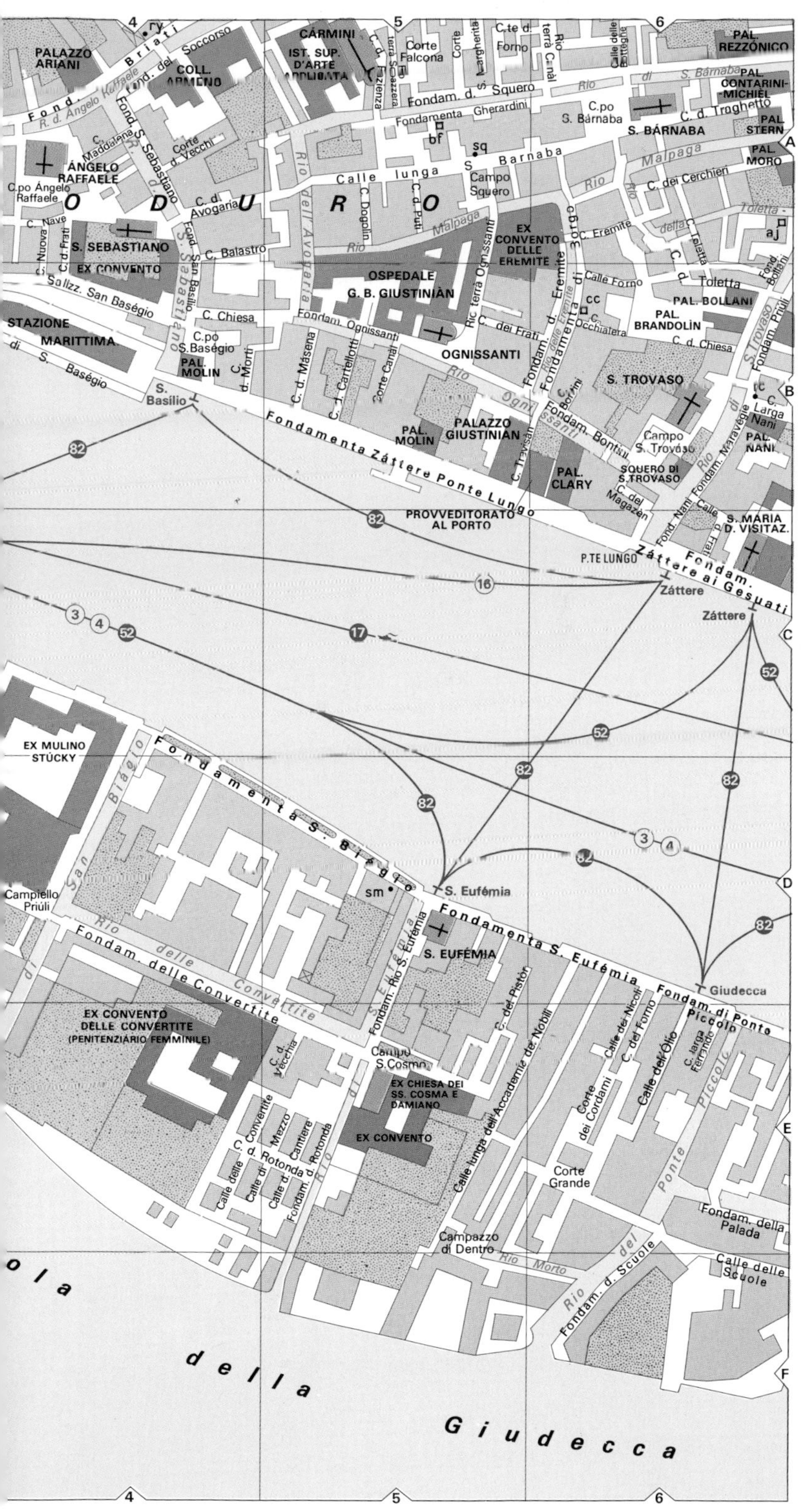
PALAZZO ARIANI
COLL. ARMENO
CÁRMINI
IST. SUP. D'ARTE APPLICATA
PAL. REZZÓNICO
PAL. CONTARINI-MICHIEL
PAL. STERN
PAL. MORO
S. BÁRNABA
ÁNGELO RAFFAELE
C.po Ángelo Raffaele
D O R S O D U R O
S. SEBASTIANO
EX CONVENTO
EX CONVENTO DELLE EREMITE
OSPEDALE G. B. GIUSTINIÀN
STAZIONE MARITTIMA
PAL. MOLIN
OGNISSANTI
PAL. BOLLANI
PAL. BRANDOLÌN
S. TROVASO
Campo S. Trovaso
SQUERO DI S.TROVASO
PAL. NANI
PAL. MOLIN
PALAZZO GIUSTINIAN
PAL. CLARY
PROVVEDITORATO AL PORTO
S. MARIA D. VISITAZ.
Fondamenta Záttere Ponte Lungo
Fondam. Záttere ai Gesuati
P.TE LUNGO
Záttere
S. Basílio
EX MULINO STÚCKY
Fondamenta S. Biagio
S. Eufémia
S. EUFÉMIA
Fondamenta S. Eufémia
Giudecca
Fondam. di Ponte Piccolo
Fondam. delle Convertite
EX CONVENTO DELLE CONVERTITE (PENITENZIÁRIO FEMMINILE)
Campo S.Cosmo
EX CHIESA DEI SS. COSMA E DAMIANO
EX CONVENTO
Calle lunga dell'Accademia d. Nobili
Corte dei Cordami
Corte Grande
Campazzo di Dentro
Rio Morto
Fondam. della Palada
Calle delle Scuole
Fondam. d. Scuole
Campiello Priúli
Canale della Giudecca

PAL. REZZÓNICO
S. Samuele
PAL. MALIPIERO
EX CONVENTO S. STEFANO
S. STÉFANO
Campo S. Stefano
S. BÁRNABA
CA'DEL DUCA
PAL. FALIÈR
PAL. LOREDÀN
PAL. MOROSINI
Campo S. Maurizio
S. MARIA D. GIGLIO
PAL. PISANI
Accadémia
PONTE DELL'ACCADÉMIA
CASA STECCHINI
GALLERIE DELL'ACCADEMIA
PAL. CONTARINI-DAL ZAFFO
PAL. BARBARIGO
PAL. VENIÈR DEI LEONI (GUGGENHEIM)
PAL. DARIO
S. TROVASO
Campo S. Trováso
S. MARIA D. VISITAZ.
S. AGNESE
GESUATI
Fondam. Záttere ai Gesuati
Fondam. Záttere allo S. Santo
EX OSPEDALE DEGLI INCURABILI
SPÍRITO SANTO
SALONI EX MAGAZZINI DEL SALE
CANALE DELLA
Giudecca
Ísola della
Redentore
Campo del Redentore
SS. REDENTORE
CONVENTO DEL REDENTORE
Quartiere S. Giácomo

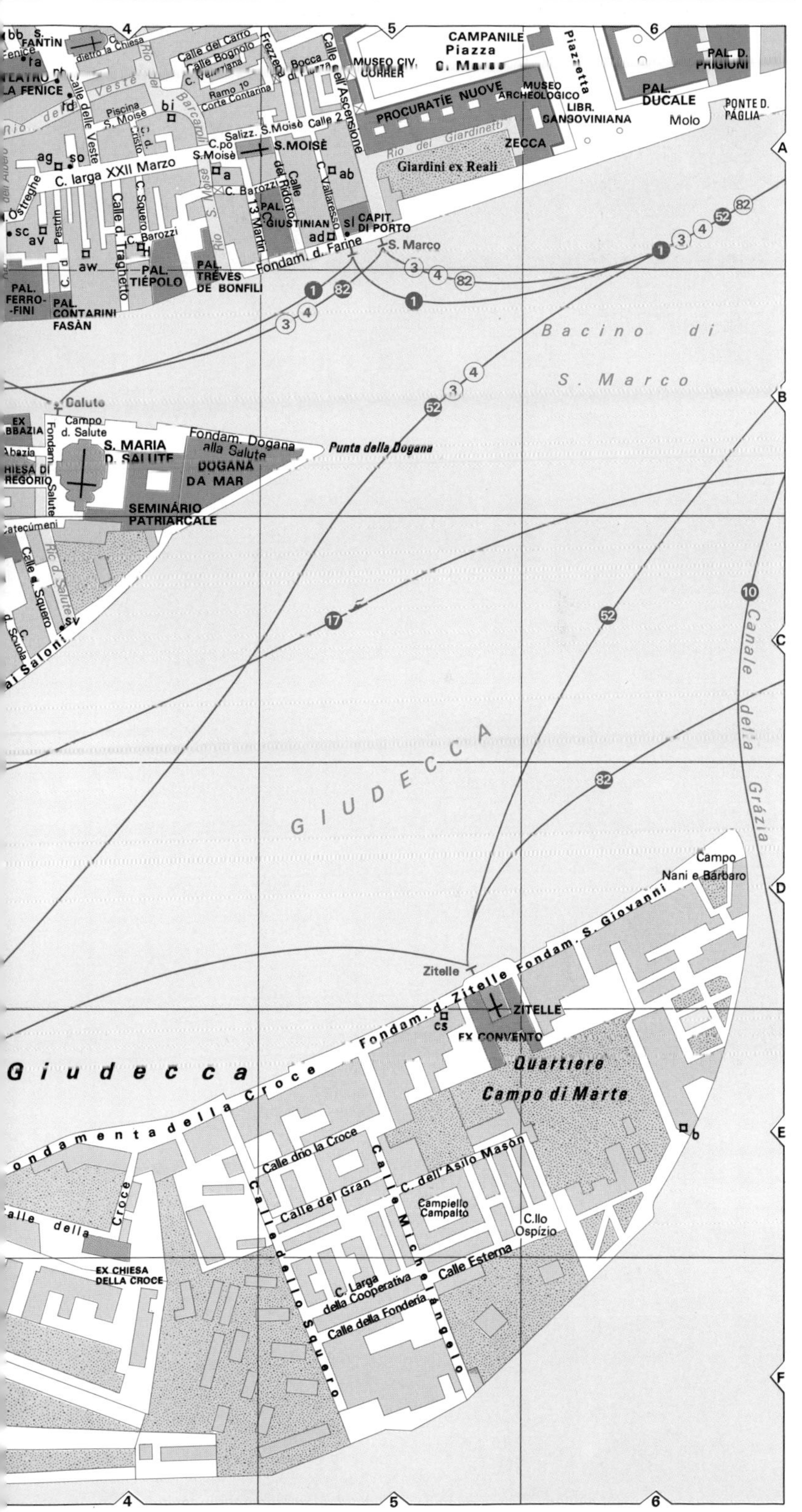

CAMPANILE
Piazza S. Marco
MUSEO CIV. CORRER
PROCURATIE NUOVE
MUSEO ARCHEOLOGICO
LIBR. SANSOVINIANA
PAL. DUCALE
PAL. D. PRIGIONI
PONTE D. PAGLIA
Molo
Piazzetta
ZECCA
Giardini ex Reali
Rio dei Giardinetti
S. MOISÈ
C. larga XXII Marzo
Calle del Ridotto
C. Vallaresso
PAL. GIUSTINIAN
CAPIT. DI PORTO
S. Marco
Fondam. d. Farine
PAL. TIÈPOLO
PAL. TREVES DE BONFILI
PAL. CONTARINI FASAN
PAL. FERRO-FINI
TEATRO LA FENICE
Calle delle Veste
Calle del Carro
Calle Bognolo
Ramo 10 Corte Contarina
Calle dell'Ascensione
Frezzeria
Bocca di Piazza
Salizz. S. Moisè
Calle d. Traghetto
Bacino di S. Marco
Salute
Campo d. Salute
S. MARIA D. SALUTE
Fondam. Dogana alla Salute
DOGANA DA MAR
Punta della Dogana
SEMINÁRIO PATRIARCALE
Calle d. Squero
Zattere ai Saloni
GIUDECCA
Canale della Grázia
Campo Nani e Bárbaro
Fondam. S. Giovanni
Zitelle
Fondam. d. Zitelle
ZITELLE
EX CONVENTO
Quartiere Campo di Marte
Giudecca
Fondamenta della Croce
Calle drio la Croce
Calle del Gran
C. dell'Asilo Masòn
Campiello Campalto
C.llo Ospízio
Calle Michelangelo
Calle dello Squero
C. Larga della Cooperativa
Calle Esterna
Calle della Fondería
Calle della Croce
EX CHIESA DELLA CROCE

 1: 6000 (1 cm = 60 m)

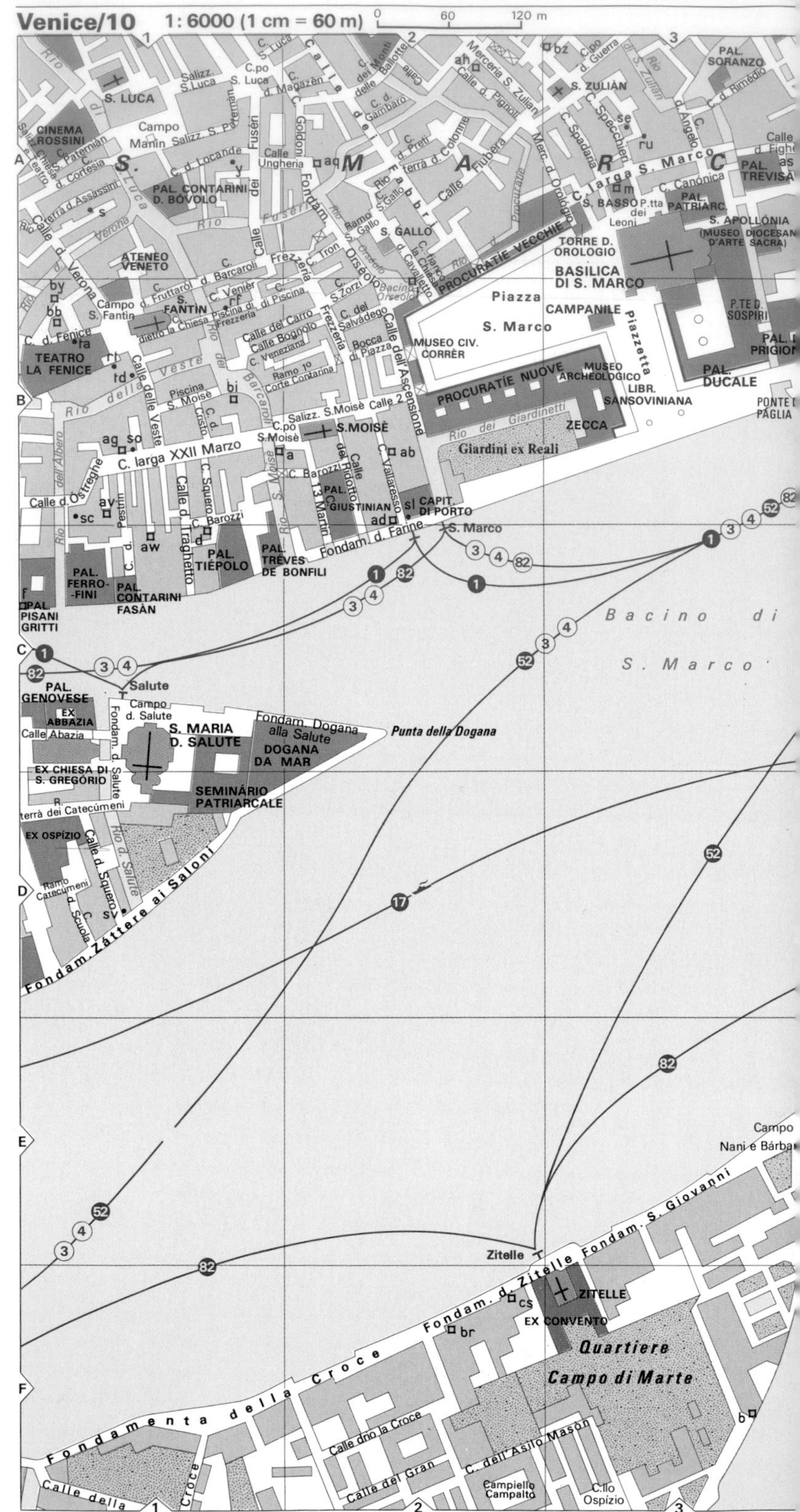

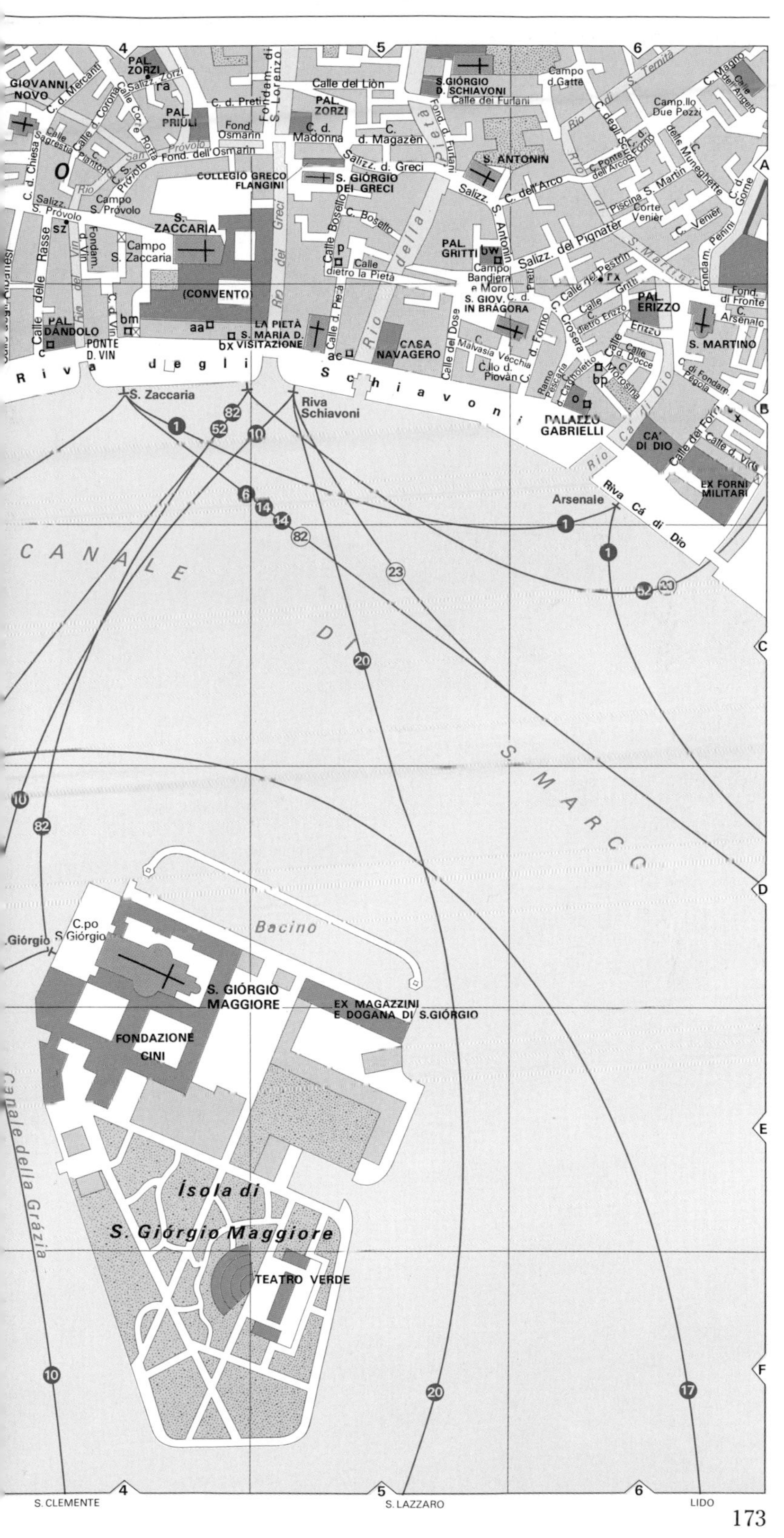
GIOVANNI NOVO
PAL. ZORZI
PAL. PRIULI
COLLEGIO GRECO FLANGINI
S. ZACCARIA
Campo S. Zaccaria
(CONVENTO)
LA PIETÀ
S. MARIA D. VISITAZIONE
PAL. DANDOLO
PONTE D. VIN
Campo S. Provolo
Calle del Liòn
PAL. ZORZI
S. GIÓRGIO D. SCHIAVONI
Calle dei Furlani
S. ANTONIN
S. GIÓRGIO DEI GRECI
Salizz. d. Greci
PAL. GRITTI
Campo Bandiera e Moro
S. GIOV. IN BRÁGORA
CASA NAVAGERO
Campo d.Gatte
Camp.llo Due Pozzi
Salizz. del Pignater
PAL. ERIZZO
S. MARTINO
PALAZZO GABRIELLI
CA' DI DIO
EX FORNI MILITARI
Riva degli Schiavoni
S. Zaccaria
Riva Schiavoni
Arsenale
Riva Cá di Dio
CANALE DI S. MARCO
Bacino
C.po S.Giórgio
S. GIÓRGIO MAGGIORE
EX MAGAZZINI E DOGANA DI S.GIÓRGIO
FONDAZIONE CINI
Ísola di S. Giórgio Maggiore
TEATRO VERDE
Canale della Grázia
S. CLEMENTE
S. LAZZARO
LIDO

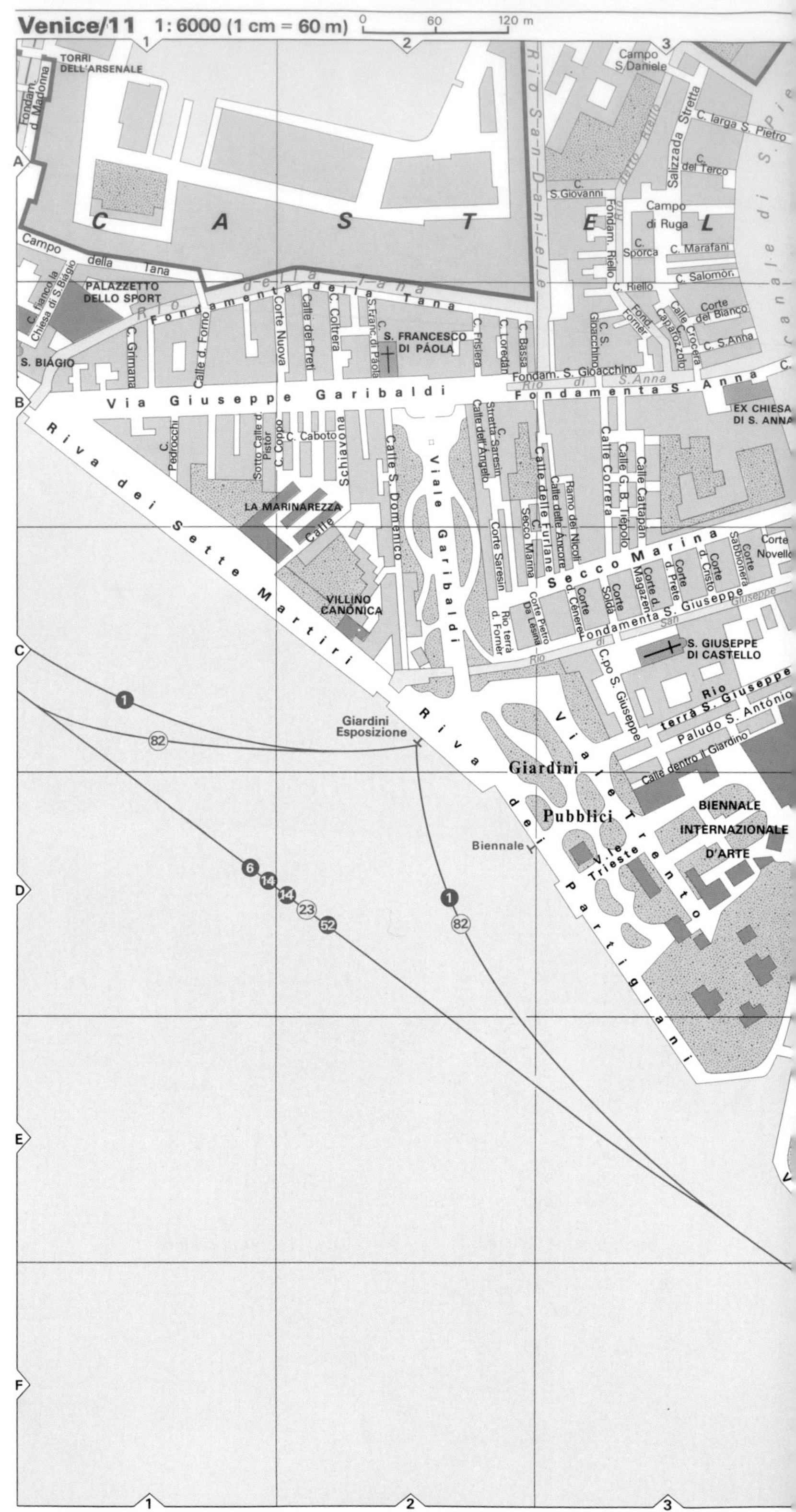

0 60 120 m
TORRI DELL'ARSENALE
Fondam. d. Madonna
C A S T E L
Campo della Tana
Rio della Tana
PALAZZETTO DELLO SPORT
C. fianco la Chiesa di S.Biagio
S. BIÁGIO
Fondamenta della Tana
C. Grimana
Calle d. Forno
Corte Nuova
Calle dei Preti
C. Coltrera
S.Franc. di Paola
S. FRANCESCO DI PÁOLA
C. Frisiera
C. Loredan
C. Bassa
Rio S. Daniele
Campo S.Daniele
Salizzada Stretta
C. larga S. Pietro
C. del Terco
C. S.Giovanni
Fondam. Riello
Campo di Ruga
C. Sporca
C. Marafani
C. Salomon
C. Riello
C. S. Gioacchino
Fond. Forner
Calle Caparozzolo
Calle Crociera
Corte del Bianco
C. S.Anna
Fondam. S. Gioacchino
Rio di S.Anna
Fondamenta S. Anna
EX CHIESA DI S. ANNA
Via Giuseppe Garibaldi
Riva dei Sette Martiri
C. Pedrocchi
Sotto Calle d. Pistor
C. Coppo
C. Caboto
Schiavona
Calle S. Domenico
LA MARINAREZZA
Calle
VILLINO CANÓNICA
Viale Garibaldi
Stretta Saresin
C. dell'Angelo
Calle dell'Angelo
Corte Saresin
Calle delle Furlane
C. Secco Marina
Calle delle Ancore
Ramo dei Nicoli
Calle Correra
Calle G. B. Tiepolo
Calle Cattapan
Secco Marina
Corte Sabbionera
Corte Novello
Corte d. Cristo
Corte d. Prete
Corte d. Magazen
Corte Solda
Corte d. Cenere
Corte Pietro Da Lesina
Rio terà d. Forner
Fondamenta S. Giuseppe
Rio di San Giuseppe
S. GIUSEPPE DI CASTELLO
C.po S. Giuseppe
Rio terrà S. Giuseppe
Paludo S. Antonio
Calle dentro il Giardino
Giardini Esposizione
Riva dei Partigiani
Viale Trento
V.le Trieste
Giardini Pubblici
BIENNALE INTERNAZIONALE D'ARTE
Biennale

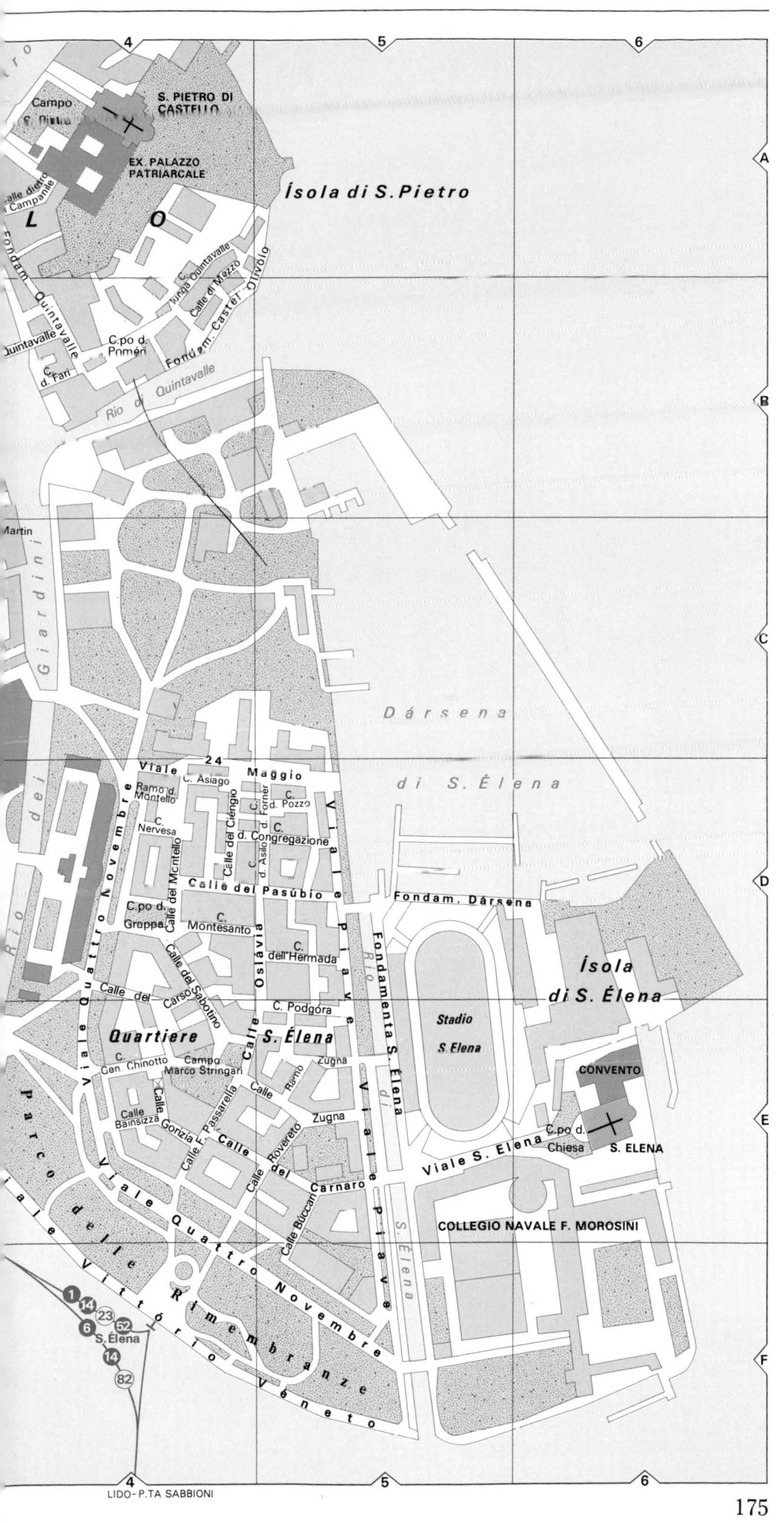
S. PIETRO DI CASTELLO
Campo S. Pietro
EX. PALAZZO PATRIARCALE
Ísola di S. Pietro
Calle dietro Campanile
Fondam. Quintavalle
Quintavalle
C.po d. Poméri
C. d. Fari
Fondam. Castel Olivolo
Calle di Mezzo
C. lunga Quintavalle
Rio di Quintavalle
Martin
Rio dei Giardini
Dársena di S. Élena
Viale 24 Maggio
Ramo d. Montello
C. Asiago
C. Nervesa
Calle del Ciengio
C. d. Forner
C. d. Pozzo
C. d. Asilo
C. d. Congregazione
Calle del Montello
Calle del Pasúbio
Fondam. Dársena
C.po d. Groppa
C. Montesanto
C. dell'Hermada
Calle Oslávia
Viale Piave
Fondamenta S. Élena
Rio di S. Élena
Stadio S. Elena
Ísola di S. Élena
Calle del Carso
Calle del Sabotino
C. Podgora
Quartiere S. Élena
C. Gen. Chinotto
Campo Marco Stringari
Ramo Zugna
Calle Zugna
Calle Bainsizza
Calle Gorizia
Calle F. Passarella
Calle Rovereto
Calle del Carnaro
Calle Búccari
Viale Quattro Novembre
CONVENTO
C.po d. Chiesa
S. ELENA
Viale S. Elena
COLLEGIO NAVALE F. MOROSINI
Parco delle Rimembranze
Viale Vittório Véneto
S. Élena
LIDO-P.TA SABBIONI